IMAGINED MASCULINITIES

Male Identity and Culture in the Modern Middle East

Edited by

Mai Ghoussoub and
Emma Sinclair-Webb

British Library Cataloguing-in-Publication Data
A catalogue record for this book is available from the British Library

ISBN 0-86356-042-3
EAN 9-780863-560422

copyright © Mai Ghoussoub and Emma Sinclair-Webb 2006
copyright for individual texts rests with the authors and translators

First published in hardback in 2000 by Saqi Books

This edition published 2006

SAQI
26 Westbourne Grove
London W2 5RH
www.saqibooks.com

Contents

Preface   7

PART I: MAKING MEN: INSTITUTIONS AND SOCIAL PRACTICES

1. Festivities of Violence: Circumcision and the Making of Men, *Abdelwahab Bouhdiba, Abdu Khal*   19

2. Circumcision, the First Haircut and the Torah: Ritual and Male Identity Among the Ultraorthodox Community of Israel, *Yoram Bilu*   33

3. 'Our Bülent Is Now a Commando': Military Service and Manhood in Turkey, *Emma Sinclair-Webb*   65
   'Military service in spite of me': Interview with L.Ş., Former Conscript   92

4. Male Gender and Rituals of Resistance in the Palestinian Intifada: A Cultural Politics of Violence, *Julie Peteet*   103

5. The Military as a Second Bar Mitzvah: Combat Service as Initiation to Zionist Masculinity, *Danny Kaplan*   127

PART II: MALE FICTIONS: NARRATIVES, IMAGES AND ICONS

6. Reading 'Wiles of Women' Stories as Fictions of Masculinity, *Afsaneh Najmabadi*   147

7. Male Homosexuality in Modern Arabic Literature, *Frédéric Lagrange*   169

8. Farid Shauqi: Tough Guy, Family Man, Cinema Star, *Walter Armbrust*   199

9. Chewing Gum, Insatiable Women and Foreign Enemies: Male Fears and the Arab Media, *Mai Ghoussoub*   227

10. 'That's how I am, world!': Saddam, Manhood and the Monolithic Image, *Hazim Saghieh*   236

PART III: MEMOIR AND MALE IDENTITY

11. Lentils in Paradise, *Moris Farhi*   251

12. Not the Man My Father Was, *Ahmad Beydoun*   263

13. Those Two Heavy Wings of Manhood: On Moustaches, *Hassan Daoud*   273

Notes on Contributors   281
Index   285

Preface

There is by now a rather large literature on the subject of men and masculine identity in relation to European, American and Australian societies. From popular psychology and self-help books, to academic studies coming from various disciplines, to social policy reports and on, this literature has taken different forms and served various agendas. Because interest in the subject has largely developed in the wake of the political project and writings of Western feminism, it is perhaps inevitable that what has been written about men and masculinity should encompass some diametrically opposed arguments, some located within gender studies, others closer to sociobiology. Those texts that have sought, often in reaction to feminist projects, to reassert various versions of a supposedly essential and true (read heterosexual) masculinity under threat of extinction will be left aside here. The more compelling literature has worked in the opposite direction to show in different ways that maleness is as socially constructed as femaleness and to demonstrate that – beyond anatomy – there is not a fixed set of determinants that establishes masculinity.

Factors of class, labour market relations, ethnicity and sexuality, as well as individual experience and relations with family and peers, are centrally implicated in the formation of men's identities, in patterns of association and in the categories men find themselves occupying and sometimes also consciously seek to occupy. Such different socialization processes and variations in how men relate to women and to other men suggest that it makes little sense to see masculinity as a single category, as though it were an 'outcome'. To take this further, there has been an emphasis in recent work on the ways in which gendered selves are also constructed dynamically (and performatively) in social interaction.

The differences between men, and between understandings of what masculinity can be, have perhaps been brought out most effectively by campaigns and projects, in the more cosmopolitan metropolitan centres of Western countries, that have opened up the discussion of sexuality and gay masculinities. Questions of ethnicity have also been increasingly brought to bear in considering the construction of male identity and in raising questions about power. Mainly demonstrating the contradictory and racist assumptions that operate via cultural and media representations, work that attempts to tie discursive dimensions to social practices and histories is still in its early stages. Between them, approaches that consider the dimensions of ethnicity and sexuality are important, too, for establishing that the subordination of women by men should not let us forget the subordination of men by other men.

Linked with feminist projects which have fought for, among other things, more equitable relations between men and women at all levels, work that has attempted to unseat essentialist understandings of masculinity has provided some grounds for being optimistic that men can and do change and that the gender order is not unshakeable. To date, the gains for women – in terms of efforts to defeat the public and private divide which has so consistently entailed women losing out in both – have necessarily been limited in societies where public provision of childcare, and efforts to make shared parenting a feasible option for the majority, has not been seriously pursued as social policy. However, admitting that does not discount us from saying that work on masculinity has shown that patriarchy is both more complex, for being *more* implicated in the structure of social relations than has sometimes been admitted, and at the same time not as monolithic as has been suggested. Focusing on masculinity should not be seen as a shift away from feminist projects, but rather as a complementary endeavour, indeed one that is organically linked.

This is not the place to attempt to summarize the work of those who have been engaged in major attempts to rethink approaches to masculinity (notably, R.W. Connell and Lynne Segal), though much of what is said here and in my own article is influenced by them.[1] In putting together this book it was decided to embark upon a rather different and more modest endeavour. For a number of reasons that will be mentioned, there is a need to open up the debate on masculinity and to introduce the research and commentary of writers focusing on a region which, with some truth, is still regarded as one of the seats of patriarchy.

The point might be made with some justice that the study of men has in fact been the traditional focus of most scholarship on the Middle East: after all, the examination of social structures, political institutions and movements, religious networks and practices, labour relations, and the historic relationship with European trade interests tended until recently to be conducted with little or no consideration paid to histories of women. Often presumed to inhabit a static, socially undynamic and even undifferentiated private sphere, women and the private sphere were simply absent or, when they were studied, were not seen as an inextricable part of dynamic social structures and political economy. Writings on gender in the Middle East have thus understandably focused largely on women and in recent years major inroads into anthropological, sociological and historical research have been made by gendered approaches. In that sense it must be seen as a real achievement that studies that take gender as central are no longer regarded as belonging to a separate sphere that can be cordoned off from mainstream disciplines.[2] Working on women in Middle East societies of course also means working on men: indeed, implicit in most studies of women's agency in Islamist and other political movements, the politics of veiling, women in the labour force – whether as homeworkers or in the public workplace – women as brides, wives and mothers, and so on, has been the presence of men. Though men have rarely been a direct object of study in these accounts,[3] most have indicated the sense in which men are there positioned at the thresholds and have often attempted to police the mobility and conduct of their sisters, daughters, companions, wives and comrades, sometimes – quite often in fact – with the complicity of their mothers and other senior women.

Turning now to this book, the plan was to bring together writings which take a variety of approaches to male identity. The emphasis of nearly all the essays is on providing informative as well as analytical readings of the gendered dimensions of institutions, social practices and cultural productions and, centrally, the power relations they entail. A preoccupation is to look at the locations where and dynamic processes through which socialization into masculinity takes place. While over half the contributions come from academics working in anthropology, political sociology, psychology and gender studies, also included are journalists and writers (three of them novelists) from and working on the Middle East. Since so little gets translated, their work is unfortunately still rarely available to readerships who do not know the languages of the region. Books which combine different approaches can sometimes end up being for everybody and for nobody. We like to think that dividing the book into sections has in some sense resolved this problem, and accordingly a brief discussion of the principles along which the essays have been grouped and a summary of the themes covered follows. Needless to say, there are many gaps in this book, many subjects not covered that perhaps should have been. Variation in assumptions as well as form also means that contributions do not 'agree'. However, being comprehensive and reaching a consensus is not the function of collections of this kind; reaching a consensus on the title of this book, indeed, eluded us! .

One of the motivations in commissioning the essays in this book was to look at areas where masculinity is most explicitly, and usually publicly, constructed. Circumcision, *bar mitzvah* and marriage perhaps provide the classic formal sites, and have since the nineteenth century preoccupied Western anthropologists. Van Gennep's work on 'initiation rites', involving tests and trials that culminate in social acceptance as a gendered adult, dates back to the beginning of the twentieth century. That its thesis is still in circulation is attested by the fact that several contributions to this book draw on it in passing, though none claim that it carries real explanatory value. The contributions are more concerned to explore institutions and practices associated with masculinity in specific historical contexts, and more work of this kind will perhaps result in a shift away from rather static functionalist models. The honour/shame thesis constructed in relation to Mediterranean and Middle Eastern societies is another such model, but one that has been substantially criticized, not least for presuming semantic fixity which an investigation of practice would immediately contradict.

With these provisos, the first part of this book groups together essays which do for the most part tackle the formal sites where exemplary masculinities are 'made', but resist attempts to generalize about such 'rituals' across a huge region. The book as a whole is, we hope, evidence of the dynamics of the local, and in each case the local is subject to marketized social relations and internationally circulating cultural idioms whose 'take up' or reworking in specific contexts in practice tends to make their origins increasingly unimportant. So much so that it is doubtful if the local in different Arab countries, in Turkey, in Iran, has ever been fixed, unsullied or authentic.

Though the book addresses some of the sites where masculinity is most evidently and ritualistically constructed, less obvious sites could easily have been chosen: studies of different sectors of the labour market and educational institutions, for example, would yield interesting results and help to break down the sense that Middle Eastern societies possess gender socialization processes that are distinct and do not find comparable versions elsewhere. Future studies will no doubt address these concerns, but it seems important to make clear that registering differences and specificities does not mean assuming that a country or region works to a different 'logic'. To illustrate the point from the reverse position, it could be added that to assume unproblematically that there is really something called 'Western ideology' that gets imposed on non-Western societies is to fall into a similar trap.

Turning to the essays that make up the first section, following a kind of chronology from childhood to adulthood, the first two both look at the earliest rituals that boy children undergo. Thus Abdelwahab Bouhdiba's discussion of circumcision among Muslims – though with mention of the Jewish practice – explores the social dimensions of the custom in Tunisian and Moroccan town settings in the period up to the early 1970s. From a novel by the Saudi writer, Abdu Khal, an extract describing a circumcision ceremony in the southern Arabian countryside in the inter-war period has been chosen. Acknowledgement of the very ambiguous sentiments at play is evident in both extracts: the boy suffers the pain and trauma of mutilation and the awful anticipation of it by being dressed up and paraded around in advance, but the event is celebrated as a joyful one by the family and local community and thus suffering brings with it social acceptance and further confirmation, in Bouhdiba's words, of the 'exorbitant privileges that go with being a male'. Both extracts reflect on an earlier time and should be read as such. How circumcision is celebrated varies widely according to region, urban or rural setting, and the social position of the family. The age of the boy also varies. It is a ceremony that also takes on the fashions of the time: videoing one's son's circumcision, for example, has become a common practice for those who can afford it in Turkey. While many boys nowadays undergo circumcision in clinics as babies and have local anaesthetics, in large cities like Istanbul local municipality councils and political parties in the summer months organize mass public circumcision events – sometimes for 1,500 boys – a populist move, partly about securing the votes of the urban poor.

The Jewish practice of circumcision generally takes place much earlier than the Muslim: customarily, on the eighth day in the infant's life. The contemporary rituals around circumcision as practised by one part of the ultraorthodox community in Israel, the subsequent celebration of the boy's first haircut three years later at the shrine of a saint, and his school initiation ceremony, are the themes of Yoram Bilu's article. Bilu provides a rich reading of the ways in which the physical practice of circumcision and the haircut are symbolically associated with the boy's induction into the world of Torah study, for males in the ultraorthodox community in theory a lifelong commitment and one which means that gendered socialization processes separating boys and girls are established in very early childhood.

Two articles look at the institution of military service in Israel and in Turkey, and a third deals with the gender dynamics of the Palestinian intifada. Julie Peteet explores the ways in which the masculine identity of Palestinian males, in the intifada context, became bound up with resistance against the far greater powers wielded by the Israeli Defence Forces. Though

Palestinian youth could not fight back in any real sense, resistance took the form of non-submission and a mode of personal conduct that emphasized resilience in the face of beatings. Young males thus began to command a level of respect and recognition from the local community generally not accorded to the younger generation. Peteet also examines the implications of this for women from the same communities and the active part they played in the process.

Danny Kaplan's article is drawn from the research he has been conducting on masculine identities in the Israeli army and shows the extent to which in that context military service inculcates versions of exemplary masculinity that are inextricably bound up with Zionism. Nir, whose life-history Kaplan interrogates, is gay and grew up in a secular liberal family. Though placed in an elite combat regiment where the majority were new immigrants to Israel who placed emphasis on religious practice, he did not reject the institution, but through a process of negotiation found means of affirming the experience and endorsing militarist versions of Zionist ideology. Kaplan's essay is important for showing, among other things, that it is not inevitable that gay masculinities resist the dominant culture.

Emma Sinclair-Webb's article looks at social meanings of military service in Turkey in the context of the seventeen-year conflict in the Kurdish areas of the country. Given the actual position of the armed forces in Turkey and a dominant culture strongly inflected by militaristic nationalism, it has been very difficult to secure popular support for anti-militarist campaigns, despite the high number of war casualties and almost half a million draft evaders. The workings of hegemonic masculinity can be explored by looking more closely at institutions like armies: the Turkish case in the current context demonstrates that within such an environment the making of exemplary masculinity entails the subordination of men by other men, quite apart from the subordination of women. An interview with a former conscript is included as a second section to the chapter and gives a suggestive personal account of the regime of degradation in one unit.

The theme of violence is one that marks the first section of the book. While this was not something we anticipated, it is perhaps fitting in relation to a region which is currently one of the most militarized and conflict-ridden.

Emphasizing diversity of practices and processes is a way to escape essentialism and stereotypes of various kinds. But since stereotypical outcomes – not least when it comes to popular conceptions of what masculinity is or is not – are resilient, get reproduced and carry social power there is no point in simply denying their truth and wishing them away. To refuse to engage with them is akin to ignoring or underplaying the power of dominant cultural values which in all societies generally prove harder to resist than to incorporate.

Another aim of the book has thus been to engage with stereotypes and essentialisms about the meaning of masculinity (and femininity) by exploring some areas of cultural production that demonstrate this process of negotiation. The essays grouped in the second section of the book, 'Male Fictions', are for the most part engaged with narratives and images of masculinity in film, novels, classical folk tales and the press. Understandings of what constitutes a desired version of masculinity can often only be asserted in relation to varieties perceived to be undesirable, deviant, effeminate or treacherous, and in relation, above all, to presumed characteristics of femininity. Thus assumptions about the 'nature' of women, their sexuality and their tricks and guiles against men are preoccupations. Homosexual masculinity, often seen primarily as deviant sexual practice rather than something categorizable as masculinity (as Frédéric Lagrange points out in his essay), provides another 'foil' against which to establish supposedly real, heterosexual masculinity. (It is clear that deep intolerance and denial of homosexuality is widespread across the Middle East and operates at many levels, with severe social sanctions that sometimes take a violent form.)

Afsaneh Najmabadi engages with some of the classical tales that have been circulating in written and oral forms for centuries and still have a certain popular currency. Given that the organizing narrative principle of many of these tales entails the wiles and tricks of a woman against a man, Najmabadi explores the function of the repetition of plot and thus how in narrative terms the disorder of women functions to shore up a homosocial 'bonding' between men. Najmabadi also engages with the question of whether in the light of this, figures like Shahrzad, the narrator of *The Thousand and One Nights*, can possibly be recuperable for feminist readings.

Frédéric Lagrange offers a survey of the representation of homosexuality in modern Arabic literature and shows, by charting different narrative trajectories of homosexual characters, the ways in which homosexuality is made to 'mean' different things: a deviant practice, associated with 'backward' societies; simply a substitute for heterosexual relations; the symptom of an ill society; a metaphor expressing the relationship between the Arab world and the West. Since sociological work on sexuality – and in particular, homosexuality – is still lacking, Lagrange sees discussion of homosexuality in cultural production as one means for opening up a wider discussion about the practice and attitudes to homosexuality in societies where 'the will not to know' has meant an enormous discrepancy between public attitudes and private practices in the realm of same-sex desire.

Turning to Farid Shauqi, a popular film-star – dubbed 'King of the cheap seats' – in 1950s Egypt, Walter Armbrust explores the various 'faces' of the star, the themes of his films, and the texts that circulated around the films and the star in the form of fan magazine articles. Armbrust's article also compares the on-screen/off-screen persona of Shauqi with the treatment of male stars in the American fan media of the same period. He suggests that Shauqi's popularity becomes more interesting and complex when one begins to think about his audience: their social position, the prevailing gender order and how they responded to the various versions of masculinity that Shauqi seemed to embody.

Starting again in Egypt, but this time in the mid-1990s, Mai Ghoussoub looks at a news story that broke in the national press which focused a whole series of social anxieties about male power and loss of power in relation to women and the foreign enemy. An innocent looking chewing gum supposedly exported by Israel to Arab countries came to be attributed with the devilish properties of rendering women insatiable and men impotent and infertile: the issue was even debated in the national parliament. Ghoussoub explores the function of such moral panics and then goes on to relate them to a whole genre of classical texts – advice books on erotic life and sexual practice – that focus on the wily nature of women and their active sexuality in relation to men. Such texts may be centuries old, but in recent times have enjoyed a popular revival and circulate widely.

The final essay in this section looks at the image of Saddam Hussein, projected through photographs, statues, monuments and a vast array of mementoes. Hazim Saghieh engages with the various stereotypical depictions of the leader which, he argues, in the end, for all their variety, have a monolithic quality, ahistorical, abstract and ultimately empty, depending only on 'a never-ending process of greater magnification' in order to sustain the project of inducing fear. Saghieh ties his discussion of Saddam's image with some factors about the social structure and modern history of Iraq that all too easily get sidelined in discussions of the Iraqi president.

The final section is made up of essays in a different genre from the rest. We have called them memoirs because each looks at the formation of masculine identity in individual lives. In at least two cases we might equally categorize them as written in a fictional form: the line between autobiographical writing and fictional writing is in formal terms a very unclear one.

Thus Moris Farhi's autobiographical short story centres on his visits as a boy with his nanny to the public baths, *hamam*, in the Ankara of the late 1940s. The pleasures of this steamy environment of voluptuous naked females and the erotic stirrings induced in the boy – until the inevitable moment of expulsion when the innocence of his gaze is questioned – are the themes of a comic tale which evokes a social world that existed until recent times and will come as familiar to many who grew up in Turkey, or indeed in other parts of the region.

Ahmad Beydoun's account turns to other memories of childhood and describes his relationship with his father – a local *zaim*, or leader, in south Lebanon in the 1950s – his separation from his father's world and its values, and choice of another direction, propelled by a secular education that became available for the first time to his generation. That he could not become his father and thus assume leadership and responsibility for the affairs of the community into which he was born, or live up to the name he had been given at birth (that of another senior *zaim* to whom his father was a 'satellite'), proved at times a painful course to negotiate. Beydoun's account highlights the importance, too, of looking at generational aspects to gender identity which intertwine with the transformation of social and economic structures.

The final essay in the book turns to that virtual institution of Middle Eastern societies: the moustache. Hassan Daoud's part memoir, part fantasy recalls the different moustache fashions of his childhood (from the neatly drawn 'Douglas' and on), their meanings for him then, and at how he and his friends imagined male handsomeness. Himself the possessor of a fine moustache, Daoud traces his version back to the late 1960s when the favoured model in Beirut, as elsewhere, was 'Che Guevara's without the beard'. As Daoud explains it, 'It was not appropriate for a young man of the left who neglected his clothes, his sleep and his food to have a moustache drawn as neatly as a woman's eyebrows.'

Thanks are due to the following for kindly granting permission to reproduce material: to the Study Centre on Turkey, Amsterdam, for permission to use an interview from their report on human rights abuses in the army in chapter 3; to the American Anthropological Association for permission to reproduce a version of an article by Julie Peteet that appeared in *American Ethnologist* as chapter 4. Although commissioned for this book, versions of chapters 6, 7, 10 and 13 have already appeared in Arabic in various editions of the journal, *Abwab*. Chapter 12 is an abridged version of an essay written for the conference on the individual in the Middle East, which took place at the Rockefeller Foundation, Bellagio, Italy, 31 May to 4 June 1999.

I would like to acknowledge the help of several friends and colleagues with the project. I thank André Gaspard and Sarah al-Hamad at Saqi Books in London; my co-editor, Mai Ghoussoub, with whom the book was edited between London and Istanbul. Thanks to Basil Hatim, Osman Nusairi, Gavin Watterson and Malcolm Williams for their translations from Arabic; to Emmanuel Sivan for his helpful suggestions for articles; to Gwynnfyl Lowe for proofreading the book and to Ed Emery for indexing it; and to Yücel Terzibaşoğlu for his engagement with this project and support for all my work.

Emma Sinclair-Webb
March 2000

Notes

1. The work of R.W. Connell on gender has been central to this effort and is notable for its combination of approaches to the subject, insisting on an empirical basis to research while placing equal emphasis on knowledge about gender in the social sciences and in political movements. See two of his books, in particular: *Gender and Power: Society, the Person and Sexual Politics* (Cambridge: Polity Press, 1989), and *Masculinities* (Cambridge: Polity Press, 1995). The work of Lynne Segal is also important for, among other things, bringing to bear conceptual debates on a socialist feminist political project: see, in the context of the subject of masculinity, *Slow Motion: Changing Masculinities, Changing Men* (London: Virago, 1990), and *Straight Sex: Rethinking the Politics of Pleasure* (London: Virago, 1994).

2. For perhaps the most explicit and articulate statement of this, see Deniz Kandiyoti's 'Contemporary Feminist Scholarship and Middle Eastern Studies', in Deniz Kandiyoti (ed.), *Gendering the Middle East* (London: I.B.Tauris, 1996), pp. 1–49, and the other essays in her book which demonstrate something of the range of fruitful new research emerging on the region.

3. An exception to this is Andrea Cornwall and Nancy Lindisfarne (eds.), *Dislocating Masculinity: Comparative Ethnographies* (London: Routledge, 1994); some of the essays relate to Middle Eastern countries.

PART I

Making Men:

Institutions and Social Practices

Festivities of Violence: Circumcision and the Making of Men

Abdelwahab Bouhdiba
Abdu Khal

In this chapter we include two extracts on male circumcision. Practised through-out the Middle East among Muslim and Jewish communities, with consider-able regional variation as to the age of the boy and the accompanying ceremonies and customs, one account comes from a study of sexuality in Islam by the Tunisian sociologist, Abdelwahab Bouhdiba, and one from a novel by the Saudi writer, Abdu Khal. It should be borne in mind that Bouhdiba's discus-sion (down to the terminology he uses) refers mainly to the rite as it was popu-larly practised in North African Muslim societies – Tunisia and Morocco, in particular – in the early 1970s when he wrote his book; he emphasizes circum-cision as a mark of inclusion in the community of Muslim believers but also comments on the violence of the custom. The circumcision episode in Khal's novel is set in a Saudi village some fifty years ago. The episode makes no men-tion of a socio-religious dimension and brings out another aspect of the prac-tice's social meaning: among other things, this is a rite that signifies the arrival of manhood.

ABDELWAHAB BOUHDIBA
SEXUALITY IN ISLAM

Translated from the French by Alan Sheridan (London: Routledge & Kegan Paul,
1985; paperback publication: London: Saqi Books, 1998), pp. 174–84. First published
in French as *La Sexualité en Islam* (Paris: Presses Universitaires de France, 1975).

[I]n the interwar period, a tribe in southern Sudan wanted to be converted
en bloc to Islam. It contacted the Islamic University of El Azhar for information concerning the doctrine, practices and laws of Islam and the procedure to be followed to complete the conversion. It was given a list of what
had to be done: at the top of the list was circumcision. When the adult
members of the tribe refused to have themselves mutilated the whole idea
was dropped.[1] This gives some idea of the importance accorded by El Azhar
as indeed by almost all the Muslim populations to circumcision, which is
regarded preeminently as the mark of inclusion in Muslim society. Indeed
this practice is more or less unanimously observed at every social level and
at whatever degree of development and acculturation. No one – not even
free thinkers, communists, atheists, or even partners of mixed marriages –
ignores the rule. Even in Tunisia under Bourguiba, which in so many re-
spects has demonstrated its openness to innovation in matters of custom
and religion, the number of the uncircumcised cannot exceed a hundred.
In the last few years Tunisia has begun to accept that a Muslim Tunisian
woman may marry a non-Muslim. This is a very brave measure, indeed one
that is unique in the Muslim world and constantly being brought up in the
Tunisian parliament. But what people find most shocking about the idea is
that a Muslim woman can sleep with an uncircumcised man, even in a
lawful marriage! Circumcision is a great deal more than a matter of hy-
giene, or of mere custom. It is deeply rooted in Islamic mores and certainly
corresponds to something fundamental. [. . .]

And yet circumcision is an act that, according to the fiqh, is in no way
compulsory. It is a *sunna* act,[2] that is to say, one that is strongly recom-
mended. The excision of girls is even less obligatory. It is a *makruma*: a
pious practice, like removing a stone from the road, clearing a public drain
or maintaining a collective watertap. The question is so secondary that
even the longest books of fiqh devote very little space to it. The *fatawa
hindiyya*, which stretches to almost three thousand pages, devotes only a
third of a page to it. Al-Ghazali deals with the question in exactly seven
lines in that summa of over two thousand pages known as the *Ihya*. As for
the great commentary of Aini on the Bokhari tradition, it is, in spite of its

nine thousand pages, absolutely silent on this matter. The Quran says nothing about it. And Sidi Khalil, the great Malekite jurist, admits that collective prayer may quite validly be conducted by an uncircumcised man.

Indeed we do not know in what conditions the Prophet himself was circumcised. He must have been so since the act is a *sunna*, that is to say, an imitation of the Prophet, yet biographers attentive to the slightest details of the life of the Messenger of God have little to say about his circumcision. It is said that he was circumcised by his grandfather when he was forty days old. According to other traditions he was born already circumcised – by angels in his mother's womb. On the other hand tradition does tell us how his heart was purified (*tathir*). Since we know that circumcision is also commonly called *tahara* (purification), it may be possible to establish a correlation between the two notions. When Muhammad was being fostered by the Beni Saouds and was not yet four years old two angels took him and weighed him in order to determine his metaphysical value. They split open his chest, took out the heart, opened it, and removed the 'speck of black blood', which is the sign of the *shaitan* [devil]. They washed the heart with water from the sacred zemzem well contained in a golden bowl. They placed *sakina*, 'peaceful quietude', which was like the face of a beautiful white cat, in the heart. They then put everything back in place. Lastly they placed between his shoulders the seal of prophecy (*khatam al-nubwa*).[3] The surgical operation had, of course, a very precise metaphysical meaning. It was intended to protect Muhammad's heart from any tendency to evil.

'Circumcision', says Ghazali, 'is practised by the Jews on the seventh day. We must differentiate ourselves from them and wait until the child's hair has begun to grow.'[4] The *fatawa hindiyya* advocate the period between seven and twelve years. There was much concern about the circumcision of the adult who had become converted to Islam. Canonically an old man in weak health could be dispensed from it, but not others. Preferably he would circumcise himself; otherwise he would pay a concubine who was specialized in this sort of operation to perform it. Indeed she alone was permitted to see and touch her master's penis. Any other person ran the risk of breaking the rules concerning *'aura*. In extreme circumstances the manager of the hammam would be allowed to perform the operation.[5]

It should be noticed that Islam distinguishes carefully between *khitan*, circumcision in the strict sense, which consists in the circular section of the foreskin, and *khasi*, which is castration obtained by the total or partial removal of one or both testicles. The latter is strictly prohibited by the *fatawa hindiyya*,[6] whereas Qadhi-Khan[7] merely declares it to be blameworthy.

[. . .]

Is [circumcision], as has sometimes been said, simply a survival from an earlier period? This is the opinion of Mazahéri, who writes: 'Christianity rejected this semitic custom and replaced it by baptism, which is of Zoroastrian origin; but Islam, believing that it is following in the supposed footsteps of the "prophet" Abraham, preserved the semitic practice of circumcision for both sexes.'[8] The explanation of survival is very convenient, but not very satisfactory, for in the Maghreb the Berbers appear not to have known it and even the Phoenicians gave it up, it seems, when they settled in Africa.[9] It was introduced in the seventh and eighth centuries by the Arab conquerors. Indeed it is difficult to speak of survival for a practice so profoundly rooted in the collective life of the Arabo-Muslim societies. Circumcision provides an opportunity for familial ceremonies that are exceeded in scope only by wedding festivities. It is a solemn festival. It is not surprising if no prayer accompanies it, since it has no canonical character. But the child is dressed in his finest clothes, always new, almost always embroidered. Everyone goes off to the marabout, or shrine, of the holy protector of the town or family, Sidi Mehraz in Tunis or Imam Shafi'i in Cairo. There is always a procession through the town.

When the moment has come, the uncle or grandfather takes the child in his arms and a barber (tahhar) performs the operation, which lasts only a second or two, with a razor or sharp scissors. Then the wound is sealed with a little wood ash, spider's web, alum or other haemostatic. Just at the moment of the operation, a large red or black cockerel must be killed and the tahhar takes it away as payment. Just as the cut is being made, new pitchers must be broken by throwing them violently on the ground. Meanwhile, in front of the door, the child's friends from the kuttab, or traditional quranic primary school, bellow out litanies, accompanied by a deafening din of drums, bagpipes and fanfares. The important thing is to make a noise, a lot of noise.

Then everyone comes in to congratulate the newly circumcised boy and give him sweetmeats, toys or coins. Then there are celebrations. Rich people, of course, make more of a show, spinning the festivities out to a week or more. There are concerts, known as hafalat tarab in the Middle East or 'auada in the Maghreb. Some of these celebrations have gone down in history: there were those of Jahya, the grandson of al-Ma'mun of Toledo, for example, or those of the son of al-Moizz Ibn Badis of Kairwan.

As for the mutilated child, he could do nothing but cry out in pain and weep in shock at the violence done to his body. This wound in his flesh, these men and women torturing him, that gleaming razor, the strident oohs and ahs of inquisitive, indiscreet old women, the jugs smashing on the floor, the cry of the cockerel, struggling and losing its blood, the din outside and finally the endless stream of people coming to congratulate the patient on 'his happy accession to Islam', that is what circumcision means to a child.

One should mention too the obsessional anxiety of the *tahhar*, kept up before, during and after the event, and the painful wound, so often slow to heal; sometimes long, painful weeks were necessary, sometimes, too, accidents caused more serious complications; infections, haemorrhages, cutting through the artery or even right through the penis, removing part of the glans.

Circumcision, secondary from a religious point of view, would not seem to be explicable from a physiological point of view either. Though sometimes necessary in treating phimosis, nothing can justify its systematic use, especially without anaesthetic. It involves enormous dangers, on both the physiological and psychical plane. It is hardly surprising if some commentators see it as a barbarous, traumatizing practice.[10] A French dictionary of sexology speaks uninhibitedly of 'bloody sacrifice' and goes on to say:

> By exposing the glans permanently, circumcision often allows it to be covered by a skin that makes it lose much of its sensitivity. The merits of this semi-anaesthetic are often praised: the man needs a larger number of coital movements to reach orgasm, thus giving the woman the advantage of prolonged excitement. One must indeed have very little self-control to require such a surface anaesthetic.[11]

In view of all this, one may well pose the problem of the significance of circumcision in Islam. In Judaism this meaning is more or less clear. Indeed Genesis says quite explicitly:

> And God said to Abraham, 'As for you, you shall keep my covenant, you and your descendants after you throughout their generations. This is my covenant, which you shall keep, between me and you and your descendants after you: every male among you shall be circumcised . . . So shall my covenant be in your flesh an everlasting covenant. Any uncircumcised male who is not circumcised in the flesh of his foreskin shall be cut off from his people; he has broken my covenant.'[12]

The meaning of Jewish circumcision is perfectly obvious. It is a sacrificial rite. It seals the covenant with the Eternal, by offering him a bloody part of one's own body. It may be seen as a substitute for a more radical human sacrifice, a purification of the pleasures of the flesh, an initiation trial through endurance, courage and mortification, a subtle way of increasing sexual pleasure, or on the contrary, as Philo maintained, a way of directing oneself away from lechery.[13]

In a more general way, ethnologists and sociologists, comparing Jewish and archaic societies, have given vent to their theories. There is a good discussion, followed by an excellent summing up by Marcel Mauss that concludes: 'For me circumcision is essentially a tattoo. It is a tribal, even national sign.'[14]

Without embarking further on a theoretical discussion of such a wide-spread practice, we ought perhaps to say that the initiatory meaning of the rite is undeniable.

This is evident in the extraordinary passage in Exodus that describes Moses' circumcision. After living among the Midianites, Moses, who, in the meantime, has married Zippo'rah and had a son by her, returns to Egypt. There then follows an episode that has embarrassed Jewish and Christian commentators for centuries:

> At a lodging place on the way the Lord met him and sought to kill him. Then Zippo'rah took a flint and cut off her son's foreskin, and touched Moses' feet with it, and said, 'Surely you are a bridegroom of blood to me!' So he let him alone. Then it was that she said, 'You are a bridegroom of blood,' because of the circumcision.[15]

Not having been circumcised Moses had been excluded from Abraham's sacrificial ritual. Returning among his people and consummating his marriage, he had to regularize his situation, that is to say, seal his covenant with God. So he did this by substitution. Zippo'rah cut off the foreskin of their common son and touched Moses' parts with it. Moses then becomes for her 'a bridegroom of blood'. Their son's blood may be regarded as Moses' own blood. In his fine book, *L'initiation sexuelle et l'évolution religieuse*, Pierre Gordon rightly concludes that circumcision is 'a communion with the divine universe . . . On the road from Egypt, the operation is carried out by a sacrosanct man, a man bearing the title of Yahweh, and who collaborates with God to bring the Prophet to his mission so that he may be better prepared to carry it out.'[16] The initiatory character of Mosaic circumcision would appear to be established beyond doubt.

Approaching the question from the Jewish tradition, Maryse Choisy eventually reaches a similar conclusion, while emphasizing the archetypal symbolism of the ritual of circumcision as exemplified in the incident concerning Moses. Having reached the Nile delta, Moses is almost swallowed whole by a python. Only his legs are left visible in the dragon's mouth. Zippo'rah guesses at once what God requires. Quick as a flash, picking up the first stone to hand, she circumcises her second son. With the blood from the foreskin, she anoints his legs.

'You are for me a *chathan dammin*,' she says.
A voice rises from the Nile:
'Spit him out! Spit him out!'
Then the serpent spits out Moses.[17]

Stressing the idea that 'the sacrifice of Abraham is the archetype of all evolution',[18] Maryse Choisy brings out the two fundamental characteristics of the ritual of Moses' circumcision; that it is performed by a woman and in a bloody manner. 'When the Bible translates *chathan dammin* by "bridegroom of blood", it loses the richness of meaning in the ritual. It stresses blood and female initiation.'[19] And Maryse Choisy concludes: 'In Genesis . . . the initiatory value [of circumcision] is not in doubt. A circumcised child is to the children of Israel what a baptized child is to Christians. A personal soul has been awakened in that spark of life. Through this sign he will survive the destruction of the flesh. By this sign he distinguishes himself from the pre-Adamites, from wholly mortal animals, which lack the divine light.'[20]

It can certainly be said that Jewish circumcision is a covenant with the Lord in the sense that it is a rite and a sacrifice intended to raise consciousness in the group and community. It is an initiation rite effecting a double passage from adolescence to the community of mature men and from the state of nature to the state of man, fertilized by the divine light and belonging to a chosen people privileged enough to maintain a dialogue with the divinity.

It is impossible not to be attentive to this Jewish constellation of the symbolism of circumcision. For Christianity was to deprive circumcision of this meaning. Apart from the Church of Ethiopia, which still practises circumcision, all the sects and Christian churches keep to the terms of St Paul's epistle to the Galatians:

It is those who want to make a good showing in the flesh that would compel you to be circumcised, and only in order that they may not be persecuted for the cross of Christ. For even those who receive circumcision do not themselves keep the law, but they desire to have you circumcised that they may glory in your flesh. But far be it from me to glory except in the cross of our Lord Jesus Christ, by which the world has been crucified to me, and I to the world. For neither circumcision counts for anything, nor uncircumcision, but a new creation.[21]

So the symbolism of circumcision is explicitly rejected by the Gospels. Baptism came to replace circumcision. Communion with Christ took the place of the bloody covenant with the Lord.

So where does that leave Islam? Are we to believe that in restoring what Christianity had abolished, Islam was quite simply returning to a Semitic tradition? I do not really think so. Canonically and theologically, circumcision has no privileged status. It is not one of the five pillars of Islam (profession of faith, prayer, alms, fasting, pilgrimage to Mecca). It is merely a *sunna*. The ritual surrounding it is loose, imprecise, and more spontaneous than organic. It is accompanied by no prayer. The age at which the operation is performed is not fixed in any strict way and may take place at any time between one and twelve years. The fiqh is hardly concerned with it and the Quran not at all. Furthermore there is a systematic concern on the part of Muslims to distinguish themselves from the Jews on this matter, whereas in other cases the imitation of Jewish practices is hardly stressed in so systematic a way. For instance, a Muslim may eat meat killed according to the Jewish ritual; whereas, among the few recommendations given by Ghazali is that not to practise circumcision at the age of seven days, 'in order to distinguish ourselves from them by postponing it'.[22] In Islam the seventh day of birth is marked only by a simple ceremony of presentation to the family and to the 'people' of the household, by which is meant the djinns. At Damascus, as at Cairo or Marrakesh, the child, bathed, scented, oiled, dressed in a thousand and one propitiatory amulets, is wrapped in a sheet. The midwife (*qabila u daya*) presents him at all the doors of the house by knocking on each one three times. She throws grilled chick peas, raisins and sweets on the ground, crying: 'The house is ours, the children are ours, here is the Prophet come to visit us.'

Circumcision, like excision indeed, is more a practice of Muslims than a practice of Islam. By that I mean that its sociological aspect, its social significance, is quite obviously more important than the clearly secondary sacral aspect. It is a question of marking membership of the group. The words 'We the circumcised' define a relationship of inclusion within the community. It is this that explains, it seems to me, the tenacity with which 'Muslims' and the less 'Muslim' cling to this practice. The festivities surrounding it are in fact ceremonies by which young children are admitted to the group. Hence the relatively advanced age at which it is practised.

Circumcision is a passage to the world of adults and a preparation; carried out in blood and pain, and therefore unforgettable, into an age of responsibilities. In terms of Muslim society and religion, it exists at the same level as the practices of the hammam.

Looked at more closely, from a different point of view, in terms of the celebrations around it, it is difficult not to regard it as a sort of repetition of the wedding ceremony.[23] The two ceremonies are structured in the same way and some of the days bear the same name. The day before the eve of the day of circumcision is called in Tunisia, like the wedding night, *wutya*, from *wataa*, to coit. The ceremonies of laying on henna, of washing in the hammam, of the visit to the hairdresser and even the day of rest (*raha*), which separate them from the act itself, have much in common in each case. It is as if circumcision were only a mimicry of marriage and the sacrifice of the foreskin an anticipation of that of the hymen [. . .]. It is as if circumcision were a preparation for deflowering and indeed is it not a question of preparing oneself for coitus, of sensitizing oneself to the genetic activity, of valorizing in a sense the phallus, which is thus in turn purified and placed in reserve? The sexual significance of circumcision cannot be in doubt. And if anyone is still in any doubt on the matter, let him remember the traditional song sung in Tunisia on this occasion:

> You begin with circumcision and you end in marriage, and still your horse neighs in the forest.
> You begin with circumcision and you end in youth, and still your horse neighs among the bachelors.
> Let us call quickly for his mother, let us call quickly for his aunt, let them come quickly and throw money on the procreative rod.[24]

The symbolism is perfectly obvious. Circumcision and marriage are marked here as the two steps, initial and final, in the single process of living. Circumcision is the open way to marriage, it is the promise of a permanent youth, in the sense that it will spare man the disappointments of old age. For in this business there is a horse that will always neigh and will always be standing, present and master of all, of the cohort of bachelors. What is this horse if not the 'procreative rod'('*ammara*) on which one asks the female relations to come and throw propitiatory money. The money must match this '*ammara*, which must be strengthened, prepared, maintained, glorified and protected from the evil eye. Circumcision is both a promise and a guarantee of a future genetic life that one hopes will be as full, as great and as durable as love.

Everything is carried out in such a way, therefore, that circumcision is seen as quite different from castration. Does it succeed? The question really should be asked. For circumcision is carried out at an age when the boy has long since been made aware of the difference between the sexes. Very often a state of anxiety is induced in the boy by his family and friends. He is soon made aware of the exorbitant privileges that go with being a male. He has been made well aware of the importance of that 'little thing that hangs down', as little Muslim girls invariably refer to it. Hence the fear that it will be cut off if it is not circumcised or, even, that what remains will be cut off after circumcision. Such a fear is part and parcel of the paradox and contradiction of childhood experience. There is a symbolic valorization of the phallus and an obsessional fear of losing it. This situation is likely to last for a long time, especially in an authoritarian society and one in which the terrifying father holds all kinds of goods, pleasures, wealth – and women – in 'trust' for him. If, in the end, everything seems to settle down without too much difficulty and heartache it is certainly because of all the forms of socialization set in train, but also because of the early age of marriage.

Notes

1. Ahmad Amin, *Qamus al 'adat wa al-taqalid wal-ta'abir al-masriyya* (Cairo, 1953), p. 187.
2. *Al-fatawa al-Hindiyya* ed. Bulaq, 1310h., 6 vols, vol. v, p. 356.
3. Moslem, *Sahih* (Cairo, 1328h., 1st edn.), 7 vols, vol. i, p. 34*ff*; Tabari, *Jama' al-bayan fi tafsir al-Quran* (Cairo, 1312h.), 30 vols, vol. i, 154; M. Gaudefroy-Demombynes, *Mahomet* (Paris, 1957), p. 63; Muhammad Essad Bey, *Allah est grand* (Paris, 1937), p. 55.
4. Al-Ghazali, *Ihya 'ulum al-din* (Cairo, 1302h.), 4 vols, vol. i, p. 132. [Editors' note: The Jewish practice of circumcision is usually said to take place on the eighth day. Ghazali, however, refers to it as the seventh day, according to the system whereby the day of birth is not counted. See Yoram Bilu's essay, chapter two in this book.]
5. *Al-fatawa al-Hindiyya*, vol. v, p. 357.
6. Ibid.
7. Qadhi-Khan, *Fatawa*, in *al-fatawa al-Hindiyya*, vol. iii, p. 409.
8. A. Mazahéri, *La vie quotidienne des musulmans au Moyen Age* (Paris, 1947), p. 47.
9. C-A. Julien, *Histoire de l'Afrique de Nord*, p. 92.
10. Ahmad Amin, *Qamus*, p. 187.
11. *Dictionnaire de sexologie* (Paris, 1962), p. 321.
12. Genesis, 17, 9–14.

13. cf. *Dictionnaire des religions*, p. 84.
14. 'The origin of circumcision according to Frazer', in Marcel Mauss, *Oeuvres* (Paris, 1968), vol. i, p. 142.
15. Exodus, 4, 24–6.
16. P. Gordon, *L'initiation sexuelle et l'évolution religieuse* (Paris, 1946), p. 68.
17. Maryse Choisy, *Moïse* (Geneva, 1966), p. 91.
18. Ibid., p. 92.
19. Ibid., p. 94.
20. Ibid., p. 96.
21. Galatians, 6, 12-15.
22. Al-Ghazali, *Ihya*, vol. i, p. 132.
23. In addition to personal experience, my main sources here are: Salah al-Rizqi, *Al-Afghani al-Tunusiyya* (Tunis, 1967), pp. 171–75; Ahmad Amin, *Qamus*, pp. 187–89.
24. My translation here is from the version given by Salah al-Rizqi, *Al-Afghani*, p. 187: 'Ulik tahhar wu 'qabiq 'aras wu hsanik ywalwal ma bin l-ghrus./ Ulik mtahhar wu 'qabiq shbab wu hsanik ywalwal ma bin l'uzzah./ Wini um l-matahhar, wini khaltu tji tarmi drahim 'ala 'ammartu.'

ABDU KHAL
MUDUN TA'QULU AL-'ISHB
(*Cities that devour grass*)

London and Beirut: Dar al-Saqi, 1998, pp. 39–43. This extract translated by Basil Hatim and Gavin Watterson.

Abdu Khal's novel is set in Saudi Arabia and, beginning during the inter-war period, tells the story of a young boy growing up in a rapidly changing society. Yahya's father is dead and he is now the male of the family and the one who will accompany his grandmother on the pilgrimage to Mecca. Before departing on this journey – which is unexpectedly to result in his separation from the rest of the family for many years, and his eventual return to the village only with the outbreak of the Yemen war in the early 1960s – Yahya undergoes his circumcision. His mother, Khadij, warns him of the importance of how he conducts himself: the reputation of the family is at stake. Related to the theme of publicly establishing the boy's right to be considered a man through a trial involving acute pain to the body, is the contradictory relationship between mother and son, in which the mother's love is at once quite overpowering and the threat that it may be withdrawn if the boy disappoints all pervasive.

The author adds a footnote, explaining this episode in the text: 'The method of circumcision practised in the regions of southern Tihama (on the southern edge of the Arabian peninsula) runs as follows: the person requiring circumcision is prepared, and stands with his hands on his hips, gazing away ahead of him without blinking until the circumcision is performed by cutting a small part of the foreskin and tying it. If the circumcised person looks at his wound, or blinks, or shows any sign of fear, it is said that so-and-so flinched (the verb used is takhabbab*), and his shame remains as long as he lives.' The place where the circumcision is performed is described as follows: 'The* makhatina *is composed of piles of accumulated rubbish which over time has made it a raised place. While such piles are found everywhere in the village, the one chosen for the circumcision podium is usually in an open area somewhat outside.'*

I never saw her yearning for me so intensely as on the day of my circumcision, and because she was yearning for me, she insisted on attending the circumcision with the men. She kept pushing me onto the dance floor and warning me:

'Be careful not to flinch.'
'___'
'Don't let people gloat over us.'
'___'
'Don't let them say you're a sissie.'
'___'
'Don't blink and so shame us and yourself.'

She poured advice into my ears as I danced my way towards the circumcision podium. The high stringed instrument shrieked, and I felt that with his bow Rayyis Khamis was kindling my heart. It was beating wildly, almost leaping out of my breast with its swift throbbing. I lost myself in the dance. Others joined me for a swift spell and then slipped away. I remained on the floor, circling with strenuous steps which I tried to do perfectly. I felt that all eyes were on me, watching every movement I made.

There were *zagarids** reverberating from afar and the sound of rifle shots pierced my ears with a high-pitched buzz. Some lowered their rifles on purpose

---

* Shrill trilling cries (ululation) made by women at many celebrations in the Middle East [translator's note].

so that their bullets flew horizontally like shooting stars, leaving behind them a wisp of smoke playing on round the muzzle of the gun. The circumcision procession was moving towards the podium slowly and with joy. I was jumping from one place to another surrounded by the drummers, the riflemen, and a group of people from the village. I felt ashamed when I noticed my mother coming behind us lovingly, and I wished I could call out to her to go back. As I danced I stole a glance at her face which wore a veil of compassion, anticipation and joy. She raised her hand from afar, her lips mouthing words, and when her words failed to reach me she loosened her tongue and chased away the wind with blazing *zagarid*s.

I arrived at the place of circumcision, jumped up on it and stood there upright. I heard rifle shots go over my head as I gazed into space. The circumciser undid my *ezar* [covering garment] and I felt the blade cut off my foreskin and sticky blood pour out. My eyes gazed firmly into the distance without being fixed on anything. I only wanted to get through this ordeal without bringing shame upon my mother. I heard Uncle Jibril cry, 'Khadij's son has enabled us to hold our heads high.'

I was seized with ardour and shouted at the circumciser without blinking, 'Circumcise, you circumciser, and cut off some more of the foreskin for my uncle!'

He reached out his sharp blade and cut off a further slice of my foreskin. A succession of shots rang out and whistled into the distance, while smoke danced about on the muzzles of the rifles. I shouted, 'Circumcise, you circumciser, and cut off some of my foreskin for my mother.'

He twisted the blade out towards my thigh. I felt sticky blood pour down the lower part of me and flow like little rivers between my thighs. It zigzagged down, some of it coagulating and some of it continuing to flow. Clamour, *zagarid*s, rifle shots and men shouting to one another, 'A man, a man from the loins of a man.'

I was seized with ardour and wanted to cut off a part of my body for all those I held dear. I was carried away with excitement, and cried, 'Circumcise, you circumciser . . .'

Before I could complete the sentence my mother snatched me from on top of the podium, letting out *zagarid*s, 'Don't kill yourself, my son!'

I slipped away from her arms, determined to complete the journey to the house dancing. That day the circumciser said, 'I have never seen someone circumcised like the son of Khadij.'

This bravery almost cost me my life. I remained in pain for three months from the wounds, which festered and spread to eat at my foreskin and branched off to reach those shameful testicles. Every time my mother noticed me in pain, she would beat her breast in dismay, 'I am the cause, I am the cause!'

My grandmother blamed her for her weakness and scolded her loudly, 'All men find that their circumcision wounds gnaw at them.'

But my mother repeated with anguish, 'My son is an orphan. If I had circumcised him at home, nobody would have blamed me.'

She remained near me all that period, blaming herself and trying her best to stop the ulceration. She tried every medicine she had heard of in the hope that it would work. She swore an oath that she would not put me in harm's way from that day on as long as I lived. In the third month after my circumcision, she had a lamb slaughtered near the shrine of Sayyid al-Makki and scattered some dust from the place over me. She was letting out *zagarid*s all along the road.

I woke up the morning we were going to travel to find my mother embracing me and sobbing quietly. It hurt her to sob since she had become hoarse, 'Yahya, it is time to travel!'

Her voice came to me, and it was as if I were in a clamorous dream. I opened my eyes, blinked and then fled back into sleep once more. She allowed me some time and retreated. She embraced me and tidied my hair. When she heard calls to hurry from my grandmother and some of those who had been preparing our camel, she shook me gently and sought to encourage me, 'Only two days and you'll be back with us.'

TWO

Circumcision, the First Haircut and the Torah
Ritual and Male Identity Among the Ultraorthodox Community of Contemporary Israel

Yoram Bilu

In contemporary Israel, the *haredi* or ultraorthodox who number about 600,000 (10 per cent of the population) are known to be the most religiously observant sector of the population. Clearly distinguished by their peculiar appearance (beards, ear-locks, skull-caps, and sect-appropriate old-fashioned dark uniform for men; wigs or head-dresses and modest clothes for women), the *haredi* are noted for their uncompromising adherence to the strictest version of Halakha (Jewish religious law). The sacred for them becomes a 'phenomenological constant' regulating every aspect of daily life.

Although unified by religious fundamentalism (Heilman and Friedman 1991), augmented by deliberate attempts to retain the socio-cultural life patterns of traditional Jewish communities in former centuries, the ultraorthodox do not constitute a monolithic bloc. In fact, they are sharply divided into many sects and factions, marked by bitter struggles over political power, material rewards and religious hegemony. The historical watershed that separated enthusiastic, mystically oriented *Hasidim* from their rationalist opponents (*Mitnagdim*) has been blurred in the twentieth century; but the two camps, and many of the parties within each of them, have preserved distinct religious sensibilities. Another historical rift, between Ashkenazi and *Mizrahi* or Sephardic Jews (of European versus Middle Eastern and North African backgrounds respectively), has been strongly maintained among strictly religious Israeli Jews, as evidenced by the persistence and growth of ultraorthodox political parties and educational systems in keeping with the ethno-cultural division. As I later show, the ritual haircutting sequence undergone by three-year-old boys is mostly an Ashkenazi phenomenon, performed in somewhat different forms by both Hasidim and Mitnagdim.

The various ultraorthodox groups also differ in their attitudes toward the Zionist state which range from reserved acceptance to total condemnation of Israel as a sovereign nation-state. The groups are united, however, in their unequivocal opposition to the secular lifestyle of mainstream Israeli society. Striving at all costs to insulate themselves from the polluting effects of modernity, they tend to concentrate in well-delineated neighbourhoods. Most of the ultraorthodox thus live in Jerusalem and in Bnai Brak, an all-religious town near Tel-Aviv. But today, because of population pressures and housing shortages in these centres, a Haredi neighbourhood can be found in many urban settlements throughout the country.

Life in the ultraorthodox neighbourhoods unfolds according to socio-cultural codes so much at odds with those of the rest of society as to fashion a sharply distinct subculture that institutes (and is being instituted by) a social reality and behavioural environment of its own. For those immersed in this subculture, the twin spiritual ideals to be relentlessly pursued are the strict fulfilment of all religious precepts and the study of Jewish sacred texts, especially the Talmud, in religious academies (*yeshivot*) (see Heilman 1986, Helmreich 1982). Women are expected to contribute to the second goal, limited to men only, by taking care of the house with its numerous children (as procreation is a cardinal commandment to be strictly pursued) and, if necessary, by becoming the breadwinner.

The puritanical character of the family is manifest in an elaborate decorum of modesty and a strict separation of the sexes. This separation launches boys and girls into entirely different socialization orbits. Three-year-old male children are already engulfed in religious study that will remain their main vocation for years to come, while the learning path of girls is geared towards more mundane jobs. Women working, alongside the community's well-established support system and state-sponsored subsidies, have together made the pursuit of religious study realizable for many young male adults. Consequently, ultraorthodox society is becoming 'a society of learners'. Outside the world of learning the most important institution for the ultraorthodox man is the synagogue where he prays three times a day. Of immense importance are also spiritual leaders of the community, most of whom are ordained rabbis, whose moral authority and advice is sought and accepted without challenge.

Despite their separatist ideology, the ultraorthodox have not been self-sufficient enough to entertain a complete disengagement from the secular society within which they are uncomfortably situated. On the contrary, their empowerment has entailed an increasing involvement in national political, economic and social issues, and a rising dependence on state resources. The outcome is a complex negotiation process with the secular world: the community seeks to maintain and even fortify its boundaries against it, but is at the same time being inevitably subtly transformed in the course of this (Ravitsky 1993). The drift of many ultraorthodox groups toward the right of the political spectrum is one of the more noticeable changes in the community in recent years. The upshot of all this is that the stereotypical image of a community averting its gaze from the swarming activity of the secular world 'out there' is far from accurate.

Focusing on ultraorthodox (*haredi*) Jews in contemporary Israel, I seek in this essay to delineate and explore one set of childhood rituals among them that I find highly important in the process of inculcating male identity values and sensibilities.

Most three year-old *haredi* male children undergo today a two-fold ritual sequence in which the first haircut (*halaka*) is associated with entering the world of study. Although less binding than the rites of circumcision (*brit milah*) and bar mitzvah, and therefore less well-known outside Jewish religious circles, the ritual complex at the age of three is an emotionally powerful rite of passage, suffused with rich cultural symbolism and involving a dramatic physical transformation. These properties make it a salient marker on the road to manhood in the ultraorthodox community, crystallized around the supreme value of Torah study. I view all Jewish ceremonies that punctuate the male life cycle, from birth to marriage, as one integrated system that encodes gender-specific prerequisites to self-actualization via learning. But the logic of my analysis leads me to decode the psychocultural meanings of the haircutting and school initiation rituals primarily in relation to their ceremonial antecedent, *brit milah*. Succinctly put, my argument is that *brit milah* takes place too early in life to provide the circumcised with all the spiritual and scholarly values conferred upon the ancient Israelite rite by classical rabbinical Judaism. Therefore it has to be repeated later in life, following the acquisition of the basic cognitive skills necessary for the rudimentary assimilation of the male ideals coalescing around Torah study. I view the ritual sequence that takes place at the age of three as a 'secondary circumcision', a ceremonial marker of the beginning of the male's ideally life-long sojourn in the textual manifestations of the sacred.

Methodologically, given the primacy of the text in Judaism, any contextual analysis of Jewish ceremonial practices has to be supplemented by the textual layers of exegesis that explicate the rites and endow them with surplus meaning. I follow this vein in my analysis, which is based on multiple observations of the rites,[1] but is also informed by a variety of biblical, Talmudic, and mystical references and later rabbinical compendia and anthologies of Jewish injunctions and customs associated with the rituals of childhood.[2] The prevalence and easy availability of the latter collections in the ultraorthodox community, together with the strong hermeneutic tradition in Judaism which flexibly construes exegeses from multiple and divergent sources, may alleviate concerns about lumping together many rabbinical sources from different schools and traditions spanning centuries. It would be no exaggeration to say that male ultraorthodox adults, members in the 'community of scholars' (Friedman 1987; 1991), are familiar with many of the sources I present here.

In the vast rabbinical literature of Talmudic and Kabbalistic exegesis, the bridging of the gap between the physical realm of the body and the discursive realm of the symbolic is contemplated through male-specific idioms. The inscription on the male body of the physical mark of circumcision is in particular viewed as the first step in this direction, designed to prepare the Jewish male for 'entering the Torah' – the universe of religious injunctions and spiritual calling conveyed by the holy language of the holy text. The idea that the symbolic emanates from the bodily is rooted in many languages in the form of a dual register simultaneously carrying physical and abstract meanings. Hebrew is no exception in this regard, as the following two linguistic labels amply show. First, the word *ot* designates 'mark' (including the mark of circumcision, *ot habrit*) and 'letter of the alphabet'. Second, the homophone *milah* connects both 'circumcision' and 'word'. The fact that the two stem from different, though related, roots did not stop the rabbinical imagination from weaving a rich associative web around their meanings.[3] Informed by these lexical associations, the rabbinical sources connect the Jewish body and the divine word in formulations that, especially in mystical texts, are replete with sexual and procreative meanings.[4]

Again, the idea that the sexual is the critical shifter underlying the move from the physical to the symbolic is not limited to the rabbinical imagination as articulated in Hebrew. It is most pronounced in the discourse of psychoanalysis, among other systems of thought. Jacques Lacan appears almost to follow the rabbinical tradition: the transition from the bodily penis to the symbolic phallus, as he puts it, is 'the elevation from anatomy to a universal semantics'. In his dialectics of loss and endless substitutions, Lacan views the threat of castration as an impetus for transforming the male sex organ into a 'useful theoretical tool' capable of eliciting 'unlimited explanatory range' (Bowie 1991: 129–30). Taking note that psychoanalysis tends to collapse the gap between circumcision and castration, my focus in this essay is on the explanatory range, also seemingly unlimited at times, brought forth by rabbinical exegesis to deal with the passage from circumcision (*milah*) to word (*milah*), that is the passage from the realm of the physical and bodily to that of the sacred.

In this article I focus on four cultural values: the child's growing awareness, gender differentiation, purity, and knowledge. The first three of these are configured as prerequisites for the fourth: the religious ideal of Torah study that contemporary ultraorthodox men pursue with unprecedented zeal. The sequence unfolds as follows: learning is limited to men; as an intellectual activity it entails a certain level of cognitive development, primarily awareness and memory; and since the texts to be learned are deemed God-sent and sacred, learning also necessitates specific acts of purification. The rituals of childhood simultaneously constitute and are constituted by this configuration.

Circumcision

As the ritual practice through which eight-day-old male infants enter the Jewish community, *brit milah* ('the covenant of circumcision')[5] constitutes an embodied representation of the covenant between God and the Jewish people. However, this spiritual meaning, emphasized by the priestly version of the Torah and elaborated in the post-biblical exegetical literature (Hoffman 1996), also encodes earlier, pre-exilic meanings of the Israelite practice related to assuring sexual maturity, virility and fertility, and emphasizing patrilineal descent (Eilberg-Schwartz 1990). These meanings draw the Jewish circumcision ritual closer to tribal initiation rites at puberty. Indeed, the suggestion that the primordial precursor of the Jewish ritual constituted a ceremonial passage to adult life has been raised by many biblical scholars (Eilberg-Schwartz 1990: 142; Goldberg 1996: 25,28; Propp 1987; 1993). This suggestion is supported by the fact that adult mass circumcision is evident in the Bible,[6] and that various associations connect circumcision and marriage in biblical narrative (Propp 1993: 508) and in later Jewish tradition.[7] This connection also has a linguistic basis: while in Hebrew *hatan* means 'bridegroom' or 'son-in-law',[8] in Arabic *khatana* means both 'to become related by marriage' and 'to circumcise'.[9]

Without going into the assumed reasons for the transfer of ancient Israelite circumcision from puberty to infancy (see Propp 1987, for a review and an original explanation), it is clear that as a ritual of passage into life, subsequent to the birth process, circumcision has been viewed as critically important for rendering the newborn human. The rabbis believed that 'circumcision was designed to repair nature', since '. . . man is not born intact and still requires fixing of body and soul' (Wilhelm 1992: 207). Moreover, circumcision was viewed as reflecting a universal law: 'Whatever was created in the first six days requires preparation, e.g., mustard needs sweetening, vetches need sweetening, wheat needs grinding, and man too needs to be finished off.'[10] Indeed, in Judaism, cutting off, removing and separating are key-idioms, a paradigmatic vehicle for transforming nature into culture, that is, for 'Judaizing' it (Cooper 1987). In this sense, circumcision resonates with a long list of laws of separation and removal related to food (for example, making meat edible by removing the vein-of-the-hip sinew), sacrifices and contributions (Rubin 1995: 16–17). The equivalence between circumcision and other ritual practices of removal in Judaism is crucial to the analysis that ensues.

Gender, memory, purity and knowledge in circumcision

In terms of gender differentiation, it might be argued that the early timing of circumcision places it as a marker of a distinct male trajectory from the beginning of life, 'a representation of the very basic cultural dichotomy between men and women' (Hoffman 1996: 44). A particularly powerful statement of the critical importance of circumcision as part of the birth process is the rabbinical assertion that the newborn's soul comes to inhabit him only upon circumcision. In raising this idea to account for the duty of the *father* to circumcise his son, it is explicitly said that circumcision is 'the extension of the creation of the son by the father' (Wilhelm 1992: 226).[11] Thus, *brit milah* appears as a ritual of pseudo-procreation (Shapiro and Linke 1996). Through the suggestion that 'circumcision is a man's birth into his cultural state whereas childbirth is "merely" a birth into the state of nature' (Hoffman 1996: 147), the rabbis symbolically assumed for themselves the superior role in procreation. The post-biblical exegetical elaboration that endowed the operation with spiritual meanings related to purity and erudition (to be discussed below) was particularly instrumental in making circumcision a superior mode of *cultural* creation.

Articulating circumcision as an all-male pseudo-procreation ritual constitutes (and is constituted by) a polarized view of men and women. The rabbinical treatment of gender differences is strongly informed by the notion of the female's proximity to 'nature' (Ortner 1996). In the rabbinical literature there are two sides to this. On the one hand, women are absolved from observing most of the Jewish precepts, and are not subjected to any physical marking or 'rectification' at the beginning of life.[12] On the other hand, since this rectification serves as induction into the covenantal community, it leaves women in a vague and culturally deficient position, unable to transcend their 'nature'. Bound to biologically determined cycles of involuntary and uncontrollable, hence polluting, bodily discharges (Eilberg-Schwartz 1990: 177–194), their temperaments too are regarded as impaired (Eilberg-Schwartz and Doniger 1995).

As a ritual of pseudo-procreation juxtaposed to the birth process, male infant circumcision is all the more understandable in this light. At the same time, however, the early timing of the ceremony poses two crucial problems from which initiation rites into adulthood are exempt. The crux of my argument is that the ritual sequence at age three may be viewed as a cultural endeavour to cope with these problems.

First, biological imperatives bind the circumcised infant to his mother and he cannot be directly launched into a separate male-specific sphere. Rituals typically chart an exemplary state of affairs, the way things ought to be. The circumcision ceremony follows this vein, but its idealized message cannot be fulfilled. Like all Jewish rituals of childhood, it constitutes a moment of male exclusiveness in which the infant is appropriated from his mother and temporarily situated in an all-male environment (Rubin 1995: 17). The degree of male participation in the ritual is illustrated by the following description of a traditional *brit milah* from a book of Jewish customs:

> The women bring the newborn to the synagogue and hand him over to his father; and the father holds him and utters [the proper prayer], and then hands him on to the *mohel* (circumciser) who lays him on the chair prepared for Elijah [the Prophet]. Then the *mohel* delivers him to the *sandak* [the man who holds the child on his lap during the operation] and performs the circumcision, and the father says [a special prayer]. And the *sheliach tzibbur* [leader of the service] makes the blessings over the wine and the spices, and the crowd smells the linen with myrtle distributed by *ba'al habrit* [literally, 'the owner of the covenant,' a ritual role sometimes overlapping with that of the *sandak*] with the help of the *shamash* [the synagogue caretaker] (Gliss 1968: 284).

Following the pre-ceremonial transfer of the infant from the women to the father, no fewer than nine different male categories are involved in the course of the ritual and include the baby, Elijah the Prophet, and the crowd. It is tempting to reinterpret the Hebrew idiom 'to cut a covenant', which appears as an oxymoron,[13] in terms of gender differentiation: circumcision is supposed to separate the child from his mother and bond him with his father (and the Heavenly Father).

It should be noted that, as with other Jewish rites of passage, this male monopolization of circumcision is historically situated. Until the thirteenth century, women had been an integral part of the ritual, but from that time on they were gradually banished from it (Hoffman 1996: 190–207). This estrangement is softened in contemporary rites, where women are normally present among the celebrants; but as in other public ceremonial arenas, they are marginal participants, separated from the males, and devoid of any ritual role.

Compelling as the ritual is, however, the biological constraint prevails over the cultural ideal of gender differentiation. After circumcision, the child is returned to his mother and, given the strict separation of the sexes, is re-immersed in a female ambience. The tension between nature and culture in the beginning of life comes forcefully to the fore when dealing with female pollution. A menstruating woman is not supposed to touch utensils in the house that her husband uses; but what about her own male baby? The permission is given grudgingly: 'Because of the pressing need (*mido'hak*), she was allowed to suckle her son' (Gliss 1968: 270). The normative period of nursing is two years, a period of intimate bonding with the mother.

Second, granted that every ritual is a significant cultural communication, in circumcision the message is lost on the infant: it is inscribed physically but, since it can never be a consciously recalled experience, not mentally. As a physical mark, indelibly permanent, circumcision may be viewed as an embodied means 'to pass down memory of social identity outside cognition and text' (Zatz Litt 1997: 22). The child cut is the child bound forever. But it is unlikely that this embodied representation, though capable of serving as a 'repository for a whole host of new meanings' (ibid. p. 23; see also Boyarin and Boyarin 1995) can register the emotional impact of the operation and its transformative significance in the infant's mind. Indeed, the fact that the injunction is not based on conscious intention and voluntary fulfilment invokes many puzzles and a plethora of commentaries in the rabbinical literature.[14] This problem does not exist in Islam (let alone tribal societies), where circumcision often takes place at an older age, although the actual age varies widely across the Muslim orbit. In his portrayal of circumcision in Morocco, Westermark states that, 'In many parts of the country it is held desirable that the operation in question will be held so late that the boy can remember it in the future' (1926II: 417). Indeed, ethnographic reports indicate that circumcision in Islam may be a highly charged, vividly recalled experience (for example, Crapanzano 1981). *Brit milah*, shaped in a religious system where commemoration of past events pervades every aspect of ritual practice (Yerushalmi 1982), may be viewed indeed as an instance of 'embodied memory'. But, in all probability, it cannot produce the type of recalled experiences engendered by genital mutilation in ritual settings where the novices are significantly older. This omission is striking when we note that in Hebrew 'male' (*zakhar*) and 'memory' (*zekher* or *zikaron*) derive from the same root (ZKhR).

In order to address the two problems that infant circumcision entails, we first have to shed light on the problematic position in *brit milah* of two other religious values that shape male vocation: purity and knowledge.

The impurity of the mother upon parturition pollutes the infant. Circumcision, taking place only after the mother's seven-day state of severe uncleanliness is over, indicates the passage from impurity to purity. Unlike the mother's blood, associated with sin, indecency and death, the blood of the operation signifies righteousness, wholeness and blessing (Eilberg-Schwartz 1990: 181; Hoffman 1996: 146). Equated with the blood of the Passover sacrifice, it was used in certain communities as a panacea (Gliss 1968: 287; Rubin 1995: 105). As against the blood of the operation, the fore-skin (*orla*), an 'excessive' body part which has to be excised to render one Jewish, is viewed as loathsome and impure. These negative meanings have been elaborated in Jewish mystical texts where the foreskin sometimes has female connotations. These ideas resonate with indigenous interpretations of prepuberty circumcision as designed to remove the feminine residue from the body to facilitate initiation into manhood (Turner 1962). Some psychoanalytic interpretations of *brit milah* have followed the same vein (Nunberg 1949; Reik 1931).

Note that the circumcision operation is composed of two acts: *milah*, removing the foreskin, and *pri'ah* ('uncovering'), pulling the membrane to expose fully the corona.[15] The second act complements the first. Physically, it makes circumcision irreversible;[16] and on a symbolic-mystical level, it assures that the external side of the membrane, equated with the 'other side', or the demonic world, will come under the control of the sacred inner side (Wilhelm 1992: 67). This two-tier notion of circumcision endows it with a dual meaning – a duality further supported by the fact that in the Bible other organs aside from the penis are depicted as having foreskin. The ears, the mouth and the heart can be *arelim*, uncircumcised (Eilberg-Schwartz 1990: 148–149). *Pri'ah*, based on exposure and disclosing, is associated with the discovery of the pure heart (Wilhelm 1992: 71). The non-penis foreskins require metaphoric circumcision. Rather than a physical cut, it entails a spiritual rectification of one's inner essence. This rectification is based on discourse: hearing, uttering and understanding the words of God. Thus, bodily *milah* and *milah*-as-word are merged together. Moreover, a mystical interpretation asserts that circumcision (*milah*) and mouth (*peh*) are related since both words have the same numerical value, 85, in Hebrew (ibid, p. 236).

Elaborating on the biblical axiom that the word preceded the world, the mystical Book of Creation (*Sefer Yetsira*) depicts how the universe was created from the 22 letters of the Hebrew alphabet. But the letters also have bodily representations, deployed in two horizontal arrays, across the lower and the upper parts of the body. The lower tier, called the 'covenant of the penis', includes the ten toes with the penis in the middle, while the upper array, called 'the covenant of the tongue', includes the ten fingers with the tongue in between. The two levels are set against each other and since, as in other languages, tongue (*lashon*) means also discourse, it is not surprising that a rabbinical exegesis argues that circumcision is also designated 'saying' or 'statement', *amirah* (ibid, p. 196).[17] Another interpretation contends that circumcision and Torah are one and the same, since external (physical) *milah* entails internal (spiritual) *milah* of the heart, which opens one to the Torah (ibid, p. 221). One has to purify his heart to enter the world of the sacred text. Job's utterance, 'Yet in my flesh shall I see God' (Job 19: 26), attributed in a *midrashic* (exegetical) commentary to Abraham, was presented as indicating that through circumcision the body is consecrated and becomes a worthy receptacle for the holiness of the Torah. Abraham was privileged to have a divine revelation only after circumcising himself (Wolfson 1987b). Purity, then, is a prerequisite for encountering the sacred, which in classical Judaism became associated with the text: '*Brit milah* has the virtue of purifying his [the circumcised's] blood and rendering him receptive to the teachings of the Torah' (Wilhelm 1992: 222). This takes us to the unsettled place of knowledge in circumcision.

According to a well-known Talmudic exegesis, the embryo in his mother's womb is omniscient. It 'looks and sees from one end of the world to the other', and 'it is also taught all the Torah from beginning to end.'[18] A metaphorical reading of another phrase in this reference – 'a light [literally, candle] burns above its head' – accounts for these prenatal prodigal capacities. The candle stands for the soul, which, as a divine spark, unconstrained by the limiting bodily habitat, is intellectually boundless. Again, this primordial omniscience is predicated on primordial purity. In the womb the embryo is fed through the umbilical chord, therefore a bodily separation between the material and the spiritual can be maintained: intellect is limitless because the mouth can be used exclusively for study (ibid, pp. 257–58). This blissful state, however, is short-lived: at the moment of parturition an angel strikes each newborn male on its upper lip, thus making him totally amnesic. This act may be viewed as the Jewish equivalent of the psychoanalytic notion of birth trauma. The first seven days of life, terminated by circumcision, are deemed a week of mourning, the reason for which is twofold: birth-linked impurity and birth-linked amnesia (ibid, pp. 86, 268). Following the erasure of the prenatal platonic traces of erudition and insight, learning becomes strained and slow. A constant process of purification is required successfully to incorporate the Torah. As we saw before, circumcision creates the preconditions for entering the world of Torah. According to Wolfson (1987a; 1987b), the mystics believed that the mark (*ot*) of circumcision was a magical seal composed of the letters of God's name. Thus, 'from the flesh of the phallus one indeed beholds the divine, for the Tetragrammaton [God's name] is imprinted on that limb . . .' (Wolfson 1987a: 110). This convergence of anthropomorphic and linguistic symbolism transforms the physical into the spiritual. Another reverberation of the association *milah-milah*, or, more to the point here, *ot* (physical marker) and *ot* (alphabetical letter), is the mystical equivalence between the bodily opening of circumcision – particularly in the act of *pri'ah* (uncovering) – and the hermeneutic 'opening' (or 'deconstruction') of the text. The two arguments are related since the Torah is the material manifestation of the divine. The range between the physical opening and the interpretive-textual one is mediated by the opening of the mouth – given that 'circumcision' and 'mouth' are numerically equivalent words – to study the Torah (Wilhelm 1992: 235).[19]

As a purification ritual, circumcision constitutes the preconditions for learning. Yet the road to achieving the cultural ideals of manhood is arduous and precarious. One interpretation of the response recited at the end of the circumcision ritual, 'As he has entered the covenant, so may he enter the Torah, the marriage chamber, and [a life of] good deeds', underscores this precariousness.[20] 'The commandment of circumcision is but an entrance; one has to invest a lot of work and effort, to be heedful, to enter the shrines of holiness and faith, to circumcise the foreskin of the heart, and to purify the rest of his limbs.'(ibid, p. 205).

The twofold predicament of *brit milah* – the lack of recalled experience (the awareness problem) and the female bond with the baby (the gender problem) – perforce suspend the attainment of the two other cultural ideals of maleness epitomized by the ritual. Learning, it goes without saying, is impossible without rudimentary awareness and basic cognitive skills. Purity, the precondition of learning, is hard to achieve as long as the child is dangerously exposed to female pollution.

The first haircutting and school initiation rituals at age three address the concerns associated with infant circumcision by reconstituting gender differentiation, purity and knowledge in novices cognitively mature enough to start assimilating the cultural scripts associated with these values. This assimilation is inchoate, indicating the very beginning of the long process of the making of the Jewish male; but age three enables some synchronization between biological-maturational and cultural rhythms that is altogether impossible at the beginning of life. Before discussing the meanings of this synchronization, a short description of the rituals is called for.

The first haircutting ritual

During the first three years of life, the hair of male toddlers of all ultraorthodox groups and sects is left untrimmed. The first haircutting is a ceremonial event usually conducted on the child's third birthday or during that year's festival of *Lag Ba'omer* – on the thirty-third day after Passover. The festival is the occasion for the *hillulah* (celebration on the anniversary of the death) of Rabbi Shimon Bar Yohai, a second-century luminary and the putative author of the *Zohar* (Book of Splendour), the canonical text of Jewish mysticism. The mass pilgrimage to Rabbi Shimon's shrine in Meron near the northern town of Safed is undoubtedly the largest annual gathering in Israel, drawing as many as 200,000 celebrants.

Two events on the eve of *Lag Ba'omer* mark the beginning of the celebration: the procession from Safed to Meron carrying a Torah scroll belonging to the family that built the sanctuary in the nineteenth century and the lighting of two bonfires on the roof of the sanctuary. The *hillulah* brings together Jewish pilgrims of diverse backgrounds. Most numerous among them are celebrants of North African and Middle Eastern extraction, but Ashkenazi Hasidim, in closed ranks, wearing black uniform and engrossed in spiritual devotional activities, are no less conspicuous. These two groups flock in and around the sanctuary, converging under the canopy of a charismatic saint; but their ways of celebrating the *hillulah* are different. Many of the *Mizrahi* pilgrims spend several days at Meron camping in a picnic-like atmosphere on the forested slopes surrounding the site. They gather there in groups of kin and friends, males and females together, feasting on slaughtered sheep, consuming large quantities of spirits, singing, dancing and recounting the miracles of the saint. The ascent to the tomb, the spiritual climax of the *hillulah*, takes but a small part of their time in Meron.

The Hasidic visitors by contrast observe strict separation of the sexes. Their stay at Meron is temporally limited to the *hillulah* itself and spatially restricted to the precincts of the sanctuary. There they engage in devotional prayers at the tombs of Rabbi Shimon and other sages and in ecstatic dances in the inner courtyard and on the roof of the shrine. Assuming the role of 'ritual specialists' they usually avoid the encampments and the gigantic colourful fair outside the shrine where the atmosphere is convivial, at times indulgent.

The *Lag Ba'omer hillulah* in Meron is the prominent setting for the first haircutting ritual, primarily preferred by mystically oriented Hasidic groups. In non-Hasidic ultraorthodox circles the ritual typically takes place at home or in the local synagogue, even though other intersections of place and time are possible too (at other shrines on *Lag Ba'omer*, in Meron on the child's birthday, or on other festive occasions). The following description refers to the paradigmatic ritual in Meron.

The popular name of the ceremony, *halaka* (Arabic for haircut) betrays its local Middle Eastern origin. Even though most of the participants are Ashkenazi Hasidim, the Yiddish designation for the ritual, *upsheren*, is less commonly used. The three-year-old novices, arriving with their families at the gates of Rabbi Shimon's shrine, are notable for their long, silky hair (freely dispersed or tied with pretty ribbons or spangled bands), ceremonial male costumes, beautiful skullcaps (sing. *kippa*), and four-cornered undergarments (sing. *tsitsit* or *talit katan*). The inner courtyard of the shrine where the ritual takes place is separated by an opaque railing into a men-only arena and a female gallery. The women watch the ceremony through tiny peepholes in the railing or from the balconies above the courtyard, which are also gender-segregated.

The *halaka* is performed against the ecstatic backdrop of Rabbi Shimon's *hillulah*. From morning to evening, dense cohorts of Hasidim, mostly *yeshiva* (religious academy) students with their rabbis, pour into the courtyard and dance rapturously to the deafening music of a *klezmer* troupe, amplified throughout the precinct. The leader of the troupe sings the praises of the great mystic in repetitive throbs and the dancers, each one holding the shoulders of the person before him, breathlessly repeat the stanzas. Perched on the shoulders of their hopping fathers, swinging and swaying with the rhythm of the dance, the children are located in the inner core of this dense whirl, surrounded by circles of male dancers. The music and chants, rhythmic motion and high seat clearly have an impact on the children. Clinging to their parents, many appear dazed and disoriented; some cry in fear, while still others seem to enjoy their elevated position. Their disorientation is lessened by the fact that they are showered with gifts and suggestions to live up to their new status as boys (sing. *yeled*) rather than babies (sing. *tinok*). Aside from the ceremonial attire and ritual garments which most of the children wear for the first time, many of them boast colourful sunglasses and hold flags and bags of candies in their hands.

From the balconies above the courtyard, the separation between the sexes is accentuated by the contrast in hues: colourful costumes on the female side; black and white garments on the male side. The children's costumes, though of glimmering, high-quality linen or silk, are usually of the same design and colours as their fathers', and this congruence makes them blend into the encompassing adult ambience.

Salient and exciting as the dancing and chanting are, they merely serve as a prelude to the ritual haircutting. The fathers are equipped with scissors, sometimes tied around their necks, a plastic bag to collect the shorn hair, and wine and cake to distribute. They hold the children in their hands while the scissors are passed around among kin and dignitaries who are granted the honour of cutting one curl each, starting with the forelock. Many fathers complete the haircut in a special hall in the shrine using electrical shavers to shear their children's heads save for the side curls. Indeed, although the haircutting appears as the crux of the ritual, it in fact serves the ultimate goal of creating the highly visible marker of *payess* (ear-locks). The physical difference between the children after the *halaka*, with their shaven heads and lengthy ear-locks, and their pre-ceremony countenance, with their long, curly hair, is striking. Often, the collected hair is weighed and then thrown into the bonfire on the top of the sanctuary. Later on, donations are given to the poor in equal amounts to the weight. One curl is usually taken home, to serve as a reminder of the event. Kept in a prayer book, it may accompany its owner throughout his life.

Two disparate hair-related practices appear to have converged in the *halaka*: the growing of ear-locks and the shearing of the head hair (Zimmer 1996). A biblical injunction, 'Ye shall not round the corners of your head neither shalt thou mar the corner of thy beard' (Leviticus 19: 27), is considered the basis for the first practice, even though this vague precept does not prescribe the timing and form of the ritual. The ritual haircut, probably modelled on the Muslim custom of shaving male children's hair in saints' sanctuaries, was practised by native Palestinian Jews (*Musta'arbim*) as early as the Middle Ages. Rabbi Isaac Luria Ashkenazi, the sixteenth-century founder of the celebrated Lurianic School of Kabbalah who assigned special mystical value to the ear-locks,[21] was instrumental in constituting the ritual in its present form. The *halaka* remained primarily a *Sephardi* (Middle Eastern Jewish) custom following Luria;[22] but in the last two hundred years it has become widespread, together with many other Lurianic customs, among Ashkenazi Hasidim. From Palestine it spread to the Diaspora communities, where it was usually celebrated in a more modest family setting. In present-day Israel, the *halaka* is ubiquitous among the ultraorthodox, though, as noted before, the spatial and temporal patterns of the ritual may vary.

Without going into the specific associations that link Rabbi Shimon to the *halaka*, it is safe to assume that the selection of the shrine in Meron stems from its unrivalled popularity as a pilgrimage centre. As noted before, other holy places may serve as minor ceremonial arenas.[23] Lag Ba'omer is a particularly auspicious time because on this day some of the proscriptions associated with the counting of the barley period (between Passover and the festival of Pentecost), including haircutting, are temporarily suspended.

The school initiation ritual

In various rabbinical sources the *halaka*, viewed as a fulfilment of a biblical injunction, is dubbed 'the beginning of the children's education' (Haglili 1988). Following it, the child is expected to cover his head, wear the four-cornered undergarment, recite the Jewish statement of faith (*Shema Yisrael*) and basic blessings, and accompany his father to the synagogue. In line with the rabbinical statement, 'Age three [is ripe] for the letters', this is also the time for entering the *heyder* (the religious pre-school), which constitutes the first step in the world of study. The first haircut is inextricably linked with entering the Torah and the world of study and commandments, as clearly indicated by the flags, decorated with the letters of the alphabet, that some children hold in their hands during the *halaka*. Many parents are anxious to perform the school initiation ceremony immediately following the *halaka*, even though Lag Ba'omer does not coincide with the beginning of study. In this case, the children are likely to undergo the ceremony twice: first individually, immediately after the *halaka*, and then collectively, with their classmates, on the first day of school (scheduled for the beginning of the month of *Ellul*, in mid-Summer).

The school initiation ceremony is a rite of passage *par excellence*. Dressed again in festive attire, the child is wrapped from top to toe with his father's prayer shawl, to guard him from impurity as he approaches the holy text, and carried by his father to the *heyder*.[24]

In the individual ceremonies, the child is placed on the lap of the *melamed* (teacher), in front of a tablet on which the Hebrew alphabet is printed. The teacher recites aloud each letter in alphabetical order, signalling the letters with his finger, and the child is encouraged to recite them after him. This exchange is then repeated backward, from *tav* (the last letter of the alphabet) to *alef* (the first letter). Next the teacher recites a biblical verse, 'Moses charged us with the Torah as the heritage of the congregation of Jacob' (Deuteronomy 33: 4), followed by a Talmudic phrase, 'May the Torah be my occupation and God my aid';[25] and again the child is urged to reiterate. The same exchange takes place with the first verse of Leviticus.[26]

The central part of the ritual is marked by a move from recital to three-fold literal incorporation of the text. First, the teacher sprinkles drops of honey on the tablet with the alphabet and the child licks with his tongue the honey from the letters. Second, a cake kneaded with honey and decorated with a passage from Isaiah (50: 4–5) depicting the skill of learning as a divine gift ('The Lord gave me a skilled tongue . . .') is brought over. In the context of the ritual, the passage is a supplication to acquire such skills. The child eats a piece of the cake following recitation of the text written on it. The third part of the ritual concerns a peeled hard-boiled egg, on which the famous verse from Ezekiel (3: 3) is written, describing the eating of the scroll by the prophet ('. . . I ate it, and it tasted as sweet as honey to me'). Again, the egg is consumed following recitation. This threefold absorption lucidly conveys the notion that just as the child 'enters the Torah', as the traditional idiom puts it, the Torah enters him. The ritual ends as it started, with the father carrying the child, wrapped in his prayer shawl, out of the *heyder*.

The initiation ceremony on the first day of school follows the pattern described here, with minor modifications ensuing from the collective character of the ritual: this time all the classmates are initiated in concert. The presence of many parents calls for a spatial organization of the classroom that accentuates the demarcation between male and female participants. The children are seated by the desks, arranged in U shape along three walls of the *heyder*, with each father sitting just behind his son. In contrast with the close physical proximity between fathers and sons, the mothers are relegated to the *heyder*'s backyard. They watch the ceremony from the outside, pressed against the grilled windows of the class.

In reciting the letters, the teacher points to a big alphabet tablet, hanging from the blackboard; but each child has his own laminated paperboard of letters, sprinkled over with honey. The fathers are quite involved in the ritual, encouraging the children to recite the letters and verses and urging them to absorb the edibles on which they are written. Before leaving, the fathers stretch several prayer shawls over the sitting children and recite a special blessing to protect them. Showered with candies by their parents, the children also receive from the teacher and his helper (*oyzer*) bags of candies designed as the four-cornered garment the children are supposed to wear after the *halaka*.

As Ivan Marcus (1996) shows, the school initiation ceremony emerged in twelfth- to thirteenth-century Europe in Jewish Ashkenazi culture (in Germany and northern France). Integrating elements of Jewish schooling from late antiquity with ancient and early medieval traditions of adult magical mnemonics and mystical Torah study, the Ashkenazi ritual 'was articulated in the "grammar of perception" of contemporary Jewish-Christian cultural polemics' (ibid, p. 16). Thus, for example, the symbolic act of ingesting the Torah is suggestive of the eucharistic devotion. The German-Jewish tradition of the ceremony disappeared and was eventually replaced in the late Middle Ages by the preliminary forms of a new rite of passage, *bar mitzvah*. This change, equivalent to the Christian banning of infant and child oblation in that era, reflected a new attitude towards childhood. Having defined majority as a necessary condition before letting children enter religious life, both religious cultures set up a new age-specific threshold for moving to adulthood (ibid, p. 17).

Hence, the historical continuity between the medieval Ashkenazi ceremony and its present-day successor is quite oblique, although elements of the ritual surfaced throughout the centuries in various localities, Ashkenazi as well as Sephardi. In terms of content, the current ritual meticulously follows most of the initiatory practices documented in the medieval texts, but some significant contextual differences between the two ceremonies should be noted. The Germanic ritual was scheduled for the festival of Shavuot (Pentecost), and this timing situated the ceremony within the context of the Sinai epiphany. Since the present-day ritual does not coincide with Shavuot, the associations that made the child's personal entry into the Torah a recapitulation of the paradigmatic biblical story of exodus are thinner today. Moreover, the novices in the medieval ceremony were at least two years older than their present-day counterparts (ibid, pp. 42-46); and, as far as we know, the initiation to the world of study was not preceded by a ritual haircut or any other ceremony.

It appears safe to conclude that, rather than an invariable ritual sequence from time immemorial, the powerful convergence of the haircutting and school initiation ceremonies around age three, particularly as crystallized in the Hasidic milieu, is a fairly modern phenomenon. For this reason, the analysis that follows is twofold. First, I focus on the significance of the two ceremonies as a psychocultural device to realign the elements of male identity associated with memory, gender differentiation, purity and knowledge that the early timing of *brit milah* rendered inchoate and incoherent. Second, I seek to contextualize the psychological explanation by highlighting the historical circumstances that have made the predicaments of infant circumcision more acute in the age of modernity.

Restructuring male identity at age three

The doctrinal efficacy (Moore and Myerhoff 1977) of the ritual sequence that takes place at the age of three derives from the symbolic multivocality and complementarity of the two ceremonies. For analytic reasons I will discuss them separately, however, starting with the *halaka*. Van Gennep's classic work on rites of passage may serve as an apposite point of departure: '[C]ircumcision cannot be understood if it is examined in isolation. It should be left within the category of all practices of the same order which, by cutting off, splitting, or mutilating any part of the body, modify the personality of the individual in a manner visible to all' (1909/1960: 71).

Following Van Gennep's track, can we view the *halaka* as a ' secondary circumcision'? As in *brit milah*, and even more so, the ideal of gender differentiation prevails in this ritual. At age three, after the mother-supervised functions of weaning and sphincter control have been achieved, the child is appropriated from the female world and placed in the centre of male territory surrounded, in the ecstatic atmosphere of *Lag Ba'omer* in Meron, by circles of male dancers. Dressed for the first time in male ceremonial garments, including the religious markers of skullcap and four-cornered undergarment, the child on his father's shoulders, often with the father's ceremonial fur-hat on his head, looks like a vertical extension of the father. In this dense moment of male bonding the child is physically repaired: his hair is shorn and he is 'equipped' with ear-locks. As in *brit milah* before and the school initiation ceremony that follows, the father transfers the child to 'ritual specialists', viewed as the father's delegates, to perform the injunction underlying the ceremony. These male protagonists are the esteemed kin and rabbis who cut the first curls in the *halaka*, the godfather and circumciser in *brit milah*, and the teacher in the school initiation ceremony. Their respective involvement in the rituals serves to convey the notion that the child is reconstituted ('reborn') in all-male public circles of descent and learning wider than the father-son dyad.

The physical transformation that the child undergoes in the *halaka* is dramatic. To illustrate the gap in appearance, let me offer an excerpt from an eyewitness account of the 1983 *hillulah* in Meron.

> [The] children moved above the crowd of black coats and hats, perched on their fathers' shoulders. The innocent overblown pink little faces – overblown with tears in one case – were girlish faces, crowned with beautiful long hair, tied on each side with pretty spangled bands, leaving the front hair curly and free. They clung affectionately to their fathers as they faced this way and that, borne in the dance to the sound of music. I was impressed at first how well the fathers were looking after their daughters. Where were the sons, though? They were supposed to be so important. Then I noticed that every one of the 'girls' was wearing pants, as well as an embroidered skullcap. These were the sons. (Turner 1993: 246)[27]

From an effeminate child, with long curly hair, the little boy following the *halaka* becomes a miniature replica of his father. He is granted, as the participants say, the figure of a Jew (*tsurat yehudi*). The distinctively Jewish countenance of the child is brought to full view primarily by the *payess* (earlocks). Even without arguing for the phallic qualities of the *payess* (see below), it is clear that 'the ear-locks have become a central part of "Jewish identity", *a modern equivalent of the ot, the circumcision of former centuries*' (Zimmer, 1996: 70; italics added). Needless to say, it is the visible ear-locks rather than the hidden mark of circumcision that serve as an instantaneous sign for identifying Jewish orthodox affiliation in daily encounters. The emotional elements of the *halaka* ritual, the multisensory stimulation, the agitation, and particularly the children's disorienting posture on their hopping parents' shoulders, literally betwixt and between – all these seem to deepen the impression of the transformation in the children's minds. Though far from the ordeal typical of tribal initiation ceremonies, the *halaka* still stands out as a uniquely salient and exciting life-event, both scary and exhilarating, tiring and invigorating. As my interviews with adult celebrants in Meron indicate, many of the children will claim to remember this dramatic episode throughout their lives. The possibility of persistent recollections from age three is bolstered by the Jewish tradition that situates the

emergence of religious awareness at this age, following the rabbinical assertion that 'Abraham was three years old when he recognized his creator'
(Serebrianski 1990: 27).[28] Thus, the 'secondary circumcision', unlike the first
one, involves some awareness and memory, rendering more congruent the
common root (ZKhR) of 'male' and 'memory' in Hebrew. More important
perhaps than the recalled experiences of a single dramatic episode is the
fact that the values inculcated in the novices during the *halaka* (and the
school initiation ceremony) are resonant with the new life regime to which
they will be exposed for ever after. Thus, the rituals of age three precondition the novices to the habitus (Bourdieu 1977) or embodied schemas (Strauss
and Quinn 1997: 46–7) encapsulating the attitudes, perceptions, sensibilities and knowledge that the ultraorthodox educational system seeks to imprint in its disciples. This resonance does not exist following circumcision.

The notion of the *halaka* as 'secondary circumcision', informed by the
suggested equivalence between circumcision and haircut, appears more likely
when *brit milah* and *halaka* are compared with their Muslim counterparts.
In Muslim societies the two practices are usually held in reverse order. In
Morocco, for example, the first haircut, *aqiqa* (see Westermarck 1926 II:
406–407), accompanied by a ritual slaughter of a goat or a sheep, is conducted on the seventh day. The similarity between *brit milah* and *aqiqa* was
noted long ago (Propp 1987: 363). According to most Muslim scholars,
circumcision (*khitan*) 'should be performed later, at the age of seven (*when
the male child, under the father's supervision, starts his systematic religious education*), age ten, or even thirteen years' (Giladi 1995: 824; italics added). Note
the association of *khitan* with the beginning of study.

The association between circumcision and the first haircut is made explicit in many rabbinical sources. The primary link is the biblical reference
(located just a few verses before the injunction not to round the corners of
the head) which is taken as the rationale for conducting the ritual at age
three. 'And when ye shall come into the land and shall have planted all
manner of trees for food, then ye shall count the fruit as uncircumcised:
three years shall it be as uncircumcised to you: it shall not be eaten off. But
in the fourth year all the fruit thereof shall be holy . . .' (Leviticus 19: 23–
24). The selection of this passage as the age rationale of the *halaka*, based on
equating the uncircumcised fruits with the first hair (see Eilberg-Schwartz
1990: 149–52), makes the association between circumcision and haircut almost categorical. The Zohar and other mystical sources deepen the association by claiming that, since in the first three years the powers of impurity
dominate the trees, the fruit is considered foreskin (*orla*). 'Hence, to shear
the hair means actually to remove the foreskin' (quoted in Serebrianski

1990: 40). Like circumcision, haircutting is viewed as an act of purification that entails external (physical) and internal (spiritual) shearing. Unlike circumcision, the shorn hair grows again naturally, but the hair of internal shearing cannot be regenerated unless the person is morally intact. This exegesis is apparently modelled on the two-tier notion of circumcision already discussed (Serebrianski 1990: 19).

As a visible part of the body, 'capable of painless amputation, infinite manipulation, and endless regeneration' (Myerowitz Levine 1995: 85), hair is a convenient symbolic device for articulating life passages and changes in identity and status. The symbolic meanings of hair and the disciplinary domains and analytic levels in which they should be deciphered have been amply debated by scholars. Without splitting hairs, I believe that Myerowitz Levine's assertion that 'hair can be used to enunciate a dialectic between nature and the norms and restraints of culture' (1995: 87) is inclusive enough to encompass most differing views on hair symbolism. This is certainly true of sexual explanations of hair practices with which my focus on the equation between circumcision and the haircut resonates. However, one should be wary of wholesale psychoanalytic statements that view the head hair as a phallic symbol the cutting of which invokes castration, without paying attention to the complexities of the peculiar cultural context in which the ritual is situated and the subjective experiences of the novices. Moreover, even within a psychoanalytic framework, hair manipulation in the *halaka* appears as a multivocal phenomenon that calls for a synthetic interpretation (cf. Paul 1990). It is not impossible to interpret the shaving of the children's head as some sort of symbolic castration (imposed perhaps as a cultural attempt to deal with Oedipal desires at the very period when they are most operative!). But the *loss* of hair is counterbalanced and compensated by the *attainment* of ear-locks which, with the same psychoanalytic leap of faith, may be viewed as providing the novices with adult-like symbolic penises. As suggested, these seemingly contrasting interpretations can be reconciled in the best tradition of Freudian multideterminism to which the charged atmosphere of the *halaka*, fusing fear, fatigue and disorientation with joy and pride, appears particularly congenial.

Without barring the possible sexual connotations of hair symbolism, the social control dimension inherent in the 'dialectic between nature and the norms and restraints of culture', appears no less pertinent to the *halaka*. Here I would follow Hallpike's (1969) structuralist argument that the meaning of hair symbolism is related to the location of the social actors 'inside' or 'outside' society (cf. Douglas 1973; Margalit 1995). Thus, the long, dishevelled hair of biblical Nazarites and modern hippies appears to be associated with loose social order, whereas the tightly collected hair of Victorian women, short cut hairstyle of Marine recruits, and shaven head of Buddhist monks and ultraorthodox women are all associated with rigid social control. In this vein, the first haircut at age three is a powerful social statement in which the male child cannot fail to perceive that the permissive non-gendered, under-socialized period of early childhood, under the protective cover of the mother, is over. The *halaka*, being a fulfilment of a biblical precept, is viewed as 'reshit hinuch hayeladim'('the beginning of the child's education'), the first step in the all-encompassing, primarily male world of the commandments and Torah.

As the child grows up, his purity is augmented to make him fit for holy Torah study, by cutting off parts of his body deemed profane and excessive. Whether the actual foreskin or the head hair, these parts are generically designated 'foreskin' (*orla*) that must be circumcised. This stage-developmental model, specifying the male path to holiness, is extended in mystical sources to bar mitzvah where the 'foreskin', now entirely metaphoric, stands for the first 13 years, dominated by *yetzer ha-ra*, the evil inclination (Adler 1983: 824). These years are 'cut off' upon the transition from boy (*yeled*) to man (*ish*) at 13. The appearance of the good inclination (*yetzer ha-tov*) at this age elevates the person in holiness and concludes the transformation which, again, is likened in the *Zohar* to rebirth. Although bar mitzvah appears as a major step toward the disembodied pole on the *milah-milah* developmental range, it is also marked by a bodily change related to hair. In the Talmud, the first signs of adolescent beard are taken as a standard indication of social and religious majority (Halperin 1993: 12; Horowitz 1994).[29]

Going back to the ceremonies at age three, it is clear that the growing purity entailed by the ritual transition to boyhood is a prerequisite for entering the world of religious learning. Indeed, the transformative significance of the *halaka* is enhanced by its associative link with the beginning of learning in the *heyder*.[30] A 'boy' rather than a 'baby', the three-year-old, twice repaired and equipped with male identity markers, is supposed to follow basic daily prayers and spend time with his father and the male community in the synagogue. As against circumcision after which the child is returned to his mother, the *halaka* marks a real, albeit partial, separation from her. 'If the girl is left out, the boy is thrust out, when he is carried from his mother to the *melamed* (teacher) – thrust out from babyhood and from the safe, enfolding warmth of the feminine world' (Zborowski and Herzog 1962: 348). Admittedly, the 'painful experience for the mere baby who is taken away from his mother's familiar presence to spend ten or twelve hours a day at study' (ibid, p. 88), typical of pre-Holocaust *shtetl* reality, is less harsh today. But the fact remains that, following the *halaka*, the boy is systematically distanced from his mother. From now up to his marriage, and often long after that, he will spend more and more of his time in the exclusively male territory of religious study. Even the *heyder*, equivalent to kindergarten in terms of age level (age three to five), is monopolized by male authority figures: the *melamed* (teacher) and his *oyzer* (helper). After two years in the *heyder*, the child will move to the primary school (Talmud Torah), going back home to his family only in the late afternoon or in the evenings. From there, at age 13, he will move to a small *yeshiva* (junior religious academy), to see his mother only at night or at the weekend; and then, at 17, to a big *yeshiva*, which as a rule includes boarding.

Against the separation from the mother, it is notable that the school initiation ceremony, to which we turn now, is replete with nurturing-maternal images (Marcus 1996). The child sits on the teacher's 'lap' or 'bosom', a typical mother-child position, and the teacher, like a nursing mother, 'feeds' the student with Torah. The association of Torah with baby food and its teaching with suckling is common in the rabbinical literature: 'Beyond Moses, the association between breasts, milk, honey, and Torah extended to all teachers of the Torah' (ibid, p. 90).[31] The representation of Torah teachers as surrogate mothers and the affecting style of the school initiation ceremony are certainly a powerful statement of parental affection. As such, the ritual, like the preceding *halaka* and circumcision at the beginning of life, is a moment of male bonding that constitutes a symbolic rebirth. The idea 'that the transmission of the Torah may be likened to procreation' (Goldberg 1987: 116) has many *midrashic* and mystical allusions. The *Zohar*, elaborating on the Talmudic comment that teaching Torah to a neighbour's son is like giving birth to him,[32] asserts that a teacher who encourages the student to attain knowledge recreates him in the same way as the anthropoid *golem* is created. The creation of a *golem* by the sages (by definition an all-male enterprise), using esoteric combinations of letters based on 'the covenant of the tongue', may be viewed as the ultimate rabbinical endeavour at pseudo-procreation (Idel 1990: 19; Liebes 1990–91: 1313).

Concluding note: between cultural universals and local context

This article has focused on the age three rituals as practised today in the ultraorthodox community. I explain the rites as a cultural device designed to transform expeditiously the child from an effeminate toddler, intimately tied to his mother, into a full-blown boy equipped with Jewish male identity markers, a beardless miniature replica of his father.

It should be noted that the child is not engulfed in an *exclusively* feminine world prior to the ceremonies, since the father is never entirely absent from the nuclear family setting; but because of the strict separation of the sexes he is not very involved either. This separation launches boys and girls into entirely different socialization orbits. Three-year-old male children are already engulfed in Torah study that will remain their main vocation for years to come. The male path to self-realization seems arduous and demanding: the vocabulary to describe the process emphasizes commitment, stamina, heroism, and draws on battlefield metaphors.

A major part of my argument has been that in Judaism circumcision takes place too early in life to furnish effectively the male infant with the values and meanings that will become the harbingers of his gender identity. The ritual complex of age three, taking place when the children are mature enough partially to disengage from their mothers and start assimilating the cultural scripts associated with masculine values, is a corrective mechanism designed to reconstitute male identity. Within this complex, the *halaka* may be cogently viewed as a secondary circumcision. Without going into the role of *bar mitzvah* in complementing the process of reconstituting male identity begun at age three, it seems that age thirteen is too late an onset for the ritual construction of male identity in the *haredi* community.

One issue that threatens to undermine the credibility of the functional analysis presented here involves the historical situatedness of the rituals of childhood. Since infant circumcision has persevered in Judaism from time immemorial, it might be argued that the predicaments of gender differentiation, awareness (memory), purity and knowledge that the early timing of the rite entails have haunted the Jewish people throughout its history. But the powerful convergence of the first haircutting and school initiation ceremonies at age three is a relatively recent phenomenon that has reached its zenith in present-day Jewish ultraorthodox communities in Israel. Why did these cultural solutions evolve so belatedly? To deal with this problem, we must situate the gender identity problem in the current context of the modern ultraorthodox community. First any perception of the ultraorthodox being an immutable relic of ancient Judaism should be dispelled. The contemporary *haredi* community, with its uncompromising adherence to the stringent version of written *halakha*, Jewish religious law, is a fairly modern phenomenon (see Dan 1997; Friedman 1991; Soloveitchik 1994). Many of its defining features have been shaped by the historical vicissitudes of this century and by current Israeli politics. The male ideal of open-ended Torah study looms high among these features, and its realization has never been so widespread. Since gender differentiation, awareness (memory) and purity are viewed as prerequisites for successfully pursuing the male ideal of learning, it is not surprising that the conservative approach towards women and the separation between the sexes are more strictly enforced nowadays.

Thus, the importance of the early and dramatic inculcation of male identity stems from a complex situation of which the separation of the sexes is but one corollary. Admittedly, gender relations do not constitute the major arena where the predicament of identity is most acutely felt in the contemporary *haredi* community. The present-day purist and stringent voluntary *haredi* community battles to defend its boundaries and reassert its values primarily against the mainstream secular society amidst which it is uncomfortably situated. In order to inoculate the children against the polluting influence of the external world, they have to be placed as early as possible in the guarded bastions of learning. This early timing of identity imprinting, which occurs when the child is still deeply engulfed in the domestic, female-governed milieu, perforce accentuates the transition to the all-male world of study even if the father is not entirely absent from the children's life before the rites.

In this respect, it is interesting to compare the elaborate ritualization of children's lives among the ultraorthodox to the medieval Ashkenazi scene where the school initiation ceremony and later *bar mitzvah* were instituted. The brutal pressures to convert, exerted on Ashkenazi Jews by the Christian majority since the first crusade, created a pressing need to inoculate the children, viewed as the most vulnerable members of the community, by subjecting them from an early age to an effective socialization regime, punctuated by dramatic rituals (Goldin 1997: 63–66). Granted that the emphasis on Torah study presupposes strict measures of gender differentiation and purification, it is not surprising that this period also saw the banishment of women from public ritual arenas. In Israel today the threat posed by the secular majority is articulated as temptation more than as compulsion, but it is felt by the ultraorthodox as no less real. As such, it might give rise to the same concern to extricate the child from the female domain as soon as possible in order to instil in him male values.

Notes

1. As I later make clear, the major arena for the haircutting ritual in contemporary Israel is the pilgrimage to Rabbi Shimon Bar-Yohai's tomb in Meron conducted on the festival of *Lag Ba'omer*. Observations of the ritual in Meron

were conducted during several pilgrimages in the early 1980s and again in the early 1990s, in the context of a comprehensive study of the folk-veneration of saints in contemporary Israel (see Bilu 1984; 1990). Observations of school initiation ceremonies were conducted in Jerusalem in an ultraorthodox school in 1996–98.

2. My major sources in covering the injunctions, customs and practices of the rituals of childhood were two recent rabbinical compendia in Hebrew. The first, titled *On the Eighth Day* (Wilhelm 1992), deals with circumcision, and the second, *The Anthology of the Haircut* (Serebrianski 1990), deals with the rituals at the age of three. Translations of quotations from texts in Hebrew are my own unless otherwise stated.

3. For a recent discussion of the *milah-milah* association, based on the classic Hasidic text, *Keter Shem Tov*, see Ginsburg (1997: 9).

4. For example, Wolfson (1987b) discusses an elaborate exegesis from the mystical *Zohar* that ingenuously links 'discourse' or 'speech', derived from the root NGD, and 'phallus', conveyed by the euphemism *gid* (sinew).

5. In Hebrew, the verb used for making a covenant is precisely 'cutting' (as in 'cutting a deal'). Thus, circumcision separates and unites simultaneously, a painful cut that binds (Boyarin and Boyarin 1995: 39; see also Kirshenblatt-Gimblett 1982).

6. See, for example, Joshua 5:2-9.

7. The symbolic equation between circumcision and marriage ceremonies is manifest in rabbinical promulgation of *brit milah* customs. For example: 'And they adorn him (the eight-day-old newborn) with beautiful garments, as on his wedding day, for it is the custom of the women to call the circumcised bridegroom (*hatan*), since he is wed to the Holy One through circumcision' (Wilhelm 1992: 37). The circumcised is designated *hatan habrit* (bridegroom of the covenant) or *hatan damim* (bridegroom of bloodiness, following the cryptic account of the circumcision of Moses' son in Exodus 4, 25–26). Note, however, that the designation 'bridegroom' is also applied to male initiates in the ritual haircutting at age three, and in the *bar mitzvah* ceremony at age 13. The refrain uttered at the end of the circumcision ceremony – 'As he entered the covenant so may he enter the Torah, the marriage chamber, and [a life of] good deeds' – bears testimony to the rabbinical view of the male rites of passage, from birth to marriage, as an integrated sequence.

8. From the root HTN which in ancient Semitic languages signifies various forms of family associations or rituals (Goldberg, 1996: 21–22).

9. In some Muslim societies, where circumcision 'is probably designed to mark the beginning of adolescence and to prepare the child for marriage' (Giladi 1995: 824), the operation is performed in various vestigial practices as a prenuptial ceremony (Propp 1987: 514–18).

10. Genesis Rabba, 11:6.

11. In this vein, the father's thoughts and ideas during the festive meal following circumcision are assumed to shape the soul of the newborn (Wilhelm 1992: 226).

12. A Talmudic sage has claimed that 'a woman is like a circumcised person' (Babylonian Talmud, Avoda Zara 26b; see also Rubin 1995: 91).

13. See note 5.

14. The common interpretation is that the voluntary fulfilment of the commandment is suspended, to be 'realized later on, when the child, now grown, permits his own child to be circumcised' (Boyarin and Boyarin 1995: 28). For other accounts, see Wilhelm (1992: 168–81).

15. *Milah* and *pri'ah* are followed by a third act, *metsitsah* ('sucking'). In the past, the circumciser sucked the blood of the wound following the operation to prevent it from clotting too early (Rubin 1995: 102). Today most circumcisers use a pipette to that end.

16. Historically, the act of *pri'ah* may have been added to *milah* in order to remove the temptation of seeking to reconstruct the foreskin under external pressure to convert or to pass as non-Jews (Rubin 1995: 101).

17. The dual meaning of *milah* appears similar to Paul's hierarchy between that which is 'in the flesh' and that which is 'in the Spirit'. For Paul, however, the latter (realized in baptism) supplants the former, while for the rabbis the two meanings are complementary and encapsulated in circumcision (Boyarin and Boyarin 1995: 21).

18. Babylonian Talmud (1959), Niddah 30b.

19. A rabbinical interpretation suggests that when Joseph sought to convince his brothers of his Jewish identity, during their first reunion in Egypt, he showed them that he was circumcised and he spoke to them in Hebrew, the holy tongue. Again, the connection between circumcision and discourse (*milah-milah*) is well established (Genesis Rabba 92: 10).

20. If 'good deeds' are associated with religious majority (*bar mitzvah*), then the response links together all the ritual markers in the male life trajectory, from birth to marriage.

21. The mystics noted that the numerical values of ear-lock (*pe'ah*) and God (*Elohim*) were identical (86).

22. In 1836, an Ashkenazi inhabitant of Safed wrote that 'for *Sephardi* Jews, this injunction [the haircutting ritual in Meron] is as important as the commandment of *brit milah*' (Friedhaber 1991: 183). An explicit link is made here between circumcision and the haircut.

23. Noted among the minor shrines is the Cave of Shimon the Just in Jerusalem. The popularity of this shrine is likely to stem from the fact that Shimon the Just is a namesake of the saint of Meron.

24. Today, when most children arrive at the *heyder* by bus or car, this part of the ritual begins only near the school entrance.

25. See Babylonian Talmud, Berakhot 16b.

26. The reason for selecting the first verse in Leviticus is related to the order of studying the Pentateuch in the *heyder*: when the children will actually begin to study the Torah, around age five, they will start with Leviticus rather than with Genesis. The rabbinical explanation is, 'Let the pure ones occupy themselves with purity' (*Midrash Vayyikra Rabba* 7: 3). It is appropriate that the little boys, innocent and pure, will begin their study with the purity laws of Temple sacrifice, discussed in the first passages of Leviticus.

27. The participants in the three-day visit to the *hillulah* in Meron in 1983, organized by Israeli anthropologist Harvey Goldberg, were Victor and Edith Turner, Barbara Myerhoff, and a group of Israeli anthropologists including this essay's author.

28. Whiting maintains that religious awareness evolves as a cultural solution to the child's feeling of being abandoned and inadequate following the birth of a sibling. 'In the crib and cradle cultures of Europe and the Middle East, the child is taught that the Judeo-Christian God is there to take over the parental role' (Whiting 1990: 363). In the ultraorthodox community, most three-year-old boys have already experienced the frustrating appearance of a sibling.

29. It is tempting to interpret the demand to cut the hair of the head and to preserve the beard (Leviticus 19: 27) from a gender differentiation perspective: only the hair that accentuates gender differences should be retained. Famous commentators have justified the sporting of a beard in these terms. For example: 'We are commanded to grow a beard so as not to abrogate the sign that God put in the male, to distinguish him from the female'; quoted in Horowitz (1994: 138).

30. The ritual sequence of age three is compatible with the general complementary pattern which involves rituals of extrusion for casting the bad and lowly out of the body followed by rituals of incorporation of the good and the elevated (Shweder 1991: 344–45).

31. For example, a *midrashic* commentary on 'Your breasts are like two fawns' (Song of Songs 7: 8) likens the breasts to Moses and Aaron. 'Just as whatever a (nursing) mother eats, the child eats when he sucks from these breasts, so too, all the Torah that Moses learned he taught Aaron' (quoted in Marcus 1996: 90).

32. Babylonian Talmud, Sanhedrin 99b.

References

Adler, Benyamin 1983: *Bar Mitzvah: Customs and Manners* (in Hebrew), Jerusalem: Feldheim.

Bilu, Yoram 1984: 'Saint Veneration among Moroccan Jews in Israel: Contents and Meanings' (in Hebrew), in: Naama Cohen and Ora Ahimeir (eds.), *New*

Directions in the Study of Ethnic Problems, pp. 144–50, Jerusalem: Jerusalem Institute for Israel Studies.

Bilu, Yoram 1990: 'Jewish Moroccan "Saint Impresarios" in Israel: A Stage-Developmental Perspective', *Psychoanalytic Study of Society* 15: 247–69.

Bourdieu, Pierre 1977: *Outline of a Theory of Practice*, Cambridge: Cambridge University Press.

Bowie, Malcolm 1991: *Lacan*, London: Fontana Press.

Boyarin, Daniel 1997: *Unheroic Conduct: The Rise of Heterosexuality and the Invention of the Jewish Man*, Berkeley: University of California Press.

Boyarin, Jonathan and Boyarin, Daniel 1995: 'Self-Exposure as Theory: The Double Mark of the Male Jew', in: Debbora Battaglia (ed.), *Rhetorics of Self-Making*, pp. 16–42, Berkeley: University of California Press.

Cooper, Samuel 1987: 'The Laws of Mixture: An Anthropological Study in Halakha', in: Harvey E. Goldberg (ed.), *Judaism Viewed from Within and from Without: Anthropological Studies*, pp. 55–74, Albany, NY: State University of New York Press.

Crapanzano, Vincent 1981: 'Rites of Return: Circumcision in Morocco', *Psychoanalytic Study of Society* 9: 15–36.

Dan, Yosef 1997: 'The Expansive Ultraorthodoxy: a Product of Secular Israel' (in Hebrew), *Alpayim* : 234–53.

Douglas, Mary 1973: *Natural Symbols: Explorations in Cosmology*, New York: Vintage-Random House.

Eilberg-Schwartz, Howard 1990: *The Savage in Judaism*, Bloomington: Indiana University Press.

Eilberg-Schwartz, Howard and Doniger, Wendy (eds.) 1995: *Off With Her Head!: The Denial of Women's Identity in Myth, Religion, and Culture*, Berkeley: University of California Press.

Friedhaber, Zvi 1991: 'The *Lag Ba'omer Hillulot* in Israel: their development and their dances' (in Hebrew), in: Issachar Ben-Ami (ed.), *Research on the Culture of North African Jews*, pp. 181–90, Jerusalem: Communauté Israelite Nord-Africaine.

Friedman, Menachem 1987: 'Life Tradition and Book Tradition in the Development of Ultraorthodox Judaism', in: Harvey E. Goldberg (ed.), *Judaism Viewed from Within and from Without*, pp. 235–55, Albany, NY: State University of New York Press.

Friedman, Menachem 1991: *The Haredi (ultraorthodox) Society: Sources, Trends and Processes* (in Hebrew), Jerusalem: Jerusalem Institute for Israel Studies.

Giladi, Avner 1995: 'Saghir', *Encyclopedia of Islam*, New Edition, pp. 821–27, Leiden: E.J. Brill.

Ginsburg, Isaac 1997: *The Structure of the Psyche According to Hasidism* (in Hebrew), Rechovot: Gal Einai.

Gliss, Yaaqov 1968: *The Customs of the Land of Israel* (in Hebrew), Jerusalem: Mosad Harav Cook.

Goldberg, Harvey E. 1987: 'Torah and Children: Symbolic Aspects of the Reproduction of Jews and Judaism', in: Harvey E. Goldberg (ed.), *Judaism Viewed from Within and from Without: Anthropological Studies*, pp. 107–31, Albany, NY: State University of New York Press.

Goldberg, Harvey E. 1990: 'Anthropology and the Study of Traditional Jewish Societies', *AJS Review* (the journal of the Association for Jewish Studies) 15: 1–22.

Goldberg, Harvey E. 1996: 'Cambridge in the Land of Canaan: Descent, Alliance, Circumcision, and Instruction in the Bible', *Journal of Ancient Near Eastern Society* 24: 9–34.

Goldin, Simha 1997: *Uniqueness and Togetherness: The Enigma of the Survival of the Jews in the Middle Ages* (in Hebrew), Tel-Aviv: Hakibbutz Hameuchad.

Haglili, Yosef 1988: *The Book of Meron* (in Hebrew), Meron: Author's Publication.

Hallpike, C.R. 1969: 'Social Hair', *Man*, n.s. 4: 254–64.

Halperin, David J. 1993: *Seeking Ezekiel: Text and Psychology*, Philadelphia: Pennsylvania State University Press.

Heilman, Samuel C. 1986: *The People of the Book*, Chicago: University of Chicago Press.

Heilman, Samuel C. and Friedman, Menachem 1991: 'Religious Fundamentalism and Religious Jews', in: M. E. Marty and S.R. Appleby (eds.), *Fundamentalism Observed, The Fundamentalism Project*, vol. 1; pp. 197–264, Chicago: University of Chicago Press.

Helmreich, W. B. 1982: *The World of the Yeshiva*, New Haven, CT: Yale University Press.

Hoffman, Lawrence A. 1996: *Covenant of Blood: Circumcision and Gender in Rabbinic Judaism*, Chicago: University of Chicago Press.

Horowitz, Elimelech 1994: 'The Significance of the Beard in Eastern and European Jewish Communities in the Middle Ages and the Beginning of the New Era' (in Hebrew), *Pa'amim* 59: 124–48.

Idel, Moshe 1990: *Golem: Jewish Magical and Mystical Traditions of the Artificial Anthropoid*, Albany, NY: State University of New York Press.

Kirshenblatt-Gimblett, Barbara 1982: 'The Cut that Binds: The Western Ashkenazic Torah Binder as Nexus Between Circumcision and Torah', in: Victor Turner (ed.), *Celebration: Studies in Festivities and Ritual*, pp. 136–46. Washington D.C.: Smithsonian Institution Press.

Liebes, Yehuda 1990–91: 'Golem Equals Wisdom in Numerology' (in Hebrew), *Kiriyat Sefer* 63: 1305–22.

Marcus, Ivan G. 1996: *Rituals of Childhood: Jewish Acculturation in Medieval Europe*, New Haven: Yale University Press.

Margalit, Natan 1995: 'Hair in TaNaKh: The Symbolism of Gender and Control', *JAGNES* 5: 43–52.

Moore, Sally Falk, and Myerhoff, Barbara (eds.) 1977: *Secular Rituals*, Amsterdam: Van Gorcum, Assen.

Myerowitz Levine, Molly 1995: 'The Gendered Grammar of Ancient Mediterranean Hair', in: Howard Eilberg-Schwartz and Wendy Donigen (eds.), *Off With Her Head*, pp. 76–129.

Nunberg, H. 1949: *Problems of Bisexuality as Reflected in Circumcision*, London: Imago Publishing.

Ortner, Sherry B. 1996: *Making Gender: The Politics and Erotics of Culture*, Boston: Beacon Press.

Paul, Robert A. 1990: 'Bettelheim's Contributions to Anthropology', *Psychoanalytic Study of Society* 15: 311–34.

Propp, William H. 1987: 'The Origins of Infant Circumcision in Israel', *Hebrew Annual Review* 11: 355–70.

Propp, William H. 1993: 'That Bloody Bridegroom (Exodus IV 24–6)', *Vetus Testamentum* 43: 495–518.

Reik, Theodor 1931: *Ritual: Psychoanalytic Studies*, London: Hogarth Press.

Rubin, Nissan 1995: *The Beginning of Life* (in Hebrew), Tel-Aviv: Hakkibutz Hameuchad.

Serebrianski, Yosef Y. 1990: *The Anthology of the Haircut* (in Hebrew), New York: Mendelsohn Press.

Shapiro, Warren, and Linke, Uli (eds.) 1996: *Denying Biology: Essays on Gender and Pseudo-Procreation*, Lanham, MD: University Press of America.

Shweder, Richard A. 1991: 'How to Look at Medusa without Turning to Stone: On Gananath Obeyesekere', *Thinking Through Cultures: Expeditions in Cultural Psychology*, pp. 332-52, Cambridge, MA: Harvard University Press.

Soloveitchik, Hayim 1994: 'Rupture and Reconstruction: The Transformation of Contemporary Jewry', *Tradition* 28: 63–131.

Strauss, Claudia, and Quinn, Naomi 1997: *A Cognitive Theory of Cultural Meaning*, Cambridge: Cambridge University Press.

Turner, Edith 1993: 'Bar Yohai, Mystic: The Creative Persona and his Pilgrimage', in: Smadar Lavie, Kirin Narayan, and Renato Rosaldo (eds.), *Creativity/ Anthropology*, pp. 225-52, Ithaca: Cornell University Press.

Turner, Victor 1962: 'Three Symbols of Passage in Ndembu Circumcision Ritual', in: Max Gluckman (ed.), *The Ritual of Social Relations*, Manchester: Manchester University Press.

Van Gennep, Arnold 1909/1960: *The Rites of Passage*, Chicago: University of Chicago Press.

Westermarck, Edward A. 1926: *Ritual and Belief in Morocco*, London: Macmillan.

Whiting, John W.M. 1990: 'Adolescent Rituals and Identity Conflicts', in: James W. Stigler, Richard A. Shweder, and Gilbert H. Herdt (eds.), *Cultural Psychology*, pp. 357-65, Cambridge: Cambridge University Press.

Wilhelm, Nachman Y. 1992: *On the Eighth Day* (in Hebrew), Israel: Derosh Noy Institute.

Wolfson, Elliot R. 1987a: 'Circumcision and the Divine Name: A Study in the Transmission of Esoteric Doctrine', *Jewish Quarterly Review* 78: 77–112.

Wolfson, Elliot R. 1987b: 'Circumcision, Vision of God, and Textual Interpretation: From Midrashic Trope to Mystical Symbol', *History of Religions* 27: 189–215.

Yerushalmi, Yosef H. 1982: *Zakhor: Jewish History and Jewish Memory*, Seattle: University of Washington Press.

Zatz Litt, Eleni 1997: 'Remembering the Covenant and the Embodiment of Belonging', unpublished paper presented at the American Anthropological Association meeting.

Zborowski, Mark, and Herzog, Elizabeth 1962: *Life is With People: The Culture of the Shtetl*, New York: Schocken Books.

Zimmer, Eric 1996: *Society and its Customs: Studies in the History and Metamorphosis of Jewish Customs* (in Hebrew), Jerusalem: Zalman Shazar Center.

THREE

'Our Bülent Is Now a Commando'
Military Service and Manhood in Turkey

Emma Sinclair-Webb

Close to and almost surrounding the Turkish parliament in Ankara are the various headquarters of the military establishment – the gendarmerie (*jandarma*), the navy, the army, the airforce. Diagonally opposite looms the building that houses those whom we might call the other, non-elected leaders of the country – the office of the General Chief of Staff (Genelkurmay). The Turkish armed forces are known to take a great interest in the political life of Turkey and their institutional relationship with the government and state confirms this: in accordance with the 1982 Constitution of the Turkish Republic, drawn up in the time of the military regime after the 12 September 1980 coup, the Chief of Staff reports direct to the Prime Ministry and the Ministry of Defence is subordinate to the Chief of Staff. More significantly, on a monthly basis the National Security Council (Milli Güvenlik Kurulu), composed of members of the government in office and senior military personnel, and backed by a secretariat whose secretary general must be of the rank of general or admiral, meet to discuss behind closed doors issues pertaining to governmental decision-making of all kinds. Article 118 of the Constitution entitles the Council to take decisions 'imperative to safeguard the peace and security of society' and its decisions and 'advice' are to be given 'priority consideration' by the Council of Ministers. A further law provides, among other elements, an extension of the scope of national security to encompass 'protection and safeguarding' of the state 'against any foreign or domestic threats to its interests in the international sphere, including political, social, cultural and economic [interests] . . .'[1]

That the Armed Services have played a very central role in modern Turkey since the foundation of the Republic in 1923 by Mustafa Kemal Atatürk, himself a military leader, is an acknowledged phenomenon, the political repercussions of which are beginning to be studied, most clearly through writings which look at the intersection between political and legal arrangements.[2] Since 29 October 1923 there have been three full military coups – plus interventions like the '28 February process' that brought down the RefahYol coalition government in 1997 – and, it has been calculated, 25 years, nine months and 18 days of martial law: in other words, 30 per cent of the life of the Republic has seen military governance imposed in one part of the country or another and sometimes throughout.[3] This does not take account of the period since 1987 which has seen provinces in the predominantly Kurdish southeast of Turkey designated an emergency zone (Olağanüstü Hal Bölgesi) and placed under a more stringent form of military governance, essentially a kind of war government.

This article looks at an aspect of life in Turkey that pertains to the important role played by the military not in political life but in the lives of half the population of the country, and with inescapable repercussions for the other half: military service is a compulsory duty for all males and has been so since 1927.[4] Military service is an institution still widely regarded by much of the population of Turkey as central to the socialization of men and, if one opts for an approach that can tend to become narrowly functionalist, clearly fulfils the criteria for being considered the classic initiation rite or process that establishes acceptance of a young man as a mature male. Since the mid-1980s the state security services have been embroiled in a situation of war[5] with the Kurdistan Workers Party (Parti Karkeren Kurdistan: PKK) in the southeast of Turkey. Building on prior understandings of the social meaning of military service in Turkey, this essay explores various responses to military service in the war context, and looks primarily at the institution of military service as a means to understanding dominant conceptions of masculinity.

Necessarily this article looks back over the period since 12 September 1980 and, in particular, from the mid-1980s and resists the temptation to link social and cultural change to the fast shifting political balance in Turkey – recently, the trial of Abdullah Öcalan, EU candidacy, apparently improved Turkish-Greek relations – or to find a direct correlation between the two. Though the conflict in the southeast may be brought to an end and some settlement sought in the coming months or years, it seems important to be aware that dominant cultural understandings of how gendered selves are made, constituted and reinforced in the practices of institutions and in the structure of social relations do not automatically disappear with the implementation of new legislation or the winning and granting of certain rights, although the latter may contribute in the longer term to shifts.

At a time when Turkey has been accepted as a candidate for membership of the European Union, the role of the armed services will in the years ahead inevitably become a subject of more open debate and discussion than has previously been possible. However, that the General Chief of Staff was quite prepared to defend its interests seemed evident in its decision, following soon after the announcement of Turkey's candidacy, to develop its own 'European Union Working Group', appointing for itself once more a central place in the process. At the same time it ominously emphasized 'historic reasons' for its role, its deep connectedness with 'the Republic, democracy and secularism', asserting that there were no grounds for its current relationship with the Ministry of Defence to change and that it was 'erroneous' to suggest that the National Security Council did not conform to democratic procedures.[6] Powerful institutions do not forsake their position willingly and, less tangibly, the culture which they have helped to create and which in turn reinforces and sustains their authority does not find expressions of resistance easily.

Military service and the law

To explain the legal side of military service in the Turkish Republic in its most simplified form, section 5 of Article 72 – entitled 'Political rights and duties' – of the 1982 constitution states that, 'National service is the right and duty of every Turk. The manner in which this service shall be performed or considered as performed either in the Armed Forces or in the public service shall be regulated by law.' This is also supported by the Military Service Law of 1927 which states in the first article that, 'According to the regulations of this law it is compulsory for every man who is a subject of the Republic of Turkey to do military service.' Women are thus excluded from this constitutional duty of 'every Turk' to perform 'national service' in the Armed Forces by the separate Military Service Law.

There is currently no possibility of opting to do civilian service in place of military service, as exists in many countries where national service is compulsory. Conscientious objection is also not recognized. In this respect the situation in Greece, which did not recognize conscientious objection and had no option of civilian service, until recently resembled that in Turkey. In 1998, however, civilian service was formally introduced in Greece, but since its duration was to be a full four years it functions as something closer to a punishment than to a reasonable alternative to military service. Its introduction in Greece came under EU pressure. United Nations Commission on

Human Rights resolutions, Council of Europe and OSCE recommendations have all explicitly linked the need for non-combatant forms of civilian service with the right to conscientious objection, and in this sense have a policy of supporting the principle of the right to partial objection.[7]

Men in Turkey are obliged to do their military service from 1 January onwards in the year that they turn 20 (that is, after turning 19, but in the year of their twentieth birthday). For those studying at university, working abroad, with serious illness, and so on, there are ways of delaying military service, and the procedure for this has to be strictly adhered to. Workers abroad can, if they can show that they are working legitimately, and for at least three years, pay around 10,000 Deutsche Mark and do one month's service. The normal period of military service is eighteen months as a private, though for those (for example, university graduates) who are eligible to do service as a reserve officer there are slightly shorter periods of service (currently sixteen months) and for those who are eligible to be reserve officers but nevertheless opt to do their service as a private the duration of military service is reduced to eight months.

Punishments for evasion of military service, non-compliance or flouting of regulations are many – entailing prison sentences of varying lengths – and fall into a variety of categories under the Turkish Military Penal Code (Türk Askeri Ceza Kanunu). In this context, it should be mentioned that criticisms of the armed services also constitute punishable offences (potentially entailing a prison sentence) and fall under various articles of the Turkish Penal Code (Türk Ceza Kanunu). Estimates vary as to the number of men currently evading military service after having been called up, but the Chief of Staff reported at the end of 1998 that the number of those who had ignored their call-up papers or not applied to delay their service had reached 200,000 at home, with a further 226,000 living abroad.[8] Coming from the central command of the institution that has least reason to boast to the general public that military service is unpopular, these figures can be taken to be the most conservative estimates available. Other estimates have put the number higher.

Precipitated by the need to raise money after the 17 August 1999 earthquake, and presumably with a view to finding a means to 'normalize' the situation of the enormous number of men officially known as draft evaders (*asker kaçağı*) – in the context of conscientious objection not being a recognized category – the opportunity for those born in 1973 or before to buy their way out of full military service (*bedelli askerlik*) was introduced. For the not inconsiderable price of 15,000 Deutsche Mark those eligible could apply – within a limited period – to do just one month's service. The pop star

Tarkan, living in semi-official exile in France because of non-fulfilment of military service duties, as well as several others (Mustafa Sandal and Çelik) all paid up and joined their regiments (I will return to the response to Tarkan's return below). This is not the first time that such an arrangement has been introduced: at other times there have been general 'amnesties' or similar solutions to deal with the back-log of non-attenders, though the numbers of those opting to evade in the past did not reach the proportions of recent times and the reasons for this will be looked at later in this article.

Making soldiers

Since the position of all military institutions is connected to issues of power internationally in relation to other armies and other nations, and also locally in relation to social groups, other institutions and focuses of power that form the particular nation of which they are a part, their social meaning – not to speak of impact – varies widely in different places and at different times.

As far as looking at militaries as repositories *par excellence* of hegemonic (and heterosexual) masculinity, more detailed 'ethnologies' of particular military institutions are needed to explore the complex ways in which their social position and power at home, along with their internal organization, together generate particular versions of exemplary or ideal masculinity.[9] This cannot be expected to be an unchanging or uniform process. Factors that count in this are the context of war versus peace, economic crisis versus stability, the balance of political power, social upheavals of all kinds, the relative strength of civil society organizations, and, indeed, all aspects of their relations with civilian society and civilian elements of the state with which they are in constant negotiation. Military institutions around the world may share similar features, but their social impact and meanings are not the same: the Turkish Armed Forces for the reasons mentioned at the start of this article undoubtedly play a greater part in the daily life of men and women in Turkey than the British Army does today in Britain or the Italian Army does in Italy and one consequence of this is that the versions of ideal masculinity generated by the army as a primary institutional site of hegemonic masculinity have a more inescapable social and cultural impact on all men – and women – in Turkey (regardless of sexuality, across social, ethnic and religious groups, and so on) than they would in the countries just mentioned. It would be interesting, however, to look at Greece as a comparative case, for though the Greek state is not engaged in a war, the (conscript) soldier as the defender of the Greek nation against foreign enemies – primarily Turkey, but also from time to time other neighbouring countries – presumably occupies a significant place in the national 'imaginary' and establishes a military version of exemplary manhood as inescapable and a marker against which other masculinities get measured.

In the case of career soldiers in Turkey, in particular those among the officer corps who have attended military schools and elite military academies, we have strong indications about the ideological training and version of masculinity that is cultivated. A book by the Turkish journalist Mehmet Ali Birand gives us perhaps the best indication of the self-perception of the army and its view of civilian Turkish society – in the period directly after 12 September 1980 when the book was researched – by quoting at length the words of junior and senior personnel. Since this is perhaps the only book where the army explains itself by reflecting somewhat less formally on its role and on the formation of its personnel, I will draw substantially on some of the themes that get aired.[10] In addition to elaborating on the ideology of both the training curriculum and the culture of the military institution, reflection on constructing or remaking the individual male into a soldier occupies a significant place, and a continual preoccupation with comparing soldiers with civilians runs through the whole book. Typical is a remark made by a commander in relation to the training process: 'Using the same clay, we craft a fine vase at the military schools. Civilian schools produce jugs of poor quality.'[11]

Drawing on such comments, Birand confirms that the process is less about bringing out innate qualities and more about making good what are self-critically seen as the flaws of Turkish society: 'The [military] Academies are trying to create an entirely different kind of Turk from the raw material they get, an ideal Turk, the kind of Turk one dreams of. He is free of all the maladies thought to afflict Turkish society: he is extremely well-informed, trustworthy and has all the social graces; he is also a proud and honourable warrior, a man of discipline and integrity.'[12] Overcoming the 'maladies thought to afflict Turkish society' is indeed the continual focus of concern for those interviewed throughout the book. Flying in the face of notions embedded in Turkish nationalist discourse (as in other nationalisms) about the inherent qualities and superior make-up of the Turk and the Turkish nation, implicit in the army personnel's view of things is a need to overcome what they regard as inherent Turkish characteristics. A continual point of comparison is made between the 'jugs of poor quality', the civilian population that makes up 'Turkish society', and the institution of the army, which implicitly is presumed to have somehow transcended Turkish society. The civilian world is disorderly, and civilians, however interested or concerned they may be, are finally irresponsible. One lieutenant tells Birand, when asked what the difference is between the two of them: 'It's perhaps that I'm so concerned with the future of the country. I have the feeling I'm more concerned with it than you are.'[13]

The version of masculinity that is being promoted here is thus one of superiority over civilians – who are not even differentiated as male or female but occupy an almost non-gendered childlike position – a greater sense of responsibility and self-sacrifice and an ability to repress instinctive and 'disorderly' behaviour in oneself. Since an officer has been 'trained' and remade, he has the right to identify himself unproblematically with the collective body whose mission is to guide the Turkish nation.

But there is another side to this infantilizing and contemptuous view of the civilian population. Despite the fact that Birand's interviews were conducted at a time when the Turkish army's sense of self-assurance clearly ran very high, detectable throughout is an awareness of the relatively weaker position of Turkey in relation to Western Europe and the USA. At various points comparisons with other societies are evoked to suggest, along classic modernization theory lines, that Turkey suffers from the spectre of 'backwardness'. Turkish officers can be positioned in the army's view of things as superior to civilian males, though the sense that the entire population is born inferior and in need of correction and re-fashioning threatens that superiority. Comparison with other armies who are thought to be made of better 'raw material' raises the concern that some Turkish soldiers constitute a 'parody' of the ideal, and a 'parody' presumably of the ideal male.[14]

These brief remarks about the elite sections of the military perhaps demonstrate the difficulties of unproblematically treating even institutions of hegemonic masculinity as repositories of well-defined and exemplary masculinity. In a country that suffers from underdevelopment and poverty, even elites cannot escape the ways in which power is relational and the question of their own position in relation to other (foreign) elites. As a means of avoiding comparison with other nations, leaders and armies, it should be added here that since 1980 there has been a heightened emphasis on one ideal male whose meaning is liable to regular renewal and re-invention to suit the needs of the time: Mustafa Kemal (Atatürk) is a home-grown 'ideal-type' whose leadership, military skills and 'ideology' – though consciously inspired by certain attributes perceived to signal a process of 'Westernization' – generally escape the charge of being viewed as imported or foreign-derived, and thus essentially alien. Though requiring a much fuller discussion than can be attempted in this article, viewed by the army as offering a whole guiding system of thought, administration and governance for every aspect of life in a modern nation-state, the perpetuation of 'Atatürkism' (and the inwardness this entails) also assists in the perpetuation of the military institution.

Given the ambiguity about Turkish civilian society, it is perhaps less surprising to find that the army's relationship with conscripts doing their military service is also a deeply ambiguous one. While conscripts in Turkey are seen by the civilian population as real soldiers and a part of the army for the duration of their service, evidence shows that they are treated with much of the same suspicion and reserve with which the civilian population tends to be viewed. In a sense perhaps the reservations about Turkish society are expressed thoroughly in relation to conscripts. Birand quotes a retired senior sergeant:

> A large proportion of our conscripts come to us poorly educated, cowherds straight from the fields . . . The poorer the education the harder it is to discipline them in the initial period. Yet, within two months at the most we have them thoroughly straightened out, and then we have to deal with the educated ones who resist a little longer. They too finally see the light of course. There is no other way out. Nobody likes beatings but there is no other way to establish discipline. You know our people, as soon as you act a little softly, they walk all over you . . .[15]

From what we know of the regimes of discipline in other armies, the sergeant's resort to violence, expressing a mistrust bordering on fear, is obviously not specific to the Turkish context. Also not specific is the principle of infantilizing the conscript: in Turkey the common designation is 'Mehmetçik' ('Little Mehmet'). Birand's description of the conscript is worth quoting at some length for the sense in which it reproduces the army's ambiguous sentiments and a complex attitude towards the conscripts as bearers of male identity.

> [The Mehmetçik] is the backbone of Turkey and of the Turkish Armed Forces. Throughout the eighteen months of his compulsory military service he will perform any act of self-sacrifice without batting an eyelid.
> Invariably, he regards the army as a school . . . Young men of all sorts leave their homes and come to the army from the four corners of the country. When they finish, they take back with them unforgettable memories as well as certain new ideas and value judgements ranging

from Atatürkist principles to the meaning of the motherland and their loyalty to it. Some of these prove impossible to assimilate, others are soon forgotten, but the commander and barrack-room friendships are not easily forgotten . . .

For some of the conscripts . . . [t]hey find in the army things that they had never actually seen or even heard of before. For many, this is an interlude in which they have a balanced diet of 3,500 calories a day and receive necessary medical or dental care. It is very much as if they are receiving their first lessons in a civilized way of life . . .

The private soldier is considered an extremely important person, particularly by the high-ranking officers. He is addressed as 'my son', and his welfare and protection from any unjust treatment is of serious concern.[16]

Suffused with class contempt, this description can be quite readily translated to, for example, the British context. Replace 'Mehmetçik' with 'Tommy soldier' and the sentiments expressed here can be similarly read as the portrayal of the regular soldier as an ordinary and uncomplicated 'chap' from the 'lower orders' by the commissioned officer (who in the British context is still more likely to be his social superior). Ready to 'perform any act of self-sacrifice without batting an eyelid', keen to receive their 'schooling' in a 'civilized way of life' and to be fed properly and kept healthy: less than human or at best children, the conscripts are certainly not regarded individually as the heroic 'real men' of the nation, though they are collectively described in the same breath as the 'backbone' of Turkey and of the army.

R.W. Connell's work on gender has perhaps resulted in one of the fullest accounts of the variety of masculine identities as 'organized social relations' and 'deeply enmeshed in the history of institutions and of economic structures'.[17] In considering how hegemonic masculinities are produced, he draws attention to the unequal power relations between men and sometimes between men 'in the same cultural or institutional setting':

We must also recognize the *relations* between the different kinds of masculinity: relations of alliance, dominance and subordination. These relationships are constructed through practices that exclude and include, that intimidate, exploit, and so on. There is a gender politics within masculinity.[18]

I will return to this point at the end of this article, but will first turn to some of the dominant implications of military service for men in Turkey today.

The social impact and meaning of military service

In the Turkish case, some clear aspects of the social meaning of military service for males can be traced in the combination of practical and notional sanctions that apply to those who have not discharged their duty to the nation. Unless a man has completed service he faces the prospect of being blocked from many kinds of employment. Employers in different fields consistently advertise for male employees who have completed their military duties, and discrimination on the basis of not having done so operates widely when it comes to entering permanent employment: in particular when it comes to professional work environments, as vacancies advertised in newspapers attest. It is likely that this operates too in semi-skilled positions on the factory floor of large companies. For example, all males applying to work in any capacity for Koç Holding, one of Turkey's two largest holding companies together with Sabancı, are asked in the general application form which applies to graduate-level entry vacancies in finance or marketing sectors of the Koç companies, down to assembly-line factory work in production for Arçelik, producing household appliances and electricals, to supply detailed information about their status as regards military service. It seems highly unlikely that male applicants would be offered permanent employment for Koç without having fulfilled their military duties, and it should be added that a company would presumably be in breach of the law if it were found to be complicit in employing men who fall into the draft evader (*asker kaçağı*) category.

A social restriction of a different and less formal kind also operates in the case of marriage. While it is much harder to generalize about this, many families – and women themselves – would not favour marriage until the prospective husband has completed his service. In these two senses military service becomes a rite of passage to manhood: most of the time a man is not accepted as a permanent employee, and is therefore unlikely to find a means of becoming economically independent of his family, and in addition may not be regarded as fit to be a marriage partner unless he has passed through military service.

Beyond this a young man wanting to leave the country even if he manages to secure the requisite visa will be unlikely to get beyond passport control unless he can demonstrate that he is going abroad for the purposes of study (language courses or university) and has delayed his military service accordingly. Not having done military service thus poses a further limit on mobility by legal means and, more significantly still, efforts to avoid military service generally mean avoiding various kinds of registration of residency and the impossibility of even obtaining various kinds of official documents like passports, or of subsequently renewing them. The implications of this are many and deserve a much fuller account than can be attempted here. In short, some of the most basic rights of the citizen are withheld: with no officially registered residency, inclusion on the electoral register, and hence the right to vote, is denied. In all senses, the army slogan 'Önce vatan' ('First the homeland') is real for males in Turkey.

The call-up to military service for those who have completed their education, are not able to postpone their service for reasons of entering further education, and whose whereabouts are known, comes in clockwork fashion. Since all Turkish citizens possess identity cards, giving date and place where their birth was registered, names of parents and so on, and by law citizens are required to register their place of residence with the local *muhtar* (elected local neighbourhood representative), draft papers are usually delivered to the door at the appointed time. (As mentioned above, not having one's address registered with the *muhtar* is one relatively easy and very common means of obscuring one's whereabouts.)

The moment of departure for military service has for many years been the familiar stuff of Turkish films and soap operas. Like everything else, how it gets marked depends on the social position of the family. The popular and less inhibited version sees the gathering at bus stations all around the country of great family parties, sometimes with musical accompaniment in the form of *davul* (drum) and *zurna* (a wind instrument), or a gypsy band leading the way, with dancing, songs, cheers and the waving of Turkish flags, and the boy hauled up and swaying on the shoulders of elder brothers and uncles, looking like the overwhelmed and bemused adolescent that he usually still is. As far as the attention he suffers and the energy of the occasion he will probably not have experienced anything like this since the hours before his circumcision (known in Turkey as *sünnet*), some twelve to fifteen years earlier, when he was paraded around relatives and shrines in the embroidered finery of his 'little prince' costume with turban-like hat, fake fur-trimmed satin cloak and sash proclaiming in big letters 'Maşallah' ('As God wishes'), clutching a toy sceptre in one podgy hand and a bag of sweets in the other and, before facing the terrifying moment of mutilation, encouraged to feel his full importance over his sisters in the eyes of doting parents and senior relatives.

The night before a young man departs for his service is often spent with friends, and resembles nothing so much as a stag night before marriage, with a nationalist flavour to it, or an ecstatic group of football fans after the match. Large groups of young men hanging out of the windows of cars which race dangerously through the centre of town decorated with huge Turkish flags and hooting their horns, shout 'En büyük asker bizim asker' (meaning both 'our army is the greatest' and 'our soldier is the best soldier', since *asker* means both army and soldier), or more ominously, 'Askere gidecek, geri dönecek' ('He is going to the army and he will return'). This nationalistic frenzy is often the preferred send-off of those who have ultra-nationalist political leanings: making the wolf's head sign often goes with this and its meaning is not lost on spectators (I once saw a group of defiant Kurdish children playing football in the street answer these threatening gestures with their own fearless victory signs and a reckless attempt to aim their ball straight at the passing car).

Among many petty bourgeois and middle-class families in big cities today the send-off is passed in more restrained ways, without the possibility for purging those feelings of anxiety that are certainly part of the whole ritual of being carried along in a riotous night of celebration. Indeed, in describing the ways departure for military service is marked and the social meanings the institution is inscribed with, social divisions are inescapable. As has been shown in various studies of masculinity, class background is highly significant when it comes to questions of how different images of masculinity are valued: physical endurance and stamina which go with labouring or factory-floor jobs are inevitably more valued qualities among working-class men for whom their bodies and the skill of their hands are their main economic assets than they are for white-collar men working in office environments where 'knowledges' of certain technologies and or-ganizational principles are what are valued. In this sense, it is perhaps con-ceivable that those who have had the advantages that generally go with their class of prolonged education and immersion in a cultural formation that prepared them not for physical work, but taught them to view their identity as deriving its meanings – masculine and other – from different kinds of 'knowledges' and sources of 'cultural capital', proof of masculin-ity through the physical endurance tests of military service holds less ap-peal. However, to argue along these lines is to risk underplaying the powerful associations of masculinity with militarism that undoubtedly enjoy wide currency across class divisions.

In some poor neighbourhoods of cities military service is publicly cel-ebrated with a nationalistic jingoism and macho posturing: in a district of Istanbul like Balat, for example, which has a population today largely origi-nating from the Black Sea region (Samsun, in particular), on the walls of many houses lists of names of local boys who are doing their service are roughly spray-painted, presumably by their mates: 'Memo, Oktay, Uğur, Cebo: Onlar şimdi asker: 79/2' (the names of the boys followed by 'They are now soldiers' and the year they were born, 1979, and their draft period).

Sometimes there are slogans – 'Bizim Bülent şimdi komando' ('Our Bülent is now a commando'), surrounded by roughly painted pictures of Turkish flags and guns. Bülent, like the millions of others faced with bleak employment prospects who form Turkey's growing urban poor, is momentarily transformed into Bülent the heroic commando (a role in a specially trained combat unit, that is prized or to be avoided at all costs, depending on your point of view) and defender of the nation, but the resonance of such messages is never entirely convinced or convincing. In a context of war, behind every Bülent the commando rises the spectre of Bülent the cannon fodder. Perhaps the function of such slogans is also to exorcise fear.

Nevertheless, nationalistic and macho posturing aside, perhaps some messages of this kind should be understood as signalling strong local support for ultra-nationalist politics – whether of the MHP (Milliyetçi Hareket Partisi, Nationalist Action Party) or the other right-wing parties more generally – and a certain lumpen flexing of the muscles before other sections of the population who share the neighbourhood and are liable to be regarded as disloyal fifth-columnists. Falling into this category, in particular, would be Kurds, who also now live around Balat, as well as those belonging to non-Muslim communities – Greeks, Jews and Armenians – all of whom still have a small presence in an area where historically they were large communities. Indeed the feelings of these groups towards military service – although the case of Kurds is quite different from the others – are certainly likely to be ambiguous when not openly hostile.[19] And it should be added that there are significant numbers of Turkish leftists who would share that feeling.

Military service also features prominently in family photograph albums, alongside the fading photos of family groups taken on the occasion of births, circumcisions and marriages. Grandfathers, fathers and sons all appear in uniform posing with guns, arms slung around the shoulders of their fellow countrymen and grinning inanely for the photo that gets sent home to the family from the other side of the country.

Talking to the fathers and grandfathers of young men who are today of an age to do their service, consistently striking is the fact that military service is generally remembered as having been personally important to them in their growing up. A first opportunity to be separate from the family, to see a different part of what is after all a vast country, often the first possibility of leaving the village of their birth in the days before the mass migration to cities and greater mobility, of meeting guys from different backgrounds, of being taught to read and write: the memories are generally quite fond ones even if the reality was harsher than they like to suggest and their descriptions are inflected strongly by dominant cultural understandings which construct military service as a character-building and 'manly' activity, and certainly the fulfilment of a debt or duty to the nation.[20] The time spent as a rank and file conscript was indeed referred to in a jocular and fond way by different classes until very recently, as we saw with Birand's characterization of the 'Mehmetçik'. War undoubtedly changed that to generate more polarized and ideologized views of the institution, though still the friendships and the hardships faced are topics more readily invoked in interviews than reflections on war or the meaning of military service or militarism more generally.

The current context

Since the beginning of the systematic military assault on Kurdish nationalism which began in earnest in the mid-1980s with the Turkish state's efforts to eradicate the armed struggle waged by the newly-formed guerrilla army and command structures of the PKK, military service has taken on a dimension that it did not have in earlier days, despite earlier experiences of war and combat situations (in Korea in 1950–53 and in Cyprus in 1974). That Kurdish nationalism among the Kurdish population of Turkey has a far longer history and did not begin with the PKK has been discussed at length elsewhere.[21] In the course of the 1980s and 90s, however, the Turkish army rapidly reorganized itself to fight what amounts to a fullscale war over large regions of the southeast of the country and also at times rather further afield, not least into northern Iraq where troops have regularly made large-scale incursions.

Of the estimated 525,000 conscripts doing military service at any one time,[22] it is generally estimated that 40 per cent do their service, or a part of it, in the 'emergency zone'.[23] Over 200,000 conscripts a year, then, have served in that region and a proportion of them will have seen some form of active service in the form of 'operations' against the guerrillas of the PKK and a few other much smaller Kurdish nationalist and far-left organizations who also wage armed struggle; and also against vast numbers of civilians suspected of harbouring PKK links or the many thousands – even hundreds of thousands – more who have been caught up in the emptying of villages and depopulating of the region which has been confirmed as a systematic policy by several independent observers and international human rights organizations.

Along with the units of the regular army, the *jandarma* and special teams who are trained in the tactics of contra-guerrilla warfare in a mountainous terrain, the Turkish army also introduced a system of recruiting villagers into their ranks, in an effort to discourage villages from actively supporting the PKK or from providing shelter and food to guerrillas. Some willingly joined and others found themselves under pressure to join the 'village guard' (*korucu*) system which supposedly provided them with the army's protection, some guns and payment in return for their co-operation in countering the activities of the PKK and joining in the army's 'operations' when called upon to do so. Needless to say, the existence of the 'village guard' system itself provoked violent PKK reprisals against those villages that chose the 'wrong' side. Since research into the whole way in which the war has been fought has been extremely difficult to carry out under prevailing conditions in Turkey, with heavy censorship operating at all levels, 'histories' of the last seventeen years will take many years to write.[24]

While in the first half of the 1990s reporting through state and private television channels and through print media regularly paraded captured 'live' guerrillas – standing heads bowed and hands clutched in front of them, 'humiliated' in front of the Turkish flag, their weapons lined up before them – as well as the corpses of the guerrillas 'captured dead' ('ölü ele geçirildi', in official parlance: literally translatable as 'brought to the hand/ caught dead'), there was a clear move away from this triumphalist style of reporting. Heavier restrictions on journalists reporting from the war zone seem to have resulted in an almost total news 'black-out', with reports being much more tightly controlled and showing every indication of carrying little more than the abbreviated and selective content of army-issued press releases. Funerals of the soldiers who had died in active service, consistently referred to as 'martyrs' (*şehit*), continued to be shown on television, but the 'terrorists' themselves had almost completely disappeared from the scene. Without knowing the precise reasons for this shift in the way the conflict was reported, one might speculate that the brutality of the style was perceived as counter-productive. That some of the abuses and atrocities committed by the 'special teams' (*Özel tim*) were also beginning to be reported – a series of photographs showing soldiers posing alongside the severed heads of guerrillas reached an international audience when they were published in *The European* newspaper – seems a possible reason, among other reasons connected with a significant shift in military strategy in about 1992.

While the impact of the war on the young guerrilla soldiers, male and female, and their families and communities is barely acknowledged by the Turkish press and ill-documented for reasons of the heavy censorship and restricted access operating,[25] the impact on conscripts, officers, and their

families has not been disguised. Funerals of 'martyrs' and visits by politicians to the rehabilitation centres of the physically and mentally disabled
war veterans (known by the honorific title of *gazi*, hero warrior) are regularly shown on television. These traumatic images alongside a complete
absence of information on the war through Turkish press channels has left
the Turkish public in general ill-informed on the issues entailed. There are
indications that official lines that warn against the dangers of separatism
and the presence of internal and external enemies are widely accepted and
have even cowed much of the population into willed ignorance on issues
such as human rights abuses and the notion of minority rights which might
throw into question rigidly Turkish nationalist arguments and 'security'
practices.

To counter the negative impact of funerals and images of traumatized
female relatives collapsing in grief beside the graves of their sons, several
state and private television channels began to show regular 'Mehmetçik'
programmes, along the lines of TRT's 'Mehmetçikle Elele' ('Hand in hand
with little Mehmet'). Aimed as morale-boosting events, in which conscripts
were shown clapping along to performances by well-known singers, and
being congratulated and encouraged in their task of defending the nation,
with scenes of them going about their training proudly, with a song in
their hearts and a smile to the cameras, it seems unlikely that programmes
with such a predictable message and so forced a cheeriness could command
high ratings. The awkwardness of the exercise and the scenes of hundreds of
faces whose youth and inexperience are perhaps the most striking aspect of
the spectacle does not seem the most compelling means of conveying to the
viewer the moral certainty of the cause.

Perhaps the ultimate success of the army in controlling responses to
and inducing consent among much of the population becomes evident in
the lack of criticism of the army by even those who have lost conscript
sons. Indeed with the trial of PKK leader Abdullah Öcalan, the *şehit yakınları*
(relatives of the martyrs) began to be systematically organized and used to
voice anti-PKK sentiments at every opportunity – most notably in the court
where some of the *şehit* families sat while Öcalan was being tried.[26] The
increasing focus in the course of the 1990s on the relatives (particularly
mothers) of soldiers who died in action was also in some sense perhaps an
attempt to match and counteract the visibility that the relatives and friends
of the 'disappeared' had commanded in their 'Saturday Mothers' (*Cumartesi
Anneleri*) campaign, based on the Argentinian Mothers of the Plaza de Mayo
campaign, and treated at least by the Turkish police and courts as a front
for 'separatist' activities.[27] The image of a mother grieving for her dead son

should be emphasized as carrying a resonance and impact in Turkish society (as in other places) that favours its appropriation for political ends.

It should be mentioned here once again that social divides in Turkey are pronounced when it comes to exploiting mechanisms for ensuring that a young man is not sent to the war zone and passes his service in an unrisky location and role. Unsurprisingly, those who themselves have power or have access to the institutions of power (via personnel in the army, politicians and the like) are said regularly to use this *torpil* (influence) to ensure the safety of their male relatives.

To return to military service, and to correct the bleak impression that dissenting voices have had no impact at all, I will turn now to some of the significant efforts in recent times to open up the issue of the impact of the war on those among the approximately 40 per cent of conscripts who have seen active service and to question the compulsory status of military service.

The Izmir War Resisters' Association (İzmir Savaş Karşıtları Derneği) was set up in February 1994 with the aim of 'fighting war, militarism and racism . . . of helping to promote a pacifist and free culture in place of the [prevailing] hegemonic racist-militarist culture'.[28] Back in December 1992 an earlier organization called the War Resisters' Association (Savaş Karşıtları Derneği) had been set up, but was officially banned in November 1993. At the centre of both organizations has been the campaign to establish the notion of the right to conscientious objection (*vicdani red*) and to support cases of men who have been called up but are resisting all aspects of service on these grounds. The case that really brought conscientious objection to public attention was that of Osman Murat Ülke. As early as 1992 an enquiry was made following an article he published which fell foul of article 155 of the Turkish Penal Code which makes it a punishable offence to 'alienate the people from military service' ('halkı askerlikten soğutma'). According to Ülke, it was this episode that prompted him to focus on the issue of military service and take the decision to resist it, along with a group of fellow co-resisters, in the knowledge that there was 'neither a conscientious objection movement, nor any other type of anti-militarist organization' in Turkey at that time. Possibly the only exceptions to this had been the announcements made in the journal *Sokak* back in 1990 by two men – Tayfun Gönül, and a few weeks later, Vedat Zencir – that they were objectors. Zencir had been charged under article 155 and acquitted. Reflecting on the initial decision to start a campaign, Ülke remarked in a later interview: 'In fact we were really afraid, because a few marginals like us appearing and making an announcement like that attracts no public attention and we thought, who knows, we may even be disappeared. We were a bit naïve of course at that time.'[29] It should be added here that in Turkey a culture of anti-militarism has been almost entirely lacking in the different strands of the left: for many armed struggle – at the discursive level when not in practice – has been central. Pacifist anarchist groups have historically been quite negligible in Turkey. This must have contributed to the difficulty of introducing the notion of conscientious objection even to those who were already critical of the Turkish state's treatment of the Kurdish question and of hardline security policies in the southeast. For these reasons and the punitive legal sanctions operating, the Izmir group's work has remained a limited campaign.

It was not until Ülke brought the principle to public attention by holding a press conference on 1 September 1995 at which he publicly burnt his draft papers and declared himself a conscientious objector that the campaign attained some visibility and Ülke just over one year later was arrested, charged and imprisoned, facing a variety of sentences for different offences, and the İzmir Savaş Karşıtları Derneği subsequently formally outlawed. Vedat Zencir, mentioned previously, publicly repeated his statement that he was a conscientious objector on 1 December 1997 and was subsequently charged under three articles of the Penal Code (155, 312 and 159), but acquitted on all charges.

The only conscientious objector to be prosecuted, Ülke spent in all two and a half years in prison, and was released on 9 March 1999. He continues to work for anti-militarism and to support the other declared objectors (currently about 30 men), but since following his release he should officially have gone to the barracks himself and reported for duty, he faces the prospect of being imprisoned once again at any moment as a deserter who has not responded to call-up. In his words, 'That means that there is (at the moment) no way to end this vicious circle for conscientious objectors.'[30]

The War Resisters' Association has faced a difficult campaign given that criticism of the Armed Forces and acts of civil disobedience (*sivil itaatsizlik*) against them are offences punishable according to rather a large number of articles of the regular Penal Code and the Military Penal Code.[31] The issue of being a conscientious objector has not in itself been the grounds for prosecution, but since the category is not recognized actions taken in line with being a conscientious objector (for instance, not responding to call-up) constitute punishable offences.[32] Since this has been a campaign which has fundamentally challenged what are understood constitutionally to be obligations and duties that go with being a male citizen of the Turkish Republic, the issues the association has addressed entail a reconceptualization of what it means to be a male in the current context. It can be argued that implicit in the challenge to the law comes a challenge also to military service as a socially sanctioned part of being a man or attaining manhood, though the directions and possibilities of this are far from clear.

In April 1999, a challenge of a different kind came to the institution of military service in the form of a book which consisted of the testaments of 42 men who had carried out their service in the southeast of Turkey. Nadire Mater, a journalist who had investigated the issue for several years, collected and edited her interviews as *Mehmedin Kitabı: Güneydoğu'da Savaşmış Askerler Anlatıyor* (Mehmet's Book: Soldiers who have fought in the southeast speak)[33] and, breaking the virtual silence on the issues through personal narratives of a traumatic and harrowing kind, certainly had an impact, reflected in the fact that in the first two months of publication the book went through four reprints and received positive media coverage. While other books and reports by human rights organizations had focused mainly on the impact of the war on civilians,[34] the emphasis of Mater's book has contributed a different perspective by showing that the impact on Turkish society must also be understood as being about the trauma (war syndrome) suffered by the young male conscripts who are returning from the war zone. The rejection of the heroic image of the soldier, the disillusionment with the institution and culture of the military, the sense of the futility of perpetuating a war in the southeast of the country, and attitudes to the Kurdish population, are themes running through the narratives of those who speak about their experience. The inability to adjust to life after military service and the condition of (untreated) post-traumatic stress disorder – the likely diagnosis in some cases of the variety of symptoms that the men describe experiencing[35] – attest to a side of war prohibited from being publicly voiced by powerful political and social sanctions. Most of the men also admit that they have been completely unable to talk about their harrowing experiences with friends or relatives.

Countering the nationalist and propagandistic view of the war perpetuated by the different arms of the state, governments, media channels and in everyday life situations where through a mixture of fear and induced consent the culture of authoritarian nationalism is regularly endorsed, it comes as no surprise to learn that the book has fallen foul of the law and at the time of writing this article the author and publisher were being prosecuted under article 159/1 of the Penal Code for 'demeaning and caricaturing the army' ('orduyu tahkir ve tezyif etmekten').

While the Izmir campaign has certainly challenged the prevailing military culture, Mater's book has also been significant in lifting the taboo on speaking about the subject. However, given the difficulty of turning anti-militarist campaigns into wider social movements in the current context, the association between military service and masculinity in Turkey seems likely to endure. Perhaps this essay highlights above all the problem of sustaining a discussion of masculinity in this case without continual reference to the workings of the different arms of the state, plus legal sanctions, and the political culture/s of Turkish society. Lest this seem too social determinist a conclusion, I turn now to looking at the encounter between the military and an individual whose sexuality and loyalty to the nation were, according to elements of the mainstream popular press, both in question.

The pop-star Tarkan returned to Turkey from France in January 2000 to do his military service under the one-month paid military service scheme. Tarkan, like thousands of others, had ignored his call-up papers, having no legal means of delaying service. Under the guidance of Ahmet Ertegün, the legendary Turkish co-founder of Atlantic Records in the late 1940s and the promoter of some of the great names of rhythm and blues, and later soul and rock, in the United States, the 27-year-old singer has recently begun to be 'marketed' to an international audience and now has a growing following in other Middle Eastern countries and in Europe. Tarkan's identity as a performer has increasingly been promoted as androgenous, embodying a light-hearted hedonism and sex appeal clearly aimed at both sexes. In much of the Turkish press this has prompted a great deal of speculation about his sexuality: suggestions that he is gay are loaded with the crude understanding of homosexuality as deviant, always effeminate, 'alien' in the various senses of the word, and not becoming of Turkish men.

The arrival of Tarkan in Istanbul was much hyped and reported. Endless speculation about his sexuality does not prevent him being a star with a huge following. From the Atatürk airport in Istanbul he was escorted to a police station – a routine presumably intended to remind everyone of his status as a draft dodger. He was not detained and was to leave shortly afterwards. Closely followed by the press, as he entered the police station the singer was asked by one TV reporter what his words to the viewers were: 'Ne mutlu Türküm diyene' (How happy is he who says 'I am a Turk'), came the response with a half-satirical, half-sheepish laugh, parroting the saying of Atatürk's that appears on public monuments and is learnt in every classroom in the land. From the building opposite, supporters of the MHP had gathered to shout at Tarkan: 'Every Turk is born a soldier' ('Her Türk asker doğar'), 'Duty to the fatherland is a duty of honour, the martyrs do not die, the homeland will not be divided' ('Vatan borcu namus borcu, şehitler ölmez vatan bölünmez'). There is little doubt that in this heavy climate, in which the solemn belief for some was clearly that Tarkan's military service was the fulfilment of an overdue debt, with the implication behind it that he had now to prove he wasn't a traitor, the question mark that hung over his sexuality was heavily implicated. Tarkan's cosmopolitan and camp civilian masculinity was in some way being measured up to a nationalist 'real man' local version, magnified by being militaristic.

Tarkan himself even used the performative aspect of self-transformation into a soldier in the concert he gave in Istanbul a couple of days before his service was to begin: in the middle of the show he disappeared from the stage to re-emerge with a soldier's short-back-and-sides haircut and an outfit that hinted of the army and in this new garb continued the performance with its strong emphasis, as ever, on uninhibited dance. By one reading this was a gesture that in its playfulness and sense of camp parody could be said to be about unseating and caricaturing the macho-in-uniform stereotype, by another reading evidence of a certain conformity to dominant cultural codes around military service and duty to the Turkish nation. For the audience it was no doubt something of both, but the slogans shouted and the flags waved at the moment of his appearance in this transformed state suggested that the response to Tarkan's gesture in this context (Istanbul, not New York City) and at this time can be better explained by the second reading than the first.

I do not want to claim that the fate of one pop-star can be generalized to account for the experience of other men: it can't, since artists and performers occupy a strange place and, particularly in socially conservative Middle Eastern countries, can to a certain extent flout social codes which the majority can't. However, it is interesting to note here that even those who can caricature and 'subvert' dominant cultural norms on issues such as sexuality and persisting notions of a normative heterosexual masculinity can only do so in certain contexts. There are many male TV presenters, game-show hosts and singers in Turkey whose performative style is camp or clearly not conventionally heterosexual-masculine.[36] However, it is when challenges to normative male identities are matched against the codes of exemplary masculine identity promoted by an institution such as the military that the military's position as the repository of dominant cultural values, with recourse to means of violent sanction, becomes most evident and the space and possibility for transgression severely limited.

So then the status quo is re-established and hegemonic masculinity manages once again, through being widely endorsed in the practices and discourses of everyday life by much of the population and enforced institutionally at many levels, to carry the day. Tarkan's mother sheds tears on seeing her son and his regiment swear their oath to lay down their lives for the Turkish nation and claims that this is a very proud moment for her. Notions of exemplary masculinity can also, let it not be forgotten, find reinforcement from women.

Concluding remarks

Although essentialist assumptions that men are inherently or necessarily prone to violence and thus closer to militarism than women have been thoroughly challenged by many writers on gender issues, it is worth briefly returning to them. Essentialist arguments are often predicated on accepting that because the instruments and apparatuses of violent coercion sanctioned by states (and carrying social endorsement) are male-dominated, men are 'naturally' – whether for cultural or biological reasons – more suited to such tasks than women.[37] However much the weaknesses of such formulations are exposed, though, their social currency persists and indeed their reinforcement in numerous ways and by various channels can only help to legitimize the privileged place held by militaries in certain societies: along these lines military service becomes naturalized as befitting of men.

In Turkey, the association between military service and 'becoming' a man, being socially accepted as a man, has, as this article has attempted to show, received a fresh impetus of a rhetorical kind in the context of the conflict in the southeast, but has also been hit. The messages are mixed: military service is publicly celebrated and associated strongly with manhood and 'manly' duty and sense of self-sacrifice for a nation whose very existence is said to be under threat. Privately, though, young men's feelings about it are much more ambiguous, with a large number simply avoiding their service. Some of those who are evading it are against it for political reasons of varying shades, though almost no political group that wants to survive has dared link resistance with politics openly; other young men have a general distaste for the whole thing that is not expressed in a particularly political way and they may, indeed, be quite confused about the politics involved (more than sixteen years of Turkish television coverage of the issues have not been enlightening). Despite great poverty and a disparity between rich and poor that is acknowledged to be growing, the attractions of fashion in the form of clothes, music and so on – to which since the late 1980s there has been growing access for greater numbers – presumably also provide other more pleasurable means by which young men may derive different identities and self-images. Families of young men faced with service are obviously also often disturbed by the reality, though once again ideas about the subject are confused and few Turks would argue against military service as such and fewer still against decisions and policies promoted by the widely supported institution of the armed forces. Resisting dominant practices that one may find horrifying is not straightforward.

Once militarism is looked at as a category that deserves detailed analysis as a historical phenomenon and set of practices, tied in closely with questions about how dominant cultural understandings (received ideas) preserve their dominance precisely because they are able to secure consent and adapt themselves to changing contexts, it becomes possible to explore a fuller range of issues around gender in relation to it. Militaries and militarism should not only be seen as sites where notions of masculinity are established to exclude women. Questions about power exercised by senior men over subordinate men, about heteronormative sexuality against homosexuality, or simply power exercised over men who for political or other reasons reject the military regime, should not be sidelined if we are to resist categorizing all men in an army as equally part of a hegemonic masculine order.

Viewing masculinity in over-deterministic ways allows little space for opposition to military practices and institutions, and furthermore overlooks the historic efforts of some men who, in ignoring their draft papers and opposing the politics of the state that calls them up for active service, have refused to abide by the social code operating in wartime that equates joining up with being a man and a good citizen (in this context, resistance to fighting in Vietnam among American males being a prime example). Perhaps by looking more closely at the practices and discourses of institutions of hegemonic male power we can at least discover via this unlikely route a means by which to argue strongly that masculinity/male identity is invariably multiple and that it is in interaction with the most essentialized and hegemonic versions of it that its multiplicity becomes most clear.

Notes

Acknowledgements: For incisive comments on this article and for drawing my attention to some important sources, I thank friends in Istanbul. Thanks also to Osman Murat Ülke for clarification on certain points and for helpful information about the work of the İSKD in conscientious objection and anti-militarism, a campaign that continues in very difficult conditions and at personal cost.

1. This additional law is the Law on the National Security Council and the Secretariat General of the National Security Council (no. 2945, 9 November

1983). Most of the information included here is taken from the TÜSİAD (Turkish Industrialist's and Businessman's Association) report authored by Bülent Tanör, *Perspectives on Democratization in Turkey* (Istanbul: TÜSİAD, 1997; available in Turkish and English on the TÜSİAD website: www.tusiad.com); among the recommendations of the report are the repeal, in the interest of furthering the democratization process, of article 118 and the law mentioned above.

2. See, for example, Hikmet Özdemir, *Rejim ve Asker* (The regime and the army), Istanbul: Afa Yayınları, 1989; Serdar Şen, *Silahlı Kuvvetler ve Modernizm* (The armed forces and modernity), Istanbul: Sarmal Yayınevi, 1996; Muharrem Balcı, *MGK ve Demokrasi: Hukuk, Ordu, Siyaset* (The National Security Council and democracy: Law, the army, politics), Istanbul: Yöneliş Yayınları, 1997; Zafer Üskül, *Siyaset ve Asker: Cumhuriyet Döneminde Sıkıyönetim Uygulamaları* (Politics and the army: the working of martial law in the republican period), Ankara: İmge Kitabevi Yayınları, 2nd edn. 1997; Şaban İba, *Ordu, Devlet, Siyaset* (Army, state, politics), Istanbul: Çiviyazıları, 1998.

3. Quoted from Üskül, *Siyaset ve Asker* in the Study Centre on Turkey report, *Türkiye'de Ordu ve İnsan Hakları İhlalleri: TSK ve uygulamalarına ilişkin 1998 yılı panoraması* (The army and human rights violations in Turkey: a survey of the Turkish armed forces and its activities in 1998), Amsterdam: Study Centre on Turkey, July 1999: e-mail: sot@antenna.nl, p. 1.

4. It was also compulsory before in different forms under the Ottoman empire: universally for all males, Muslim and non-Muslim, after 1856, though in practice the non-Muslims tended to continue to opt for *bedelli askerlik*, payment in place of military service, which was not an option for Muslims.

5. Predictably the war has been described in different terms by different parties: the army at one period referred to it as a 'duşuk yoğunluklu çatışma' (low-intensity conflict), but also as 'bölücü terör' (separatist terror) or 'terörle mücadele' (struggle/war against terror), terms which most Turkish media channels also use. The PKK and Kurdish media and organizations term it 'kirli savaş' (dirty war) or 'özel savaş' (special war), or may use Kurdish nationalist formulations: see *Türkiye'de Ordu ve İnsan Hakları İhlalleri*, p. 59.

6. 'Genelkurmay AB için çalışma grubu kurdu', *Radikal*, 11 January 2000.

7. Thus, the United Nations Commission on Human Rights, recognized in its resolution 1989/59 of 8 March 1989 and reaffirmed in Resolution 1993/84 of 10 March 1993, 'the right of everyone to have conscientious objections to military service as a legitimate exercise of the right to freedom of thought, conscience and religion as laid down in article 18 of the Universal Declaration of Human Rights as well as article 18 of the International Covenant on Civil and Political Rights'. On 11 March 1993 the European Parliament adopted a resolution in respect of human rights in the European Union. In the section on conscientious objection it 'Considers that the right of conscientious objection, as recognized by Resolution 1989/59 of the UN Commission on Human Rights on conscientious objection to military service, should

be incorporated in the legal system of the Member States' (§ 46). It also: 'Condemns the trials and imprisonment of conscientious objectors in the Member States, many of whom have been regarded as prisoners of conscience by Amnesty International' (§ 50). Turkey is a Member State of the Council of Europe and of the OSCE and in December 1999, as mentioned above, became recognized as a candidate for full membership of the European Union. Source: Amnesty International.

While the organizations mentioned above support the right to partial objection, those who support total objection, the policy of many war resisters' organizations, do not accept that civilian service should merely be presented as an alternative to military service and that the notion of conscientious objection disappears once a civilian service option has been introduced.

8. Reported in *Hürriyet*, 21 December 1998.

9. For R.W. Connell, in *Masculinities* (Oxford: Polity Press, 1995), the notion of hegemonic masculinity is central to understanding how the variety of masculine identities are constituted in relation and opposition to one another: see pp. 77–81 for definition of the term 'hegemonic masculinity', and p. 214 for the production of exemplary masculinities as 'integral to the politics of hegemonic masculinity'.

10. Mehmet Ali Birand, *Shirts of Steel: An Anatomy of the Turkish Armed Forces*, translated from the Turkish *Emret Komuntanım* (Istanbul, 1986) by Saliha Paker and Ruth Christie (London: I.B.Tauris Publishers, 1991). For a book about the 1980 coup which represents the views of the army and also reveals much about their self-perception and relationship with politics, see *12 September in Turkey: Before and After*, 'prepared by the General Secretariat of the National Security Council [no author stated] (July 1982, Ankara)', (Ankara, 1982).

11. Birand, *Shirts of Steel*, p. 11. In terms of facilities, class sizes and standard of general education, that military high schools offer a better level of all-round education than many regular Turkish *lise*s is probably true.

12. Ibid., pp. 29–30.

13. Ibid., p. 87. The Armed Services' criticisms of the civilian society is another subject altogether, but suffice to say here that implicit in many of their public addresses and 'recommendations' to the government is their mistrust of self-interested politicians and all 'ideologies' (except their own which they do not regard as ideological and tend to naturalize). In Birand's book, researched in the aftermath of the 12 September 1980 coup, commanders openly air views about the pervasiveness of Turkey's enemies within and without, the gullibility of the population and the army's superior role in maintaining the achievements of Atatürk. See, in particular, chapters 7 and 8 which focus on the army's relationship with politics and isolation from civilian society.

14. Ibid., p. 30.

15. Ibid., p. 120.
16. Ibid., pp. 122-24.
17. R.W. Connell, *Masculinities* (Oxford: Polity Press, 1995), p. 29.
18. Ibid., p. 37.
19. Experiences of military service vary and, based on available sources, it is not possible to claim that any minority is systematically or necessarily discriminated against in the army. Presumably, however, the *prospect* of doing military service for an Armenian or Greek male cannot be particularly welcome, given that both groups – in particular the former – are still popularly invoked in certain contexts as national enemies, regardless of their self-perception as Turkish citizens (cf. the interviews with former conscripts, one Greek and one Armenian, in Nadire Mater, *Mehmedin Kitabı: Güneydoğu'da Savaşmış Askerler Anlatıyor* [Istanbul: Metis Yayınları, 1999], pp. 27–30 and pp. 196–201 respectively, in which both mention their preconceptions/fears about the treatment awaiting them in the army in their first days.) The prospect of military service and the actual experience of it for Kurds may be dependent on political inclinations or perceived loyalties once in the army, but the subject merits a full study to ascertain the extent of the level of discrimination, which in recent times must be assumed to be higher than that experienced by other groups.
20. For a quite typical reflection on military service by someone who did his service back in the 1950s and views the post-earthquake one-month *bedelli askerlik* opportunity, taken up by Tarkan and others, as an insufficient trial, see Hakkı Devrim, 'Biz yaptık oldu, dediniz. Yirmi sekiz günde olacak şey değil!' ('You are saying, "We did it and it's done." But it's not something to be done in just 28 days!'), *Radikal*, 20 February 2000, p. 7.
21. See the extensive literature by Martin van Bruinessen, R. Olson, Hamit Bozarslan, David McDowall, among others.
22. Number of conscripts estimated in Study Centre on Turkey report, *Türkiye'de Ordu ve İnsan Hakları İhlalleri*, p. 59, based on figures quoted by International Institute of Strategic Studies report, *Military Balance 1996/1997*.
23. In all, the authors of *Türkiye'de Ordu ve İnsan Hakları İhlalleri* estimate that in 14 years of war some 1,500,000 soldiers served in the war zone: ibid., p. 59.
24. A brief article by Hamit Bozarslan, 'Research guide: Kurdish studies', *Middle East Review of International Affairs* V. 4/2000 no. 2, Jan 2000, confirms the difficulty of research in this area and suggests the disciplinary strengths and weaknesses of existing work.
25. Estimates of the overall death-toll since the beginning of the war vary widely. During the Öcalan trial the figure of 30,000 dead was widely quoted by the Turkish press, but as was pointed out to me, this figure was also being quoted at the beginning of 1997, before one of the largest military manoeuvres in Turkish history saw the incursion of some 50,000 Turkish troops into northern Iraq in the spring of that year (see interview with L.Ş. that follows this

article). The majority of the dead (estimates range from 18,000 to 26,000) are said to be PKK guerrillas, with estimates of 5 to 6,000 dead from the security services (including village guards), and around 5,000 civilian deaths. Injuries are obviously much higher. Since the circumstances of these deaths must be regarded as impossible to substantiate, all numbers quoted (including those of military personnel who died 'accidentally' and who may therefore not figure in the statistics which generally refer to 'martyrs') seem to be unreliable.

26. See Tanıl Bora, 'Şehit yakınları: Evlat acısıyla oynamak', *Birikim* 123, July 1999, pp. 12-15.

27. Among the journalistic books on the Cumartesi Anneleri are Yıldırım Türker, *Gözaltında Kayıp Onu Unutma!* (Istanbul: Metis Yayınları, 1995); Berat Günçıkan, *Cumartesi Anneleri* (Istanbul: İletişim Yayınları, 1996); Ece Temelkuran, *Oğlum, Kızım, Devletim* (Istanbul: Metis Yayınları, 1997).

28. Source: İSKD brochure: no date.

29. Source: interview by Coşkun Üsterci with Osman Murat Ülke in *Firari* (Deserter) newsletter, November 1997, no. 3, newsletter of the London-based Campaign Against Compulsory Service in Turkey.

30. Source: personal correspondence with Osman Murat Ülke, 24 February 2000.

31. The İSKD in an article entitled 'Vicdani ret ve yasal düzenlemeler' (no date) lists the relevant offences for conscientious objectors as: TACK (Turkish military penal code) articles 63, 66/1, 81, 86, 87/1 and TCK (Turkish penal code) articles 155, 312, 159/1.

32. See 'Vicdani ret hakkının tanınmasını talep etmek suç değildir' (Demanding the recognition of the right to conscientious objection is not a crime), a one-page press release by the İSKD (no date) which comments on the military court's 9 December 1997 verdict (97/156–294 no'lu karar) which deemed conscientious objection in itself not a crime punishable under article 155.

33. Nadire Mater, *Mehmedin Kitabı: Güneydoğu'da Savaşmış Askerler Anlatıyor* (Istanbul: Metis Yayınları, 1999).

34. For a discussion of human rights organizations in Turkey, see Gottfried Plagemann, 'Turkish Human Rights Organizations in Various Cultural Milieus', in S. Yerasimos, G. Seufert & K. Vorhoff (eds.), *Civil Society in the Grip of Nationalism: Studies on Political Culture in Turkey* (Istanbul: Orient-Institut, forthcoming 2000).

35. See, on war syndrome and post-traumatic stress disorder among soldiers, the extensive study of the condition in the report, *Türkiye'de Ordu ve İnsan Hakları İhlalleri*, pp. 57–94, and the interview with a former conscript, L.Ş., extracted and translated from that report, which follows this article.

36. Among camp game-show hosts is Aydın, who hosted the popular ATV show 'Kaynana-Gelin' (Mother-in-law and Daughter-in-law) in which two teams made up of a woman and her mother-in-law would compete. Aydın, who played the over-touchy and bitchy 'queen' in the proceedings, would send

up family values, while simultaneously reinforcing them. Aydın, who is also a singer, can be thought of as one of the 'heirs' of the actor and singer, Zeki Müren.

37. A full critique of the commonly unquestioned association between men and violence, and a discussion of women's capacity for violence, can be found in Lynne Segal's *Slow Motion: Changing Masculinities, Changing Men* (London: Virago, 1990), pp. 261–71. Segal, a socialist feminist, also addresses related issues in an earlier book, *Is the Future Female? Troubled Thoughts on Contemporary Feminism* (London: Virago, 1987).

'MILITARY SERVICE IN SPITE OF ME':
INTERVIEW WITH L.Ş., FORMER CONSCRIPT*

L.Ş. was born in a western Anatolian town near Izmir. He finished college and worked in several jobs before doing military service, which he evaded for some years but finally had to do in the Autumn of 1996. Married, with a daughter (prior to service), he subsequently worked for a few months in the work place of an old friend, was then out of work, and separated from his wife.

L.Ş. died on 9 February 1999 in a traffic accident. The authors of the report for which this interview was made harbour some doubts about the circumstances: though the police enquiry categorized it as an accident, the authors do not discount the possibility of suicide. L.Ş. had been having psychiatric help since returning from military service.

What were your feelings in the first days of your military service?
I experienced very clear trauma in my first days of being in the army. You are shocked when as soon as you arrive you face the curses and the contempt. Then you feel like you're beginning to sink. The senior privates (*usta erler*) do that to you. They roll you helpless to the edge. All the things that are done are meant to erase your personality and produce a new identity. No laughing, no place for a smile. The senior ones were always severe. Just as for a

---

*   Interview taken from the report *Türkiye'de Ordu ve İnsan Hakları İhlalleri: TSK ve uygulamalarına ilişkin 1998 yılı panoraması* (The army in Turkey and human rights violations: A survey of the Turkish Armed Services and their practices in 1998), pp. 81–87, published in Turkish in July 1999 by the Study Centre on Turkey, Amsterdam (e-mail: sot@antenna.nl) and translated and edited by Emma Sinclair-Webb from the Turkish by permission.

pious person, a believer, everyone is a sinner, for the state every citizen is a potential criminal, and in the army too the same logic prevails. This makes a person lose his self-confidence. In the new recruits' unit (*acemi birliği*) we were made to feel complete alienation and mistrust. You feel you can do absolutely nothing without your superior or commander. In short the aim of the army training is, I think, to completely empty the mind and feelings and later also to make individuality shapeless, and to force you into the single mould prepared by them. To put it another way, at the end of this education a person learns not to question in any way and to be absolutely obedient.

What are the incidents that you remember?
In the recruits' unit we were trained by the senior privates. They had come to the unit only a few months before us and, in spite of having suffered the same bad treatment only a short time before, were very harsh and cruel. The difference in hierarchy between us recruits and them was very great. When they were training us they continually spoke in a severe tone and shouted. Their orders were absolute and final. Insults, curses and a rough beating were the most common means of training. Because the number of recruits was so many it wasn't possible for them to learn our names. They mostly used to call us by our physical attributes like 'weedy', 'fatty', 'glasses', 'fat head'. Maybe that too was a way of making us have no identity, I don't know. As I said curses were very common, but as befits the typical macho tradition there was absolutely no swearing on mothers and wives.

The source of my personal uneasiness was the fact of my having over a long period dodged the army and my late arrival in the unit. There were 20 to 30 more men beginning their military service late for reasons like mine. From the first day onwards all of us were continually accosted and degraded by the officers and privates with terms like 'those who are against the state', 'traitors to the nation'.

When I was in the recruits' unit, out of fear I never had a bath. The time given for having a bath was very short. It was impossible for us to stay there long and if you exceeded the limit you were immediately beaten. Since it was such a stress to have a bath I didn't have one for 32 days. The majority were like me and were afraid of going to the bathroom.

In general as a punishment for their mistakes new recruits preferred to get beaten (as the lesser of two evils) rather than get a legal recrimination. Because I was older than the others and with subtle measures got round the rules – or as in the bath example avoided the reason to be beaten – I didn't get beaten. However, actually when I compare it with the stories I heard before being in the army, I think that the use of beatings is less than it used to be. Nowadays psychological pressure has a much greater place.

When I look at all the things that were done, I think that there is no irrationality about the army. On the contrary, the way in which you are immersed in an aggressive atmosphere which equips you with violence is very systematic. On the one hand, as I said, it brings absolute obedience and means bowing your head before authority. On the other by inducing the feeling of 'protect yourself, don't be crushed' it makes severe and aggressive behaviour of each against the rest compulsory. In fact because the privates became so worn down before authority they were put in competition with each other and were very pitiless. Generally I'm a quiet person. However, before doing military service I, too, would from time to time quarrel and fight with others. But it had never reached violent proportions. In the army, however, I fought with three people and it reached the point where I nearly killed them. In general the new recruits' unit was like that . . .

My senior unit was in Urfa. I was an infantryman in the Second Mechanized Infantry Regiment. Naturally it was much easier there than in the new recruits' unit. Due to my age and my status I was given relatively easy duties that were not viewed as risky. But again too a relationship based completely on crush and be crushed was dominant.

What did you feel when you first went to Urfa?
How alone I was. To the very core I felt a cold loneliness. In spite of examples of instinctive solidarity where those in the same draft or from the same region would protect each other, in the army you suffer a frightening isolation. You are continually badly treated and trauma is thoroughly established. You start military service as if it were a game and you end it as if it were a game, but what you go through is real. After finishing military service, the ones who first swore at you and degraded you would say, 'We got on well', and send you off with a pat on the back.

How did you spend your days?
There my days passed in a monotonous and boring way. In spite of all efforts, the daily vocabulary is no more than fifty words. There is almost no possibility of reading and being alone. You feel yourself to be worthless fodder. Pleasure and feelings are reduced to nothing. That I understood much better in the period when I was on leave. On leave even the most ordinary things seemed wonderfully attractive to me.

There in my monotonous life the continually exalted basic theme was 'manhood, power and the gun'. It was possible to observe the image of men in Turkey from every aspect.

The feeling of being degraded is constant. Everyone is degraded. The level of degradation is such that if one person is degraded even more than the rest, for the others this situation is the source of a kind of comfort and happiness. For instance, when someone who has made a mistake is beaten or reprimanded everyone makes a special effort to see it. In fact, the commanders also consciously carry out the actions in front of everyone so that it may be an example to the other privates. Instead of being distressed or worried when their mates are being humiliated astonishingly the privates voluntarily watch what's going on and with faces expressing that they're virtually in orgasm.

When you went to Urfa did you feel the war? What was people's behaviour like?
When we were in Urfa everyone was talking about going on duty. Our unit was organized according to the requirements of non-regular warfare. It was a contra-guerrilla type formation organized for internal operations. Silopi, northern Iraq, Kulp, Lice and Diyarbakır's other districts were the operation zone for my unit. And what was called duty meant going on operations. Those returning from an operation would sometimes throw us out of our beds. Because they had returned from 'saving the country' the beds were their right. We slept in between the bunks. For one month I slept on a campbed, I mean a kind of stretcher. It was very cold, I was suffering from backache. But I couldn't explain my problem.

What was the state of mind of those returning from an operation like?
It was completely like they were drunk. As if they had succeeded in carrying out a very big job, their adrenaline was up, they were decked out in the feeling of greatness. They would recount to each other the things they had done in difficult conditions in an exaggerated way. I think that the clearest definition of this state is that it was a type of drunkenness. However as time passes this slowly fades. The high ranking ones would behave more softly to the soldiers preparing to go into the field. Generally in operations the hierarchy was relatively broken. When they were returned from an operation, in order to ensure the soldiers' observance once more of the former disciplinary rules, the existing discipline was again reinforced. Two or three days afterwards order was re-established, everything was normalized. I think that this was at the same time aimed at delaying the negative effects of trauma created in the soldiers from the operation.

Did they give special training to soldiers to heighten determination and courage when they were going on operations?

Normally twice a week from 20.00 in the evening till morning training was given. Training groups were formed in the field. A special sergeant (*uzman çavuş*) explained how security in the base area is achieved, what is done when you are ambushed. In short, in fifteen days a low-intensity, non-regular war training was given. What was more emphasized was how to save ourselves.

Did you too join in operations? What did you go through?
It was said that we would go to Diyarbakır for an operation. It had been just a month since we came to the trained unit. In the place we went to it was dirty everywhere and there was nowhere to lie down. Hurling themselves here and there the other privates searched for beds for themselves. I thought they looked like animals trying to carve up a carcass. With sorrow, tiredness and bitterness inside me I found a corner and slept. We were supposed to go to Lice for the operation. They left me in Devegeçidi [also in the Diyarbakır province], the place where we were staying. I said that I wanted to go to Lice on the operation. I wanted to see Lice and what was going on there. But for some reason I was not sent on duty and I stayed in Devegeçidi. After staying there I felt I had entered a completely different world. It was the Sikorsky helicopter passing over us that gave me the first feeling of war. At that moment I really felt myself to be in a war zone. News of clashes came from Lice. Among those who went on the operation was a dear friend of mine; I was concerned about his fate and was very anxious about him. I was waiting for news to come from Lice. After [hearing] the news that 200 guerrillas were coming I began to be much more concerned about my friend. During the operation he was always in my mind.

Our friends came back four or five days after going off on the operation. I was shocked that they had suddenly changed. In their general appearance they had all darkened from being weathered by the cold and the snow. I also noticed the same darkening of their souls. My friend who I was concerned about during the operation was also behaving like he was drunk. He was saying things like, 'The dishonourable terrorists escaped, we weren't able to corner them, we couldn't kill them.' He was from Istanbul, a city kid. During the operation the guerrillas had retreated. As a result, it was a short-lived operation which resulted in no losses on either side, but there, in Devegeçidi, feeling the war through the sound of the helicopters, seeing the change in my friends after the operation, and particularly in the friend I was talking about, I was very affected. A few days later we returned to Urfa. The weather was very cold during those days. I was cold, I was having nosebleeds very often. I was feeling both physically and mentally unwell. [. . .]

We returned to Urfa and on the first weekend we went on 'shopping' leave. We went to the market dressed the same in army clothes. All the privates became children. They came close to feeling human. Privates who were continually alienated from everything and had been turned into monsters, at that moment became children. It was the first time I went to the market and it was the first time I observed their state. When I was at the market I thought about myself and military service and the things I was going through, and I asked how much my life belonged to me. I used to take notes from time to time when I felt the need to clear my head from this kind of state. I used to try to write.

How was your relationship with the other soldiers?
The other privates found my actions a bit strange. Our superiors also said it. Because I behaved more casually it attracted attention. I mean I wasn't inhibited. One day I went up a tree. I was very bored from doing the same things every day and for the sake of a change I climbed a tree. In fact I was getting used to everything with time. At the beginning when I entered the dormitory it used to smell very dirty to me. Later my nose began to get used to the smell. With time my body and soul got used to a lot of things. When I got outside the army unit, I mean when I went on market leave, when I saw other people everything looked very different to me. In the army the uniform, the smell, the way of behaving are all the same. The roles are clear from start to finish – we had roles. But in time I got used to them and they got used to me.

Later did you join in other operations or clashes?
Yes, I joined a big operation that took place in Spring 97 in northern Iraq. Our whole unit joined in the operation. First in a region near the border we were massed. We stayed there for a while. While going into the region where we were massing I was very affected by the state Cizre was in as we passed through. That city was virtually like an open prison. Everywhere there were police stations and check points. The concentration of the army was much more than that of the civilian population. It was now impossible not to feel the war and above all it felt as though you were in another country.

A few days after coming to the massing zone, PKK guerrillas attacked a *korucu* (village guard) village near the zone where the unit was. In the raid several village guards apparently died. Although the village the guerrillas attacked was outside our unit's firing range, the sound of gun fire enveloped us on every side. Who was firing at whom and from where was not clear. Among the soldiers there was big fear. Everyone left the tents and threw themselves to the ground. A while later in spite of the clash stopping no one could sleep again. Getting through that night was hard for everyone. The privates could not now rant and rave like before. Words implying bravery and greatness were no longer used. Apprehension and fear were more evident in our conversations. The guerrillas weren't sworn at as much as before. To eradicate their fears and to comfort themselves they were rationalizing the situation, even saying that the PKK guerrillas, whom they had described as cut-throats before, in fact didn't want to kill soldiers, but wanted much more to kill officers and high-ranking commanders.

In the middle of May our unit entered northern Iraq. There were attacks on nearby units and peshmerga stations; war raged all around us. We saw clashes, rocket fire. Out of great luck the place where I was wasn't attacked directly. But everywhere fear reigned. One night guerrillas opened fire on the other division of our regiment. In response to the guerrillas' firing four or five times, all guns from our units, including anti-aircraft fire and mortars, were blindly fired for 45 minutes. About 30 mortars were launched.

Over the following days our unit advanced further into northern Iraq. From time to time we were very close to the PKK. Very close to us another regiment tried to climb the mountain (Zagros mountains) ahead of us but guerrillas repelled them. On one occasion our canteen vehicle was fired at with machine gun fire. The mountains around us were continually being shelled. We were able to watch the guerrilla groups' actions with fieldglasses. Once our brigade retreated. We felt the heat of the war and the guerrillas breathing down our necks at every moment. [. . .]

In the operation zone everywhere was mined. When they were retreating the PKK guerrillas left booby traps and mines behind them. Of course there were also the mines that our units left. It was said that a lot of soldiers got wounded for this reason. I was scared and tried to be careful. When I was throwing out the unit's rubbish I wasn't brave enough to go very far or to new places. One evening while throwing petrol over the rubbish that I'd thrown out, wanting to burn it, suddenly there was an explosion and my arms and face got burnt. For two days I was made to wait in that state in the field without any serious treatment. And after waiting for one day too at the Haç Billeting Centre I was sent by helicopter to Diyarbakır to the military hospital. In the helicopter there was a child with his right arm and left leg gone and on the point of death. Next to him was his father who was a village guard. The doctor was making every effort to keep the child alive. Also opposite me was sitting a special operations man who had been shot in the left eye at close range. We travelled together for 40–45 minutes. Those were frightening moments, I don't know how they passed.

What did you see during the time you stayed in the hospital?
The horror of war, the savageness of it. I stayed in hospital for about 10 or 12 days. Later I was given leave and a change of scene (*hava değişimi*) to get better. In the period I spent in the hospital some days, more or less every day, there was at least one funeral. Everywhere was full of soldiers who had lost arms and legs or with faces in an unrecognizable state. There were one or two events that I will never forget.

One of those was the telephone call that a soldier from Eskişehir who had lost two feet because he had stepped on a mine was making to his family. The soldier was talking with his mother on the phone. While he was saying that not a thing had happened to him, tears were streaming from his eyes. That young person's outlook was deeply humanistic and peace loving.

Another incident that I remember was the situation of one family that paid a visit to the hospital. The family consisted of a father, mother, a little boy and a young girl. When the family entered the room where we were lying, the girl felt sick and began to cry. The look of us lying in the room was really unbearable. But looking at the girl, I began to laugh. I couldn't control myself. I hid my head under the covers and continued to laugh. During the time the girl remained in the room she was unable to talk to her big brother. Because a [normal] human being can't stand such a sight, doesn't laugh, couldn't have laughed . . .

When my leave finished I returned to my unit. My burns had healed. The leave was good for my spirits and physically good. But from the first day that I stepped back into the unit very quickly somehow everything began once more to overwhelm me. With all its irrationality military service was continuing in spite of me.

What type of incidents did you encounter?
One incident comes to mind. Perhaps this can explain the goings-on best. The event happened one day when we got our wages – although we were not professional soldiers every month pocket money was given to us. According to the rules, after taking our wages we had to salute the squadron commander (*bölük komutanı*) and take our leave. In spite of one soldier having given a salute after taking his wages, the commander didn't like the salute given by the private. Because of this he stopped the giving of wages and dismissed everyone. The following day all the privates were gathered together in an area and were forced to give salutes to the trees. Until noon we continually saluted the trees. This is a very good example of the general practice. We were continually put through similar nonsense. Now I remember another incident. From our division one private apparently saluted a brigadier general (*tugay*

komutanı) a bit late. For this reason our division was punished. For a whole day we did ceremonial marching on the training ground.

Apart from these nonsensical things were there also practices like insults and beatings? Because I was careful I didn't suffer from such things. But in full view when there was absolutely no reason, purely to say, 'We are watching your every move', they would beat a lot of soldiers. Sometimes this had bad results. There was a private called Ahmet Seven. It had been three days since he'd arrived – I think it was the beginning of January 98 – and one of the special sergeants apparently cuffed him. Because this man couldn't take it, he attempted suicide by jumping from the window. He jumped and when he fell hit a car tyre and then the ground. He didn't die, we learnt that his ribs were cracked. However, he stayed a long time in Diyarbakır Military Hospital. He had a three-month change of scene. The senior ranking ones had contempt for him and would say about this private, 'He harmed himself in order to skive off military service.' And while talking about him they always used to curse him. After that incident the pressures increased: they began to enforce the rules more firmly.

There was a private from Istanbul whom I got to know well and became friends with. He also had two children, and we used to talk about our children to each other. He was knifed and killed by a private who had just arrived. As far as I remember between the two there was an exchange of insults and because of this apparently a fight had started. Kemal Eren was his name. He was in the 76/4 draft. We were told that he died from loss of blood. However, I think he died because the necessary treatment was not given: during the time he was to be taken to the hospital he was made to wait up to four hours to complete the red-tape. As always bureaucratic red-tape had to take its course. He went back and forth to the hospital two or three times. In the end while being taken to Diyarbakır he died on the road near Siverek. In spite of the dead man being my friend I was unable to define my feelings properly. I also didn't hate the killer. Straight after the incident I phoned a friend in Izmir. Apparently I was telling him about the incident and laughing. When I became aware of this state I began to understand that I had lost my usual balance. I, too, had become adapted to this *Mad Max* world. At that time something that also caught my attention was that neither of the two events got reported in the press. After these events our situation became even worse. The pressure greatly increased.

You said that after each of the two incidents the pressure increased. What were the most prominent differences?

It was required that all rules be completely complied with. Previously after the evening meal we used to go to our beds and were able to rest. However, later they began to make us wait till 21.00. For example before the prayers at the meal it was even forbidden for us to lift a spoon. The market leave was limited. The soldiers became like a powder keg ready to explode at any moment. Everyone became aggressive towards each other.

How did the privates react against, on the one hand, the stress of the operations, on the other, the arduousness of military service. What resistance did they develop?
Among the privates the use of cannabis and pills was very widespread. Alcohol consumption was not inconsiderable. Although this stuff was used a lot, there weren't searches made and people caught. The environment was very conducive to it. I think that this was the answer they gave to the arduousness of what they were going through. In order not to use that stuff I restrained myself with difficulty.

What have been the direct or indirect effects on you of what you went through?
A lot of negative consequences and disturbance . . . In the last months of my military service I began to have acute headaches. For this reason I went to the infirmary and the doctor established that my blood pressure was very high. Following the examinations I spent two weeks in Diyarbakır Military Hospital. They said that my unstable blood pressure was stress related. I was prescribed certain drugs but they didn't make me completely better.

Before doing military service I had never thought about killing anyone. But now, although I don't like war and violence I could very easily kill someone. I reached the state where I could very easily harm people.

There are incidents that I remember, and that I still see, that never go away. What I lived through during military service later on showed its effects. A while after being discharged while I was wandering around the Karşıyaka district in Izmir I ran into a soldier friend of mine who was in a later draft than mine. We greeted each other and talked a bit. A short time after leaving my soldier friend, I began to hear the rising sound of a helicopter coming towards me. It was the sound of a Sikorsky helicopter. Suddenly I saw myself in the helicopter that I had been taken in when wounded. Opposite me was the wounded child of the village guard. At the same time I was hearing the voice of my own child. Though I stopped in the middle of a huge road in the city centre I didn't register anything including the traffic around me. I was entirely cut off from my surroundings and what I had lived through came to life before my eyes like a film reel. When the two friends beside me saw my state they apparently got worried. They were calling to me but I was hearing nothing. Quite a long time later I slowly began to hear their voices and to come to my senses. This condition continued until the morning of the next day in varying intensity and at intervals. I was covering my ears but I was continuing to hear the sound of the helicopter. It was as if I was permanently inside that helicopter.

FOUR

Male Gender and Rituals of Resistance in the Palestinian Intifada
A Cultural Politics of Violence

Julie Peteet

At the time of writing this article,[1] around 40 per cent (approximately 2,100,000) of Palestinians lived under Israeli rule, either in Israel proper (around 645,000), in the West Bank and East Jerusalem (around 938,000), or in the Gaza Strip (around 525,000).[2] From the beginning of the intifada in December 1987 through December 1990, an estimated 106,600 Palestinians were injured.[3] Beatings are not isolated in these statistics, so it is impossible to calculate with any certainty the numbers involved, though one would have been hard pressed to find a young male Palestinian under occupation who had not been beaten or who did not personally know someone who had been.[4] This article examines the attainment and enactment of manhood and masculinity among Palestinian male youths in relation to these beatings and detention in the occupied West Bank. The beatings (and detention) are framed as rites of passage that became central in the construction of an adult, gendered (male) self with critical consequences for political consciousness and agency.

Under the political and military authority of a foreign power, Palestinians possess few, if any, political rights, nor do they possess or have access to technologies of domination. Their powerlessness is all the more pronounced given their occupation by a major military power. The juxtaposition of technologies is striking. Offensively and defensively, Palestinians wield stones, one of the earliest forms of weaponry known to humankind. As part of the natural environment and landscape, the stone bears minimal, if any, application of human technological skills.

The occupying authority continuously displays the potential for and the actuality of violence to stem opposition and to imprint upon the subject population its lack of autonomy. In spite of more than two decades passing and a generation of youths who have known no other way of life, Israel has not been able to 'normalize' its power relations with those under occupation. Since the beginning (in 1967), resistance has been common.[5] The inability to establish a 'naturalness' to occupation has meant a continued recourse to physical violence along with the standard forms of structural violence.

One quickly discerns that beatings are a common occurrence. The anticipation of an encounter with occupation authorities that might lead to a beating influences the daily mobility of young men. They decline evening social invitations that necessitate driving after dark. Military personnel at roadblocks stop cars and randomly pull out men for beating. Parents hesitate to allow adolescent boys to go downtown unaccompanied, or even on short errands, fearing they might be pulled over for an identity check and in the process roughed up. In the alleys of the camps, children now are more careful to stay close to home because, on their daily patrols, soldiers occasionally chase, manhandle and detain them for several hours until their parents pay a stiff fine.

Beatings have thus been a part of the apparatus of domination since the beginning of the occupation, both in public and as an integral part of the interrogation process. How then do pre-intifada and intifada beatings differ? While framing beatings in the context of time periods, one must not draw too distinct a boundary. In the first weeks of fieldwork in a refugee camp in the West Bank, I would pose many of my questions in terms of a distinct set of time frames – 'pre-intifada' and 'intifada'. Finally, one woman kindly, but with some exasperation, told me: 'Look, we've been having an intifada here for 40 years, since 1948! The difference now is the rest of the population of the occupied territories is involved, and the continuity of resistance is being sustained! Though this word intifada is new to us, we've been resisting for 40 years.'

Before the intifada, beatings were less public, usually taking place while in custody.[6] They were an integral part of an interrogation procedure, designed to break the will of prisoners and to extract confessions as to their alleged deeds and those of their acquaintances and to possible externally-based political backing and material support for resistance against the occupation.[7]

Soon after the launching of the intifada in December 1987, beatings became an explicit policy of the occupation authorities. On 19 January 1988, Defence Minister Yitzhak Rabin announced a new policy of 'might, power, and beatings' to quell the uprising. The international witnessing of the public beatings and bone-breaking evoked widespread alarm among Israel's supporters, particularly in the United States. Subsequently, Likud ministers barred the media from the territories. Until the ban (Spring 1988), the beatings were featured prominently on nightly news broadcasts in the USA and Europe. In diminishing the external witnessing of the infliction of pain, the occupying authorities were attempting to create a fictitious reality of non-violent techniques of control for external consumption.

For the Israelis, the beatings were an encoded medium intended to convey a message regarding the consequences of opposition. The young male is a metonym for Palestinian opposition and struggle against domination, the idea and symbols of which must be rooted out and silenced: the Palestinian population must be made acquiescent to the colonizing project. Israeli violence proceeds on the assumption of collective guilt and responsibility among Palestinians. In the occupied territories, violence is directed at individual bodies as representations of a collective transgressive other.[8] This collective other, however, is denied a national identity. The pre-given defining power of the collective Palestinian body, which requires a violently negating intervention, lies precisely in its assertive national identity, which in its very existence denies the mythical Zionist landscape of Palestine. Taussig draws our attention to torture and terror as 'ritualized art forms' that 'far from being spontaneous, sui generis, and an abandonment of what are often called the values of civilization . . . have a deep history deriving power and meaning from those very values' (1987: 133). Unbowed males signified an assertive resistance to the colonial project and a Zionist self-identity.

The walking embodiment of power, the Israeli soldier, totes the modern technology of violence: automatic rifle, pistol, grenade, hand-cuffs, tear-gas canisters, and batons. Anthropologist and Israeli army captain Ben-Ari remarked that some soldiers, given their training for warfare, were very uneasy with their task of policing heavily civilian areas (1989: 376).[9] This unease, he suggests, should be understood against the images soldiers had of the uprising. The mass media presentation was one of 'mass demonstrations, concentrated rock throwing and tyre burning, and the constant use of Molotov cocktails'. Ben-Ari frames the behaviour of soldiers in the territories in terms of the metaphor of masks and disguises. He suggests 'that for the limited period of milium (reserve duty) the reservists cease to be the normally identified, circumscribed, constrained members of Israeli society who must be concerned with how they are regarded by themselves and by others' (1989: 378).

Donning masks and disguises facilitates construction of 'highly delimited – spatially as well as temporally – episodes during which they become another person' (Ben-Ari 1989: 378–79). Rather than 'donning masks' and becoming 'an other', I would cast their behaviour as more analogous to what Taussig referred to as 'colonial mirroring', where 'the terror and tortures they devised mirrored the horror of the savagery they both feared and fictionalized' (1987:133).

Tolerance of physical abuse of Palestinians was underwritten by a regime of knowledge that cast them as lawless and socially primitive and violent – terrorists, threats to law and order, bands, gangs – and thus as amenable to violent extrajudicial measures. Beyond the pale, Palestinians were cast as possessing a fundamentally different set of morals and knowledge – commonly stated as 'they only understand force'. Their human status does not correspond to that of others. Israeli military announcements do not use the Hebrew word for 'child' when reporting injuries or deaths of Palestinian children in confrontations with the military. The Israeli Palestinian writer Anton Shammas commented that 'for twenty years now officially there has been no childhood in the West Bank and Gaza Strip . . . [A] ten year-old boy shot by military forces is reported to be a "young man of ten"' (1988: 10). Military discourse bypasses childhood, collapsing male Palestinian life-cycle categories. This regime of knowledge, together with a widespread ideology of the rights of the occupiers to Palestinian land and resources, constitutive of a claim to an Israeli national identity, and a judicial system that tolerated systematic human rights violations, if not indeed encouraged them as Amnesty International (1991) argues, fostered an atmosphere where inflictions of bodily violence flourished.

Whether pre-intifada or intifada, the intent behind the beating was to reconstitute the Palestinian male as a non-resistant, though certainly not consenting, subject of colonization. Stone throwing, tyre burning, demonstrating, or displaying symbols of Palestine, such as the flag or its colours, could bring a swift and violent response. But rather than being mute repositories or sites on which the occupier exhibited and constructed power and affirmed its civilization and identity, the meaning of the beating has been appropriated by the subject in a dialectical and agential manner.

Before moving on to look at the social meaning of violence to the body in the specific context of the intifada, a few remarks on manhood and rites of passage in the Middle East are in order. Masculinity is neither natural nor given. Like femininity, it is a social construct. Herzfeld argues that, in a Cretan village, there is more stress on how rather than on what men do – what counts is 'performative excellence' (1985: 16). Gilmore notes that a 'critical threshold' is passed by various forms of tests and ordeals (1990: 11). While cautious of the perils of essentializing the category of gender, male or female, it is fairly safe to say, on a reading of the anthropological literature on masculinity in the Arab world[10] and its conflation with the deed, that this conflation conforms to Gilmore's criterion of being 'something almost generic . . . a ubiquity rather than a universality' (1990: 2-3).

Arab masculinity (*rujulah*) is acquired, verified and played out in the brave deed, in risk-taking, and in expressions of fearlessness and assertiveness. It is attained by constant vigilance and willingness to defend honour (*sharaf*), face (*wajh*), kin and community from external aggression and to uphold and protect cultural definitions of gender-specific propriety.[11] Since elaborate, well-defined rites of passage to mark transitions from boyhood to adolescence to manhood are difficult to discern, a loose set of rites marking the route to 'manhood' must be accompanied by performative deeds to convince and win public approval.

In the Palestinian context, the occupation has seriously diminished those realms of practice that allow men to engage in, display and affirm masculinity by means of autonomous actions.[12] Frequent witnesses to their fathers' beatings by soldiers or settlers, children are acutely aware of their fathers' inability to protect themselves and their children.[13]

Manliness is also closely intertwined with virility and paternity, and with paternity's attendant sacrifices. Denying one's own needs while providing for others is such a signifier. Resistance to occupation and the consequences of such resistance constitute a category of sacrifice with long-term implications for the autonomy and security of the community and larger national collectivity.[14]

Several anthropologists have referred to the concept of honour as a defining frame for masculinity. Abu-Lughod's work on the Egyptian Bedouin, emphasizes the notion of control as crucial: control is the lack of 'fear of anyone or anything', for to exhibit such fear 'implies that it has control over one' (1986: 88). 'Real men' are able to exact respect and command obedience from others while they themselves resist submitting to others' control (Abu-Lughod 1986: 88–90). Among the Berbers of Algeria, Bourdieu locates the man of honour in the context of challenge and riposte. A challenge confers honour upon a man, because it is a cultural assumption that the 'challenge, as such, requires a riposte and therefore is addressed to a man deemed capable of playing the game of honour'

(Bourdieu 1977: 11). The challenge provides an opportunity for males to prove their belonging to the world of men. A point to which I shall return later concerns Bourdieu's contention that challenges directed to men who are unable to take them up dishonours the challenger.

I shall also return more generally to some of these questions about the construction of masculinity and rites of passage after an ethnographic discussion of inscriptions of violence on the Palestinian male body.

Bodies on display

The bodies of those under occupation are continuously called forth to present themselves to outsiders. Visits to families are punctuated by the display of bodies with the marks of bullets and beatings and are social settings for the telling of beatings, shootings, verbal exchanges with settlers and soldiers, and prison stories. After several visits to Um Fadi, I noticed that her children were always in the house or in the walled garden around the house with the gate locked. Once when I had to knock very loudly several times for the children to open, she rushed to open it and explained that she no longer leaves the gate open or allows her children to play in the alleys of the camp. After we were seated in the house and drinking tea, she quietly motioned her 11-year-old son and 13-year-old daughter to come stand in front of us. With the reluctance of children their age, they silently did so. In a subdued and controlled tone, she related how they once were caught by soldiers while playing in the alley. Soldiers regularly patrol the streets and alleys of the camp, and occasionally groups of children throw stones at them. Four soldiers claimed they had been stoned by children in the vicinity and accused Um Fadi's son and daughter. Both were beaten with batons and rifle butts directed at the kidneys, arms and face. When he got up to run, the boy was shot in the side. She asked him to raise his T-shirt to show me the scar. During this telling, several women neighbours were present as well as friends of her children. There was hushed silence as she told the story. The older women would periodically interject, almost inaudibly: 'In the name of God – how can they do this to children!', 'What can we do?', 'What kind of people are these!' The act of telling lends dramatic narrative form to a dialogic process. For the listener, a sense of community is evoked through empathy. Many families have experienced such pain, and for those who have not the possibility looms large.

The physical marks of beatings, rubber bullets and live ammunition constitute crucial elements in dialogue with others, particularly Americans whose near official silence on the matter of Palestinian human rights violations by the occupying authorities is seen as a form of complicity. Given the levels and continuity of US financial support for the occupying power, they consider it all the more appropriate to display the physical signs of their suffering to Westerners. The battered body is a representation fashioned by the Israelis but presented by Palestinians to the West. To the Palestinians, the battered body, with its bruises and broken limbs, is the symbolic embodiment of a twentieth-century history of subordination and powerlessness – of 'what we have to endure' but also of their determination to resist and to struggle for national independence.

A representation created with the intent of humiliating has been reversed into one of honour, manhood and moral superiority. But bodies do more than represent. Torture and beatings are ordeals one undergoes as sacrifices for the struggle (*qadiyyah*). It should be firmly stated that this argument in no way is meant to imply that Palestinians make light of physical violence. It is rather to try to understand how culturally they make sense of it. Displaying physical marks of violence, that one is usually powerless to avoid, stands as a 'commentary on suffering' (Keesing 1985; Peteet 1991) but also, I would suggest, as a commentary on sacrifice. As such they are poignant communicative devices. These displays are powerful statements belying claims of a benign occupation and resonate with the honour that comes from unmasking and resisting.

Becoming men

> One sign of things to come – amidst the jokes and nervous laughter there were signs of genuine excitement by some soldiers at the prospect of 'teaching them not to raise their heads'. [Israeli soldier in the occupied territories, quoted in Peretz 1990: 122]

I first had an inkling of the meaning of the beating and imprisonment as rites of passage when Hussein, 24 years old and resident in Jalazon refugee camp, remarked casually and with a hint of resignation that, on his first evening home from a nine-month stint in prison, a neighbour had come to ask his help in mediating a dispute he was involved in with another neighbour. Hussein pleaded fatigue and the crush of visitors to avoid assuming this mantle of community responsibility, a responsibility that carries with it substantial moral authority. To be a mediator is a position and task usually the preserve of well-respected, older men known for their sagacity and even temperament. Such men are thought to have attained *'aql* (reason or social common sense).[15]

Hussein did handle the matter the next day, talking to both parties, eventually hammering out a compromise solution. Like many young men of his generation and experience, he suddenly found himself faced with responsibility for managing community affairs, mainly such tasks as mediation in disputes and participating in popular tribunals to try suspected collaborators.[16]

During visits to Hussein's family, I began to notice the deference paid him by his father, an unusual state of affairs in Arab family relations where sons are usually deferential to their fathers. Much about hierarchy and submission can be read in seemingly mundane, everyday gestures. Seating patterns in Arab culture are spatial statements of hierarchy. Those who stand or sit closest to the door are usually subordinate, younger males, while those farthest from the door and centrally positioned are older, respected men who are able to command obedience. The spatial arrangement of visitors and family members when congregating at Hussein's home did not conform to the traditional pattern. Indeed Hussein often was centrally positioned with his father clearly on the periphery. During conversations where his father was present, along with other family members and friends, his father deferred to Hussein in speech, allowing his son to interrupt him. Hussein's father listened attentively as his son talked for lengthy periods of time before interjecting himself. In short, he gave Hussein the floor. When Hussein would describe his prolonged torture at the hands of the interrogators, his father was quiet, only occasionally to interject, 'Prison is a school, a university' and 'Prison is for men.'

In observing resistance activities in camps, villages and urban neighbourhoods, it was clear the older men played little, if any role. It was the preserve of the young (under 25 years of age), and as such they embodied the prestige and respect that come from, and yet give one access to, leadership positions. It did not take long to realize that Hussein was a member of the local underground leadership. He had spent 19 months in jail on charges of organizing local forms of escalation, such as stone throwing and barricade building. Chased and publicly beaten in the camp's alleyways before being thrown into a jeep, he was then taken to prison and subjected to 18 days of interrogation. Naked, deprived of food, water and sanitation facilities for the first three days, he was subjected to beatings with fists, pipes and rifle butts, which alternated with questioning over an 18-day period.

Once interrogation procedures are completed, prisoners join their fellow inmates in daily prison routine. Palestinian political prisoners are highly organized. Classes are conducted daily in a variety of subjects ranging from foreign languages to maths, science and history. Classes in political theory and practice are the high points in this educational project. For this reason, it is commonplace in contemporary Palestinian discourse to hear the comment ,'Prison is a university.' A leadership hierarchy emerges, and as young men are released they take up the leadership mantle of those who are newly detained. In this way, young men circulate between prison and leadership positions. This circulation of young men ensures a leadership in spite of the campaign of massive arrests and detention of young males.

Upon his release, Hussein returned home to several days of visitors – kin, friends and neighbours – and new responsibilities in the camp leadership. Within the prisons, recruitment to political organizations flourishes, and leaders of each political faction emerge to lead their followers. From the prison they can have some voice in the daily actions and policies of the intifada as they confer instructions and ideas on prisoners about to be released. Upon returning to their communities, young men like Hussein have acquired the stature to lead. They have withstood interrogation and not given away information or become collaborators. More importantly, however, they return 'educated men'. Hussein and other released detainees spoke of prison as a place where they learned not only academic subjects, but also about power and how to resist.

Another young man I became acquainted with in the West Bank was Ali. Ali's experience of bodily inflictions of violence began substantially before the intifada. Within a five-year period, he had been detained 17 times. Politically inactive before he was taken away from home in the middle of the night during his last year of high school, the soldiers assured his frightened parents that they would just ask him a few questions and let him go. Handcuffed and blindfolded, he was placed on the floor of a jeep where he was repeatedly kicked and hit with rifle butts. He recalls that the jeep stopped and picked up someone else. Once they started beating the other fellow, and he screamed, Ali realized it was his friend Sami. Sami told him: 'Don't cry or shout. Don't let them know it hurts.' He told me:

At first, of course, I was scared to death, and then once you're in that room and they slap your face and start hitting you – that's it, it goes away and you start being a different person. All of a sudden you have a power inside you – a power to resist – you want to resist. You can't help it; you feel very strong, you even want to challenge them, though basically I had nothing to tell them since I had done nothing.

After his release several days later, he returned home. Two weeks later, soldiers appeared again and detained him, this time for about two weeks. Upon his release, he decided to join the underground resistance movement and after several months was active in the local-level leadership. He now had stature in the community as a result of the beatings, arrests and interrogations. He was effective in mobilizing others to join in demonstrations, national celebrations, and the resistance movement on the university campus he later attended.

Physical violence can be construed by its recipients as a 'bridge-burning' activity (Gerlach and Hines 1970). One often hears comments such as 'I've nothing left to lose' and 'I've already paid the price, I might as well be active.' Palestinian males need not necessarily do violence to become political agents as Fanon (1969) argued for the Algerian revolution. As its recipients, they acquire masculine and revolutionary credentials. Marks on the body, though certainly unwanted, signal a resistant, masculine subjectivity and agency. The pervasiveness of beatings/detention, their organizational format, and their construal by recipients as entry into the world of masculinity make possible their casting as a rite of passage.

In his classic study of rites of passage, Van Gennep (1909/1961) identified three characteristic stages: separation, marginality, and aggregation. A logic of sequences is apparent in the transformative process of physical violence. In the initial phase, the individual is physically detached from the group. He is either taken from his home and family to the jeep and then the interrogation room, or he is detached from the crowd in public and held by soldiers or settlers who try to keep at a distance those who would intervene. The second, or liminal, stage is a state of marginality and ambiguity and is one fraught with dangers. The young novice exists outside of social time, space, and the categories of the life cycle. Social rules and norms are suspended. Interrogation, with its applications of physical violence, is such a liminal stage during which social hierarchies of age and class are diluted. Oppositions between normal social life and liminality (Turner 1977) can be applied to the one being beaten, especially those in custody who are frequently naked, in a state of humility and without rank or status, and who silently undergo pain and suffering. Imprisonment is also a liminal period because communitas is achieved and expressed in the emergence of new hierarchies that rest on an ability to withstand physical violation and pain, political affiliation and rank, and ability to lead in the prison community.

The final sequence, aggregation or the post-liminal re-entry into normal social life, is verified and enacted by the family and the community at large.

The return home is marked by a fairly well-defined celebratory etiquette. Relatives, friends and neighbours visit for several weeks to show respect to the released detainee and his family. Special foods, usually more expensive meat dishes, are prepared by the women of the household both to strengthen the detainee's often poor health as well as to show appreciation and respect for his endurance. New clothes are bought to mark re-entry into the community. The respect shown by deferential gestures to the former prisoner or beaten youth all mark his re-entry into society with a new status of respect and manhood.

In emerging from the beating unbowed and remaining committed to resistance activities, young men exhibit generosity to the point of sacrifice that asserts and validates a masculine self. The infliction of pain reveals, in the most intimate and brutal way, the nature of occupation and strengthens them, they contend, to confront it.

Endowed with the qualities of adulthood, honour and manhood, emergence from the ordeal dovetails with access to power and authority. In a reversal of meaning, the beating empowers the self and informs an agency of resistance. Palestinians, as participants in and as audience to the public spectacle of beatings, have consciously and creatively taken a coherent set of signs and practices of domination and construed them to buttress an agency designed to overthrow political hierarchies.

The intifada: tremors in the construction of masculinity

The term intifada comes from the Arabic root n-f-d, which indicates a shaking, as in shaking the dust from (Harlow 1989: 32). It implies a shaking off of foreign occupation and ties of economic and administrative linkage. While its eruption was fairly spontaneous, the intifada was the culmination of years of accumulated frustrations and outrage. A decade of grassroots political and social organizing undergirded its direction and ability to sustain itself (Hiltermann 1991). The intifada brought to the forefront of international diplomacy an internally-based Palestinian leadership. Equally, it signalled a generational shake-up. The young, armed only with stones and facing death and pain, were to sweep away the older generation in terms of political relevance and actual leadership. Shaking off also implicates forms of internal domination embodied in age, class and gender hierarchies. The continuity created by life-cycle transitions such as marriage, employment, and reaching the state of 'aql were destabilized by the actions of young boys.

The assertion that the male under occupation is reconstituted via violence implies that the creation of meaning is a matter of Palestinian control. The transformative power of the ritual lies in the individual who consciously commits himself to political action and in the community's ability to confer adult status. Ritual mediates between relations of violence and domination and political agency by subordinates in such a way as to defy any notion of directional unilineality between oppression and resistance. As Feldman argued in his discussion of political violence in Northern Ireland, 'Political agency is not given but achieved on the basis of practices that alter the subject' (1991: 1). Yet it is political practices by boys, many undertaken willingly and often spontaneously rather than given, that lead to further political agency via ritual.

As rites of passage, beatings and imprisonment are procedures that are not controlled or overseen by the family or kin group. It is an individual experience within a collectivity of young men. Thus a critical rite of passage into adulthood, with its corresponding privileges of power/authority/respect, is now accomplished earlier and is initially out of the bounds of the kin group. Indeed, it underscores the powerlessness of the kin group to protect its youth.

To return to Bourdieu's mapping of the relationship between masculinity and honour, we can now pose the question, what happens to the cultural categories and concepts around which honour is organized and expressed when challenge and riposte take place not between members of the same social group, but between a colonial entity, and its apparatus of force, and a subjugated, indigenous population? A man dishonours himself when he challenges a man considered incapable of 'taking up the challenge' (Bourdieu 1977: 11). When Israelis pursue and engage Palestinian youths, the cultural interpretation available to Palestinians is to consider the Israelis as lacking in the emotional and moral qualities of manhood. Only men of little honour and thus dubious masculinity would beat unarmed youths while they themselves are armed with and trained in the use of modern implements of warfare. Because little or no effective riposte is possible at the instant, there is no challenge – and the encounter degenerates into mere aggression (Bourdieu 1977: 12). Such aggression deprives its practitioners of claims to honour and morality.

Palestinians construe these aggressions as cowardly and immoral, rather than a challenge. But what has all this to do with manhood? Palestinians have changed the cultural categories of the encounter so that manhood comes from a 'riposte' not to a challenge but to what Bourdieu distinguished as 'mere aggression'. It is against this backdrop of aggression then that Palestinians are reconstructing defining elements of their culture and society. This will take on more meaning when read against the following scene.

Moral superiority: affirming cultural and national selves

On my way to an office in east Jerusalem, I was rushing to avoid the 1:00 p.m. closure of all commercial activity in the Palestinian sector of the city in observance of the general strike. Children were returning home from school, and shop shutters were hastily rolling down. As I rounded the corner, I saw two jeeps and about six or seven heavily armed soldiers. They had a 10-year-old mentally handicapped boy pressed against the stone wall, were slapping him in the face, shaking him, and yelling in broken Arabic for him to admit throwing a stone at them. Being mentally handicapped, the boy could only whimper and cry – he was incapable of talking. I ran into our office to tell the others that they were beating the boy who lived across the alley. By this time several neighbourhood women, by and large middle-class Jerusalemites, had also appeared. One of these women, fluent in English, calmly walked up to the group, which had now expanded to four jeeps and about 15 soldiers. She politely asked why they were bothering this boy who was retarded and could barely speak. She kept repeating to the soldiers that the boy could not understand and speak like a normal child. By now, she had a slight mocking smile on her face and appealed to the soldiers with a kind of sarcasm: 'Can't you see he's retarded? It takes all of you soldiers and four jeeps to question a retarded boy?' The other women were smirking and exchanging comments on what it was that could possess these people to beat retarded children. Several of the soldiers were clearly embarrassed and physically distanced themselves, turning their backs on the boy and the two soldiers roughing him up. They smiled sheepishly to the women gathered there and shrugged their shoulders as if to say, 'What can we do?'

An audience of women defused a potential escalation of violence through mockery and joking. The imbalance of forces is so patently absurd that Palestinians find an almost comic relief in watching soldiers engage in such morally revealing behaviour. In imposing interpretation and meaning on the violence of the occupiers, Palestinians are (re)constituting themselves in a moral sense. Violent encounters where Palestinians are both participants and audiences are public scenes where their moral qualities are dramatically juxtaposed against those of the occupiers.

The reconstitution of a moral self via violence involves both men and women. To some extent, however, a gendered distinction appears in the practice of violence. While women have been active in all arenas, a task assigned to them early in the intifada, and one in tune with cultural notions of female propriety and 'natural' concerns and mobility constraints, was to intervene in violent encounters. In other words, women were to witness and defuse rites of violence. A leaflet (*bayan*) distributed on 8 March 1988, and signed 'Palestinian Women in the Occupied Territories', said, 'Mothers, in camps, villages, and cities, continue confronting soldiers and settlers. Let each woman consider the wounded and imprisoned her own children.'[17]

Despite a gendered division of roles, the moral reconstruction consequent to violent acts does indeed permeate gender boundaries. The reconstituting moral self, whether male or female, is a cultural category, in this case one with a national content, constructed as it currently is vis-à-vis a foreign other. As the witnessing audience, women provide a running commentary intended to shame soldiers to cease a beating or to stop an arrest. 'Don't you people have children?', 'Has God abandoned you?' is screamed at soldiers while entreating them to desist. While women's moral self is enacted and affirmed publicly in this act of witnessing, the male being beaten or arrested is also positioned performatively to place himself against another. But how are non-participants positioned such that they also ultimately are enabled to construct a moral self? I would argue that the 'telling', punctuated by moral and evaluative judgements that circulate throughout Palestinian society as people visit one another in the course of daily life, is one such event in which a moral constitution of the self unfolds.

Israeli behaviour is considered rude and boorish. Palestinian discussions are punctuated by surprise at their bad manners: 'These are supposedly educated people – why do they behave so obnoxiously?' They are regarded as lacking in ethics and morality. Most significantly, they are seen as deficient in empathy with the suffering of others.[18] In contemporary constitutions of self vis-à-vis their occupiers, Palestinians have recourse to a 'poetics of contrast' (Comaroff and Comaroff 1987: 205). Clear and defining distinctions are drawn between their behaviour and the occupiers'. Palestinians consider themselves polite to others and reserved in public, personal qualities that are central to a Palestinian etiquette. Images of contrast are rhetorical devices that lend meaning to the occupiers' behaviour. The moral nature of these images provides Palestinians with the stuff of which they construct a collective self-image in a situation of subordination and an absence of autonomy.

Transforming hierarchies: class and generation

In the historical encounter, socio-cultural systems are simultaneously transformed and reproduced (Sahlins 1981). Inscriptions of bodily violence and their construal as rites of passage both transform and reproduce certain structural, relational and cultural features of Palestinian society. The intifada has had profound implications for class and generational structures and relations in the occupied territories. While the intifada is a popular uprising, those in the forefront of resistance to occupation are subaltern male youths from the refugee camps, villages and urban popular quarters who are usually under 20 years of age and can be as young as ten.

The power and status of the older generation were eclipsed. Young males took over the tasks previously the preserve of more mature, often notable men. For example, disputes were mediated in new judicial tribunals organized and staffed by the underground leadership. A common lament was that the young were out of control, displaying little or no respect for their parents. It reached such a pitch that several leaflets in 1990 called for parents to reassert control and for youth to heed the voices of their parents and teachers.

The older generation, those over the age of 35, played little, if any, visible role in the daily activities of the intifada. A telling incident occurred one day in a service (shared taxi) ride from Jerusalem to Ramallah. There were six passengers, myself included. As we approached a roadblock manned by soldiers, we could see several other cars stopped with young male passengers being searched and questioned. No one in our car seemed particularly worried or concerned. Our car came to a halt and the soldiers peered in, gave each of us a searching glance, and then motioned the driver to proceed. My husband commented to the rest of the passengers, 'Why didn't they ask to see our identity cards or search us?' The other men in the car, none of whom appeared to be younger than 30 or 35, turned around in their seats and looked at him with incredulity. One of them said, 'You think you're a boy! They aren't interested in men our age!'

Bodily inscriptions of violence are more prevalent in camps and villages and thus are somewhat class bound. The politically active urban elite, often from notable families, who have traditionally striven for leadership, are not usually exposed to bodily inscriptions of violence, though they may well undergo periods of administrative detention. Indeed, they can be subject to derision for assuming a mantle of leadership when they have not been credentialized by violence. Um Kamel is a 40-year-old mother and activist in a refugee camp. Her husband is in jail serving a ten-year sentence on the grounds of organizing anti-occupation activities. One son has spent considerable periods of time in prison, and a 16-year-old son has been shot twice in the stomach. Twice she has had homes demolished, with only a few hours notice, because of allegations of her sons' political activism. She commented sarcastically of the urban-based leaders: 'What do they know of suffering? Who are they to lead? They and their sons aren't beaten and they rarely go to jail. Their sons study here and abroad while our sons are beaten, shot and imprisoned!'

Reproducing hierarchies: gender

Contemporary rites of initiation into manhood articulate with and set in dramatic relief the social reproduction of asymmetrical gender arrangements, while a hierarchical male identity and notions of selfhood and political position are reaffirmed in these rites of passage.

Given the casting of the beating as a zone of prestige for young men, what does it mean for women? The number of women beaten, arrested and detained is small, and their status afterwards is more ambiguous than heroic. The number does not index women's level of involvement in the uprising, which has been extensive. It does indicate, however, their less visible role, and the tendency of the Israeli Defence Forces to go for males first. Ambiguity devolves for the women from the shame of having bodily contact with strange men, a stark transgression of the code of modesty and shame. Foremost on everyone's mind is the question of sexual violation. Women who violate the modesty code by engaging in illicit sexual activities (pre-marital sexual relations or adultery after marriage) risk incurring reprisals by kinsmen. But when the violator is a common enemy in whose face one's kinsmen hold no power and few means of recourse, ambiguity sets in. Ambiguity arises from the notion of will and intent. Arab women are seen as possessed of an active sexuality. When transgressions of the sexual code occur, the woman can be held responsible. Yet, if a woman's nationalist activity sets in motion a series of events that culminates in a beating and detention, and an interrogation procedure that includes sexual torture, it is difficult to cast her as having violated the modesty code. The nationalist, patriotic cast of her intent and actions precludes the usual cultural interpretation. By the time of the intifada, ambiguity was giving way to a cautious respect for the woman detainee.

While femininity is no more natural than masculinity, physical violence is not as central to its construction. It does not reproduce or affirm aspects of female identity, nor does it constitute a rite of passage into adult female status. Women frame their physical violation as evidence of their equality with men and wield it to press their claims – 'We suffer like men, we should have the same rights,' quipped one former prisoner who had undergone a lengthy detention and was tortured during interrogation. While the violence visited upon males credentializes masculinity, that visited upon women indicates a potential equality of citizenship (Peteet 1991).

Women experience the phenomenon of beating from a multiplicity of subject positions. The 'mother' saving boys from soldiers' blows is one of the most widespread and enduring images to emerge in the intifada. Mothers of the subaltern are extolled as the 'mothers of all Palestinians'. Known in the camp as 'a mother of all youths', Um Kamel explained her actions in intervening in public beatings: 'I feel each and every one of those boys is my son. If it was my son, I would want other mothers to try to protect him.' The mothers intervene during beatings, at once screaming for the soldiers to stop and pleading with them to show mercy. They hurl insults that highlight the soldiers' denial of the humanity of others: 'Have you no compassion and pity?', 'Aren't we human beings, too?', 'Don't you have mothers and sons – how would your mother feel if you were treated this way; would you like to see your sons beaten like this?', 'What kind of a people takes the land of another and then beats them when they protest?' This protective action of middle-aged mothers accomplishes several things: it can create a diversion that allows boys to escape. The noise and confusion it generates can quickly mobilize large groups of passers-by and nearby residents to surround soldiers and try to intervene. But above all, it casts shame on soldiers by scrutinizing their moral qualities in a dramatic, public narrative. Women as mothers of all are a collective moral representation of a community testifying to the abusive nature of occupation.

Thus women are not silent witnesses to everyday violence. Witnessing is itself a form of political activism. When the occasional foreign journalist enters a camp, a delegation comes from abroad, or the anthropologist such as myself comes, the 'mothers', those who risked their own safety to protect others, are called forth. Much like the vaunted position of the 'mothers of the martyrs' in areas where Palestinian resistance takes the form of armed struggle (Peteet 1991), they are called upon to tell their stories, to assume the position of communal witnesses and tellers of suffering. The experience of a beating may not affirm a feminine identity and selfhood, yet it does evoke some female traits – stoicism and silence, to protect the community.

While beatings reproduce a masculine identity, they also reproduce men's authority and physical domination in the family. Asymmetrical gender relations may be reaffirmed as a result of a young man's assumption of adult tasks and authority that in this case are assumed through violent rites of passage. Young wives and sisters complained that their husbands and brothers returned from interrogation and detention with a new authoritarianism expressed in attempts to assert control over their mobility. Style of dress was another arena of conflict, as women were pressured to wear head scarves. Domestic violence, wives and social workers claimed, was on the rise. Some men who were subjected to beatings and torture return home and inflict violence upon women.

Conclusion

The meaning of the beating is central to new conceptions of manhood and ultimately access to leadership positions. Violence has almost diametrically opposed meanings. For one, it is an index of a fictionalized fear and image of inferiority of a subject population and is intended to control and dishonour; for the others, it is constitutive of a resistant subjectivity that signals heroism, manhood, and access to leadership and authority. Practices that intimately situate Israelis and Palestinians are construed by Palestinians as transformative and agential. How did the experience of physical violence become construed as a rite of passage into manhood with its associated practices? In other words, can we identify a dynamic interplay between meaning and agency? The categories of experience, meaning and agency should not be arranged in a unilinear manner so as to identify a direction of transformation. A more fruitful line of inquiry would cast these categories as existing in a relationship of mutual constitutiveness.

While beatings, bodies and rites of passage are texts and structures of meaning, they are also historically grounded social constructions derived from particular signs and practices that galvanize a community to action. The call to action derives less from the actual structure of the ritual and more from its performative essence, in which the audience plays a crucial role in reversing the meaning intended by the dominant performers. The intifada abruptly and violently signalled an end to what Scott has referred to as the 'public transcript . . . the open interaction between subordinates and those who dominate' (1990: 2). Israel's public performances to exact submission are no longer efficacious.

The act of incorporating beatings and imprisonment into a cultural criterion of manhood and assigning them status as a rite of passage is a 'trick', if you will, that reverses the social order of meaning and leads to political agency. To let bodily violence stand as constitutive of an inferior and submitting social position and subjectivity without interpretation and challenge would be to submit to the dominant performers' meaning. For the anthropologist, to interpret it otherwise would leave it as a textual rather than an agential problematic.

The occupying authorities, with constant attention directed to detecting ripples of change in Palestinian cultural categories and social relations, have by now caught on to the way applications of bodily violence and imprisonment have empowered a generation committed to resistance. A new element seems to be emerging in their regime of pseudo-knowledge of the subject population. Interrogation procedures now contain a sexual practice designed to thwart the meaning and agency of physical violence as rites of passage to masculinity and manhood. Rape during interrogation is now being more widely discussed among some released prisoners, as is fondling by interrogators with photographs taken of these incidents. Sexual forms of interrogation deprive young men of claims to manhood and masculinity. One cannot return from prison and describe forms of torture that violate the most intimate realm of gendered selfhood. If knowledge of such sexual tortures circulates widely, the power of violence and detention to contribute to a gendered sense of self informing political agency will be diluted.

Notes

1. This article was completed in November 1992 and is here reprinted in an abbreviated form with small modifications by permission of the American Anthropological Association (not for further reproduction). It has been decided not to attempt to 'update' the original article or to change tenses throughout to reflect the fact that, with the institution of the Palestinian Authority, there have been changes in the status of some Palestinians. The article first appeared in *American Ethnologist* 21:1 February 1994, and research for it was carried out in the West Bank during 1990. Funding for a year of fieldwork was generously provided by the Fulbright Islamic Civilization Program. The Palestinian Academic Society for the Study of International Affairs (PASSIA) graciously provided institutional support and hospitality. I would like to extend my appreciation to Mary Hegland, Yvonne Jones and William Young for comments on an earlier draft and to the four anonymous reviewers for *American Ethnologist* for their helpful comments and suggestions for revision.

2. See Hajjar and Beinin (1988). This is a primer designed to provide a very basic overview of twentieth-century Palestinian history and society.

3. This encompasses injuries sustained from live ammunition, which includes plastic bullets, rubber bullets, metal marbles and tear gas.

4. The Palestine Human Rights and Information Committee (PHRIC) cautions that the figure of 106,600 should probably be doubled, especially the beatings. They receive their information from hospitals and clinics, and many people do not seek medical care. Moreover, they do not receive figures on beating cases treated in emergency rooms, in local or private clinics, or by the medical communities. The figures from the Gaza Strip for the month of December 1990 indicate 273 reported beatings (66 were of women, 45 of children) (Palestine Human Rights and Information Campaign 1990).

5. See Aronson (198 days of the occupation).

6. Their actual numbers are somewhat harder to estimate because, with the intifada, human rights organizations began making a concerted attempt to keep monthly and annual figures on human rights violations, breaking them down into distinct categories.

7. Amnesty International (1991) states that in the occupied territories, Palestinian detainees are: 'typically subjected to forms of torture or ill-treatment, with the aim of obtaining information as well as a confession . . . Torture or ill-treatment seem to be virtually institutionalized during the arrest and interrogation procedure . . . The practices relating in particular to interrogation procedures have been officially endorsed or are generally condoned, and therefore effectively encouraged, by the authorities.' (p. 45)

   Amnesty's report also questions the 'fairness of military court trials' because of the prominent role of confessions and 'the apparent reluctance by judges to investigate claims of coerced statements' (p. 49). The report states that 'the substantial evidence available indicates the existence of a clear pattern of systematic psychological and physical ill-treatment, constituting torture or other forms of cruel, inhuman, or degrading treatment which is being inflicted on detainees during the course of interrogation' (p. 58).

8. Zionist fictionalizing, and I would add, fear of collective Arab sentiment and action, goes far in explaining why the shooting of an Israeli diplomat in London could be presented as justification for the 1982 invasion of Lebanon and yet why Israel has usually insisted on bilateral negotiations with Arab states.

9. See Peretz (1990) for a discussion of the complexity of views among soldiers serving in the occupied territories.

10. Literature devoted explicitly to masculinity in the Arab world is rare, but the topic surfaces in a variety of works, not exclusively but largely based on ethnography in North Africa (Abu-Lughod 1986; Caton 1985, 1987; David and Davis 1989).

11. Unlike masculinity in the Mediterranean, especially Spain, public displays of lust and sexual bravado are not explicit components of Arab manhood. Indeed self-mastery of lust and romantic emotions is crucial to the construction and maintenance of Arab manhood (see Abu-Lughod 1986; Gilmore

1990: 40). In Muslim thought, unregulated sexuality can lead to *fitna* (social chaos).

12. Autonomy is more than simply the ability to provide physical protection. It is also the ability to support one's family through labour. Adequately to explain how the Palestinian economy has been harnessed to that of the occupying country, and in the process how labour categories, relations, and patterns have been transformed is beyond the scope of this article.

13. In a study of the dreams of Palestinian children, Bilu (1991) noted that in nightmares of violent encounters between their families and Israeli soldiers or settlers, parents are unable to protect children from violence, whereas in Israeli children's nightmares of violence emanating from Arabs, salvation arrives in the form of fathers, families, and the army. In one case the nightmare is resolved, in the other it is simply a nightmare from which the child can find no escape. A study discussed by Peretz had a similar conclusion. In a study of Palestinian children's dreams, a prominent theme was the presence of soldiers in their homes, smashing furniture and beating parents. Peretz commented that: 'a major conclusion was that these children regard themselves as victims of violence initiated by armed men and that the family no longer provides security. The father almost never figures in these dreams; according to the analysis, he has lost his authority.' (1990:116) His source is Amos Lavav 'Jewish-Arab Psychoanalysis', *Sof-Shavooa*, weekly supplement to *Maariv International Edition*, 23 December 1988.

14. See Peteet (1991:105–7) where I argue that, among the Palestinians in Lebanon, rituals of martyrdom for guerrillas were testimonials of their honour and immortality in the collective consciousness. Moreover, their celebratory spirit signalled defiance of death and the subordination it was supposed to overcome.

15. For an extensive discussion of the concept of *'aql*, see Rosen (1984). *'Aql* has been described as the 'faculty of understanding, rationality, judiciousness, prudence, and wisdom' (Altorki 1986:51). Males begin to acquire *'aql* around the age of 20. While acquisition of this quality has no definable starting date, it does grow with marriage, and most men attain it fully 'no earlier than 40, or mature adulthood, when men are perceived to have achieved sufficient capacity to deal with the complex problems of social existence' (Altorki 1986:52). Milestones along this path to adulthood are circumcision, educational achievements, marriage, income earning, the birth of children, and the acquisition of wisdom that comes from knowledge of one's society and its customs. See Granqvist (1931, 1935, 1947), for a description of circumcisions and weddings in Mandate Palestine.

16. For discussion of Palestinian popular tribunals and popular justice committees during the intifada, see McDowell (1989) and Peretz (1990). A similar process of legal development occurred in Lebanon under the PLO (Peteet 1987).

17. Leaflets are printed several times a month by the underground leadership of

the intifada. They contain a listing of the strike days and days of confrontation, and additionally exhort people to boycott Israeli goods, actively to participate in popular committees, in general, to support the uprising.

18. Jewish theologian Mark Ellis suggests that 'Holocaust theology' – emergent since the creation of Israel in 1948 – is a self-absorbed phenomenon based on a joining of religious heritage with loyalty to Israel. Such self-absorption diminishes Jewish capacity for empathy with Palestinian suffering (Neimark 1992:21; see also Lewis 1990).

References

Abu-Lughod, Lila 1986: *Veiled Sentiments: Honor and Poetry in a Bedouin Society*, Berkeley: University of California Press.

Altorki, Soraya 1986: *Women in Saudi Arabia: Ideology and Behavior among the Elite*, New York: Columbia University Press.

Amnesty International, Israel and the Occupied Territories 1991: *The Military Justice System in the Occupied Territories: Detention, Interrogation and Trial Procedures*, New York: Amnesty International.

Aronson, Geoffrey 1987: *Creating Facts: Israel, Palestinians, and the West Bank*, Washington, DC: Institute for Palestine Studies.

Ben-Ari, Eyal 1989: 'Masks and Soldiering: The Israeli Army and the Palestinian Uprising', *Cultural Anthropology* 4: 372-89.

Bilu, Yoram 1991: 'The Other as Nightmare: The articulation of aggression in children's dreams in Israel and the West Bank', paper presented at the 90th Annual Meeting of the American Anthropological Association, Chicago.

Bourdieu, Pierre 1977: *Outline of a Theory of Practice*, Cambridge: Cambridge University Press.

Caton, Steven 1985: 'The Poetic Construction of Self', *Anthropological Quarterly* 58: 141–51.

Caton, Steven 1987: 'Power, Persuasion, and Language: A Critique of the Segmentary Model in the Middle East', *International Journal of Middle East Studies* 19: 77–102.

Comaroff, John L. and Comaroff, Jean 1987: 'The Madman and the Migrant: Work and Labor in the Historical Consciousness of a South African People', *American Ethnologist* 14: 191–209.

Davis, Susan, and Davis, Douglas 1989: *Adolescence in a Moroccan Town*, New Brunswick and London: Rutgers University Press.

Fanon, Frantz 1969: *The Wretched of the Earth*, Harmondsworth: Penguin Books.

Feldman, Allen 1991: *Formations of Violence: The Narrative of the Body and Political Terror in Northern Ireland*, Chicago: University of Chicago Press.

Gerlach, Luther, and Hines, Virginia 1970: *People, Power and Change: Movements of Social Transformation*, Indianapolis: Bobbs-Merrill Educational Publications.

Gilmore, David 1990: *Manhood in the Making: Cultural Concepts of Masculinity*, New Haven and London: Yale University Press.

Granqvist, Hilma 1931 & 1935: *Marriage Conditions in a Palestinian Village*, 2 vols., Helsingfors, Finland: Societas Scientiarum Fennica.

Granqvist, Hilma 1947: *Birth and Childhood among the Arabs: Studies in a Muhammadan Village in Palestine*, Helsingfors, Finland: Soderstrom & Co.

Hajjar, Lisa, and Beinin, Joel 1988: 'Palestine for Beginners', *Middle East Report* 154: 1 7–20.

Harlow, Barbara 1989: 'Narrative in Prison: Stories from the Palestinian Intifada', *Modern Fiction Studies* 35: 29–46.

Herzfeld, Michael 1985: *The Poetics of Manhood: Contest and Identity in a Cretan Mountain Village*, Princeton, NJ: Princeton University Press.

Hiltermann, Joost 1991: *Behind the Uprising*, Princeton, NJ: Princeton University Press.

Keesing, Roger 1985: 'Kwaio Women Speak: The Micropolitics of Autobiography in a Solomon Island Society', *American Anthropologist* 87: 27–39.

Lewis, Mark 1990: *Beyond Innocence and Redemption: Confronting the Holocaust and Israeli Power*, San Francisco: Harper & Row Publishers.

McDowell, David 1989: *Palestine and Israel: The Uprising and Beyond*, Berkeley: University of California Press.

Neimark, Marilyn 1992: 'American Jews and Palestine: The Impact of the Gulf War', *Middle East Report* 175: 19–23

Palestine Human Rights and Information Campaign 1990: *Palestine Human Rights and Information Campaign* 3:13, Human Rights Update.

Peretz, Don 1990: *Intifada: The Palestinian Uprising*, Boulder, CO: Westview Press.

Peteet, Julie 1987: 'Socio-political Integration and Conflict Resolution in a Palestinian Refugee Camp', *Journal of Palestine Studies* 16(2): 29–44.

Peteet, Julie 1991: *Gender in Crisis: Women and the Palestinian Resistance Movement*, New York: Columbia University Press.

Rosen, Lawrence 1984: *Bargaining for Reality: The Construction of Social Relations in a Muslim Community*, Chicago: University of Chicago Press.

Sahlins, Marshall 1981: *Historical Metaphors and Mythical Realities: Structure in the Early History of the Sandwich Islands Kingdom*, Ann Arbor: University of Michigan Press.

Scott, James 1990: *Domination and the Arts of Resistance: Hidden Transcripts*, New Haven, CT: Yale University Press.

Shammas, Anton 1988: 'A Stone's Throw', *New York Review of Books*, March 31: 10.

Taussig, Michael 1987: *Shamanism, Colonialism, and the Wild Man: A Study in Terror and Healing*, Chicago: University of Chicago Press.

Turner, Victor 1977: *The Ritual Process: Structure and Anti-Structure*, Ithaca, NY: Cornell University Press.

Van Gennep, Arnold 1909/1961: *The Rites of Passage*, Chicago: University of Chicago Press.

FIVE

The Military as a Second Bar Mitzvah
Combat Service as Initiation to Zionist Masculinity

Danny Kaplan

Despite growing criticism of the military and of militarism more generally, the Israeli Defence Forces (IDF) still hold a central place in Israeli society today. Military service is a core aspect of this and is considered almost a prerequisite for entering adult life. A variety of studies conducted in recent years have demonstrated the military's predominant role as an agent of socialization into Israeli society in general (Azarya 1983; Lieblich 1989) and into hegemonic masculinity in particular (Lomsky-Feder 1992; Ben-Ari 1998; Kaplan 1999). This article explores combat culture and its underlying Zionist ideology as they powerfully shape the masculine identity of Israeli Jewish youth.

Although the IDF is the only conscript army with compulsory service for women, the military is based on a regime which intensifies gender distinctions (Izraeli 1997). Regular service begins at the age of eighteen. Men are recruited for three years whereas women are discharged after a year and nine months or less. Only men may participate in combat-related activity and are called up annually for varying periods of reserve duty throughout much of their adult life. Functioning as the all-Israeli 'melting pot', the military attempts to mould all men in a uniform guise of masculinity. It does so through an organizational culture that encourages ideal assets of soldiery such as physical ability, endurance, self-control, professionalism, sociability, aggressiveness and heterosexuality. These traits tap on masculine performance by contrasting them with images of 'otherness' such as femininity, homosexuality and the Arab enemy. For example, the curse 'Go find yourself a red-headed Arab to shake your ass about' denotes a man who is submissive enough to be penetrated, and not just by another man, but by an Arab – the national enemy – and a red-headed one at that: the ultimate expression of biological otherness. These various images of the 'other' are all related and serve to construct the hegemonic images of Israeli masculinity.

The IDF is also bound by underlying Zionist ideology. The Zionist revolution entailed not only the return of the Jewish people to their 'old-new' homeland, but also an emancipation of the Jewish man. The image of the Jewish man was now to be rid of associations with its Diaspora version that spelled a dislocated, 'sheep-like' passive-effeminate existence and replaced with images of physical strength, labouring, prowess, harshness and sexuality. Zionist masculinity was reconstructed as a masculinity of body, realized through territorial settlement and self-defence, accomplished through military power (Biale 1992; Boyarin 1997a). Influenced by other European national movements, the Zionist project endorses what Mosse (1990) called the 'myth of participation in war'. This view crystallized with the 1948 generation of the 'Sabra'[1] – the Israeli-born male youth (predominantly of Eastern and Central European origin) who fought for the establishment of the Israeli state. The Sabra represented everything that the old Jew lacked: youth, strength, health, physical labour and deep-rootedness (Rubinstein 1977). The Kibbutz agricultural settlements, inspired by socialist ideology, were a major force in the Zionist revolution and the Kibbutz-born youth, who participated in quasi military activity, came to embody the Sabra ethos (Almog 1997).

Following the founding of the IDF, the image of the Jewish warrior has been reinforced as a state institution. The IDF has become the dominant socialization agent. Military training attempts to remodel the new recruits coming from various sub-cultures of segmented Israeli society and to mould them through one common denominator – that of hegemonic Zionist masculinity. Despite an official policy of universal conscription, in practice different arrangements prevail for different groups of citizens within Israeli society. Their positioning is determined by their relationship to masculinity, Judaism and Zionism. Women are excluded from most combat roles, the archetypal 'manly' activity. Ultraorthodox Jews who hold non-Zionist views rarely serve and, if they do, are usually confined to religious service jobs. While most Muslims and Christians of the non-Zionist Arab minority are excluded from service altogether, men from the Druze, Circassian and some Bedouin communities, who are minorities within the Arab minority, are eligible for combat service, yet are channelled to specific posts (see Lomsky-Feder and Ben-Ari forthcoming). In contrast, *Mizrachi* men (originating from Middle Eastern and North African Jewish communities), men of national-religious affiliation, and some of the new immigrants (predominantly from Russia), being both men and fully Zionist, are closer in their starting position to the hegemonic Sabra and thus are gradually assuming a more central place in military ranks. All that it takes is an effective 'melting pot' process to have them qualify for the hegemonic ideal.

Since active service of three years is an obligatory and self-evident stage for most Jewish-Israeli youths, it is the much smaller group of male soldiers who serve in combat units and risk their lives on a daily basis who attract adoration. These men, stationed in a variety of units, are trained to be fighters, and engage in operational duty on the borders, in south Lebanon and in the Palestinian territories. Combat roles are the archetype of the military organization: they are the organization's most important roles, claim the highest status, and define the meaning of military service both on a personal and collective level (Devilbiss 1994: 143). Through their very participation in combat duty, individuals act according to various values of the Zionist masculine ethos.

I shall demonstrate how present-day Israeli men establish their multifaceted identity using a case study of informants who hold a unique position in this culture – combat soldiers who have developed a homosexual identity. I will focus on the story of one soldier, Nir (pseudonym), born and raised in a Kibbutz, who served in an elite unit of the Giv'ati infantry brigade. Like most gay soldiers, Nir refrained from disclosing his sexual orientation in the military (see also Segal, Gade and Johnson 1993).[2] He acted as a full participant in combat culture, with no distinctive patterns of behaviour and with no overt conflict with his surroundings. In other words, unlike other minorities who serve in the Israeli army, his otherness within military culture remained invisible. Yet, having a strong internal notion of himself as different prior to joining the army – he regarded himself as bisexual at the time – his military experience became a voyage of self-exploration. By probing his own evolving identity as an invisible 'other' vis-à-vis hegemonic military masculinity, his case serves to point out and elucidate underlying processes by which various aspects of cultural identity are negotiated by all men in the military.

My analysis will be based on the conceptualization of current Israeli mainstream society as a civil religion. This concept, elaborated by Liebman and Don-Yehiya, refers to a system of sacred symbols expressed through belief and practice which 'integrate the society, legitimate the social order and mobilize the population in social effort while transmitting the central values and world-view that dominate the society' (Liebman and Don-Yehiya

1983: 24). Within this framework, the 'religion of security' (a term coined by Arian, Talmud and Hermann 1988: 49) serves as a core unifying force of Israeli society. The pervasiveness of security issues has put the military in a position of sacredness. Aronoff (1989: 132) has made the explicit observation that service in the IDF is 'the primary rite of passage that initiates one into full membership in the Zionist civil religion'.

Using Nir as a case study, I shall demonstrate how the military, as an ongoing initiation rite based on sacred symbols, works on the *individual level* – how in Israel it mobilizes a young man and proceeds to transmit and simultaneously legitimize to him the central values of Israeli society. I will discuss, through Nir's narrative, various negotiations of male Zionist identity: negotiation of militarism, the enemy, left-right politics and religion, all combined within the initiation rite to masculinity.

Nir's story

Nir, aged 20 at the time of the interview, wanted to join a combat unit from the very beginning. As he explained to me, the Kibbutz ideology strongly indoctrinates its youth to participate in combat service. Most of his older fellow men in the Kibbutz, as well as his father and brother, had served in combat units. He and his peers had been preoccupied with listening to stories about various prestigious units that had partaken in military warfare. In his high school class all but one male student had indeed made it to fighting units. Nir's own dream was to join the most prestigious reconnaissance unit, Sayeret Matkal, which is involved in secret operations behind enemy lines.[3] After failing at the second stage of the meticulous and arduous screening process, he was referred to the more conventional infantry unit of Giv'ati, where he passed yet another selective screening and was assigned to an elite unit in one of the Brigade's special companies. He underwent the four months of initial training and two additional months of advanced infantry training which together formed his basic training as a combat fighter. He was then assigned, together with his platoon members, to Giv'ati's operational duties in Israeli-controlled territories in the Gaza strip and later on the Lebanese border. In between stints of operational duty, his unit took part in exercises and large-scale drills.

Giv'ati, a relatively new brigade, has specialized in recent years in recruiting new immigrants from Russia as well as from national-religious circles. The latter have become known for their motivation, and their numbers in elite combat units are constantly increasing. In his own platoon,

Nir was one of the few 'secular' soldiers and the only one from a Kibbutz. Kibbutz men are more prone to enlist in the well-established and highly acclaimed Paratroopers brigade, a unit that is still identified with the founding principles of the IDF, and with the Sabra ethos. He remembered his puzzlement on first arriving in Giv'ati's boot camp: 'I scratched my head and thought, "What is this Giv'ati, what on earth am I doing here?" The human composition seemed to me very odd. Everybody was either religious or a new immigrant.' From this point onwards Nir had to negotiate his position, his attitudes and his identity in relation to the surrounding environment. The striking feature of his narrative is a constant shift between partial criticism of some aspects of his military experience, especially that which opposes his initial belief and value system, and a rhetoric of full identification with his unit and its underlying military ideology. The result of this tension is a growing adherence to the one binding force of Israeli society – the religion of security.

Starting with the issue of military training and socialization, Nir recounts: 'Let me tell you how your day starts in Giv'ati boot camp. Every morning when you wake up, the first thing you hear is the Giv'ati hymn, "He who has dreamt Giv'ati", ten times in a row, coming from huge loudspeakers. Every morning. You get a heart attack from that. As soon as you hear it you know your short sleep has ended and another day of drilling and harassment is coming your way.' Yet, after this rather critical picture of military training as brainwashing, he immediately switches to a rhetoric that defends this method of drilling: 'They try to look after the soldier's health. Nobody in our unit ever got injured from getting the run around. Okay, you crawl in the disgusting sand for an hour, you get yourself all covered in mud, it's physically difficult, but it's not dangerous.'

Nir was assigned to a prestigious and highly sought-after weapon in the platoon – a heavy machine gun. It became a source of satisfaction to him: 'I was especially keen on the firearm drills. I was like Rambo. I was in charge of a heavy machine gun. There is competition over some of the tasks and that's one of them. I loved the special role the heavy gun plays in ambush procedures. That's the real action of combat service.' The size of the heavy machine gun requires physical ability and strength beyond that of other weapons (see also Sion 1997), and winning this prestigious position singled him out and reinforced his masculine image.

The process of becoming a combat fighter of the Giv'ati Brigade is marked by a final forced march of around 90 kilometres from the unit's base to the official Giv'ati memorial site. The march terminates with a ceremony where the soldiers take an oath to the military and get presented with the unit's purple beret. Nir recounts the ceremony as, 'one of the most exhilarating experiences of my life . . . You feel like you finally made it, you got your own special beret, after all my pals in the Kibbutz were laughing at me for being in Giv'ati. It was a divine feeling . . . There were really important people at the ceremony, including the legendary chief commander who built up the unit. He is still a role model for Giv'ati soldiers, especially the religious ones. They got as excited as if they'd seen the Messiah in flesh and blood.'

This last comment is again one of mixed feelings – a tremendous pride in his new unit combined with some criticism towards the adoration, bordering on sacred worship, of the chief commander. It also raises another important arena of negotiation in Nir's narrative – his position as secular and 'leftist' compared with his religious- and conservative-inclined fellow platoon members. This issue arises in particular in relation to his unit's participation in policing Palestinian civilians in the Gaza strip.

Nir was first deployed in the territories during the unit's advanced training period. Asked how he felt serving there, he described the activity in professional military terms: 'Operational duty in the territories is different. It's LOTAR [Israeli military acronym for anti-terrorism combat techniques]. It's combat in built-up area conditions.' Yet, when I asked him in what way it was combat, he reflected in a more reserved way: 'You can call it combat. In good conscience, I can't shoot a ten-year-old who is confronting me and throwing stones at me. I remember each and every stone that hit me . . . It's insulting. It's one thing if the religious guys get hit, but me with my leftist ideology – wanting to get the hell out of there and leave them to have their own state – why do I deserve to get stoned? Why do I have to be there and run after ten-year-old kids?'

Nir complained about the prolonged training period, recalling how he waited month after month eager to start the real action – that is, to participate in operational activity in Lebanon. He describes his first entry to a post in the Israeli-controlled area of south Lebanon: 'We rode in a convoy, under the back-up of artillery shelling from behind us. Shells fell 200 meters away, it's very scary at first. You almost piss in your pants, sitting in the armoured personnel carrier and looking all around you. It's definitely frightening, but it's part of a routine you get used to, it's your job.'

Later he started to participate in ambushes against Hizbollah guerrillas. His initial description of the first encounter with the enemy is technical and report-like in nature: 'During that period we had one encounter, nothing serious. We were expecting them to come. There was no surprise factor. It was an ambush in a classic design. Each one took his place, I was with my machine gun in a cover position. When they arrived, the commander yells,

"Fire", and that's it, it ended very quickly. I think our snipers took down the first two in a matter of seconds. A third one tried to hide under a rock and got a bullet in the leg. I don't know if it was my shots that killed them, but they were totally full of holes.' Understanding that he had actually seen the bodies, I asked him about it, upon which he responded: 'They were all torn apart. When you stop and think about it, he is a human being too. Was a human being a minute ago.' Yet in practice, one didn't stop and think about it, but kept in mind only one thought: 'You know that it's either you or them, so why not do it? At the minute we first spot them you don't stop to think at all. You shoot.'

This description is typical of the way military logic works to accomplish its missions through a process of dehumanization. The enemy is depersonalized and objectified – as a target to be hit or as an obstacle to be dealt with. Focusing on the technical, machine-like performance of military action against the enemy reduces the human aspect of another man's death (Ben-Ari 1998). But the machine-like operation is not devoid of strong emotions. Nir recalls his feelings during the act and reflects on the atmosphere in his platoon after the successful assignment: 'Your heart starts beating strongly. I think it was one of the most thrilling experiences I ever had in my life. Everybody was in a state of ecstasy. When you think about it it's not so difficult, forty men against a few *mehablim* [guerrilla fighters; literally, saboteurs]. But the morale was high. People really got high on it – the fact that our guys got to do the job, and not another Brigade, that we actually killed *mehablim*.' Here is another aspect of military performance. Through inspiring pride in the unit, competition with other units, and focusing on the end result of the operation – the number of casualties to the enemy – the activity is perceived as if it were like winning a match. In addition, the feelings triggered in combat activity as a joint group endeavour evoke, in case of victory, a quasi-religious atmosphere of ecstasy which plays a major motivational role for the participating individual.

The importance of the military performance as a collective endeavour is especially noteworthy in Nir's case: not only in terms of his sexual identity but, perhaps more importantly, with his secular background he was somewhat of an outsider to the group. Coming to the issue of his place among religious soldiers, Nir explained:

My home is especially anti-religious. For example, if I had told my mother, not that I am gay, but that I intend to become religious, she would have taken that much more severely. So there was a lot of alienation. I was prejudiced against religious people. It turns out that I was wrong about many things. In practice they are a bunch of great guys. We were very much united. On the Sabbath [the Jewish day of rest], I'd even attend Synagogue prayers with them at base. The 'distance' between the commanders and the soldiers would tend to break as well, since the commanders are religious too and come to Synagogue to pray. I consider it a foreign custom, but it was nice. They have fun, they have this commitment to being happy on Friday nights. They stay up and sing till late. There is a problem as they come from various traditions – Ashkenazi, Mizrachi, and Hasidic [one of the ultraorthodox religious streams] – each one with its own songs. So the best thing was to stick with the Giv'ati songs. They would sing Giv'ati songs all the time!

Sion (1997) has demonstrated how the ceremony of breaking 'distance' between soldiers and commanders serves to strengthen the new soldier's identification with the military. In the above example, the same process operates at a much deeper level, incorporated as it is within a ritual that has a strong emotional resonance. The traditional Jewish Sabbath singing ritual is animated by jovial group activity performed in a new, non-religious context. The ritual in turn is reinforced by the particular context of its performance in military life: the harsh discipline of basic training is suddenly broken and replaced by a friendly social atmosphere. Being able to integrate the men of various backgrounds under the Giv'ati songs bolsters the military as a unifying religion that all can identify with, regardless of their views towards Jewish tradition.

Another broad issue Nir addressed was homosexuality and masculinity. First, he explained why disclosing his gay identity to military officials was out of the question, for fear of being marked and possibly denied future promotion. Second, he told of his hesitation to disclose himself to friends in his unit: 'There's no one to talk to. For religious people, homosexuality is the end of the road. Something which the Torah [Jewish Old Testament] condemns to death.' He did, however, tell another secular guy who became his best friend and a source of support within the unit. What is more interesting is how his resolution to join combat service to begin with singled him out from among his existing group of gay friends. These friends, with their antipathy to military Zionism, represent for him another strain prevalent within Israeli society among secular-liberal urban circles: 'If I am gay, it means that I am leftist, that I won't do combat service, all the typical things. I can't justify that . . . In the Kibbutz, it's in their blood, they educate for Zionism and combat service more than in the city. In the city nobody appreciates you for serving there, they see it as a waste of time.'

To conclude, Nir needs constantly to manoeuvre his multi-faceted identity between various opposing positions within Israeli discourse. The only way he can make sense of his socialist Kibbutz upbringing on the one hand, of a national-religious inclined unit on the other, and of his new reference group of secular-liberal urban gay men, is to adhere to the one binding force available for him – his identification with the military. This identification immediately draws on the question of masculinity: 'Perhaps someone who defines himself as gay to begin with would not go to combat service. Indeed I have. But I wasn't looking for my masculinity . . . I was like this before the army, I'll be the same after it. I won't adopt feminine behaviour just because I'm gay.'

It is obvious that Nir's identification with militarism is embedded deeply in his Kibbutz upbringing and cannot be attributed solely to his conscript military service. Military-like activities are a hobby among his peer group, as Nir mentions: 'In my Kibbutz there is a tradition that you gather unused bullets from your army drills and bring them back home, and on Saturday all the guys get together and go to the Kibbutz shooting range. Everyone tries out other people's weapons.' Yet Nir's narrative demonstrates how the very expectation and eventual participation in the combat military ordeal gives this early indoctrination its meaning and fulfilment as a man. In order to negotiate between various aspects of his own unique identity, Nir relies on the imagined Zionist masculinity achieved by combat military service.

The military as an initiation rite

Van Gennep (1909/1966) provided a framework for interpreting the transition of youth to adulthood through a set of socially constructed and gendered initiation rites that mark a change in status and in identity. In the case of men, they symbolically signify the death of childhood and the rebirth of the individual as a man. In warrior societies around the world, rites of passage typically involve the dramatic enactment of trials on a public stage. The youngsters display their courage when faced with pain and mortification before their community. Similarly, soldiers must display qualities of fortitude and endurance through practices enacted before their superiors, peers and underlings (Ben-Ari, forthcoming).

At a more general cultural level, participation in the military, and in combat service in particular, can be viewed as a prolonged initiation rite for becoming an adult, an Israeli citizen and a man. Four motivational factors underlie the rite of passage of Israeli youth in the military, and in combat service in particular. The first component is the perception of military service as developmental, as a major stage for identity crystallization (Orr et al. 1986) and self-discovery (Ben-Ari, forthcoming). The trials and tests experienced in military service enable the youth to examine his ability to withstand physical and mental hardships. It also shapes the attainment of personal, professional and social attributes associated with self-growth, and expansion of horizons (Lieblich 1989). As Nir concludes: 'I look at people who haven't served and they are still kids. I look at myself – I feel it made me more mature. It's not just pure machismo, it's a process of maturation.'

A second aspect involved in military participation is the normative aspect – the universality and centrality of military service shape it as a normative, indeed taken-for-granted, stage for Israeli youth. Establishing a prestigious military record, such as serving in an elite combat unit, is considered a better entrance ticket to mainstream Israeli occupational circles (Mayseless & Gal 1990). On a deeper level, it shapes the sense of belonging to Israeli society, as another soldier from the Nahal infantry brigade puts it: 'It's an integral part of Israeliness, of the Israeli way of life. Much of Israeli humour, many concepts, stem from the military experience. Someone who has not been in these situations will not understand what's going on. I think he would be less Israeli, he wouldn't belong.'

Yet as an organized, collective and normative rite of passage, the military defines not only a new stage in the life cycle, nor only a new position in society, but also a new role as a man. A third component of military service is its genderedness. It evokes the culturally recognized and legitimate themes identified with hegemonic masculinity. Conceptualizing masculinity in terms of an initiation rite underscores the universal notion that hegemonic masculinity is not given, but an ideal that needs to be accomplished. The recurring theme in many cultures is a constant attempt to affirm and prove one's masculinity (Connell 1995; Gilmore 1990; Roper and Tosh 1991). This need to prove one's masculinity is further enhanced in military culture. How military indoctrination acts as a powerful tool in the socialization process of the male has long been discussed (Arkin and Dobrofsky 1978). Barrett (1996) demonstrated how male officers in the US navy attempt to secure a masculine identity through multiple strategies of assertion and differentiation. The soldiers are likely to experience degradation and humiliation as a result of the constant surveillance and the testing and gruelling life conditions that are constructed as part of military training. Constantly exposed to the possibility of failure, their investment in masculine discourse becomes a way of compensating for the bad experience, reinterpreted as a series of challenges whose attainment leads to the accomplishment of an ideal masculinity.

On this basis combat activity is construed as the ultimate test of masculinity (Badinter 1995: 68). Ben-Ari (1998) offers an explanation of how this gendered role of combat is structured in the military through a logic of action he refers to as 'combat schema'. The combat scenario depicts a threatening situation of extreme stress and uncertainty in which individuals perform their assigned tasks, under command of officers, by mastering their emotions. Admittedly, less than 20 per cent of men in the Israeli military are combat soldiers, and far less have ever encountered combat situations. Yet, the military provides a continuum of situations that simulate combat and use the same criteria to inspect men's performance and abilities. From basic training, through specialized expertise training, through officers' courses, to the various manoeuvres and exercises – all these events are based on their similarity to combat. Being able to act as a soldier in battles encapsulates the notion of a man mastering a situation and passing a test. It epitomizes the achievement and reaffirmation of manhood.

Officially, of course, there is no title of 'man' conferred upon the soldiers, nor can the individual soldier attribute it to himself. However, as Nir comments on the issue of his being a macho: 'Maybe it's a reputation I got among friends within the [gay] community. Not that I think I am. It's a title they gave me. I say thank you and just carry on.' As with other graduation ceremonies, manhood must be conferred by others. In Nir's mind, it is a gay reference group that crowns him a macho, a 'real' man. Yet, as the present discussion reveals, being regarded as a man through accomplishment of military service must be seen as having much wider social currency.

Finally, we must turn to the context of Zionism and what is perceived as the national-ideological cause. Israel's political and security conditions in the Middle East, with its history of repeated wars, and its founding in relation to the Jewish Holocaust, have made military service seem like an essential factor in the security of the state of Israel and a prime national goal. This view is accepted by most Jewish Israeli citizens. As Ran, a Nahal brigade infantry soldier, puts it: 'It is definitely something which connects you to this country, the link of the people to their land, all those slogans . . . I remember myself sitting in the patrol vehicle and really telling myself "It is me in this job who is guarding the northern border, only me." Yes, you feel that.' This national aspect of military service can be further elaborated in relation to current Israeli society, an issue I address in the ensuing discussion.

Security as religion and combat service as Bar Mitzvah initiation

How is military socialization and its underlying Zionist ideology culturally expressed within Israeli society? My suggestion is twofold. First, the various aspects of Zionist identity that men such as Nir negotiate in the military – issues such as militarism, the Arab other, left-right politics, religion versus secularism – are linked through one binding ethos, the quasireligious ethos of security. Second, this ethos is sustained at the *individual level* through integrating men of various backgrounds through a unifying initiation rite of masculinity, performed through ritual.

Here I adhere to a broad definition of ritual in social context as 'rule-governed activity of symbolic character which draws the attention of its participants to objects of thought and feeling which they hold to be of special significance' (Lukes 1975: 291). The ethos is transmitted to the would-be men through various ritualized sites and activities that sanctify values of security. Memorials to commemorate fallen warrior heroes; long marches across the land of Israel terminating in swearing-in ceremonies; singing of anthems; ecstatic-type representations of combat experiences: all these have a performative role in assimilating security values as sacred. Such practices take place not only in the military itself, as depicted in Nir's story, but also in the educational setting, in youth movements, in the mass media and in state ceremonies. Thus, all Israeli-Jewish men, regardless of their actual participation in the military, are exposed in one way or another to the ritual of security and must relate to it. Both the concrete participation of combat soldiers in the military, as well as the *imagined* participation of other men, sets the stage for the military as a collective and sanctified initiation rite to be experienced by each man individually. This rite shapes the ideal attributes of the imagined Zionist masculinity – the attainment of personal, professional and social competence on the one hand, and a growing commitment to Zionist ideology on the other.

Gilmore (1990: 124) distinguishes between structured and non-structured cultures, in the way adulthood initiation is acknowledged for both sexes. For men, many traditional societies provide collective rites of passage that usher the youth through sequential stages to an unequivocal manhood. The masculine transition is 'dramatized' and ritualized through rigid chronological watersheds, often accompanied by magical incantations and sacred paraphernalia. In contrast, Western industrial societies seem to be more loosely structured and offer no public markers and no unified form of recognition for the coming of age. He notes the American case which, according to some scholars, offers a bewildering range of options for men at every stage of life, creating 'dilemma', 'crisis' and possibly resulting in 'makeshift masculinity'. Gilmore notes the Jews as an interesting example of ritual dramatization within modern Western societies. Like many traditional cultures, the construction of masculinity in (Orthodox) Judaism is publicly acknowledged, regulated and celebrated as a set of rites, rich with masculine symbolism: the *brit milah*, the circumcision ceremony at the age of eight days, and the *bar mitzvah*, the first reading of the Torah and an official admission to the religious obligations of adult Jewish men. From this point onwards the adolescent is committed to carrying the burden of commandments (*ol mitzvot*). The *bar mitzvah* is held for each individual separately when he reaches the age of thirteen, but it is celebrated publicly by the entire congregation. It also marks a developmental task. Davis (1995) analyses the *bar mitzvah* ritual in contemporary American Jewish families as a coping mechanism of adolescent transition. Compared to the invisibility of this transition in contemporary culture, it is an affirming public performance where the individual is surrounded by the goodwill of family and friends in a trance-like state of 'communitas'. When compared to other traditional initiation rites, the Bar Mitzvah evokes not the typical masculine performance associated with warrior societies, but rather an intellectual competence in reading the sacred text. Yet, it is still a marker of the acquisition of male power since it singles out the most important difference between men and women in Jewish culture – the privileged position men have in relation to reading and studying the Torah and in performing religious commandments. Thus, like other affirmation rites of masculine ability, it is a test that centres on mastering the dominant values of the society (Gilmore 1990).

Over the last century the ceremony has gradually developed into a festive event celebrated by family and friends, often outside the Synagogue. Its religious meaning for non-orthodox Jews, especially in Israel, has faded. Yet, behaviourally, it is still the most persistent symbol of tradition performed by 80 to 90 per cent of the Israeli-Jewish population. In contrast, less than 25 per cent of the population pursue the responsibilities that the rite demands and follow the rule-governed everyday life of orthodox Judaism (Katz 1997). I suggest that a more significant transition to adulthood emerges in Israeli society at the age of eighteen in accordance with modern civil law, and more importantly through participation in the military. Since the Zionist shift within Judaism aimed at ridding the image of Jewish masculinity of its historic associations with effeminate, dislocated Jews who surrendered themselves to the study of the Torah, and transforming it into an identity associated with fighting men in the land of Israel, it is hardly surprising that Zionism has institutionalized combat military service as a dominant developmental marker. As Van Gennep (1909/1966) noted long ago, initiation rites marking the child's admittance to adolescence rarely converge in time and content with the issue of physical puberty, but rather occur at various ages in different groups, in some instances up to the age of eighteen. The military has replaced the *bar mitzvah* as the meaningful initiation rite for men in the new Israeli religion of security.

This transformation does not require a withdrawal from tradition. On the contrary, Jewish tradition has assumed a more positive place in present Israeli society in comparison with the days of the more revolutionary secular stance that marked the initial Zionist enterprise. While early Zionism – as envisioned by central European Jews such as Herzl – was based on secular-liberal principles, the subsequent establishment of the Israeli state entailed a need to consolidate a sense of national consciousness. With the mass immigration of Jews from North Africa and Middle-Eastern countries traditional trends were strengthened (Liebman 1992: 425) and religious embellishments were gradually added to the secular-nationalist ethos. While most Israelis do not observe Jewish tradition, their notion of their culture is constituted through its symbols and an identification with its underlying rhetoric. Tradition, in this context, refers to Jewish continuity and history and to the central myths of Judaism that evoke a sense of identity and commitment among most Israelis. It is also connected to the notion of a hostile and anti-Semitic gentile world that has persecuted Jews across history. Thus, tradition socializes Israeli Jews to the expectation of security threats, and concern over security in turn reinforces commitment to tradition (Liebman 1997).

The current civil religion of Israel resonates with Jewish tradition yet does not take its authority from transcendent sources of power, but rather rests on the power of state institutions. It has adopted a strategy that Liebman and Don-Yehiya (1983) coin 'reinterpretation'. Traditional symbols penetrate the culture and, instead of being rejected, are reinterpreted and assigned values that meet contemporary needs. The aim is to legitimize these new values by linking them to a consensual tradition. From the beginning of the nation-state the Zionist narrative has glorified military service and participation in war through recourse to biblical referents. Soldiers were deemed successors to the tradition of courage first revealed in the biblical period. A term such as assuming the 'burden of the commandments' (*ol mitzvot*), derived from the *bar mitzvah* rite, was used to express loyalty and commitment to state institutions. The IDF, in particular, attained special sanctity: it has been referred to as the 'guardian' of Israel, a synonym for God in Jewish tradition. A banner in an army base read: 'In the beginning the IDF created the soldier, and the soldier created the nation.' (Liebman and Don-Yehiya 1983)

To recapitulate, a quasi-traditional civil religion, which commands a certain commitment from the majority of the population, is sustained through the centrality of the security ethos in Israeli culture. This ethos is maintained through the structured initiation rite of military service, which follows the earlier rites of the *brit milah* and the *bar mitzvah* in symbolically shaping a collective form of masculine identity. Unlike the 'open' developmental process that may characterize Western cultures, the modern Israeli 'tribe' has created a structured set of public rites of passage that usher youths through sequential stages to an unequivocal manhood. Furthermore, no matter how unique the self-identity that may emerge during the process, the all-encompassing new Israeli religion of security seems to predominate.

That being said, it may be surprising how little in this process relates to the wider cultural context of the Arab Middle East. Apart from a general depiction of the Arab as the 'national other', portrayed through a variety of stereotypes, specific perceptions of Palestinian and other Arab men do not seem to play a dominant role in the cultural construction of Israeli masculinity. This disregard may derive from the complex colonial position of early Zionism as well as from the military logic that held sway in subsequent Israeli perceptions. Boyarin (1997b: 305) suggests that Herzlian Zionism imagined itself as a colonialism whose mission was to transform Eastern European 'native' Jews into 'white men' in the fashion of 'civilized' Western Europeans. In the process no recognition was given to 'the very existence of already existing natives in the place where the Jewish colony was to be founded'. Almog (1997) observes how later on the Arab presence was virtually repressed from the consciousness of the Sabra generation, both in the educational setting and in the evolving military culture. To the present day, the IDF, in keeping with military organizational logic of mastering excessive emotions of hatred, refers to the enemy in a removed and depersonalized way. This is in contrast to the rhetoric common in other modern militaries that tends to demonize and debase the enemy by emphasizing its negative cultural characteristics (Ben-Ari 1998). Perceived through the eyes of 'neutral' military tasks, 'Arabs' – whether as *mehablim* (saboteurs), as 'civilian population', and even as 'women and children' or 'neighbours' – become an abstract entity devoid of cultural meaning, lacking identity, colour, ideology and religion. For example, the term *mehablim* refers in an undifferentiated way to individual Palestinian guerrilla attacks within Israel and to Hizbollah guerrilla fighters in south Lebanon.

In this respect, Israeli men manifest both a sense of defensiveness and of repression with regard to their position in the Middle East. Not only do they feel threatened by their condition as a 'Western' Jewish entity foreign to the region, but they tend to repress this very condition. Their cultural initiation rites could just as well take place in Uganda or Argentina (two alternatives for early Zionism), or in Canada. In one of the only passages in my interviews that goes so far as even to mention the Middle East, another IDF veteran sums up the place of military service within the Zionist narrative: 'I was brought up in a Zionist, secular house, and was raised to believe that this is the last home for the Jewish people . . . If I could, I would have chosen to be born blond, Christian, in Canada, and not Jewish, Israeli, and gay at that . . . But this is my house. To guard the physical existence of the house, given the present circumstances in the Middle East, we need to go to the army, to combat units, and to fight . . . There was no doubt about it, and it still holds today.'

Notes

1. The *sabra* is the name of a fruit imported into the region two hundred years ago. It also refers to a person who is rough and prickly on the outside, yet rich and tender inside (Almog, 1997: 15).
2. Since 1993 the Israeli military has had a non-discriminatory policy towards the enlistment of homosexuals and officially they may serve in any unit. For an elaborated discussion of homosexuals' experience in the IDF, see Kaplan (1999), and Kaplan and Ben-Ari (2000).
3. The two recent prime ministers in Israel – Binyamin Netanyahu and Ehud Barak – served in this very unit and eagerly mention the fact time and again.

References

Almog, Oz 1997: *Ha-tzabar – dyokan* (The Sabra – a profile), Tel Aviv: Am Oved.

Arian, Asher, Talmud, Ilan, and Hermann, Tamar 1988: *National Security and Public Opinion in Israel*, Boulder, CO: Westview Press.

Arkin, Williams, and Dobrofsky, Lynne R. 1978: 'Military socialization and masculinity', *Journal of Social Issues* 34, (1), 1978.

Aronoff, Myron J. 1989: *Israeli Visions and Divisions*, New Brunswick, N.J.: Transaction Books.

Azarya, Victor 1983: 'Israeli armed forces', in M. Janowitz and S.D. Westbrood (eds.), *Civic Education in the Military*, vol. 2, pp. 99–127, California: Sage.

Badinter, Elisabeth 1995: *On Masculine Identity*, New York: Columbia University Press.

Barrett, Frank J. 1996: 'The organizational construction of hegemonic masculinity: the case of the U.S. navy', *Gender, Work, and Organization*, vol. 3, no. 3, pp. 129–42.

Ben-Ari, Eyal 1998: *Mastering Soldiers: Conflict, Emotions and the Enemy in an Israeli Military Unit*, Oxford: Berghahn Books.

Ben-Ari, Eyal (forthcoming): 'Tests of soldierhood, trials of manhood: Military service and male ideals in Israel', in: Daniel Maman, Zeev Rosenhek and Eyal Ben-Ari (eds.), *Military, State and Society in Israel: Theoretical and Comparative Perspectives*, New Brunswick, N.J.: Transaction Books.

Biale, David 1992: 'Zionism as an erotic revolution', in: H. Eilberg-Schwartz (ed.), *People of the Body: Jews and Judaism from an Embodied Perspective*, pp. 281–308, New York: State University of New York Press.

Boyarin, Daniel 1997a: 'Masada or Yavneh? Gender and the arts of Jewish resistance', in: Boyarin, D., and Boyarin, J. (eds.), *Jews and Other Differences: The New Jewish Cultural Studies*, pp. 306–29, Berkeley: University of California Press.

Boyarin, Daniel 1997b: *Unheroic Conduct: The Rise of Heterosexuality and the Invention of the Jewish Man*, Berkeley: University of California Press.

Connell, R.W. 1995: *Masculinities*, Cambridge: Polity Press.

Davis, Judith 1995: 'The Bar Mitzvah balabusta: Mother's role in the family's rite of passage', in: Maurie Sacks (ed.), *Active Voices: Women in Jewish Culture*, pp. 125–41, Urbana: University of Illinois Press.

Devilbiss, M.C. 1994: 'Best-kept secrets: A comparison of gays and women in the United States armed forces', in: W.J. Scott and S.C. Stanley (eds.), *Gays and Lesbians in the Military: Issues, Concerns and Contrasts*, pp. 135–48, New York: Aldone de Gruyter.

Gilmore, David D. 1990: *Manhood in the Making: Cultural Concepts of Masculinity*, New Haven: Yale University Press.

Izraeli, Dafna N. 1997: 'Gendering military service in Israel Defence Forces', *Israel Social Science Research* 12 (1), 129–66.

Kaplan, Danny 1999: *David, yonatan, ve-chayalim acherim: Al zehut, gavriyut, ve-miniyut be-yechidot kraviyot be-tzahal* ('David, Jonathan and other soldiers: Identity, masculinity, and sexuality in combat units in the Israeli army'), Tel-Aviv: Ha-Kibbutz Ha-Meuchad (Hebrew).

Kaplan, Danny, and Ben-Ari, Eyal 2000: 'Brothers and others in arms: Managing gay identity in combat units of the Israeli army', *Journal of Contemporary Ethnography*, 29 (4).

Katz, Elihu 1997: 'Behavioral and Phenomenological Jewishness', in: Charles S. Liebman and Elihu Katz (eds.), *The Jewishness of Israelis: Responses to the Guttman Report*, pp. 71–83. Albany: State University of New York Press.

Lieblich, Amia 1989: *Transition to Adulthood during Military Service: The Israeli Case*, Albany: State University of New York Press.

Liebman, Charles S., and Don-Yehiya, Eliezer 1983: *Civil Religion in Israel: Tradi-*

tional Judaism and Political Culture in the Jewish State, Berkeley: University of California Press.

Liebman, Charles S. 1997: 'Cultural conflict in Israeli society', in: Charles S. Liebman and Elihu Katz (eds.), *The Jewishness of Israelis: Responses to the Guttman Report*, pp. 103–18, Albany: State University of New York Press.

Lomsky-Feder, Edna 1992: 'Youth in the shadow of war – war in the light of youth: Life stories of Israeli veterans', in: Wim Meeus et al. (eds.), *Adolescence, Careers and Culture*, pp. 393–408, The Hague: De Gruyter.

Lomsky-Feder, Edna and Ben-Ari, Eyal (forthcoming): 'The "people in uniform" to "different uniforms for the people": Diversity, professionalism and minority groups in Israel', in: J. Soeters and J. Van Der Meulen (eds.), *Managing Diversity in the Armed Forces*, Purdve University Press.

Lukes, Steven 1975: 'Political ritual and social integration', *Sociology* 9, 289–308.

Mayseless, Ofra, and Gal, Reuven 1990: *Motivatzya shel banim le-sharet be-tzahal: Noar israeli be-tkufat ha-intifada* ('Male youth motivation to serve in the IDF: Israeli youth during the Intifada'), Zichron Yaakov: Israeli Institute for Military Studies (in Hebrew).

Mosse, L. George 1990: *Fallen Soldiers: Reshaping the Memory of World Wars*, Oxford: Oxford University Press.

Orr, Emda, Liran, Edna, and Meyer, Joachim 1986: 'Compulsory military service as a challenge and a threat: Attitudes of Israeli twelfth graders towards conscription', *Israel Social Science Research*, 4 (2), 5–20.

Roper, M., and Tosh, J. 1991: 'Introduction: Historians and the politics of masculinity', in: M. Roper and J. Tosh (eds.), *Manful Assertions*, pp. 1–24, London: Routledge.

Rubinstein, Amnon 1977: *Le-hyot am chofshi* ('To be a free people'), Jerusalem: Schoken (in Hebrew).

Segal, David R, Gade, Paul A., and Johnson, Edgar M. 1993: 'Homosexuals in Western armed forces', *Society* 31, (1), 37–42.

Sion, Liora 1997: *Dimuyey gavriyut etzel lochamim: Ha-sherut be-chativot chel raglim ke-tekes ma'avar me-na'arut le-bagrut* ('Images of manhood among combat soldiers: Military service in the Israeli infantry as a rite of initiation from youth to adulthood'), Shaine Working Papers, no. 3. Jerusalem: Hebrew University (in Hebrew).

Van Gennep, Arnold 1909/1966: *The Rites of Passage*, London: Routledge and Kegan Paul.

PART II

Male Fictions:

Narratives, Images and Icons

Reading 'Wiles of Women' Stories as Fictions of Masculinity

Afsaneh Najmabadi

'Wiles of women' stories – *makr-i zanan, kayd al-nisa'* – constitute a very important literary genre in Islamicate cultures.[1] These stories may form an independent cycle of tales, such as the *Sandbadnamah* and the *Tutinamah*,[2] be integrated in a larger story cycle, such as many stories told within (and including) the frame story of *The Thousand and One Nights*, or circulate as oral folk tales.[3] They also appear in other forms of classical writing: for instance, as morality tales told within the genre of advice books.[4] With the advent of print and the emergence of the novel and short stories, this genre may be considered as no longer centrally implicated in the production of contemporary notions of gender in Islamicate cultures. Yet, not only do they continue to circulate in the oral story-telling tradition, but they have attracted the attention of literary critics interested in promoting a shift in contemporary notions of gender which continue to construct guile as an essentially female characteristic.[5]

At the core of these stories is a notion of insatiable female heterosexual desire. It is the insatiability of this desire that drives the narrative unfolding of these tales: women cheating on their husbands, fooling other figures of patriarchal authority, committing crimes of all kinds, tricks of all sorts in search of more and an ever bigger phallus. Or as Malti-Douglas has put it in the case of *The Thousand and One Nights*, it is 'the adultery of the royal wives, which [is] the initial principle of disorder in the medieval text [that begins the chain of disorders].'[6] As Adrienne Rich suggested in her classic essay of 1980, however, the notion of an insatiable female heterosexual desire can be read as the fear of male redundancy, rather than as a realistic hypothesis about female sexuality: 'It seems more probable that men really fear not that they will have women's sexual appetites forced on them or that women want to smother and devour them, but that women could be indifferent to them altogether.'[7]

The reading possibility I will pursue in this essay is a different one.[8] It is to read these tales as cultural fictions equivalent to the Oedipus story in Freud's narrative. Abdelwahab Bouhdiba has suggested the Jawdar story from *The Thousand and One Nights* as the cultural equivalent of the Oedipus story for Arabo-Islamic culture.[9] I am suggesting that it is not any single story but a whole genre of stories centred on the theme of woman's insatiable heterosexuality and guile – to which the man is forever subjected and from which he needs perpetually to escape – which works in a similar way to the Oedipus story. As much as to plot, I want to draw attention to the work of *repetition of plot* in so many stories that circulate in a culture. The Oedipus story in Freudian psychoanalysis works to produce a particular script for 'the founding distinction of [our] culture': that is, 'sexual difference'.[10] Despite the universalist claims of modern psychoanalysis, the power of this fiction can, as many critics have argued, best be appreciated within its own cultural historical context. The working of the Oedipus story in psychoanalytic narrative is dependent, among other things, on particular kinship, marital and child-rearing practices of modern Euro-American cultures. Yet the larger insights provided by Freud's theory – that femininity and masculinity are cultural productions, rather than natural attributes; that they are performances and enactments that never fully achieve their ultimate aims, and thus continually depend on repetition and revisitation; and that there is always an excess, a surplus of meaning, that cannot be fully accessed and displayed even by the omniscient analyst – do offer us useful approaches for other places and times.

It is this approach that I am interested in bringing to a reading of 'wiles of women' stories. Though what we know of pre-nineteenth-century kinship and marital relations and child-rearing practices in Middle Eastern societies remains sketchy and speculative,[11] we can safely say that sons, like daughters, grew up in a 'women's world'. By this I mean not necessarily a physically segregated space (which would have been affordable to rather a small fraction of the population), but a social space created through female socializing practices. Even in urban lower class or peasant households, the common family space became a female space during the day while men were at work or in the fields. It became a male space when they returned and female members withdrew to the kitchen or corners of rooms. More importantly, the female social space extended to neighbours and to alleys, a socializing space occupied by women of a neighbourhood in daytime. It extended beyond that to women's festivities, to the public baths (the women's hour or day off), and to the women's section of the mosque. These spaces were all open to the son up to the 'age of recognition' – a pre-puberty age somewhere around eight or nine which constituted the beginning of a transition for sons. This transition was marked by a scene of expulsion, by exclusion of the son from these hitherto accessible women's spaces; in fact, importantly, it took shape through *repeated* acts of exclusion, most often starting with the women's baths and gradually, over a number of years, extending to women's festivities and the mosque. The full transition to the world of men was thus a gradual process.[12] The expulsion from the baths happened often at the taunting instigation of other women who would chastise the mother for having brought a 'man' to a women's space with such telling remarks as, 'Why don't you bring his father along next time?'[13] The women may have felt under the 'wrong' gaze of the growing boy, may have imagined his penis larger and/or erect, may have felt the 'wrong' touch or even a pinch of the flesh in the baths. Significantly for the boy, the process of expulsion is marked by a sense of betrayal by *other-than-mother-women* who have instigated his exit. But since his mother, however, has to go along with it, she becomes complicit in this betrayal. Both mothers and other-than-mother-women are stock figures of betrayal and of complicity in plotting against men in 'wiles of women' stories.

The grown-up man may later recall this moment of loss, of expulsion in many ways. In a similar cultural context, the Tunisian sociologist, Abdelwahab Bouhdiba, has written about it in these terms:

It would be enough for the young man to make some thoughtless gesture or say something out of place for the manageress to come up to the boy's mother and say: 'Your son has grown up, don't bring him with you any more.' What Arabo-Muslim [man] has not been excluded from the world of naked women in this way? What Arabo-Muslim [man] does not remember so much naked [female] flesh and so many ambiguous sensations? Who does not remember the incident by which this world of [female] nakedness suddenly became forbidden? We have been given more than a memory. One could not stop himself pinching that big, hanging breast that had obsessed him. Another was banned for being too hairy, for having too large a penis, buttocks that protruded too much, a displaced organ . . . For a boy the hammam is the place where one discovers the anatomy of other and from which one is expelled once the discovery takes place.[14]

The memory of the lost mother's world, and in particular the women's baths, gets recalled, for instance, in those artistic representations which depict strange islands populated by naked women,[15] and in narratives of paradise populated by countless female beauties.[16] As Bouhdiba has argued, as the transition from 'an exclusive "maternalism" to a "paternalism"' takes shape, the mother's world becomes a dream-aura, 'an idealized past . . . enveloped in fantasies', with the infantile, the feminine, the playful and the fanciful becoming condensed.[17] 'The most mature man,' Bouhdiba continues, 'the most masculine, will never miss an occasion to re-create, to restore, or to rediscover the uterine milieu – whether through memory, mimic, dream or imagination.'[18]

The experience of expulsion from the world of women is above all an experience of a lost sight, lost vision. Having entered the world of men, the boy's gaze becomes subjected to *ahkam-i nigah*, rules of looking. Not only is the unlimited fullness, the plentitude of sight lost, but the limited occasions in which the man may gain the sight of a woman's body become structured by laws of the father, to ensure that these occasions do not become moments of re-enactment of fullness of sight, moments of imaginary reunion with the world of mother. The ever-present danger of losing the son to the ecstasy of immersion in the world of the mother is thus kept in check by rules of looking.[19] Not only do these rules forbid a man to look at any part of a woman's body with the *intent* of pleasure, but he is forbidden to cast a gaze even under circumstances that may be potentially conducive to engendering pleasure.[20] Sighting itself is thought of as magically powerful and hazardous. Should a transgression of rules of looking occur, the transgressor may fall madly in love, facing abjection (like Shaykh San'an), or else madness (like Majnun).[21]

In such cultural contexts, boyhood is a transitional, intermediate state.[22] The boy, initially part of the women's world, is marked to exit that world to the world of men. He is treated as a temporary being in the women's world. As he grows up, he is sometimes pulled back by his mother, who knows that she will finally have to push him out.[23] He is treated as an 'other' by women, who will, for instance, joke about his genitals. Entering the world of men obligates the boy to prove that he has indeed left any mark of his previous world behind. To become a man, he has to prove that he has outgrown his originary contamination with womanliness, has ended his in-between-ness, through denouncing the women's world, at times through becoming contemptuous of it or even hostile towards it. A boy becomes a man by repudiation, by disavowal of femininity.[24]

Upon the expulsion from the world of women, the young boy faces challenges of entry into the domain of the father. Commonly at this stage, fear of rape is cultivated in young children.[25] In fact, fear of rape is cultivated in both young girls and young boys, and works to produce control and self-policing, control of one's sexuality to preserve presumed bodily integrity. But whereas the fear of rape in girls controls them largely spatially – don't go to men's quarters, including streets, stay close to mother and women – it works differently for boys and becomes a highly conflicted ritual of manhood. To become a man, a young boy must join the world of men, the domain of the father. Yet that means entering the realm of sexual danger, the possibility of being an object of desire for adult men. The *shahid* of Islamo-Persian poetry (the young man as witness to God's beauty) becomes a haunting witness to the passage of the boy into manhood. Through his expulsion from the world of women, the young man is projected as a heterosexually desiring subject who must thus become external to the world of women. Yet he enters the world of men celebrated as the most desired figure of male homoeroticism. The challenge of manhood is the production of a heteronormative sexuality within the domain of a male homosociality that is always already marked by homoeroticism and is forever under the threat of eroticization. The world of the father turns out to be an ambivalent, if not dangerous, zone. This fearful ambivalence contributes to engendering a desire to return to the world of the women, to the presumed safety of the domain of the mother (imagined as a lost paradise). To become a man, the boy needs to fight off this desire for return and to enact repeatedly his disassociation from the feminine.[26]

If production of adult masculinity in this cultural context is marked by the inter-related workings of repudiation of the feminine and disavowal of desire for the world of mother, as I have so far argued, how do literary texts, and in particular the genre known as wiles of women stories, participate in this cultural production?

To begin with, we have the body of literature, in particular philosophical allegories, in which all-male utopias are constructed. Fedwa Malti-Douglas, in her ground-breaking work, *Woman's Body, Woman's Word: Gender and Discourse in Arabo-Islamic Writing*, in chapters titled 'Flight from the female body: Ibn Tufayl's male utopia' and 'Sexual geography, asexual philosophy', has analysed a number of these male utopias.[27] Her focus is to explicate the deep-seated misogyny of these texts in their common preoccupation with producing a world of men free of any female presence; the narrative drive is provided by 'the flight from sex, the female, and corporeality'.[28] Concluding her analysis of two versions of the story of Salaman and Absal, she writes, 'Both Salaman and Absal stories represent flights from the female, whose existence can only threaten to destroy the harmony of a male-centered universe. In one case, the woman is the object of love who, nevertheless, must be ultimately destroyed. In the other case, the woman is the pursuer who never attains her quarry. She is also destroyed.'[29]

Though I agree with much of her analysis, I would shift that focus somewhat by arguing that the general misogyny and 'flight from the female' that she has so eloquently analysed are consequential effects of a prior work in these texts: namely, the narrative labour to produce a particular type of adult masculinity centred on male homosociality/sexuality. Furthermore, to read male sexual aversion to woman as 'flight from sex' precludes reading it as male homosexuality. Let me elaborate this distinction by a discussion of the Salaman and Absal story.[30]

This is a story about a near perfect king, whose only problem is that he lacks an heir. The problem is complicated by his lack of desire for women.[31] The *hakim* (wise consul) resolves the king's problem by taking his semen and placing it in 'a place other than a womb' which nonetheless after nine months produces a perfect male child, Salaman. He is entrusted to a wet-nurse, a most perfect and beautiful young woman, Absal. She devotes herself to his care until he reaches puberty, at which point her passionate love for him 'emerges' and she attempts to make him love her – a Zulaykha-type project at which she succeeds with no Yusuf-like resistance on Salaman's part. On the contrary, as prophesized by the wise *hakim* in his earlier diatribe against love of women, Salaman becomes virtually addicted to union with Absal and gives up on his interest in the affairs of the kingdom for which he has been prepared – a rather disastrous situation from his father's point of view.

No amount of scolding by his father or sermonizing by the *hakim* suffices to produce the desired effect of separating the young man from this mother-figure-turned-lover/beloved. To both men of authority, Salaman responds that his love for Absal is out of his control. He becomes so annoyed at their persistent scolding and advice that, with Absal, he leaves home and they settle on an island of paradisal bliss. The father, by looking into his all-seeing vase, finds out their whereabouts and proceeds to use yet another level of his magical powers to rid his son of his uncontrollable desire for Absal. A clear battle for control of the young man ensues: which world does he belong to and whose desire is he ruled by? His adult masculinity is crafted through the process of his father and the wise *hakim* using their every power to detach Salaman from the overwhelming desire for a woman that has overtaken him. Salaman must be wrenched out of the paradisal union/island in which he lives with Absal. His father casts a magic spell on the young man so that even as he continues to desire Absal intensely he can no longer satisfy that desire. He suffers like a thirsty person next to water yet incapable of drinking. Realizing that this state has been induced in him by his father, Salaman returns to him, only to be treated to a lecture about the character required of a man for rulership.

Thoroughly fed up with his father and his scoldings, and as a final act of suicidal frustration, Salaman ventures through fire with Absal. In a final act of paternal power, however, the king makes him survive the fire but lets Absal burn to death. As Jami puts it, Absal was the impurity on the gold of Salaman and, as the fire burns away the impurity, Salaman is left as pure gold. The message that women are the contamination of manhood could not be more explicitly stated. For the young man to become an adult man, worthy of inheriting the mantle of his father, he has to be radically detached from the motherly figure whose love has engulfed him. Salaman and Absal is a tale of decontamination. In Malti-Douglas's words, 'She [woman] must be excluded from the male universe of governing and ruling. Her presence soils this exclusive world of men.'[32]

The story does not end here. Salaman continues to grieve for Absal. The *hakim* at this point takes charge of the final stage of curing the young man of even the memory of the love of the mother/woman. He begins to tutor him and whenever Salaman shows any sign of distress for Absal, the *hakim* provides him with 'a liking of Absal', introducing him to the celestial figure of Venus, and thus slowly displacing his love for Absal – a process which sees the thorough 'transference' of love for an earthly object to a heavenly object. At the end of this Salaman is declared fit to become ruler.

As Malti-Douglas points out, the story of Salaman and Absal is usually analysed as a philosophical allegory. In place of this, she offers not a latent (*batini*) but a manifest (*zahiri*) gender-conscious reading of the text. The point, of course, is not to deny the allegorical possibilities of the tale, as explicated by philosophers and poets, enjoyed by many readers, or argued by contemporary commentators. But for the claimed allegorical meanings to work, something must be going on at the level of literal meaning production. What literal meaning is produced to make the allegorical meaning possible? And what does it tell us about notions of masculinity in the culture? How is adult manhood (equated with reason at the allegorical level) to be achieved? What in turn is the effect of equating reason with adult manhood? Reading the Salaman and Absal story with these questions in mind, it seems to me that it is a story about the immense difficulty imagined by the world of the fathers in the transition of a young boy to ultimate manhood. In that sense it is not simply one more misogynous tale that 'fantasizes a world without women'.[33] It is a tale about how a boy becomes a man. Malti-Douglas, for instance, asks why the text needs a wet-nurse at all. Like Hayy ibn Yaqzan, she argues, the child could have been reared by a gazelle. Her answer – 'Simply, the problematic "mother" is at work again'[34] – only hints at the larger problem the world of fathers faces. Read as a tale of transition from boyhood to manhood, **the presence of**

Absal is critical. For the tale to work as a tale of the trials and travails of that transition, the figure of mother/wet-nurse is the critical figure against whom detachment and disavowal needs to be performed. The figure of Absal is thus far from redundant or replaceable. Nor is she just a foil against which to build the misogyny of the text. Read as a fiction of masculinity, she is of central importance in making the process of transition to manhood all about a critical break with the love of the mother/wet-nurse/woman. The misogyny of the tale comes as a consequence of this drive. To (over)simplify, one could almost reverse the argument: it is not because the tale is misogynous that it calls for the death of the woman. Rather the reverse: it is because it needs to rid the young man of any and all association – seen as contamination – with the female that it needs to become a misogynous tale. Absal has to be there and has to be done away with.

In an important sense, the Salaman and Absal story differs from the more popular fictions of masculinity centred around the figure of 'the lustful step-mother'. Though there is some hint that Absal causes the young man's initial infatuation for her, throughout the story it is his desire for her that drives the narrative; nor does she engage in any beguiling activity. Quite the contrary: it is the king and his wise consul who are openly and frantically using all their powers – paternal, tutorly, psychological and magical – to wrench Salaman away from his object of desire. In more popular tales, the young man is not so will-lessly entrapped by the love of an older woman. Though in some stories (such as *Yusuf and Zulaykha*) the young man is tempted by the woman, but with far less strong or direct opposing intervention on the part of paternal authorities, he succeeds in resisting the temptation.[35] In these stories, the narrative is plotted around the active intriguing labour of a beguiling woman, 'the lustful step-mother'. This represents a displacement of desire through reversal. The step-mother – in Persian *namadari*, literally not-mother – as the reverse figure of mother, as un-mother, becomes the insatiably desiring woman. To distance and disavow one's desire for mother and 'the world of women', for which the not-mother metonymically stands, the plot is inverted, with the male protagonist becoming the object of desire of not-mother(s). It is not he who is longing to return to the world of women, it is not he who desires mother, but the lustful not-mother/step-mother who desires him. Yusuf-like, he is forever running away from the scene of seduction-temptation, rejecting and disavowing woman, thus proving his loyalty to the world of father, his suitability to join the world of men, attributing lust and guile to women. Yusuf's flight from the scene of seduction is one of most frequently depicted episodes in illustrated versions of the Yusuf and Zulaykha story.

This reversal provides the possibility for a masquerade. In the Salaman and Absal story, Salaman clearly constitutes 'an object of desire' for the *hakim* and the father. The two male figures are engaged throughout the text in a battle for winning Salaman away from Absal. When the location of desiring subject in the text is shifted onto the woman, male homoeroticism can masquerade as the desire of a woman for a young man. That is, the occurrence of heterosexual desire in the text could be generative of homoeroticism for (presumed male) writers, readers and listeners of these stories – a point to which I will return. In this sense, 'the flight from women' and its many repetitions stand in for disavowal of not only the man's desire to return to the world of women, but also implicitly of his own desirability in the eyes of other men.

If the Oedipus story, as read by Freud, provided a suitable plot for analysing the psychodynamics of masculinity in late nineteenth-century urban middle class European culture, with a nucleated family at the centre of the drama, the plot of the youth and the lustful step-mother has performed a similar function in the Islamo-Iranian context. Whereas the Oedipus story works to produce heterosocial heteronormativity,[36] the core plot of wiles of women tales – seduction–temptation–resistance–rejection–vengeance – I am suggesting circulates to produce a heteronormative male homosociality – an ideal state in which a man could love and even desire another man without having sex with him, while having sex with a woman (to beget children) without loving or perhaps even desiring her. These tales constitute working-through texts for the disavowal of femininity, repudiation of the world of women, while distancing from male homoeroticism to construct a homosocial adult manhood. The repeated circulation of the wiles of women stories in so many genres and contexts produces an Irano-Islamic plot of masculinity. But since this is a state never fully achieved or achievable, its repetition is a necessity. The masculine state is always threatened by the desire of even the 'most masculine man' to return to the maternal, argues Bouhdiba and, I would add, by being the object of desire for other men.[37]

The core plot of these stories brings together three central elements that Malti-Douglas has analysed at length in the case of *The Thousand and One Nights*, namely, woman's sexuality, woman's speech and woman's guile.[38] At its simplest, the plot involves a young man, an older and often more powerful woman (mother/step-mother) who is infatuated with the young man and attempts to seduce him. His refusal to submit to her sexual advances (often he is tempted, yet loyalty to other men prompts his rejection) then makes him the target of her intrigues, which often arise from her insidious speech. It would be all too easy, of course, to expect a simple and uniform articulation of these elements in all such tales. To begin with the end, as far as the fate of the central female character is concerned, we have at least two diametrically opposed types of closure: at the one extreme, there is the presumably happy ending, the 'Queen Mother' syndrome, which is the fate of Shahrzad in *The Thousand and One Nights*, and at the other, there is the gory fate suffered by Kanizak at the end of the *Sandbadnamah*. Zulaykha's fate seems to fall between the two: she first suffers punishment and eventually is redeemed and rewarded by marriage and motherhood.[39]

What are these different endings about? Zulaykha's initial punishment and later redemption into a believer and a humble woman is rewarded by marriage to Yusuf. In my reading of these tales as productive of male homosociality, this closure becomes directed not so much to women – who ought to learn from Zulaykha's punishments to desist from seducing men. Rather, it becomes directed to men: reject the mother-world, its seductions and your desire for it; become a real man by proving your loyalty to other men; you will then be rewarded not only by power and wealth, but also by a different (from mother) kind of woman: a young subdued one moulded to and through your desire and your power. She will become your wife and the mother of your sons. Zulaykha thus emerges as an *incidental* prize of masculinity, next to prophethood and kingship which Yusuf also enjoys.

The reassuring closure of *The Thousand and One Nights* could also be revisited along the lines of this reading. Is it reassuring to women that avoidance of seduction and cheating, and being a wise narrating wife night after night, get rewarded with the prize of becoming queen mother? Let me probe this query, by first revisiting another paradox of the *Nights* that has been noted by a number of authors: the apparent incongruity between Shahrzad's persona – as good woman, healer, good lover, mother, powerful story-teller – and the highly misogynous content of the stories, many of which are in fact wiles of women stories, that she tells. How does one reconcile Shahrzad's telling of such misogynous tales with her own persona as the wise and knowledgeable woman who saves not only her own life but those of all other women? In my reading, this problem actually disappears as a paradox, since the very work of narrating those misogynous stories becomes part of her 'healing' work that Jerome Clinton has explored.[40] If we consider the effect of the repeated narrations of wiles of women stories to be productive of male homosociality, of instigation of the break from the world of women, and of the rejection of its seduction and pull on the man, then the figure of Shahrzad acquires a different significance. Shahrzad, the female narrator of some of the wiliest wiles of women tales, becomes self-implicated: the only safe woman is a complicit woman. A woman who narrates these 'healing' tales is enacting a plot of masculinity production.

Far from being the heroic female who saves herself and her kind through the power of her words, she turns out to be the vehicle for the production of male homosociality and is in this sense *the incidental woman*, comparable to Zulaykha in Jami's story. The reassuring ending now becomes reassuring in a different sense: the only safe woman for a man to marry is the complicit woman, the woman who repeatedly performs the healing narratives of women's wiles. Shahrzad's power of speech, her gift of being an unrivalled story-teller, in this reading, turns out to be yet another patriarchal ruse!

From this point of view, despite repeated attempts to reclaim Shahrzad as a feminist foremother for contemporary women writers and story-tellers, Shahrzad – the wise knowledgeable story-teller/healer contained and captured by the narrative closure as queen mother – seems an unsuitable character for feminist recuperation.[41] Nor can we turn to the slave girl Kanizak as a literary foremother. Though she defeats through her speech seven wise viziers, she is eventually defeated by the speech of the prince, and subsequently severely punished and turned into an outcast.

The *Sandbadnamah*'s frame story, different from that of *The Thousand and One Nights*, is closely linked to other wiles of women stories such as *Sudabah and Siyavush*, and *Yusuf and Zulaykha*.[42] Instead of the homosocial couple – the two brothers in *The Thousand and One Nights* – we have a much larger male homosocial group, composed of the king, the son, his tutor (Sandbad) and the seven wise men.[43] The prince, the only child of the age-ing king, shows no sign of being able to learn anything from his tutors. His road to knowledge is mysteriously blocked. He is eventually entrusted to Sandbad, the wisest *hakim* of the realm, who takes him away from the presumably distracting life of the king's palace and builds a special cubical space for himself and the son, a male homosocial space for *pir* and pupil, the ephebic space of knowledge transmission. This is incidentally similar to Firdawsi's account of Rustam taking Siyavush away for complete education of mind and body. The removal of the adolescent male from affinity with and proximity to the world of women seems to be a prerequisite for attainment of masculinity.

Sandbad is given six months for the education of the prince. He succeeds in his task, but the day before they are due to go back to the king, he foresees that if over the next seven days the prince speaks to anyone he will be in mortal danger. Sandbad is faced with a grave challenge: if he takes the young man back to his father and there he speaks a word, Sandbad will have knowingly endangered the prince's life. On the other hand, if he does not take him back to the king, Sandbad himself will be subject to punishment. Thus he instructs the prince to keep completely silent for seven days and in the meantime goes into hiding.

Upon returning to his father, the prince remains silent in front of the viziers and the king, no matter what they ask. Thinking he is perhaps awed by the seven wise viziers, and too embarrassed to speak out, they send him to the harem to chat with the women, the people of the veil (*ahl-i pardah*).

In contrast to the pure cubic space of the prince and his tutor – that space of knowledge production and transmission – is this female world of sexuality and intrigue. The son is entrusted to the care of the women of the king, re-entering their female homosocial space, thus becoming subject to Kanizak's seduction and later her trickery. The female figure is a slave girl – a concubine of the king – with the additional diminutive '-ak', emphasizing her double social and gender 'littleness'. This re-entry stages a trial – similar to that of Yusuf – a testing of the prince's manhood: can he resist Kanizak's sexual overtures, disavow his own erotic desirability (albeit through a heterosexual screen), and prove his loyalty to the world of the father? Has the wise hakim Sandbad's regime of knowledge production/transmission succeeded in changing the prince from a transitional being – an adolescent boy contaminated by femininity – into a man? Kanizak, we are told, has been in love with the prince for a long time, ever since upon the death of the prince's mother she took care of him and gave him motherly love. In fact, it is because of this original caring relationship that the king agrees that perhaps if she were given a chance to look after him again the prince might begin to speak. If the trauma of transition to manhood has silenced the prince, perhaps a brief return to the fold of womanhood may cure him. Ironically, he is sent back to the realm of women to acquire speech.

Kanizak takes the prince to her private chamber, tells him of her love and offers him her hand, saying that she will see to it that he becomes king. Here apparently is the first trick she successfully plays on him. Though remaining silent in front of his father and seven wise men, the prince is tricked into speech (thus endangering his life) and asks her how she can accomplish that? She will poison the king, she responds, and will put the crown of the land on his head. The prince of course refuses such transgressions as unworthy of manly *futuvvat*.[44] Yet he is caught in a dilemma: if he says a word of this event to his father in the next seven days, it will further endanger his life, he contemplates. He will wait till these days of ill omen are over. He leaves the chamber of Kanizak. Kanizak, realizing she has made a mistake that may cost her dearly, goes to the king and plays Zulaykha: she tears her clothes, messes up her hair, scratches her face, accuses the prince of transgression towards her, and asks for his punishment.

The king consults with his seven viziers who try to dissuade him from such punishment by telling him stories about women's guiles and about the ill consequences of rash judgements. This begins the cycle of the story-telling for the next seven days. The success of the first vizier in stopping the king from any punishment of the son brings Kanizak back to tell her story and for the next few days each side uses various tales to move the king from one state of mind to the other. Kanizak has no accomplice, such as the sister in *The Thousand and One Nights* or the town women in *Yusuf and Zulaykha*. She narrates alone, but she does not have the monopoly of story-telling. Kanizak is engaged in a narration contest with the seven wise men – and almost wins. The wise men produce stories about women's wiles and the ill consequences of the king listening to a diminutive slave woman, rushing into executing his son, and the futility of regret after the act. Kanizak counters their stories with stories of the guiles of men, the ill consequences of kings not being just and not carrying out the proper punishment for a severe crime. Each day she narrates one story, the effect of which is to neutralize the work of the two stories told by one of the wise viziers. Does this work as evidence that a beguiling woman's tongue is doubly powerful? Or is it that the woman's share of narrative time/textual space is half that of a man?

The contest itself is thematically significant: guile against guile, justice against patience and consideration. Unlike Shahrzad, Kanizak's stories are not stories of women's guiles to please and heal a murderous king; they are not working-through tales. Hers are told to save her own neck through the ruse of pretending innocence and seeking vengeance.

Significantly, she defeats narratively the seven wise men, but then the seven-day curse is over and the prince can now tell his story, which has more weight than all those told by a mere slave girl! His speech removes 'the dust of hatred' that she has brought between father and son, and makes the king's 'mirror-like mind . . . shine with love and kindness' – a scene of male homosocial bonding between father and son, between mature adult and young maturing manhood.

Not only does it take the collective work of seven men to help the young male to manhood – a theme shared with the Salaman and Absal story – but the final fate of the female transgressor is determined through an all-male dialogue and interchange. The king asks his viziers what punishment is suitable for this crime. As if in recognition of the visuality of sexual desire, one suggests to take out her *jahanbin* (literally 'world-seeing', and also meaning insightful and wise) eyes, because if the eye does not see, the heart cannot desire. As if to emphasize that transgression resides in the domains of speech and action rather than in desire itself, a second vizier suggests cutting out her tongue so that she cannot tell lies. A third suggests cutting off her legs so that she cannot take a wrong step. A fourth proposes to take out her heart so that she does not follow her passion. The punishments thus inscribe the qualities that are considered culturally unfeminine: a seeing eye, a speaking tongue, a moving leg, and a desiring heart. At this point Kanizak interrupts their consultation by telling yet another story, pleading that her heart be spared: she can tolerate any punishment, she pleads, except for her heart being opened up.

Following Kanizak's story-telling and plea for mercy, in a repetition of the previous order of speech, the king turns to his son and asks what punishment he would recommend. The prince suggests, and evidently his suggestion is followed through, that they cut off her hair, blacken her face, seat her on a donkey and show her around the town, with the *munadi* telling every one that this is what happens to a person who is treacherous to her master.[45]

That Kanizak uses the power of female speech to serve her own cause and almost wins is perhaps related to the closure of this cycle – in contrast to that of *The Thousand and One Nights*. Whereas Shahrzad succeeds in her literary ruse, heals the king and saves her own life and becomes queen mother, Kanizak fails in the end; she loses the battle of narration and becomes subject to severe punishment.

The *Sandbadnamah* and other wiles of women stories are of course highly complex tales and I do not wish to suggest that the reading I have so far offered – focusing on the sense in which they promote heteronormative male homosociality – exhausts their dense sedimented content. In fact, I would like to conclude this essay by considering a 'counter-labour' that these tales perform, that is, their simultaneous work in engendering male homoerotic desire. As I have already hinted, the heteronormativity of Irano-Islamic male homosociality is a highly tenuous and threatened project. It is continuously threatened with being destabilized by the homoeroticism that remains contiguous with it. Let us recall that at the centre of these stories is the intense, insatiable, heterosexual desire of an older woman for a younger beautiful man.[46] As Dick Davis has suggested in reference to the Yusuf story, according to one reading the desire circulating in and out of the text is only seemingly about heteroeroticism. The heterosexual desire in the text, 'the desire for a supremely beautiful young man', could be seen as productive of homoeroticism in the presumed male reader and expressive of the homosexual desire of the male poet. In the Yusuf story, for instance, Zulaykha can be understood as a rhetorical figure that produces intense male homoeroticism, as opposed to standing literally for the heterosexual desire of a woman.[47] The figure of Zulaykha, in other words, is a screen through whose desire the (male) reader comes to desire Yusuf. Not only does her love for Yusuf stand in for the sufi love for the divine, but it is a heteroerotic desire standing in for homoeroticism, not only between the sufi and the divine, but between the male poet and the presumed male reader of the text and the figure of Yusuf. Zulaykha mediates male homoerotic desire by circulating within the text and between the reader's and the poet's fantasies.

The suggestion that the narrative work of female heterosexual desire is to produce homosexual desire between the male reader and the male object of desire is supported in some of these stories by explicit use of descriptive categories drawn from male homoeroticism, such as describing the male object of desire of the female protagonist as a *javan-i nawkhat* (a youth with a hint of recently growing moustache), or even more explicitly as *amrad-i bajamal* (beautiful young desired male).[48] The female figure thus works as a screen in a different sense as well: her femaleness masquerades. It protects against male homoeroticism threatening heteronormative presumptions and demands of the larger culture. It allows homoeroticism to masquerade itself through heterosexuality.

Davis's suggestion recalls Sedgwick's proposition concerning erotic triangles in English literature.[49] Expanding on the work of René Girard, Sedgwick argues that in the triangles where two males are rivals for one female, the homosocial bond between males is constructed through the 'trafficking' female figure. Though my argument here is deeply indebted to Sedgwick's work, it is an extra-textual move. Whereas Sedgwick is concerned with erotic triangles within a text, Davis's suggestion prompts me to speculate about erotic desire circulating within imaginary triangles between figures-in-the-text/author-writer-storyteller/readers-listeners. The triangle of desire suggested by Davis between a male reader, Yusuf (standing for a desired male) and the figure of Zulaykha is but one. For female readers/listeners, a different kind of triangle could be imagined between them, Zulaykha and Yusuf: through the heteroerotic rivalry for Yusuf that the story evokes, a homosocial bond between them becomes formed – similar to the female homosocial bond constructed within the text of the story between Zulaykha and the 'women of the town'. In fact this scene, perhaps the most-frequently depicted episode in illustrated copies of the story, condenses many of the themes that have preoccupied this paper. Textually (and visually, in the case of painted representations), the beautiful young Yusuf is the single male figure in this scene, object of the gaze of an all-female desiring group. The intense desire that is invoked in this scene for Yusuf – the women of the town all desire him so intensely as to lose sense and cut their own hands instead of the fruit they are holding – can certainly be imagined to be productive of the kind of homoerotic desire in a male reader/listener/viewer that Davis has suggested. However, it is at the same time productive of a sense of solidarity for Zulaykha's predicament not only in the women of the town (changing their initial contempt for her to one of rivalrous empathy) but in an imagined female reader/listener/viewer. It is in this scene that Yusuf appeals to God in the same words with which he appealed to him when first approached by Zulaykha, needing divine help to ward off his own desire for her. Against the female bond established among the women, he turns to a male figure of divinity. Their collective heteroerotic desire for him can be warded off by recalling his desire for God.

Several Sedgwickian triangles exist within the text of the Yusuf story as well. First, there is the triangle of desire between Yusuf, 'Aziz of Egypt and Zulaykha – is 'Aziz angry at Zulaykha for betraying him or for coming between him and Yusuf? After all, in a number of versions, he is said to have purchased Yusuf for himself; Zulaykha's virginity at the time of her marriage to Yusuf is explained by 'Aziz's lack of desire for women. Then, there is the triangle established between Yusuf, God and Zulaykha. At various points in the seduction scenes of that story there is repeated displacement of Yusuf's heterosexual desire for Zulaykha on to his (homosocial) desire for God. A third triangle of desire is that between Yusuf, his father Ya'qub and Zulaykha. Yusuf is the intense object of desire for both Ya'qub and Zulaykha. His separation from the first sets the scene for entrance of the second. Towards the end of the story, his reunion with Ya'qub and his beloved brother, Benjamin, has temporal and narrative precedence over meeting Zulaykha again and the final recuperation/marriage episode.[50]

A more thorough study of the desires circulating in and constructed by tales of this genre would provide us with critical insights about the construction of masculinity and femininity in Islamicate cultures. In this essay, I have considered the ways in which 'wiles of women' stories work to produce masculinity within a cultural context structured by the homosociality of daily practices. Perhaps the twentieth-century decline of the popularity of these stories is related to the changing cultural context, to the heterosocialization of urban space and emergence of more nucleated urban families.[51] It may also speak of the emergence of women's individuality as an aspect of modern femininity in which individual initiative and movement into previously masculine domains has become more crucial than homosocial plotting with other women within the female world.

If these observations have any ground for persuasion, then the whole project of producing feminist versions of these tales becomes a problematic enterprise. Rather, for such an endeavour one may need to explore whether different 'working-through' texts for the production of new masculinities and femininities have been called forth by the socio-cultural transformations of modernity.

Notes

Acknowledgements: An earlier version of this essay benefited greatly from comments and criticism in my graduate seminar on 'Gender and sexuality in Islamicate cultures', Columbia University, Spring 1998. My thanks to Aneesa Sen, Judy Chen, Alessandra Ciucci and Elisabeth Eaves. It was presented as a paper at the second biennal Iranian Studies Conference, 22-24 May 1998, and at the Ohio State University conference, 'Sex, lies, and Persian texts', 8 April 1999. On both occasions I received invaluable comments and criticism. A different version of the essay, with a focus on women's readings of these stories, will appear in a special issue of *Iranian Studies* on 'The uses of guile: literary and historical moments'. I wish to thank Jerome Clinton, Kathryn Babayan, Farzaneh Milani, Dick Davis, Margaret Mills and Emma Sinclair-Webb for critical observations and suggestions on earlier drafts. Finally, my very special thanks to Houman Sarshar for numerous productive provocations that have shaped many of the arguments in this paper.

1. The term 'Islamicate' was introduced by Marshall G. S. Hodgson. Whereas 'Islamic', he suggested, can be understood as '"of or pertaining to" Islam *in the proper, the religious, sense* . . . "Islamicate" would refer not directly to the religion, Islam, itself, but to the social and cultural complex historically associated with Islam and the Muslims, both among Muslims themselves and even when found among non-Muslims.' Marshall G. S. Hodgson, *The Venture of Islam: Conscience and History in a World Civilization: The Classical Age of Islam* (Chicago: University of Chicago Press, 1974), vol. 1, p. 59: emphasis in original.

2. The most important among these tales is perhaps the *Sandbadnamah*, which is considered to be the 'mother-tale' of many related ones of this genre, such as the *Tutinamah*, and the *Bakhtiarnamah*. The most intact Persian version of the *Sandbadnamah*, by Muhammad al-Zahiri al-Samarqandi (12th c. AD), is now available in several editions. The version edited by Ahmed Ateş (Istanbul: Milli Eğitim Basımevi, 1948) contains an Arabic and a Turkish version of the *Sandbadnamah*. An early English translation of the *Sandbadnamah* was published in 1884 in Glasgow ('privately printed'), *The Book of Sindibad*, translated by W. A. Clouston. The French translation is from al-Zahiri's version, *Le livre des sept vizirs*, translated by Dejan Bogdanovic (Paris: Sindbad, 1975). For a discussion of the origins of the *Sandbadnamah*, see B. E. Perry, 'The origin of the Book of Sindbad', *Fabula: Journal of Folktale Studies*, 3 (1959): 1–94.

3. See, for instance, *Qissah'ha-yi Mashdi Galin Khanum* (Stories of Mashdi Galin Khanum), collected by L. P. Elwell-Sutton: Ulrich Marzolph, Azar Amirhosseini-Nithammer & Sayyid Ahmad Vakilian (eds.) (Tehran: Nashr-i markaz, 1995); Monia Hejaiej, *Behind Closed Doors: Women's Oral Narratives in Tunis* (New Brunswick: Rutgers University Press, 1996).

4. See, for instance, Nizam al-Mulk, *The Book of Government or Rules for Kings*,

translated by Hubert Darke (London: Routledge & Kegan Paul, 1978), chapter xlii, pp. 179–87, 'On the subject of those who wear the veil'. See also Denise Spellberg, 'Nizam al-Mulk's manipulation of tradition: 'A'isha and the role of women in the Islamic government', *The Muslim World*, vol. lxxviii, no. 2 (April 1988): pp. 111–17.

5. For one example of such efforts, see Katayun Mazdapur, *Rivayati digar az Dalilah-'i muhtallah va makr-i zanan* (An/other narrative of the beguiling Dalilah and the guile of women) (Tehran, Rawshangaran, 1995). For further discussion of these points, see Karen Merguerian and Afsaneh Najmabadi, 'Zulaykha and Yusuf: whose "best story"?' *International Journal of Middle East Studies*, 29 (1997): 485–508.

6. Fedwa Malti-Douglas, 'Shahrazad feminist', pp. 40–55, in Richard G. Hovannisian, George Sabagh & Fedwa Malti-Douglas (eds.), *The Thousand and One Nights in Arabic Literature and Society* (Cambridge: Cambridge University Press, 1997), quote from p. 44.

7. Adrienne Rich, 'Compulsory heterosexuality and lesbian experience', reprinted in Henry Alcove, Michèle Aina Barale & David M. Halperin (eds.),*The Lesbian and Gay Studies Reader* (New York: Routledge, 1993), pp. 227–54: quote from p. 236. For a feminist critical reading of the notion of female sexual insatiability in Islamicate cultures, see Fatna Sabbah, *Woman in the Muslim Unconscious* (New York: Pergamon Press, 1984).

8. To emphasize the nature of my endeavour here, the interpretations of wiles of women stories in this essay are not claimed as the only ways of reading these texts; nor do I claim them as a better, much less more scholarly or authentic, interpretation than other readings of the same works. I offer them as a reading *possibility* that within the larger context of the Islamicate cultural world may open up one layer of meaning sedimented in the works under discussion. Since literary texts are sedimented layers of meaning, my venture here is perhaps more akin to that of the archaeologist who uncovers one particular layer of artifacts and from that level of sedimentation *speculates* on a possible world of social meaning.

9. Abdelwahab Bouhdiba, 'The child and the mother in Arab-Muslim society', in L. Carl Brown & Norman Itzkowitz (eds.), *Psychological Dimensions of Near Eastern Studies* (Princeton: The Darwin Press, 1977), pp. 126–41, and *idem, Sexuality in Islam*, translated by Alan Sheridan (London: Routledge & Kegan Paul, 1985), pp. 225–30.

10. Teresa de Lauretis, *Alice Doesn't: Feminism, Semiotics, Cinema* (Bloomington: Indiana University Press, 1984), p. 145.

11. For European observations about kinship relations and child-rearing practices in nineteenth- and early-twentieth-century Iran, see Carla Serena, *Hommes et Choses en Perse* (Paris, 1883); Eustache De Lorey and Douglas Sladen, *Queer Things About Persia* (London: Eveleigh Nash, 1907); M. E. Hume-Griffith, *Behind the Veil in Persian and Turkish Arabia* (London: Seeley and Co., 1909); Ella C. Sykes, *Persia and its People* (London: Methuen & Co., 1910). For more

recent surveys, see Erika Freidl, 'Child rearing in modern Persia', pp. 412–16, in *Encyclopaedia Iranica*, edited by Ehsan Yarshater (Costa Mesa, CA: Mazda Publishers, 1992); Erika Freidl, *Children of Deh Koh: Young Life in an Iranian Village* (Syracuse: Syracuse University Press, 1997); and Elizabeth Warnock Fernea (ed.), *Children in the Muslim Middle East* (Austin: University of Texas Press, 1995).

12. See Muhammad 'Ali Islami Nudushan, *Ruzha* (Tehran, 1984), vol. 1. Islami Nudushan, for instance, stopped going to the baths with his mother around the age of eight, while he continued to go to the women's section of the mosque for a number of years more and shared a bed with his mother. He would also be allowed to attend the women's section of weddings and socialize with women in summer outings until he was almost fourteen.

13. For one fictive account, see Ja'far Shahri, *Shikar-i talkh* (Tehran: Amir Kabir, 1968), pp. 302-8. See also, Moris Farhi's account: chapter 11 of this book.

14. Bouhdiba, *Sexuality in Islam*, p. 168. The Tunisian/French movie, *Halfaouine, Boy of the Terrace* (Ferid Boughedir, 1990) also powerfully depicts a young boy's conflicting desires of wanting to become a 'man' and yet not wanting to leave the pleasure of going to the baths with his mother. See also Naguib Mahfouz's *Palace Walk*, translated by William M. Hutchins and Olive E. Kenny (New York: Doubleday, 1990), pp. 67–9, for the son's memory of expulsion from his mother's bed. I would like to thank Rachel Goldenberg for bringing this passage to my attention. See also Miriam Cooke, 'Naguib Mahfouz, men, and the Egyptian underworld', pp. 96–120, in Peter F. Murphy (ed.), *Fictions of Masculinity: Crossing Cultures, Crossing Sexualities* (New York: New York University Press, 1994). For a discussion of some of these issues within a contemporary Egyptian context, see Mervat Hatem, 'Toward the study of the psychodynamics of mothering and gender in Egyptian families', *International Journal of Middle East Studies* 19: 3 (August 1987): 287–306. See also Bouhdiba, 'The child and the mother'. For a discussion of some of these issues within the context of modern masculinities, see Deniz Kandiyoti, 'The paradoxes of masculinity: some thoughts on segregated societies', chapter 12 in Andrea Cornwall and Nancy Lindisfarne (eds.), *Dislocating Masculinity: Comparative Ethnographies* (London: Routledge, 1994).

15. See 'The queen of the island of Waq-waq enthroned with her naked women courtiers', (Isfahan, 1632 AD), reproduced in B. W. Robinson, *Persian Paintings in the John Rylands Library* (London: Sotheby Parke Bernet Publications, 1980), p. 302. For other scenes of imaginary naked female creatures, see p. 76, 'Iskandar Sultan peeping at the sirens as they sport by a lake', and p. 150, female tree dwellers from Qazvini's *'Aja'ib al-Makhluqat*, in Basil Gray, *Persian Painting* (Skira, 1961); see also 'Iskandar and the Sirens', in Colnaghi's catalogue of *Persian and Mughal Art*, plate 14xxi, p. 108, and 'Ladies' bath' ('Abd al-Razzaq, 1850) in the same catalogue, plate 79, p. 163. That the women's baths remains a site of 'primal fantasy' is confirmed by the poetry that frames the painting. The verses are addressed to, 'O you who have not seen

beauty / except for when you look into the mirror', and sing praise of the beloved as a body of cypress stature with 'grass in the middle', her hennaed hands and feet making her analogous to the sun. Though the poet and the painter would have seen the bath scene only as young boys, they envisaged it now as adult men. Having gone to the hammam with their mothers, they now re-enter it in the realm of poetic and visual fantasy as a lover imagining his beloved there. In fact it seems that most Persian paintings of naked females depict *groups* of naked women, reminiscent of the women's baths, rather than individual woman. See Nimat Allam Hamdy, 'The development of nude female drawing in Persian Islamic painting', pp. 430–38, in Atken des VII. Internationalen Kongresses Für Iranische Kunst und Archäologie, München, 7–10 September 1976 (Berlin: Dietrich Reimer Verlag, 1979). The one famous exception is Khusraw's sighting of Shirin, from Nizami's *Khusraw and Shirin*, yet she is also bathing in this scene, often alone, but sometimes accompanied by her maids. The popularity of depiction of this scene perhaps speaks to the same desire: of peeping back in fantasy into the world of naked bathing female flesh. In other words, the voyeuristic vision that incited the original narrative of the verbal text may also be at work in the popularity of the choice of subject from the text for illuminations. See Farzaneh Milani, 'The politics and poetics of sex-segregation: nannies and gypsies as figures of mediation in Persian literature', paper presented at the international workshop, 'Discourses on gender/gendered discourses in the Middle East', Ben-Gurion University of the Negev, 6–7 January 1997.

16. See Fatima Mernissi, *Women in Moslim Paradise* (New Delhi: Kali for Women, 1986). One may even be tempted to see the male prerogative and desire to create a domestic space populated by numerous wives and concubines as an attempt to re-enact in later years the memory of the all-female world to which the single male patriarch has the exclusive right to enter.

17. Bouhdiba, 'The child and the mother', p. 131.

18. Ibid., p. 133.

19. On this issue, see Mohamad Tavakoli-Targhi, 'Zani bud, Zani nabud: bazkhwani-i *Vujub-i niqab* va *Mafasid-i sufur*', in *Nimeye Digar*, 14 (Spring 1991): 77–110. See also Farzaneh Milani, *Veils and Words: The Emerging Voices of Iranian Women Writers* (Syracuse: Syracuse University Press, 1992), pp. 24–6; Bouhdiba, *Sexuality in Islam*, pp. 37–9; and Fatima Mernissi, *Beyond the Veil: Male-Female Dynamics in a Modern Muslim Society* (Cambridge, MA: Schenkman, 1975), p. 83.

20. See Sayyid Mahmud 'Alavi Tabrizi, *Al-hijab va al-Islam* (Mashhad: Firuzian, 1956); Murtiza Mutahhari, *Mas'alah-'i hijab* (Qum: Sadra, nd), pp. 164–66. In a related move these rules constitute the whole of a woman's body, that upon which a man is forbidden to set eyes, as the potential site for inciting disorder. See in this connection Sabbah, *Woman in the Muslim Unconscious*.

21. See Milani, 'The politics and poetics of sex-segregation'. One could argue that the popular belief that sighting the genitals of a woman may cause

blindness is also a related fear of transgression of the rules of looking.

22. For boys as 'transitional beings', in yet a different cultural context, see Gilbert H. Herdt, *The Sambia: Ritual and Gender in New Guinea* (New York: Holt, Rinehart, and Winston, 1987).

23. On the complicity between the son and the mother, both excluded from the world of men, and the value of this relationship to the mother – the son acting as 'a precious antenna', as messenger, as an agent of mother in the world of father – see Bouhdiba, 'The child and the mother', p. 132.

24. Ibid., p. 130.

25. I am not discussing here the fact of rape and its consequences on the development of adolescents in this context. Neither is this to deny the reality of rape or to mark it only as a fear.

26. It is tempting to conclude that it is this fear of a lapse into the world of the mother that also informs the marking as effeminate of an adult man who refuses heterosexuality. In this sense, homophobia within the world of men can be considered as a fear of collective lapse. Thus the flight from women becomes simultaneously productive of misogyny and homophobia.

27. Fedwa Malti-Douglas, *Woman's Body, Woman's Word: Gender and Discourse in Arabo-Islamic Writing* (Princeton: Princeton University Press, 1991).

28. Ibid., p. 7.

29. Ibid., p. 105.

30. For a detailed summary and analysis of Hunayn ibn Ishaq's version of this story, see Malti-Douglas, *Woman's Body*, pp. 96–105. In the following, I have used Jami's version, which is very close to that of Hunayn's. The variations are important for a more thorough comparative study, but for my present purposes I have largely ignored them. For Jami's version I have used Nur al-Din 'Abd al-Rahman Jami, *Masnavi-yi Salaman va Absal*, edited by Zahra Muhajiri (Tehran: Nashr-i nay, 1997).

31. Malti-Douglas reads this aversion as hatred of women but, at least in Jami's version, the king displays no such hatred. I am more inclined to read it as a veiled reference to the king's homosexuality. It is his wise consul, the *hakim*, who translates the king's lack of desire for women – a desire unfortunately necessary for begetting a child – into open misogyny by expounding at length about the ill consequences of desiring women, socializing and having intercourse with them.

32. Malti-Douglas, *Woman's Body*, p. 100.

33. Ibid., 99.

34. Ibid., p. 100.

35. For a discussion of these paternal interventions to rescue Yusuf from a desire for Zulaykha and 'women of the town', see Merguerian and Najmabadi, 'Zulaykha and Yusuf'.

36. For 'the heteronormativizing power of Oedipus', see Daniel Boyarin, *Unheroic*

Conduct: The Rise of Heterosexuality and the Invention of the Jewish Man (Berkeley: University of California Press, 1997), pp. 211–12.

37. By focusing on the work of guiles of women stories in the production of Iranian masculinity, I do not mean to suggest that these stories are the only site, or even a privileged site, for that production. The production of Iranian masculinity takes place through many cultural domains and sites of performance, literary and otherwise. My focus is on the beguiling woman as a cultural fiction, the work that this fiction performs, and what makes it possible.

38. See Malti-Douglas, *Woman's Body*, chapter 1.

39. For a plot summary and analysis of *The Thousand and One Nights*, see chapter 1 of Malti-Douglas, *Woman's Body*. For that of Yusuf and Zulaykha, see ibid., chapter 2; and Merguerian and Najmabadi, 'Zulaykha and Yusuf'.

40. Jerome W. Clinton, 'Madness and cure in the Thousand and One Nights', in Ruth B. Bottigheiner (ed.), *Fairy Tales and Society: Illusion, Allusion, and Paradigm* (Philadelphia: University of Pennsylvania, 1986), pp. 35–51.

41. See, in this connection, Malti-Douglas, 'Shahrazad feminist'. See also Milani, *Veils and Words*, pp. 178–80.

42. See Jerome W. Clinton, 'Joseph, Yusuf, Siyavosh: Reflections on the Chaste Youth as Culture Hero', in *Edebiyat* 1: 1 (1987): 90–102.

43. In Yusuf and Zulaykha, the male homosocial group is composed of Yusuf, his father Ya'qub, 'Aziz of Egypt and God.

44. On *futuvvat/futuwwa*, see *The Encyclopaedia of Islam* (Leiden, E. J. Brill, 1965), entries by C. Cahen and F. Taeschner, pp. 961–69.

45. The expressions for these punishments continue to be used for marking transgressively shameful behaviour, especially for women, in today's Persian: *gis-buridah*, a woman with cut-off hair; *ru-siyah*, a person with a charred/shamed face; *rusvay-i kuy va bazar*, someone whose dishonour is publicly known.

46. For a useful anthology, see John D. Yohannan, *Joseph and Potiphar's Wife in World Literature: An Anthology of the Story of the Chaste Youth and the Lustful Stepmother* (New York: New Directions, 1968).

47. Dick Davis, correspondence with author, 9 November 1997.

48. See, for instance, the fifth story in the *Sandbadnamah* cycle, p. 50, in Muhammad ibn Ali Zahiri Samarqandi, *Kitab-i Sandbadnamah*, edited by Ja'far Shi'ar (Tehran: Khavar and Ibn Sina, 1954).

49. Eve Sedgwick, *Between Men: English Literature and Male Homosocial Desire* (New York: Columbia University Press, 1985).

50. I am grateful to Houman Sarshar for opening up these questions through numerous delightful conversations. As he observed, the Yusuf story is clearly very rich for 'queer' readings, beyond the scope of the present essay.

51. See in this connection Bouhdiba, 'The child and the mother', p. 137.

SEVEN

Male Homosexuality in Modern Arabic Literature

Frédéric Lagrange

This essay explores the various representations of male homosexuality in contemporary Arabic fiction and, in light of its pervasiveness in classical Arabic cultural production, also addresses the issue of why the subject has become relatively obscured in recent times.[1] This necessarily limited perspective is conceived as a contribution to a wider discussion of the evolution of different concepts that could be grouped under the single label of 'homosexuality' in Arab societies, to form part of a sociology of Arab homosexualities that is still badly needed.[2] Looking at the representation of social relations and intimacy in cultural production is certainly one of the easiest steps in this endeavour, for we should hope to find in it both an echo of some Arab societies' views on male-male relationships, and an indication of the ways in which conceptions are evolving.

To what extent is modern literature qualified to inform us on the construction of male identity and the sexual customs and taboos attached to it in contemporary Arab societies? If we were to ask such a question of classical Arabo-Islamic cultural production, answers should be sought both in writings pertaining to the religious domain, that inform on the *nomos* and obliquely on the frequency of its transgression, and in what was termed *adab*, the cultural baggage of the learned man. In classical *adab*, artistic prose and pleasant verses dealing with frivolous or serious matters help define the sexual ethics of the multi-faceted *Homo Islamicus*. As for the modern period, sociology, journalism or even direct and personal experience should help us. But for reasons that have to be analysed, not only are the margins of the sexual ethic, such as homosexuality, severely underdocumented in sociological essays, hushed or harshly attacked in the press, but literature itself proves much less eager to discuss pleasure in all its manifestations than it did until the first half of the nineteenth century. While in the last decade 'gender studies' has started to enter the field of Islamic studies on the ethics of sexuality and eroticism,[3] hasty psychoanalytic studies of Arab societies have flourished,[4] particularly among French-speaking Maghriban writers, and these occasionally deal with homosexuality.[5] One of the most troubling flaws of works aiming to analyse Arab attitudes toward love is the portrayal of the Arab Muslim man as an unchanging monad, unaffected by time and place, unaltered from sixth-century Hijaz to twentieth-century Morocco or Iraq.

The mere fact that there are scarce mentions of homosexuality in contemporary literature, when compared with classical poetry or *adab* literature, could be interpreted in itself as an indication of huge transformations in Arab men's relations with their bodies and desires. This is not to say that homoeroticism or themes connected to gender confusion have disappeared from the public scene in the twentieth century: the Egyptian commercial cinema, as well as present-day farcical plays, have always relied on transvestism as a comic tool, while discreet homosexual allusions have often been in evidence.[6] As for the artistically more ambitious films of Youssef Chahine[7] or Yusri Nasrallah,[8] they are filled with homoerotic winks. Coarser allusions were to be found in turn-of-the-century vaudeville plays or Qaragoz spectacles, as Egyptian society retailed some of its pre-modern tolerance for homosexuality. This is shown in the 78 rpm records of Ahmad Fahim al-Far ('the Rat'), a comedian who sold many discs, among which one finds items such as *Khenaqat el-khawal ma'a l-mara* (a quarrel between the queer and the shrew) and *Ganazet el-khawal* (the queer's funeral),[9] probably pearls of 'queer' humour that could under no circumstances be distributed with such titles in present-day Egypt.

As in all culture-related subjects, words are controversial and much debate has been aroused by the use of the term 'homosexuality' in relation to classical, pre-modern and present Arab societies. It is probable that the widespread modern Arabic term *shudhudh jinsi* (sexual deviation), and more politically correct but still seldom found terms such as *mithliyya jinsiyya* (homosexuality) or *junusiyya*,[10] coincide with the Western notion of homosexuality. However, these are recent terms and have no equivalent in local dialects,[11] which retain more of a traditional conception of the universe, nor in classical (that is, medieval) Arabic. The classical language has no word to cover the wide spectrum of same-sex attraction and sexuality and, as until recent times in the Western world, does not consider homosexuality as an *identity*. It categorizes different types of homosexual *acts*: some, like the love of handsome adolescents, are considered expectable from man as a sin-prone creature; others, such as the wish to be sexually dominated by another man, are considered pathological. The language uses such specialized terms as *liwat* (anal sex), *luti* (active sodomite who prefers boys over women, not being concerned with what modern terminology would qualify as occasional bisexuality), *ma'bun* (passive sodomite), *mukhannath* (effeminate passive sodomite), *mu'ajir* (passive male prostitute), *dabb* (active sodomite who likes raping his victims in their sleep regardless of their age), *musahiqa* (lesbian), and so on. Some acts are unheard of in medieval literature or jurisprudence, like fellatio, which has no status in *fiqh*. It is therefore natural that research on same-sex eroticism in Arabic literature has been very cautious with its vocabulary, preferring in place of 'homosexuality' terms such as 'homoeroticism' or 'same-sex sexuality', or even *homosensualité* (Malik Chebel).

Four basic notions concerning homoeroticism in classical and modern Arab societies as reflected in *fiqh* (jurisprudence), poetry and prose literature should be stressed.

The first is the acknowledgement in Arabo-Islamic culture of male beauty, even in the eye of other males, and the belief in this beauty's ability to cause *fitna* (disorder). The Quran depicts the effect of the Prophet Yusuf's (Joseph) beauty on the women of Egypt who were so seized by his charm that, on merely seeing him, they cut their hands with the knives they had been given to peel fruit and exclaimed, 'He is not a human being, he must be a noble angel.' Yusuf was subsequently to become a rhetorical trope for the depiction of young male beauty in love poetry. The Quranic paradise is filled with elements to which men are naturally inclined, but are only lawful in the Other Life: wine that 'causes no intoxication' (56:19), served by lads 'eternally young' and who, 'if looked at, seem like scattered pearls' (56:17, 76:19). But in sharp contrast to classical literature and tales such as those found in *The Thousand and One Nights*, the male body's ability to seduce is seldom alluded to in modern literature. One seldom finds any sensuality in the portrayal of a male character. An exception to this is found in the depiction of Gharib in Yusuf Idris's short story, *Hadithat sharaf* (A matter of honour, 1957):

> At night [Gharib] couldn't stand sleeping at home and would prefer the tall heap of hay in the village barn. He used to bury himself in it, fondling his thighs and his chest, talking with his friends about girls, of whom they knew nothing [. . .] There was something strange in Gharib, absent in most men. Perhaps it was his excess of manliness, or something else . . . A woman simply had to see his neck, or the string of his

saroual when he was working to start choking as if she had seen a naked man.[12]

Secondly, a consequence of the recognition of male beauty is that a grown man's appreciation of a handsome adolescent's charms is a natural tendency (admitted even by theologians such as Imam Ibn Hanbal, d. 855). This natural appreciation of beauty possibly leads to desire, according to one's tastes, but a desire which has to be resisted. The cardinal sin, in the field of *fiqh*, lies in its realization as a sexual practice. *Fiqh* does not know of sexual identities, and only deals with acts. The *hadith* of the Prophet, as reported in al-Nuwayri's *al-Nihaya*,[13] is particularly clear and harsh concerning sodomy between men: the active (*al-faʿil*) and the passive (*al-mafʿul bihi*) are to be put to death. But jurists have tended to moderate the severity of the *hadd* (legal sanction) according to the perpetrators' social status. Ibn Hazm went as far as to reduce the bachelor's punishment to ten lashes. Most of those legal dispositions have certainly remained mainly theoretical through the centuries, and it should be noted that pre-modern and colonial Egypt had no law against homosexuality, in spite of the insistence of the British that there should be one.[14]

Society as reflected in *adab*, whether poetry or collections of anecdotes, is more tolerant than the sacred law concerning this expected passage from desire to fulfilment; and homosexual intercourse, when occurring between a grown man and one who is submitted to his authority because of his age or his social status, finds its place in the social hierarchy and never jeopardizes the order. There is a similarity between *zina* (illicit intercourse with a woman) and *liwat* (equally illicit anal intercourse with a male one dominates). Everett K. Rowson's work[15] shows how the medieval categorization of vices does not create a list of same-sex relationship 'vices', but rather occasions when man's natural right of dominating his subordinates (women, boys, slaves of both sexes) is illicitly exerted in the sexual field. Although this conception, which could be labelled 'Mediterranean', is still much alive in popular milieus, it is quite under-reflected in modern literature, which adopts a slightly more 'Westernized' construction of the male gender and tends to 'denounce' what are felt as symptoms pertaining to 'underdevelopment'. It should be noted that the Arab press is simultaneously engaged in stigmatizing Western corruption.

Thirdly, man-to-man attraction is not a mere sexual phenomenon, but is also susceptible to being related to love, to passion and its subsequent dangers. Authors concerned with the effects of passion on man – such as Ibn Hazm (d. 1064) in his *Tawq al-hamama* (The dove's necklace) or Ibn al-

Jawzi (d. 1201) in his *Dhamm al-hawa* (Condemnation of passion) – do not deal with man-to-man passions any differently than with heterosexual ones, and depict similar consequences. When preparing his *Masari' al-'ushshaq*, an anthology of anecdotes (at least on first-level reading) about lovers stricken by death over losing their beloved, al-Sarraj (d. 1106) also includes male-to-male tragic love affairs scattered among heterosexual anecdotes. In contrast, while homosexual intercourse is referred to in modern literature, homosexual passion is almost totally absent.[16]

Fourthly, whereas attraction of men to boys is a commonplace of classical poetry and prose literature, the attraction of a grown man to another grown man is often underplayed, and is rarely acknowledged except in *mujun* (ribaldry) and *sukhf* (obscenity) related literature. Sexual intercourse, whether heterosexual or homosexual, does not take place between equals and necessarily involves the exercise of power. A bearded man's attraction to another adult male can only mean a desire for submission, which can be either concealed (thus providing proper material for *hija'*, lampoon) or apparent and flaunted: *khinath*, effeminacy, is the subject of many anecdotes that reveal pleasant transgressions of the norm, but never question it. A man expressing his idolization of the phallus is certainly admitting the loss of his own virility, for he relies on the other's tool instead of his own: as Ibn 'Abbad, reported by Tawhidi (d. 1010), bluntly puts it, 'Do not rely on a cock you find in someone else's pants. There is no cock but your own erect one: if you were to trust another one, it would betray you, shame you, bring scandal to your house and defame you.'[17] The upshot of this is that he indirectly confirms the dominance of the phallus.

Homoeroticism in the classical period is also to be found in works standing at the inner and outer limits of the classical notion of *adab* – for the *adib* (man of education) has the right to write and read about 'lower' subjects (*bstil, sukhf*) so as to rest his mind from seriousness, but the language used has to be that of *adab*. The *mujun* (ribaldry) version of chaste homoeroticism found in poetry was also to be found for instance in the famous treatise on erotology by the Maghriban mineralogist, Ahmad al-Tifashi (d.1253). Titled *Nuzhat al-albab fi ma la yujad fi kitab* (The promenade of hearts in what is to be found in no other book), the text is ripe with piquant and often hilarious anecdotes on the underworld of active and passive homosexuals, their argot, their classifications of the male organ according to shape and size, and their witty (often blasphemous) replies when scorned by heterosexuals or men of religion.[18] At the outer limits of *adab* lies 'popular' literature, such as the shadow plays that were widespread in Egypt in the Mamluk period. The only remnant of this type of production is a highly literary rendition of it by Ibn Daniyal (d. 1310) in three shadow plays, two of which – *Tayf al-khayal* (The imaginary shadow) and *Al-mutayyam wa-l-yutayyim* (The man stricken by passion and the little orphan/ the cause of passion) – expose a character's rowdy life, full of homosexual adventures, until final repentance and death. This image of homosexual attraction as a possible entrapment in a youth's formation is repeated in the many stories of *The Thousand and One Nights*, in which the pederast Maghriban shaykh chanting his love for the young fifteen-year-old hero represents nothing but a trap that should be avoided on the path of initiation to manhood.

But whether homoeroticism is to be found in its chaste and often symbolic versions, or on the contrary in its coarsest expression in amusing *nawadir*, it is in classical literature a pervasive phenomenon, whether connected to love or to condemnable ribaldry. If a tragic tone is to be found, it is because unrewarded love is tragic, never because of its homosexual nature. Classical literature expresses the confident view of man unchallenged in his domination over the other sex, in his rule over non-Muslim communities, and ultimately in his manhood. Even rare examples to the contrary, like Jahshaway's affirmation of his passivity, are panegyrics to the Arabo-Islamic penis.

Modern literature,[19] on the other hand, is often an expression of self-doubt, sometimes of self-hatred, and the Arab male's certainty of being at the centre of the universe has vanished. Politically, economically and culturally challenged, his power, thus his virility, cannot be exerted as it was in the age of certainties. The view of homosexuality could not remain unaffected by this major shift. The limited treatment of same-sex relationships in modern Arabic literature in contrast to classical literature is somewhat puzzling. Among the modern Arab novelists there is no Proust, Wilde or Gide whose works can be read in a 'gay' light,[20] let alone a Gore Vidal or David Leavitt whose works include openly gay content. Homosexual characters are scarce, although not necessarily depicted in derogatory terms. AIDS is unheard of and this aspect of the underworld of the great cities of the Arab world still generally remains ignored. Although the Arabic novel (if we accept Haykal's *Zaynab* as a starting point) emerged in a realist genre, striking was the absence of a whole aspect of realism: that of sentimental and erotic life. Perhaps because sexual desire, whether heterosexual, homosexual or undefined and unwilling to be defined, has to be so thoroughly concealed in Arab societies, it paradoxically cannot be restrained to special places or situations. As a result, desire is disseminated everywhere and at any time, even on the most unlikely occasions. There is a strong, almost palpable erotic and homoerotic tension obvious in such formal events as *mawlids*, as well as in daily life, on buses and other forms of public transport, in cinemas, even in the streets where gauging glances are exchanged. In the homosexual field, the non-existence (and impossibility) of a gay ghetto means that homosexual desire is to be found throughout the anonymous metropolises like Cairo and Beirut. But much of this atmosphere is suppressed, unseen or ignored in modern literature, although one can hardly imagine writers to be so blind as to miss it. The universal figure of the 'queen' is not alluded to, even humorously, in written works.

Allusions to homosexuality in modern literature can generally be seen as falling into three types: homosexuality may be represented as a typical aspect of traditional society, either to be denounced or simply neutrally described, and a secondary character may embody this conception; a homosexual character, whether central or secondary, is often represented as undergoing severe *malaise* and loss of self-worth, possibly leading to death or suicide; thirdly, homosexuality may be articulated in the traumatic relationship with the Other, usually the Western foreigner. But whether considered from a medical, psychoanalytic, pathological, traumatic, dramatic or symbolic viewpoint, homosexuality is never a matter of laughter (even derogatory laughter) or amusement. There is no happy homosexuality, or piquant anecdotes in modern literature, and there are hardly any indecent allusions. The most scabrous *nawadir* of classical literature can be read with pleasure and a smile, for they are narrated with an eagerness for wit, a grace and a frankness about the relationship with the body that transcends vulgarity. Al-Jahiz's (d. 868) introduction to the *Mufakharat al-jawari wa-l-ghilman* (Book of maids and lads) is a case in point. Amusement is seen as a most natural function of literature and the soul must be soothed with jest, for an excess of seriousness would burden it: 'some of those who flaunt piety and asceticism express embarrassment and revolt at the mention of vulva, penis and coitus. But such people are most often of little knowledge, devoid of elevation and dignity if only in this affectation of theirs.'

The queer of the hara *(popular quarter): symptom of an ill society?*

Homosexual attraction is seen by Taha Husayn in *al-Ayyam* as the coincidence between natural inclination and deprivation of the feminine element: a chapter in the third part of his fictional autobiography is significantly entitled, 'A consequence of the absence of women'.[21] But attraction felt for either females or males by the companions of the narrator (who refers to himself in the third person as *al-sabi*, the boy) in their years as Azhari students is also subtly and elegantly linked in this chapter to their literary preferences:

> They had read the poetry of Abu Nuwas and his fellows, and also the verses of early Umayyad and 'Udhri poets,[22] [. . .] and had subsequently followed their own tastes in such matters. The conservatives preferred the 'Udhri authors and their love poetry, whereas the modernists chose the love habits of the Abbasid times. They all created ideals of beauty according to their literary tastes, and addressed verses to their beloved. But whereas the conservatives had no choice but to forge utterly fictional ideals, for life had put a barrier between them and their 'belles', the modernists were more fortunate, as they could find outside or inside al-Azhar itself many pretty faces that provided them with real-life material for their poetic courtship. Some followed the path of Jamil and Kuthayyir,[23] and their fate was that of total deprivation, while the others favoured Abu Nuwas's example; they were to suffer less deprivation and gain some measure of satisfaction.

Taha Husayn's innuendo never goes beyond his last sentence's humorous understatement. One of the blind boy's friends is 'nuwasi[24] in his poetry and in his tastes', and seems to find no trouble in making interesting acquaintances in the milieu of turn-of-the-century religious students. Taha Husayn's good taste, however, means that he declines to mention whether his friend's activities go any further than reciting amorous verses to his good-looking companions during private *majalis*, as the narrator mischievously describes their encounters, using with intended vagueness the same classical term poets used, for a *majlis*-session can be anything from a chaste exchange of burning verses to putting those verses into practice. But the friend's too obvious attitude soon results in embarrassment for the whole group when they discover a malignant hand has scribbled on a wall in the Abbasid Gallery of al-Azhar those (in)famous verses addressed by Abu Muhammad al-Yazidi to the ninth-century philologist, Abu 'Ubayda:

> May the prayer of God be upon Loth and his people
> O Abu 'Ubayda, and say amen, by God,
> For I see that you are without doubt their only remnant . . .[25]

As the *nuwasi* boy's companions chose to laugh the whole thing off, we are left to wonder whether Taha Husayn's apparently non-judgemental attitude to homosexuality reflects an almost pre-modern amusement towards a sexual peculiarity that bears no greater consequence than that of a literary choice, a traditional neutrality mildly moderated by the adult writer's opinion by 1950 that male-to-male attraction derives from the strict separation of men and women in early twentieth-century society, or on the other hand whether such an attitude is simply a manifestation of this humanistic thinker's tolerance.

The first obviously homosexual *character* in a modern Arabic novel is probably the *ma'allem* Kersha in Egyptian novelist Nagib Mahfuz's *Zuqaq al-midaqq* (Midaq Alley, 1947). The author created this character with much fear of censorship at the time, but felt compelled to place him in the popular *hara* (quarter) for he 'wanted to present archetypes of all sorts of inhabitants of a popular dwelling, and this was a common archetype. The owners of coffee-shops were renowned for this thing, and rumour has it that the owner of the Fishawi[26] himself [was].'[27] The sixtyish coffee-shop owner of this novel unwisely invites his young and slightly too obvious lovers to a free glass of tea at his place, to the knowledge of the whole neighbourhood, until his crazed wife (and mother of five) decides to make a public scandal, sweeps her dazed 'co-spouse' out of the coffee-shop and insults her boy-loving husband before a company of amused customers. But when Shaykh Darwish, the cafe's local sufi, draws the moral of the scene, he simply declares, 'This is an old evil, that is called in English homosexuality, but it is not love. True love is for the Family of the Prophet.' Such a conclusion, which should not be mistaken for Mahfuz's view on homosexuality, does not seem far from the medieval mystical conception: if homosexuality is not true love, it is not because it is against nature but because true love is reserved for God. It should also be noticed that the character's use of the English tongue to define homosexuality makes it a phenomenon both widespread but so untalked of that even the common language remains mute when it comes to expressing it.

Other novels by Mahfuz portray homosexuals. In *al-Sukkariyya* (*Sugar Street*), the last part of the Cairo trilogy, published in 1957, the young and handsome Radwan uses his beauty to seduce an elderly Pasha and soon becomes a prominent figure in a right-wing monarchist party.[28] Although a mere archetype in Mahfuz's panorama of Egyptian youth in the 1940s, it is remarkable that the homosexual character is the only one that chooses the past and the aristocratic world of the Egypto-Ottoman condemned elite, almost as if to suggest that his sexual life were another remnant of *al-'ahd al-ba'id* (the ancien régime). Another notable character is Wahid, one of the heroes of *Malhamat al-harafish* (The epic of beggars, 1977),[29] a parable on the corrupting effect of power and the decay of time. Wahid restores the rule of the *hara* to the family of the founder of a dynasty of *fetewwat* (bullies), 'Ashur al-Nagi, who soon becomes intoxicated by his newly found power and turns into another tyrant, but cannot refrain from parading with his minions. When he dies of a stroke caused by his gluttony, he is denied burial at the side of his mythical ancestors. Mahfuz's vocabulary is significant as he evokes this character when asked about homosexuals in his works: 'One of the *harafish* is *afflicted* (*usiba*) with homosexuality, among other signs of his *moral decline*.'[30] There are, though, some differences between this portrayal of homosexuality as evidence of a decline in the exercise of power and, say, Abu Hayyan al-Tawhidi's attacks on the almighty Buyid vizier al-Sahib b. 'Abbad[31] for boasting his preference for boys over women in his prose as in his poetry. The medieval author does not condemn the love of boys *per se*, but the unnecessary, obscene and untimely display of this minor vice, a mere peccadillo when restricted to private circles. Mahfuz on the other hand qualifies it as an illness (using the verb *usiba*) and a sign of degeneration.

The homosexual in the contemporary Egyptian novel or short story is seldom a central figure, rather just another typical character of the popular *hara* of Cairo, who provides a vehicle for conveying stock-type representations of homosexuality which may in the process be endorsed, challenged or transmitted neutrally. Thus in Gamal al-Ghitani's novel *Waqa'i' harat al-Za'farani* (Incidents in Zafarani Alley),[32] we find Samir, a shy young man who secretly visits the Hammam al-Ahrar[33] at night to get sodomized by 'Ewes, the 'stallion' from Upper Egypt who works all night and can satisfy seven customers in a row. The social mingling that homosexual intercourse can entail is vividly evoked by Ghitani: when the hammam owner approaches 'Ewes in a café, it is in these terms that he lures him into accepting his job:

> He offered a position envied by many: he would become clean, eat meat everyday, and be accommodated if he agreed to stay all night at the hammam. He would receive a monthly salary like civil servants, and what he would have to perform would be both easy and pleasant. Every night he would meet many respectable effendis, some of them occupying high ranks in society and deciding the destiny of people. Some of them were famous, appeared on television and were interviewed on the radio, which made their coming to the hammam highly secret. If he really pleased them, they might give him a nice baksheesh. 'Ewes accepted at once.

Whereas the effendi clients of the hammam can fulfil the universal fantasy of sex with the virile worker,[34] whom they wouldn't address in normal circumstances, during the intercourse the young *fellah* can dominate those same figures of authority. When asked by a customer to insult him and hit him, he eagerly performs the act as a regular service, although with utter respect.[35] This hammam is not only a site where sexual rulings are transgressed, it is also the place where social boundaries are blurred, although only up to and at the moment of climax. It is remarkable then that 'Ewes, who has not been deterred from having intercourse with men on any moral grounds – for he had the active role – and who has found the necessary desire to perform as expected, finally fears that practising sex only with men might end up in him losing his attraction to females. When the insatiable Umm Yusuf approaches him, he finds himself unable to fantasize about her: 'As he stretched out on his bed and folded his garment into a pillow he put under his head, something began to oppress him, preventing him from fantasizing about Umm Yusuf. He couldn't make himself come. Did his work prevent him from having intercourse with women? He became alarmed. Would he after a while turn into one of his customers?' The next day those fears result in him being unable to satisfy the famous journalist who pays the owner of the hammam fantastic sums of money to ensure himself the exclusivity of the stallion's services. This enrages the owner, who has fed 'Ewes with expensive meat.

Frequency of male-male intercourse is certainly regarded as one of the indicators that allow a distinction to be drawn between socially tolerable – although undiscussed – sexual acts and a perceived flaw of character. The repetition of homosexual acts, even as the active partner, is felt by 'Ewes as jeopardizing of his virility: a mere amusement is turned into an illness, or something that could perhaps come to resemble an identity. Moreover, when a man sleeps often with other men, one cannot be sure of what really takes place between them both, and as Tawhidi mischievously said of Ibn 'Abbad: 'kam harbatin fi l-qawmi sarat ja'batan' ('many a spear has become a quiver').[36] But if there is something close to an identity, it can only be linked to the passive partner: 'Ewes is not so much afraid of becoming addicted to men, thus losing his desire for women, than of becoming one of 'them'.

As an extreme separation between sexes and deprivation of the feminine element leads to substitutive homosexual intercourse, writers are inclined to describe or denounce traditional society as a 'cause' of homosexuality. Prisons everywhere in the world also illustrate the need for any type of sexual gratification. Egyptian writers of the *adab al-sujun* (prison literature) genre have alluded to rapes occurring during incarceration, but only Ra'uf

Mus'ad, in *Baydat al-Na'ama* (The egg of the ostrich), has shown how the fulfilment of a bodily need can also lead to true affection. As his narrator evokes memories as a political prisoner during the Nasser era in the Western Desert oasis camp, where inmates could freely wander around the camp day and night and paradoxically enjoyed a certain liberty despite terrible conditions, he recalls how two inmates would gradually get closer to each other:

> Two smart eyes stare at him and share feelings he has not been able to disclose to anyone. Is it that half-cigarette they smoked together, cautiously trying to find their way in the dark? They don't trust each other yet. There's that fear of not reaching an understanding. It would mean a scandal that would isolate you from the mainstream [. . .] Small things begin to grow, each one caring about the other's daily life, creating a common oasis in those sands. Then feelings are progressively unveiled. It begins with the body declaring itself. Fingertips touch, hands feel hands, each one cares for the other's body. If the two are lucky, they won't be caught by curious and dubious glances. If they're lucky, they might even share a cell, put their mattresses alongside and be together in sleep, until one of them finally makes the long-delayed move.
>
> You would be wrong to think this is close to what happens with common-law inmates. There's no comparison. Here, the body is stripped of action, it becomes a mere condition. It doesn't secrete as much as it reveals. There is no active or passive partner. Only two equals, who equally desire to help the other 'get it out'.
>
> When the camps opened their gates, everyone went his own way, to a former or a new life, to his family, his wife (or got married and had kids). The guys might meet again afterwards (generally by chance) and talk about the present and the future. But each one of them knew that this bodily revelation had its special conditions, and even if one of them wanted to re-create them, he wouldn't find a favourable atmosphere to let the feeling grow. I only know of one exception to this rule.[37]

Although portraying himself as a womanizer in the novel, the narrator does not seem to exclude himself from an experience that goes further than substitutive homosexual intercourse and becomes substitutive homosexual *affection*. The individual subsequently represses a desire he has felt and fulfilled in particular conditions, but avoids his former lover and cannot help some embarrassment when meeting him (they speak of the present, not of the past) for they both know that in *favourable* conditions the dividing line between heterosexuality and homosexuality becomes very thin indeed, and the needs of the body might reveal some needs of the heart.

The individual's awakening

Since the modern Egyptian novel is preoccupied with society as a whole, and characters tend to be mere representative archetypes of society's diversity, there is little place for the individual, and reflections on their sexual preferences or identity are avoided. The cruelty with which the passive partner is treated can be alluded to when felt as an error of adolescence, as is the case in *al-Raqsa al-mubaha* (The permitted dance, 1981), a short story by Yahya al-Tahir 'Abdallah. A young boy caught being sodomized by a friend of his own age is killed by his father because of the shame brought upon the family, while the other boy, the 'top' (active partner) is expelled from the village. But the story is aimed primarily at stigmatizing rural society's savagery when openly confronted with sexual deviations that could simply be dealt with by means of a suitable punishment; it certainly does not legitimize the homosexual act. Yusuf Idris's (d. 1991) short story, *Abu al-rigal* (A leader of men, 1987), adopts a free indirect narrative style to convey the point of view of Sultan, the ageing leader of a group of gangsters who finds himself confronted with the unbearable fantasy of being the passive partner for one of his subordinates, *al-Tor* ('the Bull'). He remembers his village's effeminate miller, Shahin, who paid boys to fuck him in the corn fields, and dreams himself, in the ambiguous conclusion of the short story, of becoming another Shahin despite having spent a whole life as the most manly male of the community. The reader cannot clearly decide whether his fantasy of proposing himself to 'al-Tor' is realized or merely imagined, but the clear impression left by the story is that allowing oneself to be possessed by another male leads to general mockery and loss of social status.

Such a feeling is beautifully depicted in the work by Syrian playwright Sa'dallah Wannus (d. 1997), *Tuqus al-isharat wa-l-tahawwulat* (The rites of signs and transformations).[38] This is one of the finest studies of homosexual desire in modern Arabic literature. Set in an imaginary nineteenth-century Damascus, an effeminate male prostitute, Semsem, meets 'Abbas, who has already used his 'services'. 'Abbas is one of the Mufti's handymen and the city's most famous braggart. He is accompanied by his best friend, al-'Afsa, a feared swaggerer who affects disgust on seeing the catamite. Taking revenge on al-'Afsa for his contempt, Semsem reveals to 'Abbas that his best friend is really a closet passive homosexual and is dying of love for him. When confronted with this accusation, Al-'Afsa confesses his love to 'Abbas, who agrees to fuck him and swears to keep the whole affair secret. 'Abbas soon loses interest in al-'Afsa. In a key scene,[39] al-'Afsa appears before his love, 'burnt' by passion. He has shaven his face, affects effeminacy in his gestures and has turned into another Semsem: he has plucked his body hair, hoping he will be more desirable, for he has discovered in submissiveness 'a pleasure [he had] been longing for all [his] life'. He offers 'Abbas his moustache, folded in a handkerchief, for it is 'the most precious thing [he] owns'. As 'Abbas grows disgusted by such a transformation, al-'Afsa justifies what we might call his 'coming-out':

> Do not kill me, Abu Fahd! I have done this for you, for you only. And you know that what I have done has cost me much. In our country, it is like death, or worse than death. You pretend to be disgusted and angry, but you are in search of a false pretence to break what is between us. I won't be able to bear your leaving me. I can't stand it if after changing my constitution you throw me off. [. . .] My appearance is now that of my true self, I look like myself. Didn't you tell me you hated two-faced people? The only thing I've done has been to accord my appearance to my essence. I have nothing to hide any more. [. . .] Passion is what allowed me to appear to myself and to the world, and it gives me courage and life.

But 'Abbas denies that there could be any passion between men. When asked by al-'Afsa what was between the two of them, he answers:

> What was between us was mere desire, that dissipates after being completed. I took pleasure in mounting a man who was universally considered a swaggerer, watching him bend and make himself small between my legs. But now, what pleasure could I derive from mounting a stupid catamite?

While al-'Afsa goes on to boast about his love for 'Abbas around the city, his lover crudely rejects him, and he consequently commits suicide. This interesting analysis of the homosexual relationship in a traditional society shows it as non-committing for the active partner, although it paradoxically demands secrecy: 'Abbas can cope with Semsem's short allusion to the fact that they have had intercourse, as long as it flatters his virile strength, but will not bear it being repeated too often and cannot refrain from insulting him. He will certainly not tolerate al-'Afsa's revelation of his love for him either. As for the conception of homosexual desire in the play, it is represented as being entangled in a dialectical conflict between two opposite fantasies, one of virility and domination, and another of femininity and the need for affection. The active partner's desire is but a brief spark, aroused by forcing the other's virility to surrender into femininity, and dying as soon as it triumphs. 'Abbas and al-'Afsa's unrewarded love affair is a tragedy which, unlike in classical literature, is clearly portrayed as a consequence of homosexuality and not simply of unrewarded passion.

A short story by the journalist and playwright Muhammad Salmawi, *'Ashara tawila* (A game of backgammon)⁴⁰ presents an unusually encoded homosexual theme which insists, typically, on the loneliness and ephemeral quality attached to the homosexual act. On a superficial level, the story deals with a provincial young man who cannot stand his loneliness in Cairo and sets out on a rainy night for any kind of encounter:'[A]ny human being, woman, man, child, old man, whatever . . . He just needed the presence of somebody with him . . . before him . . . at his side.' He enters the coffee-house of al-Hagg Sultan, where the steaming breath of clients and smoke from the waterpipes provide the place with an eerie atmosphere, in which men seem to move as indistinct ghosts. Around each table he finds two men sitting face to face, playing *tawila* (backgammon), some being silently watched by others. He finally spots an isolated young man waiting in front of his *tawila*, and joins him without uttering a single word. He simply fetches the dice and starts playing. His hand is jerky at first, then touches the dice and the pieces with softness and a regular rhythm. Their game becomes so passionate that many spectators rally around them to watch. The dice fall on the ground, and one of the two men will have to bend to take them on the ground. Both stare at each other, then his fellow player bends and submissively presents the dice.

> He seized the dice with self-confidence noticed by the spectators, whereas the young man was staring at him in surrender. He went on shaking the dice faster and faster (*zalla yaruggu al-zahr fi sur'a mutazayida*), then threw them violently on the table *(thumma qadhafa bihi bi-quwwa 'ala al-tawila)* in front of his fellow player, as a cry rose from one of the spectators 'double-six' *(dush)*, then the game ended *(intahat al-'ashara)*. He calmly stood up and left the coffee shop silently, just as he had entered it.

The steamy coffee-shop is a metaphor for a Turkish bath, and its name obviously refers to the Hammam al-Sultan, one of Cairo's well-known homosexual meeting places in the old al-Husayn district. The couples 'playing' together clearly allude to ephemeral lovers, watched in action by excited voyeurs. It should be noted that *darb 'ashara* in Egyptian slang means 'to jerk off' and that the vocabulary used in the final sequence constantly plays on double-entendre (the verb *qadhafa* also means ejaculate; *dush* for double-six also means shower) until the climaxing conclusion. But although the key for a proper reading is given in the first lines of the text and the text doesn't make much sense if not read at this level, the whole story, so evasively homosexual, seems to be a mere intellectual game written for the 'happy few' able to decipher the allusions and recognize the subtext, in much the way that Cairo has its underworld homosexual slang (*sim al-kawanin*) known only to them.[41]

Hoda Barakat's much acclaimed first novel, *Hajar al-dahik* (*The Laughing Stone*),[42] set in Beirut during Lebanon's civil war, is probably the first and only Arabic novel with a male homosexual as main character, and ironically or significantly enough this bold step was taken by a woman. Khalil, whom the narrator observes with amorous and motherly eyes, does not realize at first that he is homosexual. He simply wonders why he is so obsessed with his visiting friend Nagi's hairy thighs, to the degree that he hardly listens to what his friend tells him. After Nagi's death, Khalil falls in silent and distant love with a militia man called Yusuf, a twenty-year-old bully who jokes with his buddies about girls, and embodies a type of virility the author ascribes to 'those who have torn off the gate of manhood' and rule people's everyday life, while older men take care of important matters. But 'those two manhoods have closed their gates before Khalil, he has remained alone in a narrow passage, on a demarcation line between two highly appealing regions, in a vegetative stillness close to submissive womanhood, when active manhoods that trigger off life's volcano are almost within reach.'[43] In a beautiful passage, Khalil wonders what he really wants from Yusuf, whose image blends, in Khalil's wild fantasy, with Prophet Yusuf as portrayed in the Quran, when he is seduced by the wife of Putiphar, Zulaykha in Islamic tradition:

> Give a single clear answer and you'll be relieved. But there was no clear answer, and no clear answer was convincing, and a clear and convincing answer was certainly not a relief . . . I desire Yusuf the way Zulaykha wanted to hold him back [. . .] All this suffering because Yusuf is handsome and because I'm a spouse of another gender. I am prompting him to commit all sorts of evil and corrupt deeds, then I slap my face in lamentation, gather my women and point at him, but they cannot see him, and only my hands are cut, while the oranges of my desire remain untouched, bright and round [. . .] Every time I touch his shirt I tear it

from behind. I have torn it thousands of times from behind, but he hasn't seen me, hasn't turned toward me, and his shirt is left untorn . . .[44]

Khalil has a longing for submission, unutterable, unrealizable, and his asexuality is in the end the exact opposite of action. Khalil is slowly realizing he is homosexual, but his sexual orientation is merely an element in his reluctance to choose virility. Being a non-man is hesitation and passivity, just as womanhood is doomed to mean passivity in a country at war, when civilization is put between brackets. Khalil is at the end of the novel offered a position by the *al-Akh* ('the Brother'), a war lord whom we understand will help him in exchange for a night spent with him. We are not told whether Khalil sleeps with the man or not, and whether he has his first physical homosexual experience with a physically and morally repulsive individual (although he seems to love Khalil sincerely) instead of the object of his desire. But 'the Brother' has the power to open for Khalil the gates to one of those 'manhoods' that seemed out of reach, specifically that of men who bear responsibilities.

In the last scene, Khalil has become a local bully himself, and he rapes his neighbour's daughter. Has he slept with 'the Brother' and got an eminent position in the party, possibly higher than 'the Brother' himself? Has he chosen another party? We are left to guess. But at last, Khalil has taken action. Confronted with the unbearable choice of being a victim or a torturer (for neutrality or isolation are impossible, as the novel shows), he has chosen the latter solution. And the end of hesitation is also the end of 'passive' sexuality: whether it be heterosexual or homosexual. Khalil is now able to impose his desire, he can rape a woman and can probably get as many Yusufs as he wishes. It should be stressed that Khalil has not 'become straight' in the last scene. The narrator does not equate homosexuality with passiveness; she equates *femininity* (under the circumstances of civil war) with passiveness. Khalil's renouncement of femininity is not necessarily a renouncement of his attraction to other men, but the narrator's beloved character has simply become, in the narrator's words, 'a man who laughs', but also a violent monster she fails to condemn.

Homosexual intercourse as a metaphor for the relationship with the West

One of the most abrasive accounts of traditional attitudes towards homosexual relationships, and also one of the best illustrations of the difference that exists in a society of separated sexes between man-to-man intercourse and a hypothetical 'homosexual identity', is to be found in Moroccan author Mohamed Choukri's fictionalized autobiography, *al-Khubz al-ḥafi* (*For Bread Alone*).[45] But this rare intrusion of pornography in an Arabic novel certainly doesn't aim at arousing the reader. Rather, it is distinctly unsettling when read in the context of the narrator's material and moral misery. Three consecutive scenes, set in the Tangiers of the early 1950s,[46] oppose the sixteen-year-old narrator, whom poverty has turned into a marginal character, to homosexuals trying or succeeding in taking advantage of him. The first man, a young Moroccan, spots him in the railway station as he unsuccessfully tries to work as a baggage holder, sits next to him and offers him food, a sip of wine and a cigarette. But when he later proposes to him that he sleep over at his place, the narrator finds that, 'His eyes are not innocent. To hell with this kind of generosity!' He declines the offer, adding to himself that he is not angry with the man for he has at least 'put the birds of his stomach to silence'. Then an old Spaniard driving a car stops besides him and invites him for a ride that ends in the suburbs.

> We were driving towards the suburbs. He's queer (*ḥassas*), there's no doubt about that. [. . .] He softly fingers my crotch. The real ride was about to begin. He slowly unbuttons my pants, switches on the rooflight and leans over me. His breath warms it. He licks it, then swallows half of it. His mouth was going back and forth, and he gave me a hard on. I didn't dare stare at him as he said: 'Bravo, bravo. Macho!'
>
> [. . .] in order to come faster, I fantasized I was raping Assia in Tetouan. I came in his mouth. He hummed with pleasure, like an animal. He took a handkerchief and wiped off his mouth, dripping with my semen. His face was red, eyes bulging, lips drooping.
>
> I crossed my arms on my chest as if nothing had happened. There's plenty of women. Why should one be queer (*luti*),[47] I thought?

After the old man gives him fifty pesetas, the narrator realizes: 'My "thing" can earn money and help me live as well. And it can also derive pleasure from this [. . .] This is the way one turns into a hustler.'

In a third scene, the narrator is forced to sleep in a stable also used as a shady hotel, and hardly escapes some drunken pederasts, who insist on calling him *ghazal* (gazelle, meaning pretty boy) and seem to take it for granted he has come to sleep with them.

Grouped in a single chapter, these adventures offer an insight into different kinds of homosexual encounters that are fairly common in twentieth-century cities of the Arab world. All are directly associated by the author with poverty and deprivation, as if homosexual intercourse were necessarily a sexuality of substitution, a *pis-aller* for heterosexual intercourse.[48] But the local Moroccan male is assumed to be a 'top', thus a danger: the narrator flees both the local man 'cruising' him at the railway station, and the beggars. He will only accept to follow the foreigner, assuming the latter is passive, and perhaps also out of fascination. Homosexual intercourse as the active partner does not make him a *hassas*, a colloquial word derived from classical Arabic 'sensitive' only applying to the passive partner. Even if pleasure is derived from the sexual encounter, there has to be a compensation in cash: the narrator can clear his conscience first by claiming he will only engage in such relations for money, and also by being the object of this solicitation. Accepting solicitation is in no way comparable to soliciting, and enables one to refuse assuming responsibility for the pleasure one has taken. It is certainly no coincidence that the old man with whom the narrator has sex, clinically described in its crudest details so as to force the reader's disgust, is a foreigner.[49]

Literature often displaces the shock of the encounter with the West into the arena of sexuality. This shift is certainly inevitable, and proves the traumatic nature of this meeting of cultures. It has affected one of the most intimate elements of human life, the relationship to the body and to sexuality. Domination and submission are symbolized through sexuality, and the effect is described in its pathological dimensions. The Arab man is symbolically or physically abused by the West, and if politically dominated, will sexually dominate in response. But even when active, being a mere object of fantasy makes him feel he is ultimately the loser, as in *For Bread Alone*. This metaphorical representation of the conflict between the Arab world and the colonizing – or post-colonizing West – as a sexual encounter and a fight for domination was brilliantly evoked by al-Tayyib Salih in *Mawsim al-hijra ila al-shamal* (*Season of Migration to the North*).[50] Many 'homosexual' counterparts are to be found with heavy symbolic resonance in the literature of 'progressive' authors. Gamal al-Ghitani, in his short story *Hadha ma gara lil-shabb al-ladhi asbaha funduqiyyan* (This is what happened to the boy who worked in a hotel)[51] presents a young university graduate who dreams of working as a diplomat, but has no future as a civil servant in Sadat's Egypt at the time of the *infitah* (economic opening up). He reluctantly chooses to work in a five-star hotel in Cairo owned by a multinational company. The young man is unaware of his extremely good looks that are naturally noticed by the Egyptian manager. The latter strategically places him at the entrance to the restaurant, and merely lets him help guests to their tables for a comfortable salary. When a Dutch woman, then an elderly American lady, try to get his attention, the manager makes it clear that the customer should be satisfied, and the young man once again reluctantly accepts. Then a Saudi tries to seduce him, recites poetry, pinches his cheeks and offers him a golden watch, which he bluntly refuses. The angry manager tries to convince him:

> 'You don't realize your interests, the interests of the hotel, the interests of the country. They've spent sixteen million on this building and they phone every day. Upsetting his excellency could affect our relationship. And then, what are you afraid of? Do you think he'll make you do anything you don't feel like doing? Of course not . . . Maybe you'll find him wearing a woman's nightie . . .'[52]

The young man refuses and resigns, but is woken up by the police the next day and informed that his 'prints are all over room 177'. This not too subtle metaphor of Egypt prostituting itself to the West and the Gulf states is also to be found in works by Sun'allah Ibrahim such as *al-Lagna* and *Sharaf.*

Sharaf (Honour, 1997) is Sun'allah Ibrahim's latest novel and its title is the (highly symbolic) name of the novel's hero. It is a return to the 'prison literature' genre developed in the late 1960s and 70s. But whereas the politically aware intellectual hero of the 70s was sent to jail as an opponent, Sharaf begins his descent to hell after having accidentally killed an American who has tried to rape him. In the opening chapter, twenty-year-old Sharaf is strolling through downtown Cairo, gaping at shop windows displaying Swatches, Nike shoes, Adidas training suits and Schott jackets, following blonde female tourists in miniskirts, hesitating between buying Marlboro cigarettes or seeing a Schwartzenegger movie. He is approached in front of the Rivoli Cinema (an actual gay cruising spot in Cairo) by John, who offers him a ticket for the show, which he declines. But since 'like all blond-haired foreigners in Egypt, he wasn't used to hearing no', John finally convinces the young man to accept his offer, then invites him to his home in the posh Zamalek district for a drink. Sharaf admits to being deprived of everything:

> The confession began like a song by Umm Kulthum – totally melodramatic: I'm fed up with my life, I want to leave this country, I wish you could take me far away.
>
> The *khawaga* (gentleman) remained silent, and simply put his golden chain around the young man's neck, then lay his hand on his thigh and started fondling it.[53]

The foreigner shows Sharaf a porn magazine, then tries to clasp him in his arms. While trying to escape, Sharaf hits the American with a bottle and kills him. This aborted rape of 'the innocent Egyptian' leads Sharaf to jail, in which other instances of equally metaphorical rapes of the country by foreign powers and corrupt nationals are exposed. It is remarkable that while jails were the setting of homosexual rapes and, at the opposite pole, long-term homosexual relations between inmates in the Oasis of Kharga in Sun'allah's first collection of short stories, *Tilka al-ra'iha* (The smell of it),[54] and in Ra'uf Mus'ad's *Baydat al-na'ama* (The egg of the ostrich), there are no such scenes in *Sharaf*. The hero of *Sharaf* escapes rape in prison, and although he seems to fall into a very close and loving friendship with a fellow inmate, their love never leads to physical fulfilment: it is as if all corruptions are actually outside the jail, despite the daily humiliation and deprivation inside. It would be hard not to notice the opening scene's utter improbability: what twenty-year-old Egyptian would be innocent enough to misinterpret the *khawaga*'s invitation, and furthermore his active rapist's attitude, precipitating the hero's fatal act of self-defence, is unbelievable. The author's overly demonstrative symbolism, only retrieved by his inimitably sarcastic tone, leads him to this dubious scene: the West is simply 'fucking' Egypt, which when acting in self-defence gets sent to jail. What a change from the first doubts expressed in the 1960s by al-Tayyib Salih: back then, the colonized African Arab took his revenge on political submission by behaving as a womanizer, turning his phallus into a weapon of sexual domination and revenge. The loss of faith in the present has gone so far in the novel of the 90s that the Arab is now, even on the metaphorical level of sexuality, the victim of the Western phallus.

But why is this articulated by means of a homosexual relationship? Stephan Guth, discussing the increasing frequency of sexual passages in Egyptian novels in the 1980s, rightly observes that, 'The taboos which are broken, however, are only aesthetic taboos, taboos on a linguistic level. It must be permissible to talk about what is going on in the surrounding reality – but that does not mean calling for a system of ethical values which is really new. On the contrary: in terms of traditional sexual mores even the "pornographic" passages are nothing but affirmative. Thus, in those scenes traditional morality is, for the time being, not questioned but only radicalized.'[55] Is it so surprising that this use of homosexual sexuality as a sign of decay should be found in the literature of leftist and nationalist writers? Hannah Arendt did warn of the formidable reactionary content of the revolutionaries' search for purity.

Invisible desire

Various explanations of the infrequency of homoerotic themes in modern literature, as compared to classical, can be suggested. The first trail to follow is obviously the close relationship between the act of writing and the socio-political context in which writing is performed. Contemporary Arab writers, whether supportive of, opposing or neutral towards the regimes under which they live, cannot fail to be cognizant of the fact that their writings can fall foul to accusations by government or opposition forces of corrupting society. Censorship and self-censorship are indissociable from writing in the twentieth century, and one cannot easily write what one knows will be denied publication or, worse, may endanger one's life.[56]

But if censorship has become so wary of the mention of homosexuality, it is because public morality has changed. The values pertaining to sexual morality in Arab societies have deeply evolved since the colonial confrontation with the West, as shown by Bruce Dunne's work on nineteenth- and twentieth-century Egypt.[57] In most urbanized Arab societies, those values that are hastily disguised as *'adatuna wa-taqaliduna* (our customs and traditions) are in fact rather new moral trends which began taking shape in the era known as the *Nahda* (renaissance), and are quite often at odds with classical (or rather pre-modern) representations of virility, as exemplified in *adab* literature which allowed for a wider spectrum of male desire. This 'modern' morality is also partly at odds with popular representations and male sexual practices – which see little harm in active homosexual intercourse – easily vilified as evidence of the residue of underdevelopment, ignorance and lack of education. The newly enforced values are a reformist construction resulting from the encounter between a theoretical Islamic ethics of normalized sexuality, the influence of colonial domination and the desire to adopt Victorian-style norms as a token of 'civilization'.

One should remember that when in 1834 Muhammad 'Ali banned the *ghawazi* (female belly dancers) from performing publicly their 'obscene' dances, female impersonators (*khawalat*)[58] legally took their place and performed at weddings and in the cafés: it was felt at that time that men casting aside their virility were less a cause of *fitna* (social disorder) than women behaving freely and sporting their charms. The public space was the exclusive domain of men and it was accepted therefore that men had the right to renounce their manhood through effeminacy (*khinath*) or passive homosexuality (*ubna*), although these were seen as illnesses. Women on the other hand could not claim what was not theirs and their appearance in the public space came to be regarded as a greater threat to the social order.

The 'modernization' of society, from the second half of the nineteenth century on, implied the banishment of homosexuality from the recognized domains where it had been in evidence (even if illicitly), and the abandonment of a tolerance that was castigated by the Europeans as the 'Oriental vice' *par excellence* (whether with disdain by the British rulers or bemused curiosity by the French travellers).[59] In present-day Arab societies, sexuality has thus come to be 'normalized' in the most rigid way, albeit that the 'Western values' that are the supposed point of reference in the field of sexual ethics have in the West evolved tremendously. But governments and authorities, the media and certainly many writers – necessarily belonging to the 'conscious and educated minority' – feel that their 'educated man's burden' makes it a duty for them to denounce society's defects and corruption (among which homosexuality gets included) and that they should participate, through literature, in the sacred endeavour to reform it.

The irony is that even when this pervasive moralism asserts itself as an expression of Arabo-Islamic identity or *asala*, the moral values referred to are those the West produced but started to question profoundly from the 1960s on. It is quite predictable that critic Ghali Shukri's analysis of the crisis of sexuality in the Arabic novel[60] is totally mute on the subject of homosexuality: modern literature prioritizes men's relationships with *women* and the regulation of virility. The defence of equality between the two sexes and the advocacy of a normalized and 'sounder' sexual life between men and women, challenging the unlimited exercise of power by a dominating male, seems at face value irreconcilable with a sympathetic view of non-normative sexuality (or simply any type of *real* sexuality, for power and domination are almost necessary components of fantasy, whether heterosexual or homosexual: the particularity of male homosexuality being the confrontation of two supposedly dominant partners, as previously discussed *à propos* the Sa'dallah Wannus play).

Censorship is also a consequence of mass literacy. Nagib Mahfuz points to differences between classical and modern literature:

Classical Arabic *adab* was a literature of pleasant conversations at night with friends, and was restricted to private salons. There was no publisher nor media. Abu Nuwas, al-Husayn b. al-Dahhak and their booncompanions would sit together and recite verses. In [twentieth-century Egypt] we've had al-'Awadi al-Wakil and his circle composing even 'hotter' verses, but those are not published. These things did not disappear, but remained in private literary circles. All the [neo-]classical poets have verses in this genre, even Hafiz Ibrahim [. . .], but when poets collect their *diwan*, they suppress such verses [. . .] The modern diffusion of works provokes self-censorship. [. . .] Publishers want the authors to respect public opinion and religious values.[61]

Novelist Hoda Barakat proposes another trail:

For a long time, the Arabic novel has dealt with the social condition, with the corruption of society, the loss of values, the exemplariness of a character in society. The character is an archetype, representing a social class, a group. One merely has to watch the morals of the Egyptian hero. Oh, does he suffer because of his morals! They are small prophets. The concern for the human condition is a relatively new phenomenon. Arabic literature now deals with the way man faces himself, not merely the way he faces society. This shift of perspective might open new fields of analysis of human sexuality.

One point remains, though: both classical and modern Arab societies have shared a common feeling that displaying one's inability to conform to standards or, worse, demanding a space of freedom to practise one's own moral standards, is a far greater offence than discreetly satisfying one's tastes in private. To this effect there is a *hadith* stating that the whole community will be forgiven except 'those who boast about deeds God has covered with his veil'.[62] This is what Stephen O. Murray has rightly named 'the will not to know',[63] and it provides a clear reason for the lack of development of a gay movement comparable to what has appeared in the West: individuals want to know everything about other individuals, but society as a whole prefers not to see the *dissemination of desire*. Modern literature seems to accept the failure to lift this mask so that honour remains safe.

However, all societies need their own 'space of transgression', and the relative absence of homosexuality in the Arab literary field still needs to be studied. It is partly explainable by censorship and the close relationship between the act of writing and existing regimes and authorities in the region. As has been emphasized in this article, the current tendency in modern Arab societies of withdrawing behind an imagined Arabo-Islamic identity – which is mainly defined in terms of a rigid sexual ethics that necessarily condemns homoeroticism – is at odds with attempts to promote a cultural revival that would include the exploration and redefinition of all traditional values, including aesthetic and ethical ones. After all, a genuine endeavour of that kind would inevitably challenge the currently restricted conception of Arabo-Islamic identity. One can also pose the question of whether Arab societies have not in fact started delegating the 'function of transgression' to the Western world, with which contact is nowadays ubiquitous: ridding themselves of the task of producing their own transgressions, and consuming imported versions, makes it all the easier to condemn what they consume as evidence of the 'moral failure' of the West when and if necessary.

Modern Arabic literature is starting to break the wall of silence and narratives increasingly include sexually explicit passages. But this opening cannot be completed unless it is accompanied by an unrestricted search of the universality and complexity of human sexuality, and a better know-ledge of one's own culture. Self-doubt is a necessary step and the first attempts at questioning the old patterns of virility are central towards improving relationships between men and women. But what about relationships between men? The building of new standards should not ignore (and cannot erase) more obscure parts of human desire.

Notes

1. Some elements of this essay are based on my earlier article entitled 'Arabic literature', in George E.Haggerty & Bonnie Zimmerman, *Encyclopedia of Lesbian and Gay Histories and Cultures* (New York: Garland Publishing, 1999) vol. 2. All translations of quotations from Arabic texts are my own unless otherwise indicated. I wish to thank Georgine Ayoub, Everett Rowson and Katia Zakharia for their countless suggestions in the course of writing this contribution.

2. 'Gender studies' and 'Gay and Lesbian studies' have mainly been concerned with the construction of a 'homosexual identity' in Western societies. Even research on sexual behaviour outside the West, such as Rudi C. Bleys's *Geography of Perversion* (New York: New York University Press, 1995), focuses on the role of the 'ethnographic imagination' in the construction of a 'countermodel' to Western masculinity. Stephen O. Murray & Will Roscoe (eds.), *Islamic Homosexualities* (New York: New York University Press, 1997) deals mainly with non-Arab societies and does not address diachronicity or the issue of cultural differences between Islamic societies.

3. See particularly Everett K. Rowson & J.W. Wright (eds.) *Homoeroticism in Classical Arabic Literature* (New York: Columbia University Press, 1997). See also Arno Schmitt, *Bio-Bibliography of Male-Male Sexuality and Eroticism in Muslim Societies* (Berlin: Rosa Winkel Verlag, 1995); Arno Schmitt & Jehoeda Sofer, *Sexuality and Eroticism among Males in Moslem Societies* (Binghamton, NY: Harrington Park Press, 1992).

4. For instance Malek Chebel, *Encyclopédie de l'amour en Islam* (Paris: Payot, 1995), or by the same author, *L'esprit de sérail* (Paris: Lieu Commun, 1988).

5. Concerning the frequent misuse of psychoanalytic concepts in this field, see Katia Zakharia, 'Usage des concepts psychoanalytiques dans l'étude du monde arabo-musulman: réflexion critique', in *Arabica*, vol. 42, 1995.

6. See Garay Menicucci, 'Unlocking the Arab celluloid closet: homosexuality in Egyptian film', in *Middle East Report*, 206, 1998 (special issue: 'Power and Sexuality in the Middle East').

7. Particularly Chahine's *Eskendereyya leh* and *Eskendereyya kaman we-kaman*.

8. Particularly Nasallah's *Mercede*s.

9. Gramophone 2-11099/100 in *Catalogue Général Disques Gramophone Arabes*, 1914.

10. *Junusiyya*, a neologism, was coined by Muhammad 'Umar Nahhas, in *al-Junusiyya, nahwa namudhaj li-tafsir al-junusiyya*, (Roermond, Netherlands: Maktab al-'Arabiyya, 1997). The author, giving new meanings to classical Arabic terms, betrays a superficial essentialist perspective in distinguishing *junusiyya* (homosexual identity), not necessarily implying intercourse, from *liwat* (homosexual intercourse). The sexual identity of the participants is thus disregarded, so allowing for 'substitution homosexuality'.

    The history of the word *shudhudh* is still to be written. It is likely that the term's semantic field was narrowed to a homosexual connotation in the course of the twentieth century, but the first use of the compound *shudhudh jinsi* meaning homosexuality might go back to the nineteenth century. As for the use of *mithliyya*, it is still widely refused by the press, as recently witnessed in *al-Majalla*'s sneering cover series of articles (24 October 1999) entitled 'The last catastrophe for Arabs in the twentieth century'.

11. For instance, Tunisian colloquial Arabic opposes *mibun*, passive homosexual, clearly derived from classical *ma'bun*, and *taffar* ('jumper', a rather positively connoted noun), a man who repeatedly seeks homosexual intercourse with young men and takes the active role. The term wouldn't apply to a heterosexual having one-time or occasional intercourse with other men and implies homosexual desire. Egyptian gay slang presents a similar pair of opposites with *kudyana* (passive partner) and *barghal*.

12. Yusuf Idris, *Hadithat sharaf* (Cairo: Maktabat Misr, 3rd edn., 1957), p. 83.

13. See C. Pellat's article, 'Liwat', in the *Encyclopedia of Islam* (Leiden: Brill, 1960).

14. See Bruce W. Dunne, 'Sexuality and the "civilizing process" in modern Egypt' (Washington, DC, Georgetown University: unpublished PhD dissertation, July 1996), pp.185, 191.

15. See Everett K. Rowson, 'The categorization of gender and sexual irregularity in Medieval Arabic vice lists', in Julia Epstein & Kristina Straub (eds.), *Body-guards: The Cultural Politics of Gender Ambiguity* (New York: Routledge, 1991), pp. 50–79.

16. With the exception of Sa'dallah Wannus's *Tuqus al-isharat wa-l-tahawwulat*, discussed below.

17. Abu Hayyan al-Tawhidi (d.1023), *Akhlaq al-wazirayn* (The castigation of the

two viziers) edited by Muhammad b. Tawit el-Tanji (Beirut: Dar Sadir, 1992), p.103: 'la tu'awwil 'ala 'ayr fi sarawil ghayrika. la 'ayr illa 'ayr tamatta tahta 'anatika. fa-innaka in 'awwalta 'ala dhalika khanaka wa-shanaka wa-fadaha khanaka wa-manaka.'

18. Ahmad al-Tifashi, *Nuzhat al-albab fi ma la yujad fi kitab*, edited by Jamal Jum'a (London: Riad el-Rayyes Books, 1992); for a partial English translation from René Khawam's French translation, see Ahmad al-Tifashi, *The Delight of Hearts or What You Will Not Find in Any Book*, translated by Edward A. Lacey & Winston Leyland (San Francisco: Gay Sunshine Press, 1988).

19. We arbitrarily use the phrase 'modern Arabic literature' to refer to fiction written in the Arabic language from the last phase of the *Nahda* (renaissance), that is, the beginning of the twentieth century until the present. This article will deal, in particular, with the novel and the short story, although mention will also be made of plays.

20. Although a re-reading of Jibran Khalil Jibran's work could be attempted. His drawings and some writings such as *The Madman* could indicate a homoerotic sensibility.

21. Although originally a separate work when published in 1950, the text was finally included in the *al-Ayyam* ensemble as a third part.

22. Poets from the tribe of Bani 'Udhra and their imitators of the seventh century are reputed, according to literary historiography, to love and die of passion for a single woman they never manage to reach.

23. Jamil and Kuthayyir were famous chaste poets of the seventh century.

24. A *Nuwasi* is a follower of the poet, Abu Nuwas.

25. The verses are reputed to have been written on a column in the great mosque of Basra: see Abu Faraj al-Isfahani (d. 967), *Kitab al-Aghani* (Beirut: Dar al-Thaqafa, 1st edn. 1995; 8th edn. 1990), vol. 20, p. 196.

26. A famous cafe in Cairo, now mainly a touristic spot, but in the 1950s one of the city's literary salons, frequented by Mahfuz.

27. Personal interview with Nagib Mahfuz, 8 August 1998.

28. Nagib Mahfuz's Cairo trilogy was first published by Maktabat Misr, Cairo. The English version of the trilogy was translated by William Maynard Hutchins & Olive E. Kenny, *Palace Walk* vol. 1, 1990; *Palace of Desire* vol. 2, 1991; and *Sugar Street* vol. 3, 1992 (New York: Doubleday by arangement with the American University of Cairo Press, Cairo).

29. Nagib Mahfuz, *Malhamat al-harafish* (Cairo: Maktabat Misr, 1977) was published in English as *The Harafish*, translated by Catherine Cobham (New York: Doubleday, 1995). For the episode described, see in the Arabic edition the chapter 'Qurrat 'ayni', pp. 259–320.

30. 'hunaka ahad min al-harafish usiba min dimn inhidarihi bi-l-shudhudh': personal interview with Nagib Mahfuz, 8 August 1998.

31. In Abu Hayyan al-Tawhidi, *Akhlaq al-wazirayn* (The castigation of the two viziers).

32. Gamal al-Ghitani, *Waqa'i' harat al-Za'farani* (Cairo, 1975; al-Hay'a al-Misriyya al-'Amma li-l-Kitab reprint, 1994), pp. 43–45.

33. The Hammam al-Ahrar is a made-up name, but the author's mention of Amir al-Guyush Street a few lines before makes it clear that the popular hammam in that street famous for its homosexual atmosphere is the reference for Ghitani's novel.

34. Al-Isfahani's *Kitab al-Aghani* reports that the Umayyad poet al-Ahwas was caught in the caliph's kitchen trying to convince the young aides to sodomize him, and al-Tifashi's *Nuzhat al-Albab* mentions many anecdotes in which a rich man is obsessed with soldiers or grooms.

35. al-Ghitani, *Waqa'i' harat al-Za'farani*, p. 98.

36. al-Tawhidi, *Akhlaq al-wazirayn*, p. 374.

37. Ra'uf Mus'ad, *Baydat al-Na'ama* (London: Riad el-Rayyes, 1994), pp. 210–11.

38. Sa'dallah Wannus, *Tuqus al isharat wa-l-tahawwulat* (Beirut: Dar al-Adab, 1994).

39. Ibid., Act II, scene 3, pp. 85–90.

40. From the collection *Bab al-Tawfiq* (Cairo: Dar al-Shuruq, 1994), pp. 87–94.

41. This use of *double-entendre* might also be compared to the coy and dated allusions to homosexuality one would find in classic Hollywood films of the 1940s and 1950s.

42. Hoda Barakat, *Hajar al-dahik* (Beirut, 1990; London: Riyad el-Rayyes, 1991); published in English as Hoda Barakat, *The Laughing Stone*, translated by Sophie Bennett (Washington, DC: Interlink, 1995; paperback edn., 1998).

43. Barakat, *Hajar al-dahik*, p.17.

44. Allusion to the Quran (12, 31), from the Marmaduke Mohammed Pickthall translation (1st edn.: London, 1938), pp. 137–38: 'And when she heard of their [the women of the town] sly talk, she sent to them and prepared for them a cushioned couch [to lie on at the feast] and gave to every one of them a knife [to peel an orange] and said [to Joseph] : Come out unto them! And when they saw him they exalted him and cut their hands [losing their grip on themselves and unable to peel their oranges], exclaiming : God Blameless! This is not a human being. This is no other than some gracious angel.' *and* (12, 25): 'And they raced with one another to the door, and she tore his shirt from behind.' Khalil portrays himself as Zulaykha, tears a metaphoric shirt but remains unnoticed, and cuts his hands like the women of Memphis did, while the biblical/Quranic figure calmly peeled her orange.

45. This novel was written in 1972, published for the first time in Arabic in Casablanca, then by Dar al-Saqi, London, in 1982. The English *For Bread Alone* was translated by Paul Bowles and first published in 1973 by Peter Owen, London.

46. Choukri, *al Khubz al-hafi*, chapter 8, pp. 103–15.

47. This 'misuse' of the classical Arabic word *luti* is pervasive in modern Arabic, where it has become an equivalent of 'homosexual' as an identity. Although

oral sex is almost never mentioned in classical sources, the narrator is the closest of the two to the medieval conception of *luti*.

48. In a fourth scene (chapter 4, pp. 65–67), the narrator has become a rapist in his turn and forces a young boy to have sex with him. He has genuine desire for him and even touches the other boy's 'thing' and makes him come. But when the boy complains to his parents, and the narrator's aunt accuses him, he makes it clear that although he loves what is 'dirty and delicious', he has chosen a boy because women are unavailable. Homosexual desire is not denied, but it is a 'second-hand' desire.

49. This scene should be linked to such films as *Rih al-Sedd* (1986) and *Bizne*ss (1992), both by the Tunisian Director Nouri Bouzid. In the first film, Farfat's homosexuality is neither a genetic feature nor a choice, but a consequence of the character's rape as a youth by the carpenter for whom he was an apprentice. In the second film, 'sex-tourists' are taking advantage of deprived youth and induce adolescents into male prostitution.

50. First published in Arabic in 1966. First published in English as *Season of Migration to the North* (London: Heinemann, 1969; republished in paperback by Quartet Books, 1980).

51. In Gamal al-Ghitani, *Risalat al-basa'ir fi al-masa'ir* (Cairo: Madbuli, 1991; 1st edn., 1989).

52. Ibid., p. 57.

53. Sun'allah Ibrahim, *Sharaf* (Cairo: Dar al-Hilal, 1997), p. 19.

54. Sun'allah Ibrahim, *Tilka al-ra'iha* (Cairo: Dar Shahdi, 1986; 1st edn., 1966), pp. 26–27.

55. Stephan Guth, 'The function of sexual passages in some Egyptian novels of the 1980s', in R. Allen, H. Kirkpatrick, E. de Moor (eds.), *Love and Sexuality in Modern Arabic Literature* (London: Saqi Books, 1995), p. 129.

56. The subject of this article being 'Arabic literature', and as our understanding of this notion implies we should limit ourselves to works written in the Arabic tongue, we shall not deal with homosexuality mentioned by Arab authors writing in French or English. But their freedom of speech, their earnest and direct approach to their sexual preferences (see in French, novels by Rachid O., or in English Rabih Alameddine's *Koolaids*) suggest that those authors feel Arabic cannot convey such freedom. One should, however, establish whether the reluctance to use Arabic is simply a tactical choice by writers who legitimately want to be read and not ostracized, or if a traumatic relationship with Arabic does explain this abstinence.

57. Dunne, 'Sexuality and the "civilizing process" in modern Egypt'.

58. Under the entry kh/w/l in the *Lisan al-'Arab*, one finds that *khawal* means 'al-'abid wa-l-ima' wa-ghayruhum min al-hashiya, al-wahid wa-l-jam' wa-l-mudhakkar wa-l-mu'annath fi dhalika sawa'un' ('male and female slaves as well as other types of servants, the word is used for singular and plural,

masculine and feminine'). Ibn Manzur (1232-1311), although never really concerned by diachronicity, seems to imply that the term is in fairly common use in his time. Since he was Egyptian and lived in Cairo and in Tripoli (Libya), we can suppose that in the fourteenth century the word had not yet gained its homosexual meaning. It is likely that nineteenth-century colloquial usage of *khawal* derives from classical Arabic, since *ghilman* (young male servants) were also quite often used for sexual gratification by their masters. But the precise connection between the thirteenth-century servants and the nineteenth-century female impersonators is unknown in its details. Progress in this field demands study of the vocabulary of late Mamluk and Ottoman texts. In its modern use, however, *khawal* is simply derogatory slang for 'queer'.

59. See Gérard de Nerval, *Voyage en Orient* (Paris: Charpentier, 1851) for a vivid account of a show given by 'khowals' (sic): also quoted in Jean-Claude Berchet, *Le Voyage en Orient* (Paris: Robert Laffont, 1985), pp. 879–81. See, too, Well Lane's classic description, in *The Manners and Customs of Modern Egypt* (London: 1836), ch. 19.

60. Ghali Shukri, *Azmat al-jins fi l-qissa al-'arabiyya* (Cairo: Dar al-Shuruq, 1991; 1st edn., 1962).

61. Personal interview with Nagib Mahfuz, 8 August 1998.

62. This *hadith* is found in the *Sahih* of Muslim, 5306: 'haddathani Zuhayr b. Harb wa-Muhammad b. Hatim wa-'Abd b. Humayd [. . .] sami'tu Aba Hurayra yaqulu: sami'tu rasula Allah Salla Allahu 'alayhi wa-sallama yaqulu kullu ummati mu'afatun illa l-mujahirina wa-inna min al-ijhari an ya'mala l-'abdu bi-l-layli 'amalan thumma yusbihu wa-qad satarahu rabbuhu fa-yaqulu ya fulan qad 'amiltu l-barihata kadha wa-kadha wa-qad bata yasturuhu rabbuhu wa-yusbihu yakshifu sitr Allah 'anhu.'

63. Murray & Roscoe (eds.), *Islamic Homosexualities*, pp. 14–54.

EIGHT

Farid Shauqi: Tough Guy, Family Man, Cinema Star

Walter Armbrust

Farid Shauqi, an Egyptian actor whose film career began in the late 1940s and blossomed in the decade of the 1950s, was an exemplary figure in the development of new images of masculinity. Before the 1950s male characters in Egyptian films and fan magazines were usually associated with a bourgeois Western-looking lifestyle. Dapper characters predominated, even if they were sometimes required to engage in physical exertion, or even fights. As Shauqi's public persona crystallized over the decade of the 1950s his screen image differed from the previous, comparatively fastidious, ideal. Shauqi's characters were tough and physically active. As a star he played auto-mechanics, fishermen, soldiers and manual labourers. These characters were intentionally oriented toward 'popular' or lower-class audiences. Once he became a star, Shauqi's brand of masculinity resonated easily with conventional stereotypes of Middle Eastern 'honour and shame' in which manly men defend collective honour in the public realm, while women remain in the protected domestic space.

At the same time, Shauqi's career in the 1950s (the decade in which he created his public image within a rapidly expanding Egyptian film industry) was more interesting than a mere correspondence between man and masculine stereotype might suggest. For one thing, his popular persona never supplanted the dapper bourgeois ideal. Rather Shauqi's masculinity had to be positioned in relation to other masculinities represented in the media in which machismo, sexual protectiveness and the depiction of lower-class occupations as heroic were much less pronounced. He had to define himself both in line with received notions of Egyptian masculinity on the screen as well as against such norms. Nor was Shauqi best positioned to fill a new niche for a 'he-man'. One could much more plausibly argue that

Omar Sharif, for one, made a better mid-1950s posterboy for a vital and youthful Egyptian national character. Handsome enough to play the bourgeois gentleman, but rugged enough to put on a peasant's *gallabiyya* or ride a horse, Sharif was 'discovered' by director Youssef Chahine and catapulted immediately into local stardom until he left Egypt for Hollywood in the 1960s. Shauqi, by contrast, had to earn his fame relatively slowly. Although he had been active in the theatre profession before entering the cinema, nobody 'discovered' him as a film star. Shauqi had to transform himself, and the process of self-transformation involved him pointedly in a broad redefinition of masculinity in which media representations were important.

A crucial tool of this transformation was the subsidiary elaboration of his image via media other than film, most particularly fan magazines. It is primarily these subsidiary images of Shauqi that this essay will address. Fan magazines take the tough-guy persona of Shauqi as their baseline, and create a much more complex and contradictory figure. Once he became a star within the commercial Egyptian cinema Shauqi was able simultaneously to invoke both a traditionalism geared to male control of female sexuality, and its antithesis, an ideal of companionable marriage based on equality between men and women. Stardom, though much maligned for its commercial context, was the perfect vehicle for him to negotiate these contradictory courses.

Enter the beast

Shauqi was born around 1919 and died on 28 July 1998, after a long and prolific career in the Egyptian cinema. He began in 1938 as an amateur stage actor. Yusuf Wahbi, one of the greats of the early Egyptian stage and cinema, offered Shauqi a place in his troupe, but Shauqi's parents didn't like the idea of their son living the unsettled life of an actor. So his father found him a job in the Department of Land Records (*maslahat al-amlak*). But Shauqi's acting urge would not be denied. He founded an amateur company, the National Union Troupe, composed of bureaucrats, and so he was able to remain on the stage, if not exactly in the market.

Then in 1946 a significant step toward professionalizing the craft of acting came with the opening of a government-sponsored acting school, the High Institute for Acting, under the auspices of the Ministry of Social Affairs. There were, of course, already many professional actors in Egypt, some of whom had been working for decades. But the existence of professional actors was not the same as the professionalization of acting. For acting to be a proper profession fit for middle-class youth like Shauqi it needed an official stamp of approval. The opprobrium attached to men working in the acting profession was of course less than that faced by women. Respectable professionalization (as opposed to performing for money, which might or might not eventually lead to popularity and social acceptance) was tied to institutionalization, and state patronage of such institutions was, at least in the middle of the century, a powerful argument for legitimacy.[1]

When auditions for the High Institute for Acting were announced three thousand applicants filed the necessary papers that would permit them to perform for a selection committee headed by no less than Salah al-Din Pasha, the Minister of Foreign Affairs, who was a known enthusiast of the art. Only fifteen of them were to be selected. Shauqi, of course, was among the lucky fifteen. His memoirs describe a stunning but inadvertent success at the auditions:

> In that huge crowd of applicants one of the amateur actors who liked my work spied me. He greeted me warmly, saying, 'Of course you'll get in, you'll be the first one.' He asked me to read the supporting role in his own audition. When his audition started I was there with him on the stage, but with only a few lines to read.
>
> Suddenly Salah al-Din Pasha, the Minister of Foreign Affairs, stopped and asked me, 'What's your number?'
>
> The secretary of the Institute said, 'He's not the one auditioning.'
>
> I tried to explain that I had filed my papers, but that all I was doing now was helping a friend with his audition. The secretary cut in again, saying, 'His number isn't here. He hasn't filed his papers.'
>
> The Minister said emphatically, 'Get him his papers. He has to formally apply, and he has to pass.'
>
> Trying to control the feeling of joy that was dissipating my initial despair, I told him, 'Your excellency, I've memorized the role of Antonio [sic] in the play Antonio and Cleopatra. I can do this part.' I was clinging to this thin thread of hope . . . I was getting ready to perform the role of Antonio so that I could prove to His Excellency, the head of the selection committee, that I could act. But the minister then said just as emphatically as before, 'Son, it's obvious from the way you look and the way you perform that you're an actor.'
>
> I said, 'But please sir, give me a chance . . .'
>
> He said, 'Son, you're in. You're in.'

Of course when one reads this description the outcome is predictable: the great man on the selection committee will be so impressed that Shauqi will be enrolled in the troupe on the spot even though another thousand or so hopefuls are still milling around outside waiting for their chance.

But the passage shows more than just Shauqi praising his own unstoppable talent. His anecdote is a microcosm of his career: he came to the audition ready to read Shakespeare, but impressed the experts as the perfect character actor. Later, the directors and the producers of most of the films he appeared in until the mid-1950s saw the same thing: a character actor in secondary roles. But Shauqi never accepted their verdict.

Shauqi's refashioning of his public image would not have been remarkable if he had merely gone from character roles to Shakespeare or some other highbrow equivalent. The idea of Antonio (or Antony) was not new.[2] The role and the plays were already recognizable icons of an emergent division between refined art and commercial entertainment. Shauqi in Shakespeare would have merely added to something that was already taking shape, or at least that cultural elites and, after independence, cultural policy planners wanted to take shape.[3] Instead Shauqi aimed to bring respectability to figures indexed to the lower reaches of the emergent cultural canon. His refashioned characters were manly men, irresistible to women, who triumphed over any adversity. Of course such an image resonates easily with the defence of feminine honour and in the 1950s, when Egypt was newly independent from colonial rule, it was a short step from defending the honour of one's women to defending the honour of the nation. Shauqi made a conscious appeal to lower-class sensibilities. He became, at a certain point in his career, the self-proclaimed *malik al-tirsu* – 'king of the cheap seats'.

Shauqi's he-men were not simply copies from John Wayne stories, or of any other variant of tough guys in the American cinema. One of the most common complaints against Egyptian films – and one of the commonest reasons for dismissing them – is that they are derivative of Western models. It is, of course, true that many Egyptian films are patterned on American films, but the degree to which Egyptian films are intentional copies of foreign models, as opposed to adaptations, is routinely overstated (just as the degree to which Hollywood films poached stories from wherever they could is routinely understated). There were important ways that Shauqi fashioned his image to fit both his own self-image, and the times in which he rose to prominence. This is only apparent if one views the scope of Shauqi's work in an expanded sense. His image was only partly a product of the roles he played in films. The other factors that produced the 'king of the cheap seats' were, first, his ability to gain control of some aspects of the production of his own films; second, the auxiliary media through which his image was elaborated, particularly fan magazines. Paradoxically, the element in Shauqi's life that ties these two things together was a woman. In other words, crucial to the construction of Shauqi as the pre-eminent he-man of the Egyptian cinema in the 1950s was the actor's relationship with a woman.

I will return to this matter shortly. First I must allay an anxiety that may be growing in the minds of readers familiar with Shauqi's career. This is that Farid Shauqi, 'king of the cheap seats' and sometime nationalist icon, is not necessarily the Farid Shauqi that comes most readily to mind. 'King of the cheap seats' was Shauqi's own preferred designation, and the title of his 1978 autobiography. However, a perhaps more common nickname for Shauqi is *wahsh al-shasha*, 'beast of the screen'. For years Shauqi's bread-and-butter role was not the masterful he-man defending feminine and national virtue, but the villain and not often a redeemable villain forced to do wrong by circumstances or social ills. Farid Shauqi played a very long string of crude thugs, petty hoods, lounge lizards, blackmailers and drug smugglers. In a series of articles published in 1957 Shauqi described what his life as 'beast of the screen' was like:

> In the film *Lover's Revenge* I played the part of a villainous bedouin highway robber. Naturally I had to dress the part – an *'iqal* and *'abayya* [bedouin headband and cloak]. The heroine was the Tunisian actress Husayba Rushdi. I worked on that film from 5 a.m. till noon.
>
> I had another role in a film called *Amal*, starring Shadia. This was being made at Studio Misr, and there wasn't enough time for me to take off my bedouin clothes at the studio. So I'd put on the clothes for the other part at the first studio, get in my car, and head to Studio Misr. I'd get into the studio without anyone noticing that I was late.
>
> In this film my role was a villain who attacks the heroine. At 4 p.m. I'd leave Studio Misr and go to Studio Galal, where I was playing another villain who threatens a happy family. That's because all the directors agreed that what I was most suited for was the character of a man who threatens young women after having tricked them into sending incriminating love letters. Then after the girls get married he blackmails them, telling them he'll show the letters to their husbands who know nothing of their pasts. The story ends with the husband finding out what sort of person I am and threatening to call the police.
>
> After a hundred such films I could do these roles with no effort. But the directors insisted on giving me those roles because they realized that I did it in a new way. (Shauqi 1957d)

Shauqi was, in fact, one of the most prolific actors in the history of Egyptian cinema. When I mentioned my interest in him to one Egyptian director, the man responded, 'At least Shauqi always stayed in the market.' He was not a Shauqi fan, and said this grudgingly. But 'staying in the market' was an understatement. According to the *Encyclopedia of the Actor in the Egyptian Cinema* (Qasim and Wahbi 1997), the most prolific figures in the Egyptian film industry are Mahmud al-Miligi and Farid Shauqi. Miligi is credited with appearing in 331 Egyptian films, Shauqi with 275. Nobody else comes close.

Mahmud al-Miligi's career makes an instructive contrast with that of Farid Shauqi. Miligi was also a character actor who specialized in villain roles. In film after film Miligi existed only to be vanquished – in quite a few famous works by Farid Shauqi. But Miligi was and remained primarily a character actor, only occasionally cast against type, and never a person around whom a film could be built, whereas Shauqi metamorphosed from 'beast of the screen' to 'king of the cheap seats'.

Cherchez la femme

I have suggested that Farid Shauqi's self-transformation was linked to his relationship with a woman. She was Hoda Sultan, with whom he appeared in many films. When they married in 1951, Shauqi was at the height of his 'beast of the screen' days. He had been considered a promising young actor, and much was made of his having been one of the first graduates of the High Institute for Acting. Critics thus chided him for his monotonous screen persona. Typical was a 1957 article in the fan magazine, *al-Kawakib*. The article complained sourly about the stagnation of the Egyptian cinema. Much blame for this alleged stagnation was put on the shoulders of the actors. The section on Shauqi in the article was quite pithy:

> In 1947 Farid Shauqi appeared in the one-act play *The Lout* at the Opera Theatre. He was one of the students who earned a diploma at the Institute of Acting. The critics thought he would rise quickly. But in less than one year he started taking villain roles. Farid Shauqi developed. He became famous. He got rich. He got fat. He married Hoda Sultan. ('Kanu . . . thumma asbahu')

This could not have been encouraging for the young man who came to his audition for the High Institute ready to read Shakespeare. Of course at the time this article in *al-Kawakib* was written it was impossible to see the larger picture of Shauqi's career. By January 1957 he had only been cast against his typical villain role a few times, but was well into the self-transformation that was to add resonance to his repetitive 'beast of the screen' roles and eventually turn him into something quite different.

For Shauqi to turn himself into a working-class hero who could plausibly be viewed as 'king of the cheap seats' rather than just a goon in the Mahmud al-Miligi mode, he had to be manly. Many of Shauqi's villain roles made him appear tough or threatening, but his roles rarely made him into an endearing, or even redeemable, character. For example, in the 1953 film *Son of the Popular Quarter* he plays a snivelling cowardly aristocrat who tries to force his attentions on his cousin. In the end he is foiled by a dashing young engineer who both gets the girl and wins a competition to build modern public housing for the good people of the *hara* – the popular quarter mentioned in the title. Among Shauqi's many villainous *tours de force*, a scene that surely belongs in the all-time 'beast of the screen' hall of fame occurs in *Hamido*. In this film Shauqi gets his unmarried girlfriend pregnant. Rather than make her an honest woman, he takes her for a boat ride and throws her over the side. The actress who played the pregnant girlfriend was his wife, Hoda Sultan.

Too physically imposing to be a comedian, and already typecast in any case, trying to make himself into a strong masculine figure was perhaps the most obvious strategy for him to follow. The cultural milieu in which Shauqi defined his manliness is often described in academic literature on the Middle East as part of an 'honour-shame' complex. Men and women conceive of themselves in a relationship of complementarity: the honour of men and their kin groups is inherently linked to the sexual shame of women. Men occupy a public realm in which honour is 'projected', while women are part of a familial 'sacred realm' that must be protected (Bourdieu 1965). Although the analytical usefulness of the honour/shame complex has been both criticized and elaborated from a number of perspectives,[4] the value of assertive male honour 'covering' female vulnerability was (and still is) relevant to Shauqi's audience. That such a value was expressed differently in various social milieux, and by men and women, does not detract from its general recognizability. Honour (and sometimes, particularly in his early career, its absence) was therefore a trope in his masculine film narratives. But in the larger context of Shauqi's public image – in both cinema and print media – his career was part of a reorganization of the pervasive gender hierarchy glossed as 'honour and shame'. This restructuring of gender hierarchy used the idiom of honour even as changes in the style and content of how men and women related to each other were emerging.

By the most obvious standards of the logic of honour and shame, Farid Shauqi ought to have married quietly and never let his wife be seen in public. Before he married Hoda Sultan he had, in fact, been married in just such a way – to Zaynab Abd al-Hadi, whom he had married when he was still a government employee in the Department of Land Records. In an autobiography published in 1978 Shauqi was kind to Zaynab Abd al-Hadi. According to him, they separated simply because she could not understand the life of an artist. He bore her no ill will, and says he came to respect her more after they divorced than he had when they were married (Shauqi 1978: 164–66). But in a 1957 memoir Shauqi was considerably more bitter at what he perceived as Zaynab's attempts to hold back his acting career. His first marriage was, he said, dramatized in the 1957 film *Glory* (Shauqi 1957d: 17).

A review of *Glory* ('al-Magd' 1957) describes a film in which Shauqi plays a famous actor whose faithless wife does him grievous wrong – ignoring her husband's career, callously killing their son in an automobile accident, and ultimately driving the man to drink. His career goes into a downward spiral until he falls in love with a beautiful actress (played by Hoda Sultan), who saves him from suicide and revives his career. The reviewer found the story, in which a man signs everything he has over to his wife and then lets matters stand after the relationship sours, a bit implausible, but nonetheless praised Shauqi's performance.

That was Shauqi's public comment on his first marriage. It came in 1957, after six years of being married to Hoda Sultan. But in 1951 the crux of the matter was that Farid Shauqi's career would not have been helped by marrying another Zaynab Abd al-Hadi. If he had done so he might well have carried on playing the monotonous role of villain, and been remembered as nothing more than another Mahmud al-Miligi. Instead he married Hoda Sultan, who was part of the same artistic milieu.

The impact of the marriage on Shauqi's public image was contradictory. One reason for this was that Sultan was simply a more valuable commercial property; in 1951, as an accomplished actress who could also sing, she was on the verge of becoming a bigger star than he. From the beginning of the Egyptian cinema in the 1930s until the late 1960s singers consistently commanded the highest fees in the business. Sultan had begun her film career at the same time as Shauqi, in 1949, but appeared in far fewer films. From the beginning, by virtue of her ability to sing, she was given better roles than Shauqi and by the mid-1950s was somewhere near the top of both the singing and the acting professions. By one estimate she was the 'second best female vocalist in Egypt' after Umm Kulthum. Granted, the source of that statement was biased – it was Farid Shauqi who said it (Shauqi 1978,

83). But it was not a completely unreasonable opinion. A 1957 article in *al-Kawakib* estimated the earning power of the stars on a per-hour basis ('Nujumuna . . .' 1957). One needn't assume the estimates were completely accurate, since there were many reasons that both actors and producers didn't necessarily want the actual economics of film making to be publicly known. But if one takes the article as a rough estimate of the relative worth of the stars, Hoda Sultan, at LE 16 per hour, was worth roughly twice Farid Shauqi, who appeared somewhere near the bottom of the chart, at LE 8 per hour.[5] Assuming that she was still on her way up by 1957, when the article was published, and others such as Layla Murad (another popular singer who appeared in numerous films) were declining, Hoda Sultan did indeed rank among the stars.

Of course the hourly fee of the stars wasn't the whole story. Shauqi was appearing in far more films than Sultan, who appeared in only 70 films (Qasim and Wahbi 1997), suggesting that she had a greater pull at the box office, but that she worked much less. On the other hand, films were not her only venue. She also gave concerts, made recordings, and presumably was given air time on the radio. By the time of their marriage both Shauqi and Sultan augmented their income with stage work. But Sultan probably had access to yet another form of income, or at least to a kind of publicity that might have helped raise her profile, and hence her marketability. This was advertising.

The idea of selling both products and films – sometimes together in a seamless package – almost surely came to Egypt by way of America. Fan magazines were quite blatant about it.[6] For example, in a 1954 issue of the American fan magazine, *Photoplay*, actor William Holden advertises Camel cigarettes: 'With so many people smoking Camels, I figured they must be good! So I tried them – found their cool mildness and swell flavor suit my taste to a T! You ought to try Camels yourself!' A photographic insert to the right of the pack of Camel cigarettes shows Holden on the telephone in a still from a film. A second text reads, 'William Holden, star of *Forever Female*, is another on the big list of Hollywood personalities who prefer America's most popular cigarette, Camel! Some others are John Wayne, Lizabeth Scott, Maureen O'Hara, Alan Ladd, [and] Maureen O'Sullivan.'

The same practice was adopted wholesale into the Egyptian cinema. For example, Soraya Hilmi, a 'monologist' (singer of light comic songs both on stage and in films) sold Ward al-Nil soap in the fan magazine, *al-Kawakib*. The text is quite similar to William Holden's in the Camel ad: 'Soraya Hilmi, star of the cinema and musical theatre, says that she never uses anything other than Ward al-Nil soap, in which she found several unique characteristics, particularly its beautiful perfumed smell.' ('Rihatuhu al-jamila tu'jibni' 1951)

The economics of these advertisements in an Egyptian context, though beyond the scope or this essay, are surely a subject worthy of analysis. How much did the sponsor pay? Was there perhaps a barter arrangement between the distributors and the producers of soap and other products – a seductive pairing of a well-known face with a product, resulting hopefully in higher box-office returns on the film and higher sales of the product? It is, however, clear that such advertising overwhelmingly featured women over men. This might be a function of the familiar relationship between the female form and commercial marketing: in which women are posited as objects to be looked at and men posited primarily as the lookers with the active gaze (Mulvey 1989).

Although I have not found any advertisements featuring Hoda Sultan, such work would certainly have been an option for her, as it was for Soraya Hilmi, as mentioned above.[7] Possibly this augmented her already formidable income from singing, recording, and acting in films. What it all boils down to is that in the early 1950s when she and Farid Shauqi got married she was bigger than he was. This was a potential problem for any plans Shauqi might have had for defining his public persona in a more complex manner than it had been up to this point. How could he be 'the man' when his wife was bringing home more of the bacon?

One way he used the unequal commercial balance between himself and Hoda Sultan to his advantage was to move into both writing and producing his own films. He never says outright in either the 1978 autobiography or the 1957 one that he was able to do this because of having access to Hoda Sultan's money. I am speculating that this was the case. What is not in doubt is that Shauqi did not start writing film scripts until the production company formed by him and Hoda Sultan started producing them. Their company was called Aflam al-'ahd al-gadid (New Era Films). The difference between Farid Shauqi's earlier work as a villain and the films that he produced and often wrote, was immediately obvious. Their first effort, in 1952, was *Boss Hasan*, which remains a classic of Egyptian cinema.[8] Shauqi plays a working-class man from the lower-class neighbourhood of Bulaq who gets seduced by a decadent rich woman from the neighbourhood of Zamalek, which is just across the Nile but vastly different in terms of its class connotations. Hoda Sultan plays his wife. The film portrays Shauqi's character as a man who is morally weak and naïve, but quite redeemable. He has, by the end of the film, been a passenger in a car driven by the rich woman that runs over his own son. Fortunately the boy appears likely to make a complete recovery, and Hoda Sultan, the good wife in the film, gladly accepts

Advertisement for *Boss Hasan* (1952), Farid Shauqi's breakthrough film. It was also the first film he produced with Hoda Sultan, whose superior star power was suggested by her dominant place in this poster. Shauqi, Sultan's husband in the film and in real life, appears in the lower left corner kissing the femme fatale, played by Zuzu Madi.

her husband's return, but not until the rich woman has been killed, thereby freeing Shauqi's character from the spell cast by her money and fast foreign ways.

Boss Hasan was also the breakthrough film of director Salah Abu-Sayf, who went on to become famous as the most important director of cinematic realism in Egypt. Aside from his role in Abu-Sayf's films, Shauqi's own brand of realism has never been as widely acknowledged, but it was nonetheless part of the same broad movement, which was particularly strong in the 1950s. And as one might expect from reading Benedict Anderson's analysis of realist literary genres, particularly the novel (Anderson 1991: 29–40), cinematic realism was congenial to the goal of producing national community. Later Shauqi turned to films that did not just make national community the implicit grounds for the narrative, but were overtly nationalist. However, before he ever made a stridently nationalist film he gradually redefined himself over a period of five years, never completely abandoning his bread-and-butter villain roles, but steadily augmenting them with alternative images. Not all of these were films in which he played positive masculine roles. For example, one of his signature films was *Hamido*, made in 1953 – the film mentioned above in which he played a thoroughly despicable drug dealer who tries to drown his pregnant girlfriend. This was a work that Shauqi wrote himself, and which he and Hoda Sultan produced.[9] But even if Shauqi's character in the film was completely reprehensible, it was a more interesting production than the standard films of the time, and was credited as a significant portrayal of social issues. Iris Nazmi, with whom Shauqi recorded his memoirs, claimed that, 'Some of [Shauqi's] films were instant translations of laws that had been made to protect society. In 1952, just after the July Revolution, a law was passed preventing the drug trade. Shauqi quickly issued *Hamido*, which revealed the dangers of trafficking in this poison.' (Shauqi 1978: 1)

Anti-drug films in and of themselves were not an innovation when *Hamido* was made.[10] For example, in the 1950 *Path of Thorns* (*Tariq al-Shauk*) Husayn Sidqi plays a drug-busting police officer. Advertisements for the film suggest a standard male role for Sidqi, who was a star of the generation before Shauqi. Sidqi appears in a dapper uniform, obviously a fine upstanding hero. *Hamido* had no such character. Both Shauqi and Mahmud al-Miligi appear in the film; both of them are utter scum. In *Hamido* there is no clean and brave image of masculinity with which to contrast the evil of the film's male protagonists. The film is pure 'reefer madness': one character ends up addicted to cocaine; the heroine gets pregnant; Farid Shauqi's despicable drug dealer ends up dead. The film that everybody remembers today is *Hamido*. *Path of Thorns* is a relic.

محمود المليجي وفريد شوقي في مشهد عنيف من فيلم «حميــــدو»

السينما حميل

'The cinema is artifice': Farid Shauqi (right) battles Mahmud al-Miligi in *Hamido* (1953).

There were others.[11] *They Made Me a Criminal* in 1954, was based on the James Cagney vehicle, *Angels with Dirty Faces. Tough Guys of the Husayn District*, also in 1954, was made from a Nagib Mahfuz screenplay, and was the first cinematic attempt to portray Mahfuz's vision of traditional society that later became part of his famous Cairo Trilogy. Then in 1957 Shauqi both produced and starred in another Nagib Mahfuz screenplay that became paradigmatic of the way lower-class traditional society was imagined. This was *The Tough Guy*, directed by Salah Abu-Sayf. Shauqi plays a rough-hewn character from the countryside who comes to the Rod al-Farag vegetable market in Cairo, which is plagued by a domineering merchant who fixes prices to nobody's advantage but himself and some powerful backers from high society. Shauqi's character does not overthrow the tyrant of the vegetable market; rather he replaces him. But only temporarily. Shauqi's character in the film is arrogant, but still likeable.

As his image developed it depended fundamentally on the portrayal of virile masculinity quite distinct from his dastardly and sometimes even snivelling villain roles. However, an actor's image is constructed out of more than just film narratives. Other narratives were developed through the elaborating imagery of fan magazines, and these too were crucially tied to Hoda Sultan. It was in the print medium that the potentially

Shauqi in an advertisement for *The Tough Guy* (1957).

'Farid Shauqi and Hoda Sultan working together to set up their happy home at the beginning of their marriage': (Shauqi 1957d).

compromising subordination to Sultan's superior star power was constantly negotiated.

For Hoda Sultan, singing had come as a family vocation, and she entered the profession after her brother, Muhammad Fauzi, also a successful singer and actor. Like her, he was somewhere in the tier of performers just below superstar singers 'Abd al-Halim Hafiz and Farid al-Atrash. But according to Shauqi, Fauzi was not at all happy at the idea of his sister entering show business. As Shauqi describes it,

> Hoda came to Cairo despite the anger of her brother, the singer Muhammad Fauzi, and married the director Fu'ad al-Gazayirli. She enrolled her daughter [from her first marriage] in a French boarding school so that she would have time for her art, and rented an apartment in Zamalek. But she feared meeting her brother, who became doubly

angry after she had defied his will and, against his advice, started working as an artist. (Shauqi 1978: 147)

Shauqi goes on to say that the opposition Hoda Sultan faced from her
brother reminded him of his first wife, whose opposition to his theatrical
ambitions he felt had held back his career.

> We found that our circumstances were similar . . . [then he starts to
> write as if he were addressing Sultan directly] So why don't we get mar-
> ried, Hoda? Your brother's anger will subside when he sees you as a wife
> tied to a man who will stand by her and support her, protect her from
> the problems and travails of the artistic milieu. What does a brother
> want for his sister other than stability? And good reputation? (Shauqi
> 1978: 147)

Anthropologist Suad Joseph argues that the real foundation of patriarchy
in Arab society comes not from the relationship of children to their parents, but from the socialization of brothers and sisters, in which siblings of
the opposite sex learn their sexual roles by 'rehearsing' for each other. Consequently, a great deal of family honour is tied to a brother's relationship
to his sister: it is often the brother who has primary responsibility for disci-
plining a woman who is perceived to have offended family honour (Joseph
1994). Joseph makes her argument in the context of Lebanese refugee camps,
and one cannot assume a perfect correspondence between the social significance of brother/sister relations in 1990s Lebanon and 1950s Cairo. However, the way Shauqi describes his role in mediating between Sultan and
Fauzi is quite reminiscent of the general outlines of Joseph's ethnography.

I have no way of knowing how much of the tension between Sultan and
her brother Muhammad Fauzi was real, and how much of it was embel-
lished by Shauqi. Sultan and Fauzi were from a village near the Delta city of
Tanta, and were products of a family described as very traditional. Tension
between the two of them is entirely plausible, but I know about the matter
entirely through Shauqi's writing. What is not in doubt is that Shauqi went
to great lengths to present himself in public as close to Muhammad Fauzi,
and willing to assume the role of being his sister's guardian. As Shauqi put
it later, in his 1978 autobiography,

> Success in both our artistic and married lives was the reason that the old
> conflicts between her and her brother Muhammad Fauzi subsided. He
> began to feel at ease because his sister was now living a stable and hon-
> ourable life with an artist and colleague that he knew would protect her

Shauqi on the cover of his memoirs, 'King of the cheap seats' (*al-malik al-tirsu*), written with Iris Nazmi (Shauqi 1978).

and distance her from the errors and dangers that could befall a woman living alone, particularly when she was a beautiful woman to whom all the wolfish men in the artistic milieu aspired. Muhammad Fauzi and his wife, Madiha Yousry, became our dear friends; we were all one big family. (Shauqi 1978: 151)

Shauqi talked constantly to the press about his life with Hoda. They had, he said, made an agreement that Hoda would resign from show business if he asked her to. For example, he describes going to Damascus for one of Hoda's musical performances and finding it quite difficult to reconcile the public's admiration for his wife with his male ego.

> When we got back to the hotel I was consumed by jealousy. Hoda saw it on my face and asked what was wrong. I told her I couldn't agree to her working as a performer, and demanded that she retire that instant to live the life of a wife and nothing more. Hoda did not resist. She just hung her head and said she would always do as I wished.
>
> How did this happen?
>
> How could I betray my love for art and my belief in it in a moment like this? All I could remember was that I was a husband filled with jealousy over the crowd's admiration for his wife. Hoda told me that her first goal in life was to be a good wife, even if it meant sacrificing her artistic future.
>
> I began to calm my nerves, and the storm of jealousy subsided. I began to think calmly and with balance. How could I be content with her denying her art when her fans held her in such high regard? When she had received just that day a down payment of fame and respect? How could I demand that she resign when I was an artist who believed in art and its calling? This was arrogance, and I had never been arrogant. So I relented. Hoda respected me for it and promised that she wouldn't appear in any film or concert without my approval. (Shauqi 1957d)

However, passages such as this suggest that there was more to Shauqi's public attitude toward Sultan than mere protectiveness. He was both playing the strict husband and signalling his willingness to treat his wife as an equal. Furthermore, Sultan was complicit (or at least was presented in public as complicit) in Shauqi's public balancing act between the strict male guardian of honour and the magnanimous business-partner husband. In one article (Sultan 1957) she related a story in which Shauqi goes out with some journalists and forgets to come home. 'I was left cooling my heels, my head on my arms, fairly burning with rage and resentment.' When Shauqi arrives at 7 in the morning she jumps up and yells at him. He tries to sweet talk her to no avail, and she goes to her sister's house for the day. He merely telephones to remind her that they have an appointment with a Lebanese distributor. He wants her at least to be there for dinner, so they don't ruin their business reputation and lose money. She tells him to go to hell. He calls again and speaks to her 'in his capacity as the producer Farid Shauqi', telling her that he has a role for her to play and he'll pay whatever she wants. The role is of a wife – his wife – hosting a Lebanese distributor for dinner. She refuses. But now she's losing the edge to her anger, and starts thinking of the money they'll lose, and the rumours that will start. So she calls back and 'takes the role'. Eventually she decides she wants to apologize to him, and while acting her 'role' starts to blur the line between acting and reality. 'I surprised Farid. He thought I was acting a role, but not living it. Indeed, he only realized that I'd forgiven him after we'd said goodbye to our guest, after which he started once again to try to appease me!'

Many of these brief sketches from the married life of Shauqi and Sultan were resolved not in favour of Shauqi's offended masculinity, but in the interests of business. Whether or not the stories were 'real', they served as an extension of the screen personae of both. The object of such elaborations was not necessarily to reinforce the screen images, but to make them more complex. This elaboration of personality outside film texts is one of the things that makes a star – which Shauqi was clearly becoming by the mid-1950s – different from an actor.

Contrary to the tough lower-class image of his many gangster films, Shauqi often presented himself as stable, modern and middle class. One instalment of his 1957 memoirs was accompanied by a photograph of him and Sultan happily piling home furnishings, presumably wedding presents, on a mattress. The caption read, 'Farid Shauqi and Hoda Sultan working together to set up their happy home at the beginning of their marriage' (Shauqi 1957d). The co-operative domesticated man in the photo makes an obvious contrast to the rogues' gallery of characters he played on the screen. A pictorial article shows him and Hoda Sultan at home in pyjamas; in one frame they are arm wrestling, a smiling Sultan appearing to be on the verge of defeating her beefy husband ('al-Batala Hoda' 1954). In his later autobiography Shauqi told elaborate stories of how well he cared for Sultan's daughter by one of her earlier husbands (1978, 152).[12] This was no retrospective memory tailored for an audience with changed sensibilities, for in the 1950s he too made every effort to let the public know that he was more than willing to care for Sultan's daughter by another man (Shauqi 1957e). When telling of his and Sultan's courtship he describes writing her a love letter and then waiting by the phone like a vulnerable teenager (1957d, 1957e). Many of his not-so-tough images were associated with his relationship to Sultan, but Sultan was not his only device for showing a gentle nature. In a feature titled 'Terror on the Set' ('Ruʻb al-Blatoh') he describes shooting a gangster scene where he and another actor must threaten each other with guns. Each becomes nervous because they've just seen a play in which the plot revolves around a murder committed on stage (in a play within the play) where real bullets are used instead of blanks. He begins this story by saying, 'Don't believe that I'm a villain, as all the directors and writers and producers want to cast me. Don't think that I'm a bloody murderer. I kill only on the screen – in real life I'm afraid of my shadow.' (Shauqi 1957a)

The essential Shauqi?

Shauqi, the tough guy 'afraid of his shadow', sought to distance his screen roles from his fan-magazine role as a modern family man. In this, his presentation was typical of not just Egyptian, but of American fan magazine conventions of the mid-1950s. Such publications provided glimpses – purportedly 'real' insights – into the lives of the stars. It is true that Shauqi had to struggle to become a star, but by 1955 he was being explicitly presented in fan magazines as such (for example, the byline to Shauqi 1955).

Film scholar John Ellis defines a star as 'a performer in a particular medium whose figure enters into subsidiary forms of circulation, and then feeds back into future performances' (Ellis 1982: 91). The subsidiary fan-magazine images of Shauqi were ambivalent – always oscillating between an imagery that emphasized his violent screen roles, and another that softened him and made him look quite tame. Disjunctions between screen image and subsidiary elaboration create a combination of distance and closeness – from glamorous larger-than-life screen personality to the 'girl (or boy) next door'.[13] The differentiation of off-screen and on-screen personalities is a common attribute of stardom: 'The star's image is not one thing, but many things. As a result, this intertexuality is not simply an extension of the star's meaning, but is the only meaning that the star ever has. In other words, the star's image cannot exist or be known outside this shifting series of texts.' (McDonald 1995: 83)

Although the general outlines of this fan-magazine convention constructing a simultaneous effect of nearness and distance were, unsurprisingly, imported from American fan magazines, there was some reworking of the conventions in an Egyptian context. *Al-Kawakib*, my main printed source for this essay, used a commercial formula for selling stars and films strongly similar to that of the long-running (since 1911) American fan magazine, *Photoplay*: adverts for products that used stars for models and mentioned films by title; elaborating imagery of what was supposed to be the stars' personal lives; detailed, yet glamorous portraits of the 'work' of making films, and of course articles about the films themselves. *Al-Kawakib* was, however, more of an all-purpose publication than *Photoplay*. *Photoplay*, an unambiguous cheer-leader for the American film industry, contained little printed material that could be characterized as 'film reviews'. The main purpose of the publication was promotional. *Al-Kawakib*, by contrast, had plenty of fluff, but also quite a few attempts at serious analysis of the problems faced by the Egyptian film industry; interviews with politicians, religious figures, and of course film makers; charts illustrating various economic yardsticks for comparing the Egyptian cinema with the global competition. It is quite possible that, although Hollywood was the dominant cinema model in 1950s Egypt, at the same time a more typically European discourse about the serious artistic potential of the cinematic medium was also present (even if Egyptian critics almost always found the home-grown product sadly lacking in artistic worth).

In terms of how masculinity was represented there were also differences between *al-Kawakib* and *Photoplay*. For one thing, *Photoplay* was perhaps less given to constructing a wholesome image for actors who played unwholesome roles. For example, a feature on Robert Mitchum suggested that the man one saw on the screen was much like the man himself: famous for playing hoods and darkly troubled men in films, Mitchum is presented (Hunt 1954: 51) as a dark and troubled hood, thus minimizing the difference between the actor and his roles. Steven Cohan, who writes on masculinity in the American cinema, notes that efforts to produce a shared identity between the screen persona and the off-screen image of actors was common in the 1950s (Cohan 1997). He suggests that the dominant representational paradigm at that time was to construct men as essential beings, no different on the screen than they were in real life. Women, by contrast, were constructed performatively – as a shifting series of masquerades. However, one of the goals of Cohan's book is to show the many ways that masculinity was also a product of performance. His point is certainly appropriate in this context as well. Shauqi's ongoing elaboration of public personality was obviously as contrived as that of any American star.

One essential ingredient in understanding how the masquerade was constructed, and to what end, was the audience to whom the images were addressed. In the case of the subsidiary star images in *Photoplay*, it was almost exclusively to women: almost every product advertised in the publication was oriented to female readers. Femininity itself was represented as a product of artifice structured by consumption. This hardly assures that the imagery featured in the magazine was not also meant to appeal to men. A great deal of the photography makes perfect sense in terms of the psychoanalytically derived dichotomy Mulvey proposes between the active male gaze and the passive 'to-be-looked-at' pleasure-inducing female object (Mulvey 1989: 25). But as Cohan points out, in *Photoplay* objectification is a two-way street. *Photoplay* and other American fan magazines contained a substantial

amount of male cheesecake: men for display; men as sexual objects. A feature on Tony Curtis, for example, shows a wholesome happily married
man at home with his wife (Janet Leigh, who of course was a fantasy object
herself). This is very similar to the way Shauqi was presented with Hoda
Sultan. However, in the case of Curtis, he is described as Marilyn Monroe
might have been described in her heyday: 'He stands 5 feet, 11 inches and
weighs 158 pounds. He has a 4–inch chest expansion and a 28–inch waist.
He enjoys boxing and wrestling, but does not like to ride horseback.'
(MacDonald 1953: 32)

There were similarities between *al-Kawakib*'s presentation of gendered
stardom and that of *Photoplay*, but there were also divergences. As previously
mentioned, the magazine attempted to include in its repertory serious analysis
of the film industry, and often extremely negative reviews of films, along
with marketing and representational conventions that were essentially adapted
from American fan magazines. In a similar vein, the advertising was much
more ambivalent (and indeed, far less plentiful) than that of *Photoplay*. In *al-
Kawakib* products designed for the consumption of women were featured
regularly, as they were in *Photoplay*, but *al-Kawakib* featured far more
advertising that was probably aimed at men: Healthtex men's underwear,
Bata men's shoes, Magnetophone reel-to-reel tape recorders, Muska cameras,
Atkinson men's cologne, and Phillips radios are a few examples. The
advertisements do not, of course, constitute proof that the audience was in
fact composed of any particular ratio of men to women. The relative lack of
emphasis in *al-Kawakib* on female consumption, and indeed the relatively
muted insistence on promoting consumption overall, suggests at least that
the producers of the magazine either were not sure who was buying the
product or that they believed their audience was mixed.

Shauqi the tough-guy villain and, as the decade wore on, heroic defender of honour, was presented in films as a physically imposing speci-
men of manhood, but he was never marketed like Tony Curtis – as a 'hunk'.
This was partly because his image was ostensibly oriented toward 'popular'
audiences for whom auto-mechanics, porters, fishermen and, by the end of
the decade, stalwart soldiers were the intended ideals of identification. The
photogenic athleticism of a Tony Curtis would have been ridiculous in
such characters. Shauqi, more like a beefy Victor McLaglen than the sleek
Tony Curtis, makes an odd candidate for 'to-be-looked-at-ness'.

Class considerations are important in the creation of Shauqi's image,
but class alone, like psychoanalytic theories of desire that purportedly explain the marketing strategies of films and fan magazines, is insufficient to
explain how Shauqi's masculinity was constructed.[14] As a star he was bound
to be a paradoxical figure, as stars are by nature composed of ordinary and

extraordinary elements synthesized by a single figure (Ellis 1982: 95). The Shauqi featured in *al-Kawakib*, unlike the screen Shauqi, was an honourable gentleman who could balance an image of manliness with a highly publicized marriage to a woman who made more money than he did and who had played a central role in helping him gain some control over his career and in attaining stardom.

The paradox is surely sharpened by the fact that for a substantial portion of Shauqi's audience the 'exceptional nature' of Shauqi's image must have been differently construed from how his American equivalent would have been construed by an American audience. Shauqi's stardom was patterned on the American star model, but let us consider his audience. Shauqi's films – particularly if the often-proclaimed popular appeal of his films were true -- were seen by audiences for whom the 'ordinary' activities of couples in bourgeois domestic situations would have been novel, and quite possibly went beyond mere novelty to a much more problematic association with imposed alien customs. This was an audience for which (in the case of male spectators) the idea of a sister going to the cinema in any company but that of a male family member was unacceptable. Consequently the 'ordinary' for many filmgoers in the 'cheap seats' may well have been Shauqi's pointed and publicly proclaimed assurances that he could protect Hoda Sultan's honour, and therefore the honour of her brother Muhammad Fauzi.

Ellis describes the idealized image of the star as an 'invitation to cinema', entailing the 'impossible paradox' of combining ordinary and extraordinary elements (Ellis 1982: 97). This was constructed differently in Egypt than it was in the United States. One element of difference lay in relation to gender norms distinct from American society. The many ostensibly intimate glimpses published in fan magazines of Shauqi and Sultan as happy partners (or sometimes as genially disputing partners) were quite at odds with the experiences of large segments of the audience. The 'extraordinary' for Ellis consists of the figure who is 'removed from the life of mere mortals, has rarified and magnified emotions, is separate from the world of the potential film viewer' (ibid.). Shauqi and Sultan, however, as the happy couple *in the public eye* – an impossibility in older forms of gender discourse – were not so much larger than life as utterly unrecognizable and certainly not the familiar image of the couple next door.

Paul McDonald notes that most star studies assume that stars and the popular films in which they operate inherently promote conservatism (McDonald 1995: 80).[15] However, in the context of Egyptian cinema it may pay to look at 'conservatism' more flexibly. A masculinity defined in relation to control of women's sexuality was the conservative social background of Shauqi's work in the cinema. Shauqi's 1950s film roles often fitted comfortably within the parameters of this notion of masculinity. Paradoxically this was what made him a potent figure in restructuring gender norms through mass media. It was one of the things that made him compelling to his audience at a certain historical juncture. But the image he and Sultan promoted in fan magazines subsidiary to their screen roles, yet integral to their public personae, was of a kind of companionable marriage very much at odds with gender relations typical of 'traditional' Egyptian society. The latter image was one that both Arab and Western feminists, as well as modernists of many different political leanings, might well favour. Ultimately such labels as 'conservative' or 'progressive' cannot do justice to the complexity of figures such as Shauqi. A tough guy on the surface, he was nonetheless a figure of creative ambiguity.

Notes

1. In Egypt the state did not involve itself significantly with film production or training (including film acting) until the 1960s. But calls for government intervention in the industry were made virtually from the beginning of Egyptian cinema in the 1930s (Shalash 1986: 80–85), and an officially recognized film makers' syndicate was established by 1943 (ibid.: 85). In music, by contrast, government resources were devoted to promoting the profession by the 1920s (Shawan 1980: 95), and music was mandatory in public schools by 1931 (ibid.: 99).

2. The Antonio in question was from either a translation of Shakespeare's *Antony and Cleopatra* or from Ahmad Shauqi's *The Fall of Cleopatra* (1954 [1917]), which lists Mark Antony in the cast notes as 'Mark Antonius', but calls the character 'Antonio' in the script. Both plays were distinct from the flourishing popular theatre of the 1930s.

3. Whether it did ever actually take shape is another matter. Virginia Danielson (1996; 1997) points out that Western notions of highbrow/lowbrow distinctions in art cannot easily be mapped onto Egyptian cultural practices. At the same time there is no doubt that modernity creates strong imperatives to define artistic canons. Even if an Umm Kulthum or a Muhammad 'Abd al-Wahhab, for example, does not make sense as a cultural analogue to Western musicians eventually defined as canonical, a great deal of cultural commentary during their lives and after their deaths attempted to do just that. Twitchell (1992) and Levine (1988) both note that even in an American context cultural canons were not sorted out until relatively recently. Shakespeare, for example, did not migrate to the lofty regions of 'high art' until after the turn of the century. Similar processes have been in operation in Egypt throughout the twentieth century.

4. For example, Herzfeld (1984) questions the usefulness of honour/shame as a spe-

cifically Mediterranean cultural trait; Coombe (1990) finds a structural-function-alist agenda pervading honour studies long after the decline of structural-func-tionalism as an anthropological paradigm; Abu-Lughod (1986) argues that women's modesty can be a form of cultural capital for expressing the dominant value of honour; Meneley (1996) finds that women's competition for honour status oper-ates parallel to that of men rather than within the confines of male control.

5. Umm Kulthum and Muhammad 'Abd al-Wahhab had retired from the cinema. The top earner was singer Farid al-Atrash at LE 100 per hour. Layla Murad, the next-highest earning star, made LE 50 per hour. 'Abd al-Halim Hafiz, then a rising star, joined Fatin Hamama, the only non-singer in the top four spots, at LE 41. Hoda Sultan, at LE 16 per hour, was tied with several others for the place of tenth highest-paid star.

6. Although both Twitchell (1992) and Lipsitz (1990) suggest some slightly less obvi-ous ways that the lines between the content of popular culture and its financing can become blurred.

7. Advertising work appears to have been at the discretion of the actresses/models, and presumably of the advertising agency or company producing the featured product. Foreign as well as Egyptian companies employed local stars in their adverts. Some of the actresses working in adverts were lesser figures than Hoda Sultan, and some were her equals, or even her superiors in terms of star power.

8. Shauqi says in his later autobiography (1978: 151) that he produced the film. In 1957 he mentioned in *al-Kawakib* that he produced the film not as a New Age Films work, but as a production by 'aflam Farid Shauqi wa Hoda Sultan' (Shauqi 1957c). However, the titles of the video copy say that the producer was director Salah Abu-Sayf, as does *The Encyclopedia of Arab Cinema* (Bindari et al., 1994). When the film was first shown Shauqi and Sultan were shown with the film's producer, 'Butros Zorbanelli' ('Akhbar musawwara' 1952b). In public Abu-Sayf and Shauqi were close friends, so I am assuming that the three of them must have worked together on the project – which all sources agree Shauqi wrote – and that the disparity between the film's published credits and Shauqi's claim to have produced it is not indicative of a serious dispute.

9. Or at least this is what Shauqi says. Again, *The Encyclopedia of Arab Films* does not list New Age as the producer. It is Shauqi's 1978 autobiography that gives New Age as the producer (1978: 151).

10. Indeed the anti-drug genre goes much further back. *Cocaine*, a morality tale about the dangers of drug addiction, was made in 1931.

11. Shauqi made many films in the 1950s – important and otherwise – that cannot be mentioned in a short article. A Farid Shauqi filmography can be found in the *Encyclopedia of the Actor in Egyptian Cinema* (Qasim and Wahbi 1997). For more detailed information on the films themselves, see Bindari, Qasim and Wahbi (1994).

12. However, in the 1950s it appears that *al-Kawakib* devoted more coverage to Shauqi's relationship with the daughter he and Hoda Sultan had together (e.g. 'Akhbar

musawwara', which shows Shauqi by Sultan's side at the birth of their daughter, Nahid, and 'Farid Shauqi yahmil . . .' [1954], which shows scenes of domestic bliss at the Shauqi/Sultan residence, including Shauqi carrying Nahid on his back, as if he were a horse).

13. Jackie Stacey suggests that for filmgoers the instability of the star image is one source of pleasure. Since the star image is never fixed, a range of responses, including emulation, identification and admiration, are potentially available to the audience (Stacey 1994: 130–75).

14. Such problems in explaining Shauqi are familiar in other contexts. Jackie Stacey suggests a number of 'cinematic identificatory fantasies' as an alternative to psychoanalytic theories of identification (Stacey 1994: 130–75). Her focus is on female spectators in wartime and post-war Britain, but she makes two assumptions relevant to the development of Shauqi's public image in 1950s Egypt: first, identification with a star figure is subject to a diverse range of processes; secondly, the 'fixing of forms' emphasized by psychoanalytical theories is a dubious assumption in the broad context of film and fan magazine consumption. Another alternative to Mulvey's psychoanalytic approach, one based on the emotions in the philosophy of the mind, can be found in Carroll (1996: 260–74).

15. The almost total disregard of Egyptian cinema by academics was long justified by a related assumption: that consideration of popular cinema begins and ends with its commercialism. Viewing commercialism as simply reactionary and dismissing commercial popular culture as vulgar now looks untenable. Indeed, the wider field of cultural studies in the United States has challenged such views in the study of metropolitan expressive culture. But the acceptance of popular culture as a complex phenomenon not just worthy of study, but of crucial importance to a full understanding of modernity, is only gradually taking hold outside the analysis of metropolitan and Western societies.

References

Abu-Lughod, Lila 1986: *Veiled Sentiments: Honor and Poetry in a Bedouin Society*, Berkeley: University of California Press.

'Akhbar musawwara' (Illustrated news [including item on the birth of Shauqi's and Sultan's daughter, Nahid]) 1952a: *al-Kawakib* 41 (May): 4–5.

'Akhbar musawwara' (Illustrated news [including item on the birth of Shauqi's and Sultan's daughter Nahid]) 1952b: *al-Kawakib* 48 (1 July).

Anderson, Benedict 1991: *Imagined Communities: Reflections on the Origin and Spread of Nationalism*, New York: Verso.

'al-Batala Hoda' 1954: *al-Kawakib* 142: 11.

Bindari, Mona al-, Qasim, Mahmud and Wahbi, Ya'qub 1994: *Mausu'at al-aflam al-'Arabiyya* (The Encyclopedia of Arab Films), Cairo: Bayt al-Ma'rifa.

Bourdieu, Pierre 1965: 'The Sentiment of Honour in Kabyle Society', in: John Peristiany (ed.), *Honour and Shame: The Values of Mediterranean Society*, London: Weidenfeld and Nicolson.

Carroll, Noël 1996: *Theorizing the Moving Image*, New York: Cambridge University Press.

Cohan, Steven 1997: *Masked Men: Masculinity and the Movies in the Fifties*, Bloomington: Indiana University Press.

Coombe, Rosemary 1990: 'Barren Ground: Re-conceiving Honour and Shame in the Field of Mediterranean Ethnography', *Anthropologica* 32: 221–38.

'Farid Shauqi yahmil mas'uliyatuh 'ala zhahruh (Farid Shauqi carries his responsibility on his back)' 1954: *al-Kawakib* 146 (18 May): 24–25.

Herzfeld, Michael 1984: 'The Horns of the Mediterraneanist Dilemma', *Man* 15: 339–51.

Hunt, James 1954: 'Why Can't Mitchum Behave?', *Photoplay*, March: 50–51, 100.

Joseph, Suad 1994: 'Brother/Sister Relationships: Connectivity, Love, and Power in the Reproduction of Patriarchy in Lebanon', *American Ethnologist* 21 (1): 50–73.

'Kanu . . . thumma asbahu' 1957: *al-Kawakib* 283 (1 January): 72.

Levine, Lawrence 1988: *Highbrow/Lowbrow: The Emergence of Cultural Hierarchy in America*, Cambridge, Mass.: Harvard University Press.

Lipsitz, George 1990: *Time Passages: Collective Memory and American Popular Culture*, Minneapolis: University of Minnesota Press.

Macdonald, Alan 1953: 'Tony Stole a Trolley!', *Motion Picture and Television Magazine*, August: 32–33, 73.

McDonald, Paul 1995: 'Star Studies', in: Joanne Hollows and Mark Jancovich (eds.), *Approaches to Popular Film*, 79–97, New York: Manchester University Press.

'al-Magd' (review of the film *Glory*) 1957: *al-Kawakib* 323 (8 October): 24–25.

Meneley, Anne 1996: *Tournaments of Value: Sociability and Hierarchy in a Yemeni Town*, Toronto: University of Toronto Press.

Mulvey, Laura 1989: 'Visual Pleasure and Narrative Cinema', in: Laura Mulvey, *Visual and Other Pleasures*, pp. 14–26, Bloomington: Indiana University Press.

'Nujumuna: Kam Yataqaduna fi al-Sa'a?' (Our stars: how much do they earn in an hour?) 1957: *Al-Kawakib* 284 (8 January): 54–55.

Qasim, Mahmud and Wahbi, Ya'qub (eds.) 1997: *Mausu'at al-mumaththil fi al-sinima al-Misriyya, 1927–1997* (Encyclopedia of the actor in the Egyptian cinema, 1927–1997), Cairo: Dar al-Amin.

'Rihatuhu al-jamila tu'jibni (I like its beautiful smell)' 1951: *al-Kawakib* (26 March): 25.

Shalash, 'Ali 1986: *al-Naqd al-sinima'i fi al-sihafa al-Misriyya: nasha'tuhuh wa tatawwuruhu* (Cinema criticism in the Egyptian press: its founding and development), Cairo: General Egyptian Book Organization.

Shauqi, Ahmad 1954 [1917]: *Masra' Kliyubatra* (The fall of Cleopatra), Cairo: General Egyptian Book Organization.

Shauqi, Farid 1955: 'Ghayyar Majri Hayati', *al-Kawakib* 201: 48.

Shauqi, Farid 1957a: 'Ru'b al-Blatoh' (Terror on the plateau), *al-Kawakib* 294 (19 March): 39.

Shauqi, Farid 1957b: 'Mudhakirrat Farid Shauqi' (Memoirs of Farid Shauqi), *al-Kawakib* 299 (23 April): 16–17, 36.

Shauqi, Farid 1957c: 'Mudhakirrat Farid Shauqi', *al-Kawakib* 302 (14 May): 16–17, 37.

Shauqi, Farid 1957d: 'Mudhakirrat Farid Shauqi', *al-Kawakib* 303 (21 May): 5.

Shauqi, Farid 1957e: 'Mudhakirrat Farid Shauqi', *al-Kawakib* 304 (28 May): 30–31.

Shauqi, Farid 1978: *Malik al-tirsu* (King of the cheap seats), Cairo: Maktabat Ruz al-Yusuf.

Shawan, Salwa el- 1980: 'The Socio-Political Context of *al-Musika al-'Arabiyyah* in Cairo, Egypt: Policies, Patronage, Institutions, and Musical Change (1927–77)', *Asian Music* 12 (1): 86–128.

Stacey, Jackie 1994: *Star Gazing: Hollywood Cinema and Female Spectatorship*, New York: Routledge.

Sultan, Hoda 1957: 'Zauga lil-igar' (Wife for rent), *al-Kawakib* 314 (6 August): 38.

'Tariq al-Shauk' (Path of Thorns [advertisement]) 1950: *al-Kawakib* 15 (April): 25.

Twitchell, James B. 1992: *Carnival Culture: The Trashing of Taste in America*, New York: Columbia University Press.

Films

Angels with Dirty Faces

Boss Hasan (al-Usta Hasan) 1952. Salah Abu-Sayf. Cairo: Salah Abu-Sayf.

Cocaine (Kukayin) 1931. Togo Mizrahi. Cairo: Togo Mizrahi.

Forever Female

Glory (al-Magd) 1957. al-Sayyid Badir. Cairo: al-'Ahd al-Gadid.

Hamido (Hamido) 1953. Niyazi Mustafa. Cairo: Wahid Farid.

Hopes (Amal) 1952. Yusuf Ma'luf. Cairo: Lotus Film.

Lies upon Lies (Kidb fi kidb) 1944. Togo Mizrahi, Togo. 1944. Cairo: Togo Mizrahi.

Lover's Revenge (Intiqam al-habib) 1951. Firnutshu. 1951. Cairo: Aflam al-Gabri.

My Heart's Answer (Rudd qalbi) 1957. 'Izz al-Din Zulfiqar. Cairo: Asiya.

Path of Thorns (Tariq al-shauk) 1950. Husayn Sidqi. Cairo: Aflam Misr al-Haditha.

Port Said (Bur Sa'id) 1957. 'Izz al-Din Zulfiqar. Cairo: Aflam al-'Ahd al-Gadid.

Son of the Popular Quarter (Ibn al-hara) 1953. 'Izz al-Din Zulfiqar. Cairo: Aflam al-Gil al-Gadid.

They Made Me a Criminal (Ga'aluni mugriman) 1954. Atif Salim. Cairo: Farid Shauqi.

The Tough Guy (al-Futuwwa) 1957. Salah Abu-Sayf. Cairo: Aflam al-'Ahd al-Gadid.

Tough Guys of the Husayn District (Futuwwat al-Husayniyya) 1954. Niyazi Mustafa. Cairo: Aflam Muhammad Fauzi.

NINE

Chewing Gum, Insatiable Women and Foreign Enemies
Male Fears and the Arab Media

Mai Ghoussoub

'No spilt blood and no battles: here is the chewing gum that unleashes sexual urges with stimulating effects that exceed the power of 30 doses of a medical sexual enhancer.' Claimed by the liberal Egyptian paper *Al-Ahrar*, back in June 1996, to be the latest weapon used by the Israelis against the 'Arab body', the story of the Israeli chewing gum presented the fearful spectre of a gum that unleashed sexual desires while bringing impotence to its male consumers and rendering them sterile. Who was the first to come up with this stunning revelation? The newspaper assured its readers that Israeli research in the field had shown that:

> . . . the sexual excitement brought about by the chewing gum is not an end in itself. The ultimate object is the negative consequences of this stimulation, for if this gum increases the activity of the sexual glands in an extraordinary way, multiplying it by at least 50 times its normal rate, the chewing of this gum, even if only rarely, causes impotence through the destruction of the reproductive organs . . . The whole thing will result in a total ceasing of sexual activity among the inhabitants of the Arab countries within a few months . . . And the aim lying behind this infamous Israeli plot is the decrease in the birth rate in the Arab countries in order to narrow the wide demographic gap between the Arabs and Israel.

Such a dramatic revelation could not be ignored by the rest of the media. The daily *Al-Arabi* (an Egyptian Arab-nationalist paper) proudly declared that it had exposed the chewing gum plot before anyone else: 'the MP [member of the Egyptian parliament] Fathi Mansour relied on our information in order to carry this disaster from a mere newspaper campaign to an actual item on the agenda of the People's Congress.'

We know all too well that the dividing line between rumour and fact can be blurred and that it may even disappear entirely. What is significant to me in the case of this magical chewing gum is not to assess how trustworthy the sources of the mentioned newspapers were, nor if the editors of these sensational articles simply seized an irresistible rumour and gave it the authority of the written word, nor, conversely, whether the conviction of public opinion fuelled the whole story and brought it to the attention of the press as 'reliable information'. What is fascinating is the power of this innocent-looking chewing gum over the imagination of the readers of the newspapers mentioned as well as over at least one active member of parliament. I am describing this chewing gum as innocent looking for I saw its picture in one of the Egyptian papers during those troubled days: printed in black and white, on thin grey paper, the gum could indeed 'be very easily mistaken' for the little white squares produced by the Chiclets company or the Lebanese Ghandour factory, as the newspapers warned us.

The story of the magical poisonous gum did not remain confined to the Egyptian press. Even the serious *Al-Nahar* newspaper in Lebanon reported it in the most solemn terms, relating the facts in a news dispatch without comment and with no mention of the words rumour, claim or allegation. 'A brand of chewing gum . . . from Israel lies behind the uncontrollable sexual excitement of Egyptian girls', ran the title of the dispatch from Cairo published by *Al-Nahar* on 19 June 1996. According to the *Al-Akhbar* newspaper in Egypt, it went on, the MP Fathi Mansour had declared that, 'the story started in one of the region's universities, where many cases of rape were reported. There were up to fifteen cases of rape. What is new is that the girls were the violators in some cases and they perpetrated the rapes because of their untamed sexual desires.' Mansour purportedly added that on investigation he had discovered that the chewing gum was smuggled in through the Israeli-Egyptian border.

If rumours draw their strength from the perception of people who believe them, repeat them and spread them, we ought to take this magical gum seriously and try to understand why the need to believe in its existence was stronger than the need to question the credibility of the whole story. After all, a real parliamentary committee was designated by the People's Congress of Egypt to study the matter and arrest the culprits. *Al-Ahrar* declared in the same famous article of 25 June 1996 that the gum had been invented by a Mossad agent working with the KGB and that Yitzhak Rabin himself had personally given the order to increase its production.

I would like to investigate the driving quest behind these rumours. What do they tell us about male fears and sense of identity? Are they signs of threatened masculinity or a symptom of the re-negotiation of gender relations and sexual attitudes in Egypt and in the Middle East today? Why chewing gum? Could it be because women are its main consumers and that the fear of the chewing gum effect is actually a fear of women? If chewing gum were to trigger a large sexual appetite among the female population, what choice would husbands be left with? While quite understandably tempted themselves to resort to this miraculous enhancer to satisfy their insatiable wives, they face the cruel dilemma: the price paid for such short-lived super-virility is eternal impotence, the end of their progeny and everlasting shame. And beyond that how was a father or a brother to preserve his honour if his daughter or sister had developed an uncontrollable sexual drive? All the male fears were exposed and challenged by these little white squares and no doubt not a few fantasies triggered, too, at the prospect of a female rapist. Acting with the swiftness and the efficiency of an invisible spy, the gum had arrived to threaten a virility that had lost its guidelines. Only the devil dressed as a superpower hiding within these tiny squares could be so cunning in his quest to emasculate the ordinary citizen. Who said it was easy to be a man?

Lately, the Arab publishing world has been prolific in 'educating' the modern reader with texts retrieved from a past that was less austere in its approach to sexuality and its pleasures. In the last ten years the writings of Sheikh Nefzawi, Ahmed Bin Selman, Jalal al-Din al-Suyyuti and many others have been published in at least ten new editions each. These manuals, written in good faith a few hundred years ago – for the honest cause of serving the Muslim faithful – have often been seized upon by the agents of censorship in the modern Arab nation-states. Confiscation has in fact had the effect of increasing their popularity and their readership, generating endless reprints of popular as well as expensive editions. Even if a few women do purchase these manuals, their readership remains above all male, and if you visit Arabic bookshops you are likely to find them piled up next to the latest Fukuyama or Paul Kennedy without either their readers or the booksellers feeling them the least bit anachronistic or out of place beside books like *The End of History* and *The Rise and Fall of the Great Powers*.

You may be asking yourselves what conceivable link there is between the Israeli chewing gum and Sheikh Muhammad Nefzawi's *Al-rawd al-ʿater fi nuzhat al-khater* (*The Perfumed Garden*), written and published at the beginning of the fifteenth century, or Ahmad Bin Selman's *Ruju'u al-sheikh ila sibah* (The Rejuvenation of the Old Man), first published in the sixteenth century, or al-Tijani's *Nazhat al-aruss* (The Bride's Promenade), or al-Suyyuti's *Kitab al-'idah fi 'ilm al-nikah* (The Book of Explanations in the Art of Fornication), or . . . – the list is becoming very long indeed.[1] How could these texts written for the glory of Muslims have anything to do with a plot 'aimed at destroying them'? Could these popular manuals, written before Christian austerity invaded the scene, have something to do with the fantasies and the fears expressed by those who spread the chewing gum rumours and an audience that was pretty eager to believe them?[2] Many centuries have passed since Sheikh Nefzawi wrote his sexual manual. No modern Arab man writing about sex would dream of thanking God for having created women's vaginas for men's pleasure and men's penises for the pleasure of women (for it is with these celebratory sentiments that the Sheikh's famous book opens). Indeed, in the 1990s when a publisher in Beirut decided to reprint the book, the 'morality police' had it banned and the edition was in principle confiscated. The result as you may very well have guessed was the appearance on the market of a multitude of other editions. Where Sheikh Nefzawi felt he was accomplishing a religious and civic duty in writing his manual (dedicated originally to a vizier of Tunis), the modern religious authorities want it banned as pure pornography.

I believe that the relation between the chewing gum story and the popularity of the centuries old sex manuals lies in the fears and fantasies of men who may have changed drastically in the last century – as far as their morality and the social norms governing their existence are concerned – but whose views on sexual performance and women's desires are often derived from notions still deeply imprinted on their inherited memory which have not adjusted accordingly. The relation lies in men's tortured conception of their own 'masculinity': its meanings, demands and projections. Let us remember that the status of women, despite all the recent backlashes in Arab-Islamic societies, has changed dramatically. Their impact and their presence in the socio-economic sphere has drastically increased, their images on the pages of popular magazines and on TV screens are limitless in their variety, and moreover this is true in even the most misogynist corners of the Arab world. Men have had to adjust accordingly, be it in one direction or another, but navigating change presents its own dilemmas.

A most revealing expression of this dichotomy is summed up in the story of the edition of Sheikh Nefzawi's *Perfumed Garden* reissued by a Lebanese publisher in the late sixties. The entrepreneurial spirit of this publisher cost him a few nights in prison, the authorities being totally blind to the explicit irony of the extremely kitsch and vulgar cover to the edition. The 'artist' who had conceived the cover had obviously cut, very roughly, an image from a fifties American fashion magazine, in which a very slim, high heeled and elegantly dressed lady, whose face is hidden under a wide sophisticated round hat, appeared holding a tray. But instead of the drinks on the tray in the original photo, for Sheikh Nefzawi's cover a picture of a large penis had been substituted. The saying 'old concepts in modern dress' had never been more to the point.

Nefzawi asserts in his *Perfumed Garden* that 'women are never sated nor tired of copulating . . . Their thirst for intercourse is never quenched.'[3] And Bin Selman writes in 'The Rejuvenation of the Old Man', confirming his predecessor's vision of female sexuality: 'Some have affirmed that women's sexual appetite is many times superior to that of men . . . The weakest sexual desire among women is more powerful than the strongest male desire.'[4] These opinions are expressed in the best tradition of story-telling: we are entertained with the tales of slaves or princesses who have made love to hundreds of males without ever tiring and who ask for more and better sex. If we take the statements of these pious men as objective and indisputable (and this is how they conceived and presented them originally), we can be sure that it must have seemed impossible for a man to satisfy a woman and to match her sexual demands. What a frightening prospect for our males if they happen to give credence to these authoritative manuals. If women have such an insatiable appetite – and this assertion is stated as a scientific reality by many of these learned men who speak with the authority of the *Fiqh* (Islamic law) and with their apparently great knowledge of biology – why would they not seek fulfilment in other, and more, men? The fear is real: it is the fear of not being up to the masculine ideal, of failing to perform like the stud women are supposed to want, to desire, and indeed to need desperately. If the seclusion of women was the answer that came easily and logically to many anguished males in the past,[5] what are they to do when the barriers between the sexes are relaxed, and these highly sexed beings – their women – are working in mixed environments? When they walk freely on the street and share the overcrowded public transport of densely populated cities? It is becoming more difficult to be a male!

Listen to Nefzawi quoting the poet Abu Nuwas to tell us that sexually aroused women 'fail to distinguish the master from his slave'.[6] Bin Selman, in 'The Rejuvenation of the Old Man', tells the story of Al-Alfiya ('the thousander') who owed her name to the thousand men she had had sex with and who had acquired unique experience in keeping a man erect for days on end. She held a salon where women gathered to seek her advice and collect recipes for that purpose. It seems that honey, onions and camel's milk were the essential ingredients against undesired lapses in men's virility. How far are these ingredients from those needed to produce treacherous small white squares of chewing gum?

Reading through these volumes of treatises on sex, one is struck by how familiar and widespread these male fears and fantasies are in all societies. Very often our authors confuse their own fantasies and dreams with their objective and 'scientific' conclusions. And this is quite natural and human. The length of a male penis is one of those obsessions that all these learned men take for granted as far as the satisfaction of their demanding and permanently aroused women are concerned. Remember, these books that dwell on the needs and desires of women are written by men: thus, when the poetess Leila al-Akhiliya is asked about the desired length of a man's penis, she answers that the ideal is twelve inches, but that if it is less than six he has to compensate with other qualities and through other means.[7] To make men's life more difficult, our manuals believe in the limitless capacity of women to concoct stories, to resort to the most ingenious ruses in order to reach their aims. Men are less shrewd, and over-sexed women with powerful brains will always triumph, for 'The wiles of women are innumerable: they can mount an elephant on the back of an ant.'[8]

The writer I like most by far among our sexologists is Ahmad Shehab al-Din al-Tifashi (born 1184): he introduces his book *Nazhat al-albab fi ma la yujad fi kitab* ('The mind's promenade in what no book will tell you')[9] by thanking God for blessing men with the capacity to have fun and to enjoy lightness. Al-Tifashi is the least misogynist among his colleagues. He mixes many literary genres in his book, telling jokes, quoting poetry and referring to science and logic in order to tell us about women, their desires, their sexual tastes and their ruses. At one point, he states the elements that constitute and produce the perfect adulterer. According to our proficient author, to be a perfect adulterer a man needs to be young, for women prefer them younger; to wear perfume, for women's desire is aroused by nicely scented bodies; to bath frequently and colour his hair with henna, which should be used in generous quantities; to carry with him many little gifts, pretty objects that are not very expensive but always available; to have among his acquaintances a *qawada* (an old woman pimp); he should also be sensitive and capable of shedding tears very easily.

Al-Tifashi is obviously more sensitive and sophisticated in his knowledge of women and the politics of desire than Sheikh Nefzawi or Bin Selman. But he shares with them the belief in an active female sexuality. Women in his book are often seeking sexual encounters, and preferably with 'another' partner (the word foreign is used in this context in the text). The women in

Nazhat al-albab will use their attributes to reach their target. The 'jealous one' will show her anger: letting the desired man or men hear how much her unfaithful husband has mistreated her, she will incite male desire by acting angry and furious. Unable to resist her, the desired male will end up fulfilling her wish and making love to her. The same will happen with all the other types of women. They are different, but they want one thing from men: the sexual act.

These manuals and sources of knowledge inevitably end up telling us much more about their authors' sexual fantasies and fears than succeeding in fulfilling their promise of helping men understand women's sexuality the better to perform their sexual duties. The rumour about the sexual chewing gum reveals similar things about those who spread it. Rumours do not emanate from facts; they are the products of a perception. A rumour is a piece of information that we wish to believe and the wish to believe is always stronger than the quest for credibility, says Jean Noel Kapferrer in his excellent book on rumours.[10] What if an internalized fear finds a way of expressing itself, an outlet through which to relieve itself? 'A rumour that alleviates a deeply rooted sentiment makes the listener less critical,' says Kapferrer. What if the failure to perform and satisfy women's presumed sexual demands is shown not to be caused by the male's shortcoming? What if the danger of sexual encounters and adultery were not the result of the unavoidable mixed nature of contemporary society. What if all these ills had in fact been instigated by an ignominious plot? Then *l'honneur est sauf* and anguish is exorcized. Who is better placed to concoct this plot and be successful in its implementation than Israel, the state that has been invincible, has won many wars against the Arabs and has an inflated reputation for efficiency? Victory in war on the battlefield becomes victory by another means, this time through a kind of biological offensive, a symbolic castration in which Arab men's virility and hopes of progeny are threatened.

'The benefits drawn from adhering to and being party to a rumour fully justifies the little consideration given to plausibility,' says Kapferrer. Rumours go as quickly as they come. A few weeks after the big upheaval and the generalized anguish, the whole chewing gum story was forgotten. It knew neither a solution nor an ending. Could this silent finale be the result of a hidden awareness, born with the emergence of the rumour, that the whole story was a necessary fantasy? Did the short-lived chewing gum episode simply evaporate after having accomplished its therapeutic role?

The Egyptian film industry has been more successful in exorcizing the feeling of humiliation in the face of Israeli supremacy through a totally opposite means: a super-woman, played by an adored Egyptian film star,

234 ~ Mai Ghoussoub

infiltrates the highest of all Israeli security posts, thanks to her smartness, beauty and courage. Nadia al-Jundi invaded Arab cinema and TV screens in the early nineties with her box-office smash-hit: *Muhimma fi Tel Aviv* ('Mission to Tel Aviv'). The film was so successful that it has generated various sequels and large posters are exhibited in video shops in even the remotest corners of the Arab world.

In 'Mission to Tel Aviv' al-Jundi plays the role of a woman who is a victim of the class system in Egypt, as well as the unfair laws towards her sex. Having lost the custody of her child, she turns lose and immoral and ends up as the lover of an Israeli agent in Paris. However, her national feelings and original honesty emerge at the most crucial time and she decides to work and use her charms and connections to serve the Egyptian cause. Since she is irresistible, she manages to bring a very high-ranking Israeli security officer to her bedroom, and before making love to him (for the spectators do not miss out on the titillating and entertaining bits in the movie) she manages to slip sleeping pills into his drink and to steal the keys of the high-security room where all the strategic Israeli military secrets are kept. She is a hero, a liberated woman who dresses in the sexiest way without losing her dignity or her sense of sacrifice for her country.

This fantasy based on an image of liberated women, drawn and filmed with fun and drama, works better as a psychological catharsis than the threatening sexual chewing gum. Instead of chewing gum being slipped by 'the enemy' into the mouths of Egyptian women, it is an Egyptian woman herself who slips pills into 'the enemy's' mouth. Here a woman's strong sexuality and charms are not attributes created to make impossible demands on local men; they are used to advance further that good cause: 'the national struggle'. Women's sexuality becomes a kind of blessing when its impact is turned to the social and national good: instead of driving women into an uncontrollable sexual mood – turning them, sometimes, into rapists – active and seductive sexuality in Nadia al-Jundi's popular thrillers is used and displayed for the best of all causes against 'foreign' enemies. Women's sexual powers and desires are no longer a sexual threat for Arab men: they have been channelled in a different direction and have become a source of power (and fun) to be shared by Egyptian males as well as females.

These episodes in the modern life of the Arab media may seem unrelated. But I see in them evidence of a chaotic quest for a definition of modern masculinity. Through fears and hopes, anguished images and courageous depiction of 'the new woman', through the revisiting of old sex manuals and their modern re-appropriation, the meaning of masculinity is being thrown into question. Who said it was easy to be a man?

Notes

1. Among the few English translations of these texts are *The Perfumed Garden of Shaykh Nafzawi* translated by Sir Richard Burton, edited with an introduction and additional notes by Alan Hull Walton (London, 1963 edn.) and *The Glory of the Perfumed Garden: an English translation from the Arabic of the second and hitherto unpublished part of Shaykh Nafzawi's Perfumed Garden*, translated by H.E.J (London, 1975 edn.). Burton's translation is a 'polite' one and H.E.J.'s (the translator's name appears only in the form of initials) is intended to fill in the gaps. In this article I have relied on an Arabic edition. Al-Suyyuti's *Kitab al-'idah fi 'ilm al-nikah* has not (to my knowledge) been translated, but a book of his dealing with similar themes was translated into French as al-Souyouti, *Nuits de noces ou comment humer les doux breuvages de la magie licite* (Paris: Albin Michel, 1972).

2. There are good reasons for arguing that Christian sexual morality has deeply impregnated modern Muslim societies and that many 'fundamentalist' rejections of 'Western' depravity are merely (albeit unconsciously) reconstructing Victorian-type attitudes towards sexuality that prevailed in pre-sexual revolution European and American societies. Suggestive sources for such a view include, among other texts, Michel Foucault's *History of Sexuality*.

   As Abdelwahab Bouhdiba demonstrates in *Sexuality in Islam* (London: Routledge & Kegan Paul, 1985; paperback edn.: Saqi Books, 1998), al-Ghazali and other Muslim religious authorities centuries ago saw women's sexual pleasure as central to the happiness and stability of the Muslim family and beyond it the whole community. That Islam makes no mention of the notion of Original Sin could perhaps be understood as one factor in explaining this more positive view of sexual life. See also in this context, Fatima Mernissi's *Beyond the Veil: Male-Female Dynamics in Muslim Societies* (London: Saqi Books, 1985). It should also be mentioned here that the secular elite in modern Muslim societies, with its particular cultural formation, tends to find the classical Arabic texts of the kind that I discuss in this essay 'blunt' and 'vulgar' in their discussions of sexuality.

3. Some of these authors' writings are collected in *al-Jins Inda al-Arab*, editor's name not stated (Cologne: al-Jamal Publishers, 1997), vol. 1, p.91.

4. Ibid. vol 2, p.151.

5. See Fatima Mernissi, *Beyond the Veil*.

6. *al-Jins Inda al-Arab*, vol. 1, p. 92.

7. Ibid, vol. 1, p. 40.

8. Ibid, vol. 1, p. 99.

9. Ahmad al-Tifashi, *Nazhat al-albab fi ma la yujad fi kitab*, edited by Jamal Jum'a (London: Riad el-Rayess Books, 1992).

10. Jean Noel Kapferrer, *Rumeurs: le plus vieux media du monde* (Paris: Editions du Seuil, 1995).

TEN

'That's How I Am, World!'
Saddam, Manhood and the Monolithic Image

Hazim Saghieh

Jean Hofanes Grigor Joukasizian was born in Turkey in 1914, studied photography in Beirut and then received his practical training in Paris. One of the hundreds of thousands of Armenians scattered through the cities of the world, Jean Joukasizian moved to Baghdad in 1937 where he started Studio Babylon Photographers, which was probably the first studio of its kind to open there. In 1958, the year of the Republican Revolution, Joukasizian was commissioned as the official photographer to the republican presidential court. The modernization of the republic afforded to the photograph a greater role than previously. As photographs of the Egyptian president, Gamal Abd al-Nasser, covered the walls of Arab cities, the first president of Iraq, Abdul-Karim Qasim, wanted to compete with him in this domain.

Years later, in 1989, Ahmad Abdul-Majid wrote a book entitled *Five Iraqi Presidents*. He tried to describe these five, who followed one another in governing republican Iraq, through the memoirs of Joukasizian and the pictures that he took of them. Pictures of the five feature on the cover of the little book, all of them dressed in military uniform, and in the middle, bigger than the others, is the picture of the present president.

Of course, the reason for this honour was that Saddam Hussein was the president of Iraq at the time the book was published, while all the others were dead, apart from Abdul-Rahman Arif, who had retired from political life after being swept away by the Baathist revolution in 1968. However, there was another reason that caused the photographer to be captivated by his president. On page 7 of the book, amidst his first photographs, there is a picture of Saddam and Jean Joukasizian together. The former is standing in all his military finery, solid as a rock, apart from the smile fixed on his

'President Saddam Hussein, the Iraqi president who most often stood in front of Jean's lens' reads the original caption to this photograph of the president with Jean Joukasizian, one of the most important photographers of the republican era (from Ahmad Abdul-Majid, *Five Iraqi Presidents*, Baghdad, 1989).

lips, while the latter is holding on to him as if seeking protection from an enemy, smiling radiantly in dignified civilian clothes. He is clasping Saddam's hand with both hands, and under the picture he has written, 'President Saddam Hussein, the Iraqi president who most often stood in front of Jean's lens.' In order to understand what he meant, it is perhaps instructive to make a comparison with another president, Abdul-Salam Arif, whom the photographer described as 'more afraid of being photographed than of being overthrown in a coup' and as 'irritated by photography'. There is no doubt that Saddam by contrast loved photography. For photographs, as well as statues, monuments and speeches were responsible for making him generally known to Iraqis and forming an image of him in their minds.

A glance at the photographs of Saddam Hussein contained in the biography of the leader by the Lebanese journalist, Fuad Matar, is sufficient to show this. Some of these pictures show him smoking a pipe, puffing on a cigar, blowing out the candles on a birthday cake. Others show him in a park with his wife, swimming with his family, and taking a boat-trip with members of his family on the waters of the River Tigris. In yet others we find him praying and performing the rituals of the Umra in Mecca, eating kebabs, and asking about goods in a shop that sells spare parts for cars. We see him visiting children in a kindergarten in Baghdad, visiting the marshes where people live in shantytowns floating on the water, going shooting, hunting deer, living in his own goat's hair tent in his hometown of Takrit, visiting soldiers, kissing children, and fiddling with his worry beads. We catch him reading the newspaper dressed as a peasant and seated in front of a tent, partaking of a meal with some airmen, and on a visit with his family to a family of peasants with whom he is drinking tea. There are even domestic photographs depicting him carrying his little girl on his shoulders, darning the sleeve of the dress of his other daughter, Raghda, while 'being careful not to wake up his daughter Rana who is sleeping in her mother's lap'. Another shows him being photographed with his son and 'daughter at their request', wearing an Arab headdress on his head and holding a cigar in his hand.

This is the way he has been portrayed in photographs, but he has also been portrayed in paintings and drawings. He has been drawn mounted on a white horse, and again with a family tree showing that his ancestry goes back to Ali bin Abi Talib, the fourth rightly guided caliph and the first imam and doctrinal authority of the Twelver Shias, who make up the majority of the inhabitants of Iraq. You can also see him on his country's stamps, on clocks and watches which bear his image, and in the form of statues and murals in the public squares from which the meanings and memories of cities are made.

In his book, *The Monument: Art, Vulgarity and Responsibility in Iraq*, Samir al-Khalil demonstrated that the famous Arch of Victory Monument in Baghdad has played a crucial role in conveying an image of Saddam. This work of sculpture was cast from a plaster of Paris mould taken directly from the arms of the president and magnified to a grand scale. In both hands he is holding a sword. The equivalent of the Arc de Triomphe in the Champs Elysées in Paris, the Baathist monument is on an altogether bigger scale. The forearms and hands of the president leap out from the belly of the earth like giant bronze tree-trunks sixteen metres high – this is the height of the Arc de Triomphe. From there the two swords rise to a height of forty metres above the ground. From the debris of the Iran–Iraq war, five thousand Iranian helmets were collected, brought directly from the field of battle and divided into two equal piles, each pile stacked up against the base of the two forearms to suggest that the arms themselves are bursting up through the earth, scattering the helmets of the defeated and humiliated Iranians. Saddam himself is represented as the ultimate victor, the very embodiment of the nation.

Saddam Hussein has indeed come to fill every space in Iraqi society. He is omnipresent through photographs, statues and portraits, on every street, in every office, in every café, and in every school. He is also there through other channels such as radio and TV, as well as Friday sermons and school textbooks. In fact, through the state's totalitarian grip on society and its infrastructure, he is present in the private, personal and domestic space of almost every Iraqi man and woman. However, because 'appearances show us less than we imagine about the good and evil' present in a person, as John Updike wrote in the introduction to one of the collections of photographs of Magnum, it becomes essential to become acquainted with Saddam to some extent before dealing with his image.

He is an orphan, and this as we know is one of the qualities often attributed to those prophets who rebel against the environment in which they grow up and clash with it as they seek to introduce something new and unfamiliar. The Iraqi president did not miss the opportunity, in one of the museums he has established in his own honour, to celebrate the state of orphancy which links him with the Prophet Muhammad. However, although the death of his father opened an early door for his self-liberation, he went about this in a somewhat roundabout manner. He clashed with his immediate family when his mother married a man whose relationship with Saddam was characterized by violence and severity. However, the wider clan supported him enthusiastically in his struggle to 'pursue learning' and in his determination not to spend his life as a common peasant. As Fuad Matar informs us, the support of the clan took a very singular form: they gave him a revolver. It appears that his role model was none other than his maternal uncle, Khayr Allah Talfah, to whom the young man fled and who undertook to bring him up. His uncle was a hero and a leader within the tribal hierarchy. How could it be otherwise when he was one of the officers who had taken part in the popular military coup in support of the Germans in 1941, a coup which in Baathist legend was later to be considered an event in Iraqi history exemplifying 'manhood and nobility'.

Thus Saddam inherited his political inclinations from the wider family, not from his immediate family: that is to say, he inherited them from his bedouin background not from his peasant background. To be a peasant is at the end of the day to be a member of a social class that can be incorporated into the modern nation-state; to be a bedouin signals non-acceptance of borders and even of the legality of the central state. The clan was not lax in offering him help in the early stages of his life and in his political ascent, not least in aiding him in his flight after taking part in the attempted assassination of the then president, Abdul-Karim Qasim.

The region where he was brought up, and whose people gave him the revolver, is rich in distinct social characteristics. Takrit, near to which lies the small village of Al-Awja, is situated midway along the line stretching north from the city of Samira' to the city of Mosul. This is an Arab Sunni corridor attracted historically towards Syria, which rivals Baghdad as a focus of attraction for the western regions of Iraq. The reason for this attraction is the relative geographical proximity and also a shared allegiance to the Sunni sect, nourished by ties of blood and marriage with the clans of the Syrian Desert region who have a similar social composition. These relationships led the clans of that region, who moved and migrated freely between the two countries, to intervene effectively on behalf of the nationalists against the communists in the events which took place in Mosul in 1959. They did so especially since they were afraid of the agricultural reform that would restrict their widespread holdings and mobility.

Thus Takrit and the surrounding area remained relatively unaffected by either the new borders established by 'colonialism' after the disintegration of the Ottoman empire, or by the capital city of Baghdad, with which the only contact consisted of sending their sons into the army. The clannish composition of the population allowed people to cross the borders in order to migrate or to engage in smuggling. This same composition also made tough combative versions of manhood central, especially since to the north and east of the region lie the Kurdish tribes with whom the Arabs of the western regions regularly engaged in warfare.

In his book, *Cruelty and Silence: War, Tyranny, Uprising, and the Arab World*, Kanan Makiya comes to the conclusion that manhood in that region during the Ottoman period became identified with a code of behaviour bearing a specific bedouin name: 'breaking of the eye' (*kasr al-'ayn*). This he sees as expressed in an attempt to rape the womenfolk of an unpopular ruler. On one occasion, the Wali (governor) of the time attended a banquet in Takrit to which he had been invited. On his return journey to Baghdad a number of young men fell upon him, his wife and his companions, and guaranteed by pure sexual aggression the subsequent pursuit of policies more to the liking of the Takritis.

From this we discover one of the two basic images of Saddam: the traditional image of the young man who seems to have weak links with the concept of the nation-state and, we might infer, a weak grasp of the principles of modern political organization, and for whom blood ties and their violent standards in the most basic sense underpin his alliances and his emotions. This set of characteristics, which many identify with or find reminiscent of southern Italy, enable us to explain many of his subsequent positions, starting with the fact that he is by origin a Baathist thug and not one the ideologues of Baathism (of whom in any case there have been very few in Iraq). Then, according to Hanna Batatu in his book, *The Old Social Classes and the Revolutionary Movements of Iraq*, his accession in 1964 to membership of the leadership of the then clandestine party contributed to the 'Takritization' of the party. More recently, we have all been made aware of how Saddam does not stint at purging relations by marriage (his two daughters' husbands, among others) and how his sons and brothers struggled among themselves in the wake of the sharp reversal of policy away from giving all jobs to clan members.

This is one side of the coin, but it does not explain the impact Saddam has had. Saddam is also a modernizer who has gathered an extraordinary harvest of oil revenues and has re-established a cohesive government and a tightly knit party. He has united the government and party in an organic mould typical of totalitarian regimes. Here we must also mention a certain conception of what it means to be 'Western': a tendency towards astronomical consumption of clothes, shoes, hats and cigars.

In fact, we cannot but notice how far Saddam has gone in promoting another form of mass consumption through multiple reproductions of images of himself: indeed Samir al-Khalil in this sense draws a parallel between the leader's promotional skills and Andy Warhol's pop art. However, the Iraqi President uses so many conflicting and opposing images of himself that he also appears to resemble Madonna in her many different incarnations, filling such a vast space that she almost exhausts all possible representations of herself and self-destructs. But while the duality of religion and sex has remained the Madonna duality *par excellence*, the image of Saddam in all its different versions rests on a single monolithic function of conveying fear to the receiver.

Intimidation, in this sense, find its roots in clan relationships, and in the financial aid, party structures, ideological apparatuses and processes of modern visual consumption that have been enlisted in its service and for which the whole country has become an arena. In protecting Iraq from Iran in his role as 'the eastern doorkeeper of the Arab nation', Saddam embodies machismo raised to the level of cliché in relation to his own country whose people, political parties, religions and social classes he has penetrated.

In a word, he has subjected the history and social fabric of Iraq to a 'breaking of the eye'. To put it in simple, perhaps clichéed psychological terms, Saddam's machismo can be seen most glaringly in his attempt to penetrate neighbouring countries: Iran and Kuwait. By the same token, the last war changed Iraq into the totally feminine entity in confrontation with the totally male who tortured her and brought her suffering. As for his experience in the party, it only strengthens the idea of 'the male', indeed the leader of the pack. Beyond this, what we know of Michel Aflaq, the founder of the Baath Party, and the other very ordinary men who were part of the leadership, is enough to discourage us from thinking that there could be competition for the title of leader of the pack. When a competitor like Abdul-Khaliq al-Samira'i appeared in the Baath Party in Iraq, or someone like Munif al-Razzaz in the 'Popular Leadership', their fate was to be hung and imprisoned until death respectively.

Recently, international politics and the media have added another dimension. Nobody ever called Hitler 'Adolf', and nobody (except the British tabloid press) addresses Milosevic as 'Slobodan'. By contrast, the Iraqi leader, with a clear message of scorn, is called just 'Saddam'. From another point of view, the use of this single first name seems to indicate that the man is innocent of any tie or significance beyond himself that might be a restraint on his behaviour. His violent outbursts, with all the thunder and lightning that they contain, pass without any form of social sanction.

For this elemental maleness to fulfil its role requires both control of a modern army and modern weapons, and also monopolistic control of their symbolism. It may of course be said that this distinction is not watertight.

Hitler regularly wore military uniform, while the democratic civilian leader Churchill wore it throughout World War II, but only during that period, and Stalin likewise. However, what is noticeable is that the Iraqi President – who, unlike Hitler and Churchill, has never been in the army – has stolen the glory of the previous military leaders of Iraq. He appears in public adorned with regalia and medals, wearing a revolver, and flanked by the special weapons he has used and in whose honour he has established a museum.

Of course, this relationship with the military establishment and with military traditions serves political and party functions: Saddam does not want a repetition of what happened at the end of 1963, when the Baath was toppled by the military. He is determined to maintain direct control of the army. Nevertheless, when we stand in front of the many pictures that exist of him in military uniform and with his revolver, we realize that personal bravery and a fierce surcharge of male drive lie behind all this. He is not satisfied with dominating the main institutions of power through his friends – as Abd al-Nasser and Abdul-Hakim 'Amir did – or through his brothers – in the way that Fidel and Raul Castro have done. Instead, he prefers to exercise personal power and is irked by the competition of his maternal cousin and nephew by marriage, Adnan Khayr Allah.

Let us reconsider the many pictures which show him with his family wearing military uniform, bearing in mind that such a grouping generally implies some relaxation of dress. As we look at them, we are reminded of the first task entrusted to the totem: to protect its square and the immediate circle before all else. This goal appears with great clarity when we look back at the traditional marriage pattern Saddam has followed: his wife, Sajida Khayr Allah, is the daughter of Saddam's maternal uncle and thus a first cousin. This blond-haired lady, posed in photos in her conservative Western dress, moreover seems to be the living embodiment of the protection granted to her and her daughters by her armed knight.

There is no doubt that the continual theatre practised by Saddam the civilian wearing military clothing serves the purpose of intimidation which we see brought out in a string of contrasts. Just as Stalin in photos carried his little daughter, Svetlana, and Hitler had many delightful pictures taken with children presenting him with bouquets, Saddam has been photographed carrying his daughter while wearing his revolver at his waist. Again, at the start of the invasion of Kuwait, at a meeting with the frightened foreign communities of Baghdad, he made a point of being seen to play with a child: the image of the scene was made famous when it was broadcast around the world by CNN.

244 ∿ Hazim Saghieh

The little boy or girl represents, in each case, the extreme need of the vulnerable for protection exercised by an all-powerful father. However, the presence of the child also says something else to us, which in its turn is an indication of how pre-existing structures get harnessed to the dictates of modernity. The image of a leader carrying his little girl, or smiling at her, or showing affection towards her is not recorded in the work of artists of earlier times, but rather is tied to the present era and has become part of its accepted, indeed encouraged and required, values. Moreover, in our present context, humility — and even brokenness — before a child enhances the 'manhood' of a man rather than reducing it. For he is not humbling himself or breaking down before another man, who by implication is equal in stature and strength. Rather, he uses this modern value of 'tender' fatherhood to strengthen and serve another value which is centrally bound up with the notion of real manhood as power.

Through his few gestures, his bodily stiffness and the slow way in which he gesticulates in front of the masses, this father never ceases to offer proof of the various meanings of power, highlighting them by means of contrast. He looks down on his people from on high and grants them feelings of stability and rootedness, thus making them feel secure: the slow movement of his hands indicates level-headedness with no hint of recklessness. Even when he carries weapons, and even in the photographs which portray him using them, he never changes: his body never bends and his face never indicates any reaction worth mentioning.

This solid appearance of his is not mingled either with the awesome frown of Khomeini, the unmistakable madness of Hitler, or the hysteria of Mussolini. Rather, his image resembles a photograph that is fixed at a single moment in time. Once all the details are put aside, photographs of the leader – who has been compared with a historical personage who goes much further back than the era of the photograph, namely Al-Hajjaj bin Yousif – refuse to yield up any other dimension than that of the capacity to induce fear. In reality, the manhood of Saddam, with its roots deep in the clan, does not offer the security that can be granted by religious manhood. He has never allowed himself to grow a beard, and when he prays he does not put a cowl on his head. No image shows him fingering the beads of the *tesbih* which never leaves the hand of the devout believer. And conversely, when on occasion he wears European hats, clothes and shoes these never become more than purely external appendages evidently worn for show.

However, the unbridled tendency towards depravity that increases the impoverishment of the image of the Iraqi leader finds ways to compensate which are more elemental. For instance, that he is absorbed in history-making is clear from the Arch of Victory, which sees the limbs of the president spring out of the bowels of the earth as though they were an elemental natural force. Like many totalitarian rulers, Saddam has been concerned to appear as an extension of nature and as the supreme crowning of a continuous national history. Continuity gives an impression of co-ordination and harmony, and this explains the concern with stone monuments and statues: they are the visible manifestations of the ruler's search for eternity.

However, here we face the difficulty that we face when dealing with any totalitarian leader of this type. This image, which is intended to serve a particular time and era, and which is intended also to be generalized throughout history in so far as it is able to capture a summary of it, falls into a historical extremism which lessens its efficacy in achieving its goal. The monolithic image of Saddam may serve to secure the acceptance of the masses of all manner of myths that legitimize his leadership, especially in times of war and severance from tradition. However, it is valid only in transitory, transitional periods. The father, or the leader, or the perfect male, soon appear as absolute and timeless constructs. Since in the end fatherhood is by nature relative, absolute fatherhood becomes totally abstract and ahistorical and is almost susceptible to mockery.

If the Iraqi leader is equal to other totalitarian leaders in terms of his 'natural' absolutism, his dilemma as far as historical absolutism is concerned is greater than their dilemma. Iraq's own history, which has seen great qualitative breaks and a complex intermingling of religious, sectarian and ethnic groups, makes overuse of the past and attempts to present a unified picture of it a stumbling endeavour. Iraqi history may pulsate with powerful three-dimensional primary colours, but it is unco-ordinated.

Looking at history in static terms does not add any knowledge to fear. However, it does bring in its wake a quantity of ignorance that confirms just how fearful it is. Saddam has made a link, for example, between the Battle of Qadisiya of Sa'd bin Abi Waqqas, a battle that took place in early Islamic history against the pre-Islamic Persians, and his own war with the Iranians (described as *Qadisiyet Saddam*). In this instance, he related the two wars by collapsing history and signalling a deeper connection summed up in his rhetorical and essentialist (but empty) assertion that, 'Men are men'. According to what Amataziah Baram says in his book, *Culture, History and Ideology in the Creation of Ba'thist Iraq, 1968–89*, this is similar to what the Iraqi Baathists did in linking the Spring festivities, which began in 1969, with Sumer and the ancient Babylonians. The selective recollection of history is always harmonized with contemporary Arab issues. Thus, a lesson was addressed to Zionists through recourse to the story of Nebuchadnezzar, who marched at the head of his armies as they transferred the Jewish prisoners from Jerusalem to Babylon. After 1980, the year when the war with Iran began, the goal of one day 'liberating' Jerusalem found a historical resonance: had not the Jews supported the Persian Cyrus in his siege of Babylon; had it not been they indeed who had opened the gates to Cyrus?

What increases the element of fear, but is at the same time impoverishing, is the fact that Saddam's image is in the end totally lacking in attractiveness. It is quite unlike the image of a Castro who defied the USA with the blaze of his revolution, along with his distinctive beard and cigar. Or the image of a Nasser, with his speeches and his characteristic laugh that accompanied the enthusiasms and dreams which his policies enflamed. Saddam, in his moments of imperial arrogance, remains nothing more than a failed imitator of the Shah of Iran. In his moments of spontaneity it does not occur to him to do what Khrushchev did when he raised his shoe above the podium of the United Nations. When he smokes his cigar he just cannot compete with Churchill, or with Guevara for that matter, in fitting the image.

In a word, the image of the Iraqi President is sterile: he is unable to match the expectations of those who seek an image, and is totally and wilfully unphotogenic. 'The monument is the sign on which a man reads something which cannot be said anywhere else, because it belongs to the biography of the artist and to the history of the society,' says Aldo Rossi. Saddam is basically unconcerned with this dialectic between social demand and the proffering of self. His golden rule is that blunt bedouin saying which the tenth-century poet, Mutanabbi, drew on: 'That's how I am, world!'

In addition to this, Saddam is not an orator, bearing in mind that oratory plays a big part in creating the image of a political leader, especially in the 'Third World'. He is rarely witnessed mingling with the crowds or even near them, although he frequently towers over them from on high. Although his inert body provides the suitable raw material from which to hew an image, it is as if it is out of commission and somehow not usable as a political investment. His speech is heavy with a particular dialect: it is difficult for it to draw the hearts and minds of people who come from outside his immediate geographical area and thus cannot really fire the Iraqi nation.

There is nothing special about his appearance. His face is nondescript, its moustache as commonplace as any other in the Middle East or Latin America, those two cradles of machismo. When seen amongst party cadres his reserved smile seems only to combine a sly foxiness and artificiality with a certain traditional cunning. In short, Saddam is not a hero, and yet nor is he an anti-hero.

Nevertheless, since cult figures and points of reference are absent in a fearful, closed, turbulent and changing society, Saddam can assume such a role for a section of Iraqi youth which is deprived of an Elvis Presley, a James Dean or a Che Guevara of its own. This tragic reality says more about the Iraq that Saddam has created than it says about the creator himself. Even conviction in totalitarian countries, as we all well know, is an expression of the pervasiveness of oppression and sham choices. Thus we are never very far from the equation of fear and terror.

Inside Iraq where it is impossible to measure public opinion exactly it is probable that the lustre on the image of Saddam remains dependent on a climate of disaster and the ensuing appeal for salvation. That is, people have become accustomed to fear, although a very small proportion of the beneficiaries of it can really find something attractive about the condition. By all accounts the Baathist establishment does not impose its power on the basis that it is the expression of a socially superior 'class' in terms of education or economic status. Rather domination of the means of power has led to the assertion of this power without any other justification.

Outside Iraq, and not inside it, there developed a certain worship of the leader which canonized him as the highest ideal of manhood and male sex appeal. However, as we know, this did not last long: no sooner had the unhappy practical consequences of the 'mother of all battles' and the 'great duel' become clear than a widespread disillusionment set in which fitted ill with the macho male and the clan-related, triumphalist language that went with him. There were of course men and women who confused an erstwhile solidarity with the Iraqi people with solidarity (implicit in the most part) with Saddam. However, they tried to dress this up with an emphasis on poverty, weakness and ill-treatment, none of which fit with the basic image which he has always wanted for himself: fear and the ability to project it into hearts. In fact, Saddam's political credit and that of the ruling party do not help much. For he has not achieved, by any measure of political effectiveness, what other dictatorial leaders have achieved. Even if we forget for a moment the link that his name has with extraordinary oppression, in the streets of the Arab cities, where the 'public opinion' of the masses is made, the Baath Party has never been forgiven for its stand against Nasser, or for the withdrawal of the Iraqi army in 1970 in the face of the Jordanian forces which were approaching to wipe out the Palestinian resistance.

What remains of Saddam's image?

The Iraqi president is a self-appointed divinity. He is a producer and a creator, but hackneyed in what he produces and vulgar in what he creates. In this self-appointment, the projection of fear is accompanied by the other monolithic dimension of self-sufficiency, and hence a self-love of a sort which is weak in responding to the desires and expectations of others. In a country with a disrupted and turbulent political history the search for tranquillity is not to be found by contemplating this self-assigned divinity whose image repels in its overwhelming self-containment. The logic of this divinity is to confiscate the roles of everyone – fathers and men, mothers and women – to hand over all to his worshippers and his national and party organizations, and to require children to spy on their families.

And yet the image of Saddam is so over used that it loses all meaning and depends only on a never-ending process of greater magnification. We are faced with something resembling a modern tyrannical paganism in which the totem becomes a meeting place for fathers whose capacity for fatherhood is restricted by force. For he is the man and the god: unconcerned with winning the hearts and minds of his servants, he crushes them, caring only that they are prevented from any attempt at resisting his worship.

Translated from Arabic by Basil Hatim and Malcolm Williams

PART III

Memoir and Male Identity

ELEVEN

Lentils in Paradise[*]

Moris Farhi

Paradise was Sophie's gift to Selim and me. She took us there frequently. I was about seven; Selim a year or so older. Paradise was the women's *hamam* – Turkish baths – of Ankara.

Sophie cherished us as if we were her own; and we loved her just as much. In fact, I can now admit, we loved her more than we loved our mothers. We reasoned that since she was under no obligation to hold us dear, the fact that she did meant we were worthy of affection. Consequently, we never believed the loose talk from parents and neighbours that, given the law of nature whereby every woman is ruled by the maternal instinct, Sophie, destined to remain unmarried and childless, needed perforce to treasure every child that came her way, even curs like Selim and me.

Sophie was one of those young women from the Anatolian backwoods who, having ended up with no relatives and no home, found salvation in domestic service in the sizeable metropolises, Istanbul, Izmir, Adana, and the new capital, Ankara. Often payment for such work amounted to no more than the person's keep and a bed in a corner of a hallway; wages, if they existed, seldom exceeded a miserable *lira* or two a month. But, in the early 1940s, when Turkey's policy of neutrality in the Second World War had brought on severe economic problems, even this sort of employment was hard to find.

My parents, I am glad to say, paid a decent wage despite the constant struggle to make ends meet. For Sophie was an Armenian, a member of a race that, like the Jews, had seen more than its share of troubles. Sophie

---

[*] First published in *The Slow Mirror and Other Stories, New Fictions by Jewish Writers*, edited by Sonja Lyndon and Sylvia Paskin (London: Five Leaves Publications, 1996), pp. 15–26.

herself, as her premature white hair and the scar that ran diagonally across her mouth testified, was a survivor of the passion suffered by the Armenians at the hands of the Turks and the Kurds during the First World War.

Selim and I never accepted the distinction that Sophie was a servant. With the wisdom of young minds we dismissed the term as derogatory. We called her *abla*, 'elder sister'. At first – since Selim was not my brother, but my friend who lived next door – I insisted that she should be known as *my abla*, but Sophie, who introduced us to everything that is noble in humanity, took this opportunity to teach us about true justice. Stroking our foreheads gently, she impressed upon us that since Selim and I had been inseparable since our toddling days, we should have acquired the wisdom to expel from our souls such petty impulses as greed and possessiveness. She belonged to both of us – what was more natural than that?

The event that led us to Paradise occurred the moment Sophie set foot in our house.

She had arrived from the Eastern Anatolian province of Erzurum. The journey, mostly on villagers' carts, occasionally, using up her few *kuruş*, on dilapidated trucks, had taken her about a week. And for another week, until she had heard on the grapevine that she might try knocking on my mother's door, she had slept in cold cellars procured for her, often without the owners' knowledge, by sympathetic countrywomen. She had washed in the drinking fountains of the open-air market where she had gone daily in search of scraps; but, lacking any spare vestments, she had not changed her sweat-encrusted clothes. Thus, when she had arrived at our flat, she had come enveloped in the pungent smell of apprehension and destitution.

My mother, seasoned in matters of disinfestation – she had attended to my father whenever he had come on leave from the army – immediately gathered, from her own wardrobe, a change of clothes and guided Sophie to the shower, our only fixture for washing. We had hardly settled in the sitting room – I remember we had visitors at the time – Selim's parents, some neighbours and, of course, Selim – when we heard Sophie laughing. My mother, who had taken to Sophie instantly, looked well satisfied, no doubt interpreting the laughter as a happy omen.

Moments later, the laughter turned into high-pitched giggles. Giggles became shrieks; and shrieks escalated into screams.

As we all ran to the hallway fearing that Sophie had scalded herself, the toilet door flew open and Sophie burst out, wet and naked and hysterical.

It was Selim's father who managed to contain her. Whilst my mother asked repeatedly what had happened, he threw a raincoat over Sophie and held her in a wrestler's grip until her screams decelerated into tearful, hiccupy giggles. Eventually, after sinking onto the floor and curling up, she managed to register my mother's question. As if relating an encounter with a *djinn*, she answered, in a hoarse whisper: 'It tickles! That water tickles!'

The ensuing laughter, manifesting as much relief as mirth, should have offended her; it didn't. Sophie, as we soon learned, believed that laughter had healing qualities and revered anybody who had the gift of humour. But it had never occurred to her that she herself could be comical. The revelation thrilled her. And, as she later admitted to me, her ability to make us laugh had been the factor that had convinced her to adopt us as her kin.

The afternoon ended well. When Sophie, hesitantly, asked whether she could finish washing by the kitchen tap, my mother promptly took her, together with the women visitors, to the *hamam*.

Thereafter, Sophie became a devotee of the baths. And she used any excuse, including the grime Selim and I regularly gathered in the streets, to take us there. My mother never objected to this indulgence: entry to the *hamam* was cheap – children went free – and Sophie, Selim and I, sparkling after so much soap and water, always appeared to confirm the adage: 'Only the clean are embraced by God.'

In those days, Turkish baths had to struggle hard to maintain their Ottoman splendour. The travail was particularly evident in Ankara. This once humble townlet which, with the exception of an ancient castle on a hillock, had barely been touched by history, was rising fast as the symbol of the new, modern Turkey. As a result some 'progressive' elements saw the baths as totems of oriental recidivism and sought to reduce their popularity by promoting Western-style amenities.

Yet, here and there, the mystique prevailed. After all, how could the collective memory forget that, for centuries, Istanbul's spectacular *hamams* had entranced and overawed flocks of discerning Europeans.

And so the tradition survived; discreetly, in some places; openly in others. And when new baths were built – as was the case with most of the establishments in Ankara – every attempt was made to adhere to the highest provision.

Two cardinal standards are worth mentioning. The first predicates that the primary material for the inner sanctum, the washing enclave itself, must be marble, the stone which, according to legend, shelters the friendly breezes and which, for that very reason, is chosen by kings for their palaces and by gods for their temples.

The second standard stipulates the following architectural features: a dome, a number of sturdy columns and a belt of high windows, a combination certain to suffuse the inner sanctum with a glow suggestive of the mystic aura of a mosque. Moreover, the high windows, whilst distilling apollonian light, would also deter peeping-toms.

Our women's *hamam*, having adhered to these standards, was the epitome of luxury.

Let me take you in, step by step.

The entrance, its most discreet feature, is a small, wrought-iron door located at the centre of a high wall like those that circumvent girls' colleges.

The foyer is lush. Its dark purple drapes immediately promise exquisite sensual treats. To the right of the foyer there is a low platform with a kiosk. Here sits the manageress, *Teyze Hanım*, 'Lady Aunt', whose girth may well have coined the Turkish idiom, 'built like a government'. She collects the entrance fees and hires out such items as soap, towels, bowls and the traditional Turkish clogs, *nalıns*.

At the bottom of the foyer, a door leads into the spacious communal dressing room. As if to prolong your anticipation, this is simply trimmed: whitewashed walls, wooden benches and large wicker-baskets for stacking clothes.

Another door opens into a passageway which has boards on its floor. Here, as you walk, the clogs beat an exciting rhythm. Ahead is the arch which leads into the baths' marbled haven.

The next moment you feel as if you are witnessing a transfiguration. The mixture of heat and steam have created a diaphanous air; the constant sound of running water is felicitous; and the white nebulous shapes that seemingly float in space profile kaleidoscopic fantasies in your mind. This might be a prospect from the beginning of days – or from the last. In any case, if you adore women and crave to entwine with every one of them, it's a vision that will remain indelible for the rest of your life.

Thereafter, slowly, your eyes begin to register details. You note that the sanctuary is round – actually, oval. You are glad. Because had it been rectangular, as some are, it would have emanated a masculine air.

You note the large marble slab that serves as a centrepiece. This is the 'belly stone'. Its size determines the reputation of the particular establishment; a large one, as that in the women's *hamam*, where people can sit and talk – even picnic – guarantees great popularity.

You note the washing areas around the 'belly stone'. Each is delineated by a marble tub – called *kurna* – wherein hot and cold water, served from two separate taps, is mixed. You note that the space around each *kurna* accommodates several people, invariably members of a family or a group of neighbours. These people sit on stocky seats, also of marble, which look like pieces of modern sculpture, and wash themselves by filling their bowls from the *kurna* and splashing the water onto their bodies. Sometimes, those who wish to have a good scrub avail themselves, for a good baksheesh, of one of a number of attendants present.

You note that, beyond the inner sanctum, there are a number of chambers which, being closer to the furnace, are warmer. These are known as a word which implies 'solitude', and are reserved for those who wish to bathe alone or to have a massage. For the elite customer, the latter is performed by Lady Aunt.

But, of course, above all, you note the bathing women. Wearing only bracelets and earrings, they look as if they have been sprinkled with gold. Tall or short, young or old, they are invariably Rubenesque. Even the thin ones appear voluptuous. Covered with heavy perfumes and henna, they carry themselves boldly, at ease with their firm, soft bodies. They are, you realize, proud of their femininity – I am speaking in hindsight – even though – or perhaps because – they live in a society where the male rules unequivocally. But if they see or think someone is looking at them, they are overcome with shyness and cover their pudenda with their bowls. You note little girls, too, but, if you're a little boy like me, you're not interested in them. You have already seen their budding treasures in such outworn games as 'mothers and fathers', 'doctors and patients'.

I feel I have related our entry to Paradise as if it were a commonplace occurrence, as if, in the Turkey of the 40s, little boys were exempt from all gender considerations. Well, that's only partly true. Certainly, over the years, I came across many men of my generation who, as boys, had been taken to the women's baths either by their maids or nannies or grannies or other elderly female relatives – though never by their mothers; that taboo appears to have remained inviolate.

In effect, there were no concrete rules on boys' admission into women's hammams. The decision rested on a number of considerations: the reputation of the establishment, the status of its clientele, the regularity of a person's – or group's – patronage, the size of the baksheesh to the personnel and, not least, the discretion of Lady Aunt.

In our case it was the last consideration that tipped the scales in our favour. We were allowed in because the Lady Aunt who ran the establishment had been well-versed in matters of puberty. She had ascertained that our testicles hadn't yet dropped and would convey this view to her patrons when necessary. The latter, always tittering cruelly, accepted her word. Mercifully, dear Sophie, incensed by this artless trespass on our intimate parts, would lay her hands over our ears and hustle us away.

Selim and I, needless to say, were greatly relieved that our testicles were intact. But the prospect that they would drop off at some future date also plunged us into great anxiety. Thus, for a while, we would inspect each other's groins every day and reassure ourselves that our manhoods were not only still in place, but also felt as good as when we had last played with them that morning, on waking up. We would also scour the streets, even in the company of our parents, in the hope of finding the odd fallen testicle. If we could collect a number of spare testicles, we had reasoned, we might just be able to replace our own when calamity struck. The fact that, in the past, we had never seen any testicles lying around did not deter us; we simply assumed that other boys, grappling with the same predicament, had gathered them up. Eventually, our failure to find even a single testicle bred the conviction that these organs were securely attached to the body and would never fall off; and we decided that this macabre 'lie' had been disseminated by women who had taken exception to our precociousness in order to frighten us.

And precocious we were. We had had good teachers.

Selim and I lived at the very edges of Ankara, in a new district of concrete apartment blocks designated to stand as the precursor of future prosperity. Beyond stretched the southern plains, dotted here and there with Gypsy encampments.

Gypsies, needless to say, have an unenviable life wherever they are. Historic prejudices disbar them from most employment. The same condition prevailed in Ankara. Jobs, in so far as the men were concerned, were limited to seasonal fruit picking, the husbandry of horses, road digging and the portering of huge loads. Gypsy women fared better; they were often in demand as fortune tellers, herbalists and faith healers; and they always took their daughters along in order to teach them, at an early age, the intricacies of divination. The occasional satiety the Gypsies enjoyed was provided by the boys who begged at such busy centres as the market, the bus and railway stations, the stadium and the brothels.

The last was the best pitch of them all. Situated in the old town, at the base of the castle, the brothels consisted of some sixty ramshackle dwellings piled on each other in a maze of narrow streets. Each house had a small window on its door so that customers could look in and appraise the ladies on offer. Here, on the well-worn pavements, the beggars set up shop. They knew that, after being with a prostitute, a man, particularly if he were married, would feel sinful; and so they offered him instant redemption by urging him to drop a few *kuruş* into their palms to show Allah that, as the faith expected of him, he was a generous alms-giver.

Some of these wise Gypsy boys became our friends; and they taught us a great deal.

Above all, relating all the causerie they had overheard from punters and prostitutes, they taught us about the strange mechanics of sex: the peculiar, not to say funny, positions; the vagaries of the principal organs and the countless quirks which either made little sense to anyone or remained a mystery for many years.

And this priceless knowledge served as the foundation for further research in the *hamam*.

Breasts, buttocks and vaginal hair – or, as was often the case with the last, the lack of it – became the first subjects for study.

Our Gypsy friends had instructed us that breasts determined the sexuality of a woman. The aureole was the indicator for passion. Those women with large aureoles were insatiable; those with what looked like tiny birthmarks were best left alone as they would be frigid. (What, I wonder today, did frigidity mean to us in those days?) For the record, the woman with the largest aureoles we ever saw was, without doubt, the prototype of lethargy; nicknamed 'the milkman's horse' by Lady Aunt, she always appeared to be nodding off to sleep, even when walking. By contrast, the liveliest woman we ever observed – a widow who not only allowed us generous views of her vagina, but also appeared to enjoy her exhibitionism – had practically no aureoles at all, just stubby, pointed nipples like the stalks of button mushrooms.

And buttocks, we had learned, were reflectors of character. They were expressive, like faces. Stern buttocks could be recognized immediately: lean cheeks with a dividing line that was barely limned, they looked like people who had forsaken pleasure. Happy buttocks always smiled; or, as if convulsed by hysterical laughter, wobbled. Sad buttocks, even if they were shaped like heavenly orbs, looked abandoned, lonely, despairing. And there were buttocks which so loved life that they swayed like tamarind jelly and made one's mouth water.

Regarding vaginal hair, there was, as I mentioned, little of it on view. In Turkey, as in most Muslim countries, the ancient Bedouin tradition whereby women, upon their marriage, shave their pubic hair has almost acquired the dimensions of a hygienic commandment.

Our research into vaginal hair, in addition to its inherent joys, proved to be a lesson in sociology. A shaven pudenda not only declared the marital status of the particular woman, but also indicated her position in society. To wit, women who were clean-shaven all the time were women wealthy enough to have leisure – and the handmaids to assist them – therefore were either old aristocracy or *nouveau riche*. Women who carried some stubble, thus betraying the fact that children or household chores or careers curtailed their time for depilation, were of more modest backgrounds.

To our amazement, as if the chore proved less of an inconvenience if performed in company, there was a great deal of shaving going on in the baths. No doubt the fact that, for a small baksheesh, a woman could get an attendant to do a much better job, thus liberating her to gossip freely with friends or relatives, contributed to the preference.

Our main study – eventually, our *raison d'être* for going to the baths – centred on the labia and the clitorises. Both these wonders, too, possessed mythologies. Our Gypsy friends apprised us.

The myths on the labia centered on their prominence and pensility. The broad ones, reputedly resembling the lips of African peoples were certain to be, like all black races, uninhibited and passionate. (What did those adjectives mean to us? And what did we know of black races?) Lean labia, because they would have to be prized open, indicated thin hearts. Pendulous ones represented motherhood; Gypsy midwives, we were assured, could tell the number of children a woman had had simply by noting the labia's suspension. Those women who were childless but did possess hanging labia were to be pitied: for they found men, in general, so irresistibly attractive that they could never restrict their affections to one individual; consequently, to help them remain chaste, Allah had endowed them with labia that could be sewn together.

The perfect labia were those that not only rippled down languorously, but also tapered to a point at the centre, thus looking very much like buckles. These labia had magical powers: he who could wrap his tongue with them, would receive the same reward as one who walked under the rainbow: he would witness the Godhead.

As for clitorises, it is common knowledge that, like penises, they vary in size. The Turks, so rooted in the land, had classified them into three distinct categories, naming each one after a popular food.

Small clitorises were called *susam*, 'sesame'; *mercimek*, 'lentils' distinguished the medium-sized ones – which, being in the majority, were also considered to be 'normal'; and *nohut*, 'chick-peas', identified those of large calibre.

Women in possession of 'sesames' were invariably sullen; the smallness of their clitorises, though it seldom prevented them from enjoying sex to the full, inflicted upon them a ruthless sense of inferiority; as a result, they abhorred children, particularly those who were admitted to the baths. Women blessed with 'lentils' bore the characteristics of their namesake, a staple food in Turkey. Hence, the 'lentilled' women's perfect roundness were not only aesthetically pleasing, but also extremely nourishing; in effect, they offered everything a man sought from a wife: love, passion, obedience and the gift for cooking. Those endowed with 'chickpeas' were destined to ration their amorous activities since the abnormal size of their clitorises induced such intense pleasure that regular sex invariably damaged their hearts; restricted to conjoining only for purposes of conception, these women were to find solace in a spiritual life. And they would attain such heights of piety that, during labour, they would gently notch, with their 'chick-peas', a prayer-dent on their babies' foreheads thus marking them for important religious duties.

I can hear some of you shouting, 'Pig – clitorises have hoods. Even if you find a clitoris the size of an Easter egg, you'll have a tough time seeing it! You've got to, one: be lucky enough to have your face across your lover; two: know how to peek past the hood; three: have the *sang-froid* to keep your eyes open; and four: seduce it into believing that, for you, she is the only reality in life and everything else is an illusion.'

So, let me confess, before you take me for a liar, that in all likelihood neither Selim nor I ever saw a single clitoris. We just believed we did. Not only the odd one but, by that unique luck that favours curs, hundreds of them. And the more we believed, the more we contorted ourselves into weird positions, peeked and squinted from crazy angles, moved hither and thither to fetch this and that for one matron or another. We behaved, in effect, like bear cubs around a honey pot.

Of course, I admit, in hindsight, that what we kept seeing must have been beauty spots or freckles or moles or birthmarks and, no doubt, on occasions, the odd pimple or wart or razor nicks.

Naturally, when we described to our friends all that we had feasted on with our eyes, they believed us. And so we felt important. And when we went to sleep counting not sheep but clitorises – we felt sublime. And when we woke up and felt our genitals humming as happily as the night before – we basked in ultimate bliss.

An aside here, if I may. We never investigated Sophie's features. She was, after all, family, therefore immaculate, therefore non-sexual. Now, looking back on old pictures, I note that she was rather attractive. She had that silky olive-coloured skin that makes Armenians such a handsome race. Moreover, she had not had children, hence had not enjoyed, in *hamam* parlance, 'usage'. Consequently, though in her mid-thirties, she was still a woman in her prime. (Sophie never married. When my family moved from Ankara, soon after my *bar-mitzvah*, she went to work as a cook in a small taverna. We kept in touch. Then, in 1976, she suddenly left her job and disappeared. Her boss, who had been very attached to her, disclosed that she had been seriously ill and presumed that she had gone home to die in the company of ancestral ghosts. Since neither one of us knew the exact place of her birth, our efforts to trace her soon foundered.)

Alas, our time in Paradise did not fill a year.

Expulsion, when it came, was as sudden and as unexpected as in Eden. And just as brutal.

It happened on 5 July. The date is engraved in my mind because it happens to be my birthday. In fact, the visit to the baths on that occasion was meant to be Sophie's present to me.

As it happened, on that particular day, the women's *hamam* was exceptionally full. Selim and I were having an awfully hard time trying to look in many directions all at once. Such was our excitement that we never blinked once. It was, in effect, the most bounteous time we had ever had. (Given the fact that it was also our last time there, I might be exaggerating. Nostalgia does that.)

We must have been there for some time when, lo and behold, we saw one of the women grab hold of an attendant and command her, whilst pointing at us, to fetch the Lady Aunt. It took us an eternity to realize that this nymph of strident *fortissimo* was the very goddess whom Selim and I adored and worshipped, whose body we had judged to be perfect and divine – we never used one adjective where two could be accommodated – and whom, as a result, we had named 'Nilüfer' after the water-lily, which in those days we believed to be the most beautiful flower in the world.

Before we could summon the wits to direct our gaze elsewhere – or even to lower our eyes – Nilüfer and the Lady Aunt were upon us, both screaming at lovely Sophie, who had been dozing by the *kurna.*

Now, I should point out that Selim and I, having riveted our eyes on Nilüfer for months on end, knew very well that she was of a turbulent nature. We had seen her provoke innumerable quarrels, not only with Lady Aunt and the attendants, but also with many of the patrons. The old women, comparing her to a Barbary thoroughbred – and, given the ease with which she moved her fleshy but athletic limbs, a particularly lusty one at that – had attributed her volatility to her recent marriage and summed up her caprices as the dying embers of a female surrendering her existence to her husband, as females should; one day, a week hence or months later, when she would feel that sudden jolt which annunciates conception, she would become as docile as the next woman.

And so on that 5th July, Selim and I had been expecting an outburst from Nilüfer – though not against us. She had seemed troubled from the moment she had arrived. And she had kept complaining of a terrible migraine. (The migraine, Sophie wisely enlightened us later, shed light on the real reasons for Nilüfer's temper: for some women severe headaches heralded the commencement of their flow; what may have made matters worse for Nilüfer – remember she was not long married – might have been the disappointment of the passage of yet another month without conception.)

It took us a while to register Nilüfer's accusations. She was reproving us for playing with our genitals, touching them the way men do. (I am sure we did, but I am equally sure we did it surreptitiously. Had she been watching us the way we had been watching the women, seemingly through closed eyes?)

Sophie, bless her dear heart, defended us like a lioness.

'My boys,' she said, 'know how to read and write. They don't have to play with themselves.'

This nonsequitur enraged Nilüfer all the more. Stooping upon us, she took hold of our penises, one in each hand, and showed them to Lady Aunt.

'Look,' she yelled, 'they're almost hard. You can see they're almost hard!'

(Were they? I don't know. But, as Selim agreed with me later, the feeling of being tightly held by her hand was sensational.)

Lady Aunt glanced at the exhibits dubiously.

'Can't be. Their testicles haven't dropped yet . . .'

'Yes. Thanks for reminding me,' yelled Sophie. 'Their testicles haven't dropped yet!'

'They haven't!' Selim interjected bravely. 'We'd know, wouldn't we?'

Nilüfer, waving our penises, shrilled another decibel at Lady Aunt.

'See for yourself! Touch them! Touch them!'

Shrugging like a long-suffering servant, Lady Aunt knelt by our side. Nilüfer handed over our penises like batons. Lady Aunt must have had greater expertise in inspecting the male member; for as her fingers enveloped us softly and warmly and oh, so amiably, we did get hard – or felt as if we did.

We expected Lady Aunt to scream the place down. Instead, she rose from her haunches with a smile and turned to Sophie.

'They are hard. See for yourself.'

Sophie shook her head in disbelief.

Nilüfer celebrated her triumph by striding up and down the baths, shouting, 'They're not boys! They're men!'

Sophie continued to shake her head in disbelief. Lady Aunt patted her on the shoulder, then shuffled away.

'Take them home. They shouldn't be here.'

Sophie, suddenly at a loss, stared at the bathers. She noted that some of them were already covering themselves. Still confused, she turned round to us; then, impulsively, she held our penises. As if that had been the cue, our members shrank instantly and disappeared within their folds. Sophie, feeling vindicated, shouted at the patrons.

'They're not hard! They're not!'

Her voice echoed from the marble walls. No one paid her any attention. She remained defiant even as Lady Aunt saw us off the premises.

'I'll be bringing them along – next time! We'll be back!'

Lady Aunt roared with laughter.

'Sure! Bring their fathers, too, why don't you?'

And the doors clanged shut behind us.

And though Sophie determinedly took us back several times, we were never again granted admission.

TWELVE

Not the Man My Father Was

Ahmad Beydoun

In the place where I grew up, the name of the first son is generally a repetition of his grandfather's. Thus repetition takes the form of a switching between two names: typically, Hussein ibn Ali ibn Hussein ibn Ali, Hussein son of Ali son of Hussein son of Ali, and so on. We do not have the Anglo-Saxon practice of repeating the same name from one generation to the next without separation, as in George I, George II, and so on. This distinction does not indicate that we have a less acute patriarchy. Rather the contrary, for when a father gives the name of his father to the newly born, this profound act performs a rite of deep structural subjection: he is declaring that it is his father, not himself, who deserves immortality and who is the role model proposed for the newly born. The latter, who is part and parcel of him and issued out of his loins, is being presented as an offering to keep granddad's firebrand kindled.

I was the eldest male, after three females born to my dad. But he did not call me after my grandfather whose name was Muhammad. My father was the youngest of his brothers, and nor did he carry the name of his grandfather. So while I did not represent a name repetition case on joining the dynasty, I was, however, invited through naming into another type of repetition and continuation of tradition also familiar to us. I was given the name of a then senior *zaim* (leader) in Jebel Amir in south Lebanon where I was born. That *zaim* was called Ahmad Bek al-Asad. Indeed it was the Bek himself, it seems, who suggested the name to my dad. As it was, two factors favoured the idea: the first was that Ahmad Bek al-Asad's dad, who had been *zaim* in his day as well, was called Abdullatif, which was my dad's name also. And so my name status became like that of the Bek; we both were Ahmad, sons of Abdullatif. The second factor was that before having a male issue, my dad had been nicknamed Abu Ali. Among us, that nickname is largely given to brave men. Chance had it that my paternal uncle had the same nickname of 'father of Ali' since his elder son, who was born years before me, was called Ali. As we were then living in the same house as my uncle, there were times when both he and my father would answer in response to the name, or one of them rather than the other. So for my dad the Bek's suggestion was a way out from that fraternal muddle. He lost one nickname indicating courage but gained another indicating leadership – which he desired. His courage, for which he was renowned in those days, was one of his means to that goal.

Thus, the name Ahmed Abdullatif was a way of sending a loud message to the poor boy who was me. I was meant to be a leader like the one who had lent me his name. This is not because everyone who carries a leader's name necessarily becomes a leader – if that were the case the country would overfill with leaders and chiefs. But it was because dad himself was to become a leader as well as a dignitary and was a subordinate, a kind of satellite, of the big chief who had blessed me with his name. As I was the eldest male in my dad's household, I was meant to succeed him in his dignified status, years later, that is to say I was meant to grow into a repetition of him. My father was meant to prepare me for this destiny and I was meant to prepare myself for it too. When he stood for parliamentary elections he was in his forties while I was only eight years old. My mates in the quarter were aware of the destiny awaiting me. They used to carry me on their shoulders and roam around the quarter, chanting:

> When souls are snatched
> With a thin sharp sword
> The leader of Syria and the Jebel [Lebanon] will be
> Ahmad ibn Abdullatif.

Naturally that profound rhyme was not made for me. But borrowing it from the private arsenal of my namesake the Bek was extremely easy. There was an element of sarcasm there too: for my dad was an adversary of his in that election.

What drove my life afterwards on a different course depriving me when older of mounting the shoulders I rode so young? What removed me from the mutual tradition to which I had been pledged, thus barring me from assuming responsibility for the affairs of the community in which I was born and from surrendering my rein to it and judging all I would do and say through its values and interests? What prompted me to be fond of a state which the pre-Islamic poet Tarfah Ibn al-Abd bemoaned bitterly when he wrote:

. . . the whole clan shunned me
And I was cast out like a scabby camel.

Probably no answer to such questions is devoid of a serious risk. One constructs a whole picture of motives, means and the conditions of one's life from left-over bits in the memory, and it may have no shape except that improvised today. Despite this I intend to answer. To begin with, I did not follow the path prescribed for me by virtue of my birth, probably because, and I say this without boasting, I was not fit to follow that course.

What appears to me now as the obstacle to 'repeating' my dad was the fact that I was in possession of neither his physical strength nor his daring. As a child I tended to be rather emaciated. Most of my mates were better built and more energetic. My poor appetite had prompted my referral – in my childhood – to the doctor at a time when children were not referred to doctors except for a very good reason. I used to do a bit of sports in and out of school, but I never distinguished myself. In fact, my dad's physical strength, which was widely known and which my imagination used to dress up in mythical fashion, was an important component of his prestige. The chief in those days was before everything else the head of a familial alliance. Such an alliance or clan had to look out and lie in wait for its adversaries. This included sometimes being ready for brawls in alleyways and village squares using stones, sticks and knives. It was not unknown though unlikely for matters to reach the use of guns. The strength of the leader, though he rarely took part in the brawls directly, was a deterrent to the other side and a desired guarantee of his prestige among his men. Members of our family – particularly mothers when the husband was away – would on the other hand complain about a boy who had done something which required punishment. My dad used to summon the boy and straighten him up. The culprit would not dare, even as an adult, not to appear before such justice. In its most extreme form, such punishment would take the form of a good dose of repeated cuffs which are still talked about by those who received them.

It was a pleasure to have to go on occasion to summon candidates for such cuffs, the impact of which I had personally experienced when the occasion arose, though that became a rare occurrence. At any rate I was ill-equipped for inheriting this trade. Naturally my father's leadership was not based solely on his physical strength. Besides fortitude, the man possessed most attributes that are in theory required of elders: generosity, earnest concern for relatives, an endless readiness to serve whenever possible, and to console. That was in addition to honesty nurtured by firmly established faith and piety, and beyond that crowning everything a deep sense of the right to be at the forefront and to follow that end within the dictates of hierarchy as traditionally received. If, for my part, I have managed to possess any of those attributes, my share of such certainty and persistence has always remained negligible.

That shortcoming manifested itself early in the fact that I remained throughout my childhood a shy boy. My father himself may be responsible in part for such lack of daring, a condition which he never ceased to treat with annoyance and a determination to cure. He would insist on my entering the *madafa* (reception hall) and, when I did so, standing upright with my chin held high to greet those present, before sitting down to take part in whatever was being talked about. All these matters remained of little interest to me until I was approaching the age of twenty, though throughout that period I became a loud noisy tease when in a company other than that of the reception hall and where my father was not present.

The man who wanted me to count for something among people used by his mere presence at home to induce in me and my brothers silence, or at least a tendency to lower our voices and utter the minimum. His authority was overpowering, driving me to the margins of his circles of family, allies and supporters, rather than to their forefront. Later, when father was older he became nicer and extremely tender. Once he was over fifty his physical strength wasted after diabetes began to hit at his health. He became less inclined to be strict in handling what he considered to be wrong. He came to be saddened by my disinclination to socialize with influential people and to attend to what he called social obligations in a circle which he, for his part, had widened extensively. I did not find in myself enough determination or desire to keep pace with the endless roving within that circle.

In fact, considering the expectations placed upon him and his inability to meet them, the boy who was me was quite likely to have fallen foul of such a predicament and reached the crisis stage which children enter when they are incapable of being what they are desired to be. It is then that they shut others off and somehow get out of earshot to declare that they will become absolutely nothing and no one. I could have become extremely disturbed or plainly ill had I not found an alternative world to that of the reception hall and its associated locations, a world apart from that of my father with its vast human network, parts of which he used to preside over, perpetuating its fabric and repeating the acts which held that fabric together and allowed it to expand. My father, who pinned his hopes on me and who desired but good for me, himself aided and abetted me in entering that alternative world, the horizons of which began to reveal themselves to me gradually: an alternative world which became the focus of my aims and the means for me to move, and which gave me a context within which to live my life. My father helped me because he used to leave me to my own devices in any matters that fell outside his circle, in other words matters that were not about my behaviour in the world of adults. I used to shrink before his stern appearance and dignified presence in his own surroundings, but he trusted me and never had an eye on my doings, disregarding problematic things I embarked upon except when they involved undermining others.

I started smoking before I was fifteen. He was aware of this, though I never lit a cigarette in his presence until two or three years afterwards. He never objected. Before turning fifteen I also used to stay until after midnight at friends' houses and out in the streets. He did not object. News of me falling in love, which I started early as well, used to reach him no doubt. He would keep quiet about it, most probably considering the matter mere child's-play. My mother was the one who widened those avenues of growth for me by asking me, on seeing me staying inside to study over the holiday, why I did not go out to play.

However, the most significant matter to record here is that my father was among those who felt the world was different from what it was when their generation had entered it: education was the big gate to that new world and their children would not be able to find their way except by other means than they had known. School, among other things, led potentially to a set of values that were inconsistent with what our fathers were familiar with. They were aware of that. They had witnessed the local people's resistance, in the days of the mandate, to the state's determination to close Quran pre-schools after curriculums and certificates were introduced and their imposition required making education exclusive to formal schools. They were also aware that among those of their generation who had been to modern schools, there were cases of blatant derailment from the straight path of religion and morals which consequently presented a challenge to the grasp of the community and its structure. There were numerous elements known for drinking alcohol, abstaining from performing their prayers and undermining the authority of the *zaim* and the religious elite. In other words, there were those who came close to possessing what I once called the individuality of the exception at a time when it was not possible for individuality to be a general rule. Despite the presence of such alarming types, our parents sent us to modern schools and we became the first generation who went to those schools and followed a principle which had gained general endorsement after having been an exception for those no more than ten years our senior. My elder sister, who is only seven years older than I, attended the Quran pre-school in its dying days before transferring to a formal school.

As for my dad himself, he had obtained no more than a limited education in one of those modest Quran schools which were just disappearing when I reached school age. Despite the fact that modern education had not yet become an indispensable tool in securing the kind of leadership my father was preparing me for, he was aware that leadership itself was in the process of changing and that lack of education would soon be a shortcoming which would slow down the progress of those who aspired to it. Schools had asserted themselves fast as a vehicle for the ambitious and, moreover, as a supplier of a corps of respectable elements; their widening range early on began to present a competing force to the system of heritage and privileges that defined the old order. For all these reasons my father did his best to see that I attained as much education as possible. Despite his leadership status, and sometimes thanks to it, the man was nearer to poverty than to wealth. Being government-run, the school did not require fees. But he used to send me separately to paid private lessons. Those who know the times and the circumstances then will no doubt be astonished to hear that such private lessons were aimed at boosting my French. I was not slower than my peers in learning that language, but my father was aware that its teaching in the whole school was poor. He even brought for me once a Palestinian teacher who assumed I would be familiar with some English, a language which was never mentioned in the governmental schools of Bint Jubail and had no wide appeal in our part of the world.

When I reached the highest grade available in the village school (I was thirteen then) my father sent me as a boarder to Deir Mashmoushah monastery school, then on to the Makaasid school of Sidon. That was a momentous decision which my dad was uncertain he would be able to follow through. Hence, before making it, he took me to the shrine of Saidah Zainab on the outskirts of Damascus, to ask God for proper guidance. The Deir Mashmoushah school, where teaching in a foreign language was central, became the first support environment to help me to extract myself from the captivity of tradition and to find a way of following the rhythms of the steps to pursue the different path without being scrutinized according to the logic of the traditional or by its watchful wardens.

This was because education in that school was significantly different from what had long been taught by the teachers at Quran schools. The difference is too obvious to require a long-winded explanation. In those schools religion had been the core of all education and the source of the status of the teacher. In no way would the religious-educated depart from the culture of the community, nor would he challenge the content of any of its classes. What he was taught would not go beyond preparing him or preparing to initiate him to settle in one of the familiar slots in the system of the local community. The religious-educated would occupy a predetermined status and rank, and to fulfil this role he would rely on being subjected to a training and set of considerations basically outside the confines of the school. Such schools would not introduce to the community new skills which were likely to upset other established ranks within the hierarchy. No unfamiliar beliefs or opinions and behaviour unknown to the community would be posed there. The potential for this was introduced by the modern school: it brought the teacher to challenge the knowledge of the religious scholar, the *fakir*, the physician to challenge the parliamentary seat of the dignitary. It opened the route for public and private employment with all the power to do good or harm that entails, and, thanks to certificates, it enabled the mobility of those from the lower depths of obscure families. So the hierarchical system, too, was unsettled.

In short, the modern school pursued the element of merit above that of inheritance as a ladder to social status and as a grounds for earning it. As such it indicated through that door a way to individualism, even though it could not secure it. An aspect of this role was the fact that the school took the traditional community outside itself by offering roles and spheres of movement which had not been part of the system of the community and would not have been accommodated within it. Another aspect of that role was that the modern school improvised for its traditional community recruits a flow of unfettered and endless new ideas and behaviour. This aspect was defined and deepened by learning the foreign language. It is of no small significance to see new names, imported from faraway worlds and from different times, entering one's cultural life to stand suddenly, or gradually, on at least the same footing as the names that have stood as the flags and watch-towers of one's community for years or centuries. The imported names were so attractive as to seem as though they were parading themselves for you to choose from. This placed them in a different position from the names taken as authority by one's own community. The old names would then seem as if they had been prepared for one before one was born, and as if their huge impact left one no choice except in some minor details. [. . .]

French was the foreign language which I embarked on from my first day at school. I should make two points about this. I grew up in surroundings which were generally hostile to France. But that hostility was saturated to its roots by a deep admiration felt and spread by the graduates of modern schools in particular. It was an admiration of various French names, objects, places and values: Paris, Voltaire, Anatole France and Gustave Lebon. The second point to mention is the fact that, among many of my generation, I commanded a view on France when its cultural arena was forefronted by a group of rebels and outsiders.

The most prominent of those were the existentialist thinkers, as they were presented in the wake of the Second World War, along with all the other men of letters and artists who were sympathetic to them or affiliated to their world. In short, those we were influenced by were among the most individualistic individuals. Being inspired by them did nothing except aggravate the rupture in our relationship with the traditional community at home. The references of traditional culture, religious and otherwise, were in no position really to mitigate the effects those writers and artists left on us. The issue of freedom, for instance, was the nearest to seizing our souls and to being established as the axis for our thought and feelings as anything which we were likely to chance upon in Arabic heritage texts (or what was abridged for us thereof) or those of contemporary Arab writers.

Religion, which had been at the core of the knowledge offered by Quran schools, became very marginal in modern schools, or at least in government-run ones. We used to pay no attention to Quran classes. The Quran teacher was considered by most of us the least prestigious of teachers. And nor were families qualified to fill the shortfall caused by the sizing down and indeed the collapse of religious education. In Shia villages there were no reliably strong structures supporting families in the face of secular education. Private Shia schools were weak and could not match Christian ones. The educational role of village *fakirs* or scholars was generally insignificant compared with that of the priest and church. Conditions then were no match for what Shia later started to embark upon with Imam Musa Sadr by way of religious and sectarian instruction, an effort which during and after the last civil war has been continued. Our families then were generally religious, but rarely had someone to help them enlighten their children in religious matters. So in my village support was restricted to the apologetic religious classes in school and the Ashura season. I may well have learnt by heart a lot more of the Quran while at the Dir Mashmoushah monastery school than I had ever done elsewhere. I had to adhere closely to some identity with which to enter the environment of the school, which was not my environment, though the people treated me cordially. Of my own free will I took to reciting the Quran so that I could have 'a book' like others, and also because it is a beautiful book. Other than maintaining a fascination with the Arabic language, my soul was almost surrendered to French devils.

I must say this for the benefit of mentioning an important matter: namely that adopting a French point of reference to formulate my case against the world did not preclude me from standing firmly on a deep-rooted pan-Arab pedigree. So my intense discontent with the French (those were the days of the Algerian war and Suez) remained as a matter of course. I was a pan-Arabist (which I remained, with some modification in format, even after I became a Marxist). I was indifferent to the fact that Sartre, Camus and Merleau-Ponty were French, despite the fact that to me France was almost summed up in being a space for their lives and works. They had to be made to transcend this type of definition. They used to suggest a loftiness, somehow, although some of their actions would undermine it in another way.

Many of my colleagues and I used to continue with persistence what had been indicated hesitantly by the graduates of the modern schools of our fathers' generation: hating political France while taking intellectual France as a point of reference in ideas and behavioural values. This duality together with remaining part of the pan-Arab orbit precluded us from changing the language world in which we had been reared. This was also the course followed by many of our Christian colleagues, with collusion from family and school. As such my tongue was not Europeanized. Rather I used to do my best in conversations to translate into Arabic all that I acquired from French and Western sources in general. So I can afford to say that the main expression of my pan-Arab commitment or affiliation became the sphere of the language. And as such, I have not ceased to this day to be increasingly infatuated with Arabic and determined to improve my knowledge of its aspects and to perfect its morphology. It has been the anchor which prevented my ventures into other languages from being a mere aimless disoriented journey into the wilderness.

When I travelled to Paris for my studies at the age of twenty I was determined to do my best to perfect French. Nevertheless, I carried in my already over-stuffed suitcase the four volumes of *Nahj al-balaaghah* (The road to eloquence). Later I wrote to my father requesting a copy of the Quran. I should add here that my father, who used to get angry if any of us went beyond the limits of what was 'appropriate' and 'respectable', never pressured us in matters of worship. For my part, I used neither to fast nor to pray. My father would always emphasize this formula as a guiding principle: 'Sports, looking after one's health and serenity, in addition to pleasing God.' On realizing that the formula was destined to prove yet another candidate for failure, he would be content to utter the prophetic saying, 'You guide not whomsoever you desire. It is God who guides whomsoever He wishes.'

In fact my progress in education was a means of further distance from the bounds of parental authority and from the traditional community to which that authority was sponsoring my affiliation. As for my father, he could only be extremely pleased with such progress, although he started to feel, as I believe, that the consequences of such progress were neither calculated nor desired. What came to my rescue in my exit act was the limited education my father had attained in Quran schools. I remember that I used to be extremely embarrassed whenever I listened to my father making infrequent public addresses. What caused my embarrassment was his poor style and his many grammatical mistakes. This was because I grew up in a town where morphology and grammar, let alone prosody, still had great value. Moreover, my dad himself began to feel that what I had learnt would lend me an authority over myself rivalling his authority over me. As he did not comprehend the logic of such authority enough to rebut it with the appropriate argument, he would retreat when he had failed to convince of something to a long-standing phrase, which was not devoid of bitterness: life had taught him a lot, although he had not stayed in school for as long as I had. I only appreciated the truth of those words after I had lived long enough to realize that life does indeed teach what is not taught in schools and that it often uses severe means towards that end.

Translated from Arabic by Osman Nusairi

THIRTEEN

Those Two Heavy Wings of Manhood: On Moustaches

Hassan Daoud

As soon as soft hair began to thicken above my lips, whenever I looked in a mirror I began to imagine myself with a complete and perfect moustache. What I envisaged was a model moustache of the kind that I would have liked to have had, not as it would actually have been. I was handsome in that moustache which I added to my face like one adds a pair of sun-glasses, though I didn't acquire a pair of those until I was past forty. Nevertheless, a moustache and sun-glasses, together with a pipe: the image was never far from my mind, though when I did adopt the pipe I only used it for about ten days. Pipe, moustache, sun-glasses, and also the overcoat which we used to imagine as the dress of secret policemen, all this combined to make up the complete man who lacked nothing.

I remember a fellow student at the university who added all these things to his person, plus a hat and a Samsonite briefcase of the type carried by airline pilots. Jamil, for that was his name, had done what the rest of us hesitated to do, in fear of appearing phoney and of our colleagues laughing at us. Jamil so overdid it that he no longer fitted in, in the atmosphere of the university. As he rushed up and then rushed away again, it began to seem as if he had found a circle of people who understood him in some other place. In his case the problem wasn't so much in his overdoing things as in the eccentric behaviour which lay behind it.

But in general, with items such as the pipe, the sun-glasses and the secret agent's overcoat a person must not in practice sport more than one of them at the same time. You either use the pipe or the sun-glasses, either the overcoat or the Samsonite briefcase. What I mean is that there is nothing wrong with adopting one of these items, but only one.

The moustache is not considered an appendage, or rather it is not considered one on the face of the individual who keeps to his own version of it. However, if it is a moustache such as the one Ahmad Halal had, a thick version of the 'Douglas' – as the type used to be called after the actor Douglas Fairbanks – in that case it is most certainly classed as an appendage. In the case of Ahmad Halal, it really did appear to be drawn onto his face. That is to say, it didn't look like it grew out of the face, but rather as if it were added. Absolutely faultless, and exactly the right distance above the lip, Ahmad Halal's moustache ruled out the possibility of sun-glasses, hat, pipe or overcoat. To understand that it was an exaggeration, I had to grow about ten years older.

The moustache by then was much more handsome, more finely drawn and more symmetrical than the face around it, which formed a spacious oval stretching from ear to ear. I mean that after those ten years the moustache was no longer in harmony with the face and body which carried it around, for it required of the face and body a particular way of moving, that they might remain in orbit around it or stay in its gravitational field. With the passing of those ten years Ahmad Halal had lost something of this: his moustache could no longer determine the movement of his whole person. On his face it was something precious but out of place, like a luxurious piece of furniture in a poor dilapidated house.

He should perhaps have reduced the beauty of his moustache as he added those ten years to his age. He could have cared for it less, leaving the hairs around it, which he used to shave, to grow a little so that they made its contours a little less sharp. Or he could have raised it a bit, as old people used to do when they found that only a refined and discreet moustache would now accord with their age. As they grew older they would come to know that their moustaches would one day resemble that fleeting trace of lower eyelash. It was as though they would reduce the number of hairs every day, starting by plucking them out from the top and then moving downwards. This was what happened in my father's day. In my grandfather's time they used to pluck their moustaches from the outside edges and move inwards. Or at least that's what I thought when I saw my grandfather's moustache, aligned with his nostrils like a bird without wings. At that time, when I was fifteen or sixteen, I thought that moustaches really could be categorized according to the age of their owners. I did not realize that my grandfather had kept this style of moustache since his youth, because it had been the fashion at that time. Had we been able to observe the youth of his time, their fashions would have seemed laughable to us, mad as we were about big moustaches which we thought were the only kind suitable for adult men.

Every epoch is characterized by a particular type of moustache. At that time, when I was fifteen or sixteen and waiting for my moustache to grow, there were still styles around dating from a time I could not pinpoint exactly. I could only really imagine the people of our mountain villages in the seventeenth and eighteenth centuries wearing that type of moustache which resembles the two forearms of someone raising his arms and tensing his muscles to show how strong he is. This was the style preferred in those two centuries, and also, I thought, prevalent in the Jahiliyya period, some fifteen centuries before. Thus the pictures of the pre-Islamic poet, Antara bin Shaddad al-Absi, that were meant to show how strong and manly he was so exaggerated the thickness and breadth of his moustache that it looked like a weight suspended there on his lip and must have been quite a burden.

In the popular sayings and folk tales that have come down to us through the ages a man swears to another man on his moustache, a symbol of his honour and nobility. Our grandfathers' recollections of their grandfathers and also the symbolic meanings which remain in us are evidence of the moustache's central place. For long centuries it remained thus and its survival in our region was helped by those sayings, tales and folklore. One version would grow thick, spreading out from the centre of that rectangular type of face to cover over a third of it and then to taper off at each end to a point. What distinguished one moustache from another was how firmly those hairs at the ends would maintain their upward twirl, appearing almost to meet in a full circle which would require just a small link to make it complete. In describing such a moustache, it was said that it was so strong that it could support an eagle if one came and perched on it. All this relates to the physical composition of the hair, which was coated one or two generations ago with a sticky substance which held the moustache in place. From the point of view of its symbolism, a luxurious moustache was a boundless treasure, given that a single hair would suffice as surety for a loan or a promise. 'Take this hair,' a man used to say to his creditor or to the one to whom he had made a promise. Up to the present time it was considered like a bond or a bill of exchange.

I do not believe that such importance could have been attributed to the moustache if it were granted to everybody to grow one in the manner described. If it had been possible for professional crooks, scoundrels and the common people to take upon themselves or settle a debt merely by offering this abstract bond, moustaches would have stopped being the distinguishing mark of men and the emblem of their eminence. There is no doubt that in those times a prevalent custom enforced by the establishment allowed for the removal of moustaches from the faces of those who did not deserve them. Indeed I can picture this as an institution equivalent to that described by the Albanian novelist, Ismail Kadare, in *Broken April*. In Albania this institution had the function of restraining and regulating blood feuds. The institution whose existence I envisage would take nobility as its sphere of competence, for I believe that blood feuds and nobility are similar.

The nobility institution would have had no building, documents and officials like the Albanian Office of Blood Feuds, but would have been rather an institution run by men well known in the towns and villages, helped by followers who attached themselves to them. It would have been sufficient simply to witness on the road somewhere a man who had thickened his moustache more than he had a right to for the sanction, 'Go and shave off his moustache!' to be put into effect. In south Lebanon villagers experienced something like this, not to do with moustaches, but with those tarboushes (or fezes) that were at one time considered, like moustaches, a sign of social status. 'Go and take his tarboush off!' the leader would say to his followers when angry with a man who had been seen wearing a tarboush which he knew he had no right to wear. Moustaches like that, then, thick and pointed at the ends, were not available to anybody who wanted to sport them, but were subject to a law which I do not think was complicated. There would be some who would have had the right and others who would not have had the right. Indeterminate cases which created confusion, and where a ruling would have to be sought, were rare. This is because a society which maintained that style of moustache as a symbol of manhood for long centuries would also have preserved the status of its leaders and its leading families for a similar number of centuries.

At the age of fifteen or sixteen, I had the opportunity to see the last specimens of those moustaches – they were very few in any case. Their symbolic value was still well known to people, but being subjected to successive campaigns of vilification had made talk about them veer between seriousness and ridicule. Of course, the weapon which had succeeded in bringing down this symbolic token – and, after all, this applies to many fallen symbolic tokens – was mockery and mockery alone. The young would show no reaction to the 80-year-old Abu Faris wearing his pressed white suit, his red tarboush and sporting a moustache dating back to a previous era. They contented themselves with stealing a passing glance at him, the height of ancient elegance, as he crossed the tentmakers' market. However, as soon as he had proceeded some distance, they would begin to wink and laugh at him. His large family retained some respect for him. However, anyone younger who attempted to adopt such a moustache would have farts trumpeted at him by young children hiding behind walls as he passed by.

In recent times, moustaches have become more commonplace, more available to those who want them. You have begun to see them on the faces of the greengrocer, the taxi-driver and the bell-boys of hotels and restaurants. You have also begun to see them on the faces of lower ranking soldiers. The military profession formerly protected its soldiers from being exposed to the scorn of stupid young boors. The leaders of the military profession found no embarrassment in their soldiers' passion for their moustaches. Rather, we used to joke, a monthly sum of money was added to the salary of all such soldiers. And this was instituted when the military institution considered in its grave manner how to make soldiers stand out in ordinary civilian places. It was not allowed, for instance, for a soldier wearing military uniform to be seen carrying his baby son on his shoulders. Nor was it allowed for him to climb into a service taxi with other passengers, whether civilians or even soldiers, in the back seat. Add to this that he was not allowed to be seen eating standing at a street-side stall and you understand something of the ethos. Military attire had to be kept clean and ironed, and chins had to be shaved daily. The military command, primly committed to order, considered the nurturing and raising (for these were the words used for caring for moustaches – much the same as for bringing up a child) of large moustaches as a clear token of military manhood. The leadership used to encourage its soldiers in this and, if they looked after their moustaches and kept them in a good state, they were each awarded fifteen pounds per month, the same allowance as was awarded for each child in a soldier's family. If he had two children, he was given thirty pounds, and if he had three children he was given forty-five pounds. At the age of fifteen or sixteen, we used to say that such-and-such a soldier had two children and a moustache, for instance, poking fun at that law we considered to be the most astonishing and defective of all laws.

For this dictate that it be taken care of seemed to us to enshrine the moustache as something separate from the face of the soldier who owned it. We imagined him carrying it around as if in a cage, as if he had to look after it as he would a parrot entrusted to him by the government, or which the army had commissioned him to devote himself to bringing up. In any case, and this is something that I continue to believe to this day, the army was intending by this stipulation to provide sanctuary for moustaches whose era had passed and to conserve those that remained in its ranks. It did this by gathering them up from the markets like merchants do when they see that their commodities are not selling.

The army realized that it had to defend the wounded honour of the moustache and protect it from becoming commonplace and subject to mockery. In a photography exhibition I visited in Beirut in the early 1980s I remember a picture of a *kabadayi* (tough guy) wearing a *qumbaz* (a full-length robe), holding a glass of arak, and behind him, perched on his shoulder, a long musket. With his index finger, the man was pointing to the middle of his head, as if saying to the photographer or to the viewer of the picture, 'I am mad, but I am free in my madness.' His opulent moustache, one of the most opulent, clearly betokened rank, just as the weapon indicated that he had encountered battles and run the hazards of war.

I think that the army felt it was responsible for protecting moustaches from changing into something like the one in the picture. When we were young we found this artifice strange, and we felt it was a strategy left over from a time we did not know and whose logic we could not understand. We felt it perhaps dated back to Ottoman days, when Lebanon fell within that sphere of influence, that it was a Turkish thing, with all the nasty connotations that our young minds attached to Turks: stubborn, stupid, harsh, backward.

Returning to civilian life, it appears that that old style of moustache has continued after the passing of its golden age along two conflicting paths. On the one hand, there is the path marked by scorn and mockery which I described. On the other hand, it has continued to retain its symbolic meaning, albeit frozen and stripped of its effectiveness. In order to clarify this second path, let me say that the sort of person who mocks the luxuriant moustache when he sees it on the face of someone he chances to meet still retains a modicum of enthusiasm when he is told stories about the pride people of old took in their moustaches, that is to say in their nobility. Following one of the defeats suffered by the Arabs at the hands of Israel, the cartoonist, Naji al-Ali, drew an Arab man with his moustache hanging down, while in the days of Arab power it had previously pointed upwards. The image was still influential in the 1980s; that is to say that the honour of the group could still be characterized in terms of the state of the moustache. In an exhibition of his paintings, the Lebanese artist Rafiq Sharaf discovered another symbolic way of expressing Arab defeat: the legendary personality of Antara with a diminished moustache is matched by his beloved Abla with her toes cut off.

So long as the time separating the Arabs' victories from their defeats is at least 700 years and not a mere ten or twenty, this use of symbols will continue to move in two different directions. That is to say, the feeling persists that the people who were defeated by Israel were not us the children of today but we the ancient conquerors who have known only victory. Or, one could say, our recent defeats are felt as the defeat of the victorious self in its essence and origin. Fie on us, then, who have established that we are unworthy of carrying the honour which was ours.

The old moustache is suitable for the people of ancient times. As for those of a subsequent era, they deserve to be trumpeted with farts if they try to affect it.

Anyway, in considering our attitude to that type of moustache, we must not ignore the tendency of recent generations to mock the anarchy of the older generations. At fifteen or sixteen we never ceased to wonder how men of those times sporting that type of moustache could possibly consider themselves handsome. We went so far as to believe that those men had sacrificed their handsomeness to the greater honour of the moustache, leaving handsomeness as the preserve of those who did not 'bring up' moustaches. The beautiful women of that time took delight in the latter, leaving the former, the moustache owners, to busy themselves with that one quality which they appeared to prefer above all other qualities. They were men who were devoted to manhood, not to handsomeness or to seduction, or to cunning or trickery. In life there are vast numbers of qualities, but those wearers of moustaches in our opinion chose just one quality as their preserve, like the person whose one delight is to have appeared in a single photograph.

So at that age as we waited for our own moustaches to become bristly, we used to think that if they attained maturity they might just become moustaches of handsomeness, not the moustaches of manhood or of *capitaines*. I looked at the down which was on its way to becoming hair and I found that all by itself it was becoming a 'Douglas'. That was the preferred type of moustache in those days, the Douglas after the fashion of Ahmad Halal. It was not long before I hurriedly changed that opinion, since handsomeness had also hurriedly moved in another direction. It was not appropriate for a young man of the left who neglected his clothes, his sleep and his food to have a moustache drawn as neatly as a woman's eyebrows.

From the mid-sixties, the moustache had to grow abandoned and neglected, to take the form which it suited it to take. Che Guevara's moustache without the beard: this was the moustache I had from 1968. It is still the one I have now, in 1998, and it will remain like this as far as I am concerned. This is in spite of the fact that I know its time has passed and it is no longer in fashion. In 1973 I shaved it off and my lips appeared embarrassing. It is well known among men that, in the first days following the shaving off of the moustache, the lips resemble one thing more than anything else: the shaved pudendum. It is also well known that, in spite of its strong suggestiveness in the beginning, this will quickly pass and the lips will soon look normal.

However, after 1973, I did not shave my upper lip again. I will say now that if I had to do without a moustache, I should not have grown it again in 1973. I am no longer the leftist I was in 1968, and leftism in any case no longer has the same behaviour and dress patterns which it had at that time. However, I still keep my moustache as it was. A relative of mine, older than my father, told me that when it became the fashion in the 1930s to take off one's fez he felt extremely embarrassed to be in the street for the first time, bareheaded, and that he ran straight back to his house to seek shelter there.

In my case I sometimes think that what is shameful in shaving off one's moustache is the initial appearance. Then there are things like my passport with a photograph of me with a moustache, and then my identity card of which it will not be easy to obtain a second copy. Then there is my driving licence, my social security card, my employment card and all the other papers.

I will keep this moustache of mine, even though I know that it is no longer in fashion. Moreover, I am completely convinced that it is not appropriate for a modern man to have a moustache. I am not a moustache-lover, but nevertheless I have a moustache. I have a moustache, no longer in order to make myself handsome, or to seduce, or to follow the fashion. It is no more than a remaining trace of the customs of a previous generation.

Translated from Arabic by Basil Hatim and Malcolm Williams

Notes on Contributors

Walter Armbrust teaches anthropology at the Center for Contemporary Arab Studies, Georgetown University, Washington, DC. He is the author of *Mass Culture and Modernism in Egypt* (Cambridge: Cambridge University Press, 1996) and editor of *Mass Mediations: New Approaches to Popular Culture in the Middle East and Beyond* (Berkeley: University of California Press, 2000). He is currently working on a cultural history of the Egyptian cinema.

Ahmad Beydoun is Professor of Sociology at the Institute of Social Sciences, Lebanese University, and Director of the Observatory of Intercommunitarian Coexistence at the Centre of Christian-Muslim Studies, Balamand University. He is the author of several books in Arabic and two in French, including: *Identité confessionelle et temps social chez les historiens libanais contemporains* (Beirut: Publications de l'Université Libanaise, 1984); *Le Liban: itinéraires dans une guerre incivile* (Paris: Karthala, 1993); *Kalamun: min mufradat al-lugha ila murakkabat al-thaqafa* (K-L-M-N: from lexical elements to cultural constructs), Beirut: Dar al-Jadid, 1997; *Al-jumhuriya al-mutaqatti* (essays on post civil war Lebanon), Beirut: Dar al-Nahar, 1999; and a collection of poems.

Yoram Bilu is Professor of Anthropology and Psychology at the Hebrew University of Jerusalem. His research interests include ethnopsychiatry, psychological and anthropological aspects of religion, and the sanctification of place in Israel. On these themes he has published many articles. He is the co-editor (with Eyal Ben-Ari) of *Grasping Land: Space and Place in Contemporary Israeli Discourse and Experience* (Albany: SUNY Press, 1997). His book, *Without Bounds: The Life and Death of Rabbi Ya'aqov Wazana*, is forthcoming from Wayne State University Press.

Abdelwahab Bouhdiba is Professor of Sociology at the University of Tunis, where he is also Director of the Centre d'Etudes et de Recherches

Economiques et Sociales. He is the author of several books, including *Sexuality in Islam* (London: Routledge & Kegan Paul, 1985; first published in paperback by Saqi Books, 1998), and (with M. Ma'ruf al-Dawalibi) *The Different Aspects of Islamic Culture: The Individual and Society in Islam* (UNESCO, 1998).

Hassan Daoud is editor of the culture and society page of the Lebanese daily newspaper, *al-Mustakbal*, and a novelist. His first novel, *Binayat Mathilde* (Beirut: Dar al-Tanwir, 1983) was published in English as *The House of Mathilde* (London: Granta Books, 1999) and also in French by Actes Sud. His other novels include: *Rawd al-hayat al-mahzun* (The sad garden of life), Beirut: Dar al-Tanwir, 1985; *Ayam Zaida* (Added days), Beirut: Dar al-Jadid, 1990; *Sanat al-automatic* (The automatic year), Beirut: Dar al-Nahar, 1996; *Ghinaa al-batrik* (The penguin song), Beirut: Dar al-Nahar, 1998, a German translation of which will be published by the Swiss publisher, Lenos, in Autumn 2000.

Moris Farhi was born in Ankara, Turkey. He has written for theatre, films, television and contributed many poems to various anthologies and publications. He is best known as a novelist. His works include *The Last of Days*, *Journey through the Wilderness* and his new novel, *Children of the Rainbow*, which was published by Saqi Books in 1999. He has been active in human rights campaigns for many years and presently serves as Chairman of International Pen's Writers in Prison Committee.

Mai Ghoussoub is a London-based artist and writer who was born and brought up in Beirut. She has written on questions of culture and on Middle Eastern issues for international journals, and is the author of several books in Arabic and a memoir in English, *Leaving Beirut: Women and the Wars Within* (London: Saqi Books, 1998).

Danny Kaplan is an occupational psychologist and is conducting research for a PhD at Ben-Gurion University, Beer Sheva, Israel. He is the author of *David, Yonatan, ve-chayalim achersim: Al zehut, gavriyet, ve-miniyut be-yechidot kraviyot be-tzahal* (David, Jonathan and other soldiers: Identity, masculinity and sexuality in combat units in the Israeli Army), Tel Aviv: Ha-Kibbutz Ha-Meuchad, 1999. His main research interests focus on men's friendships and cultural narratives.

Abdu Khal is a novelist and writer of short stories from Saudi Arabia, and the editor of the cultural pages of the Saudi daily newspaper, *Okaz. Mudun ta'qulu al-'ishb* (Cities that devour grass), was published in Arabic by Dar al-Saqi in 1998.

Frédéric Lagrange is Maître de Conférences de Langue et Litérature Arabes at the Université de Paris IV-Sorbonne. He is the author of *Musiques d'Egypte* (Paris, Actes Sud, 1996), and is currently working on the perception of male sexuality in Arab societies and in literature in the classical and modern periods.

Afsaneh Najmabadi is Associate Professor of Women's Studies at Barnard College, Columbia University, New York. Her published work includes *The Story of the Daughters of Quchan: Gender and National Memory in Iranian History* (Syracuse: Syracuse University Press, 1998), and an edited volume, *Women's Autobiographies in Contemporary Iran* (Center for Middle Eastern Studies Monograph Series, Cambridge, MA: Harvard University Press, 1991). She also writes on contemporary issues of feminism in Iran and is currently working on a book, *Male Lions and Female Suns: The Gendered Tropes of Iranian Modernity*.

Julie Peteet is Associate Professor and Chair of the Anthropology Department at the University of Louisville. She is the author of *Gender in Crisis. Women and the Palestinian Resistance Movement* (New York: Columbia University Press, 1991) and has published articles in *Signs, Cultural Anthropology, American Ethnologist*, and *Social Analysis*. She is currently completing a book on place and identity in Palestinian refugee camps. Her areas of research interest are violence and culture, displacement and identity, and gender.

Hazim Saghieh is a columnist for the Arabic daily newspaper, *al-Hayat*, and the editor of its weekly supplement, *Tayyarat*. He is the author of *al-Hawa duna ahlihi, Um Kulthum siratan wa nassan* (Love without lovers: Um Kulthum, the image and the text), Beirut, Dar al-Jadid, 1991; *al-Arab ben al-hajar wa-l zarrah* (Arabs between atomic weapons and stones), London: Dar al-Saqi, 1992; *Awal al-urubah* (Early Arabism), Beirut: Dar al-Jadid, 1993; *Thaqafat al-Khomeinyyah: fi al-istishraq* (The cultures of Khomeinism: on orientalism), Beirut: Dar al-Jadid, 1995; *Difaa an al-salam* (In defense of peace), Beirut: Dar al-Nahar, 1998; *Widaa ul-urubah* (Farewell to Arabism), Beirut, Dar al-Saqi, 1998.

Emma Sinclair-Webb is undertaking doctoral research on sectarianism and urban conflict in Turkey for a PhD in the Department of Politics and Sociology, Birkbeck College, University of London. She works as a commissioning editor for I.B.Tauris Publishers, and teaches in the School of Humanities and Cultural Studies at Middlesex University, London.

Index

Abd al-Hadi, Zaynab, 206
'Abdallah, Yahya al-Tahir, *al-Raqsa al-mubaha*, 181
Abdullatif, Ahmed, 264
Abdul-Majid, Ahmad, *Five Iraqi Presidents*, 236
Absal, portrayal of, 154
Abu Faris, 276
Abu-Lughod, Lila, 107
Abu Nuwas, 176, 191, 231
Abu-Sayf, Salah, 210, 211
adab, 169, 172, 173, 190, 191
Aflaq, Michel, 242
age of three: as turning point in religious awareness, 51, 54, 56; rituals of, 55
Al-Ahrar newspaper, 227, 228
AIDS, in Arab novels, 174
Al-Akhbar newspaper, 228
al-Akhiliya, Leila, 232
Ali, a Palestinian, 111–12
al-Ali, Naji, 278
Ali bin Abi Talib, 238
Almog, Oz, 141
Amal, film, 203
'Amir, Abdul-Hakim, 243
Amnesty International, 106
anal sex, 171, 172, 178
Anderson, Benedict, 210
Angels with Dirty Faces, film, 211
Antara bin Shaddad al-Absi, 275
anti-militarism, in Turkey, 82
Arab Muslim man, portrayed as unchanging, 170
Al-Arabi newspaper, 227
Arabs, as 'other', 141

Arch of Victory Monument, Baghdad, 239, 245
Arendt, Hannah, 189
Arif, Abdul-Rahman, 236, 238
armed struggle, in Turkey, centrality of, 82
Armenians, 251–2
artists and performers, social position of, in Middle East, 85
al-Asad, Ahmad Bek, 263
Atatürk, Mustafa Kemal, 65, 71–2, 84
Ataturkism, 72, 73
al-Atrash, Farid, 213
'auada concerts, 22
al-'Awadi al-Wakil, 191
al-Azhar university, 20, 176

Baath Party (Iraq), 241, 242, 243, 247
baptism, replaces circumcision in Christianity, 26
bar mitzvah, 49, 54, 56, 57; as coping mechanism of adolescent transition, 139; military service as, 127–44
Barakat, Hoda, 192; *The Laughing Stone* (*Hajar al-dahik*), 184
Baram, Amataziah, *Culture, History and Ideology . . .*, 245
Batatu, Hanna, *The Old Social Classes and the Revolutionary Movements . . .*, 241
baths, women's *see* women's baths
beating of Palestinians, 104, 105, 114, 120; as interrogation technique, 110; as rite of passage, 109; reproduced in intra-family violence, 119; tellings of, 108

Bedouin, Egyptian, 107
belly dancers, banned by Muhammad
    'Ali, 190
Ben-Ari, Captain, 105–6, 137
Berbers, 107; and circumcision, 22
Birand, Mehmet Ali, 70, 72, 78
birth: celebrations of, 26; trauma of, 43
bodily discharges of women, 39
body: display of, 108–9; marks of
    violence on, 117 (as signal of
    resistance, 112)
Boss Hasan, film, 208–10
Bouhdiba, Abdelwahab, 19, 148, 149–50,
    155
Bourdieu, Pierre, 107–8, 114
Boyarin, Daniel, 141
boys: admission into women's baths,
    255; expelled from women's spaces,
    149, 150, 157, 262; love of, 178
'breaking of the eye' (*kasr al-'ayn*), 241,
    242
brit milah, 35, 37, 41, 51, 139, 141; as ritual
    of pseudo-creation, 38; description
    of, 39
buttocks, as reflectors of character, 257

Cairo, homosexual slang of, 184
castration, 21, 28, 53, 233; threat of, 37
Çelik, a pop star, 69
censorship, 192, 229, 230; in Turkey, 79,
    83
Chahine, Youssef, 170, 200
challenge, as conferring honour, 107–8
Chebel, Malik, 171
chewing gum, Israeli, alleged plot, 227–
    35
childhood, abolished for Palestinians,
    106
Choisy, Maryse, 24–5
Choukri, Mohamed, *For Bread Alone*
    (*al-Khubz al-hafi*), 186, 187
Church of Ethiopia, practice of
    circumcision, 25
circumciser, position of, 51
circumcision, 19–32; age of, 21, 26, 38,
    39, 40; as communion with the
    divine, 24; as finishing off, 38; as

mark of inclusion in Islam, 20; as
    mode of cultural creation, 38–9; as
    part of birth process, 38; as passage
    to adult world, 27; as *sunna* act, 20,
    26; connection with marriage, 27,
    37; dangers of, 23; family ceremony
    of, 22; in Islam, 52; in Judaism, 23–
    5, 33–64, 139; in Turkey, 75; mass-,
    37; noise accompanying ritual, 22;
    of ears, mouth and heart, 42; of
    Moses, 24–5; process of, 21, 22, 24,
    25, 39 (two-fold, 41–2); relation to
    castration, 37; replaced by baptism
    in Christianity, 22; two-step model
    of, 53 *see also brit milah and* non-
    circumcision
civilian service, introduced in Greece,
    67–8
Clinton, Jerome, 156
clitoris, study of, 258–60
coffee shops, 183; owners of,
    association with homosexuality, 177
Cohan, Steven, 219
colonial mirroring, 106
combat culture in Israel, 124–44; as *bar
    mitzvah* institution, 138–42; as test
    of masculinity, 137; feelings
    triggered in, 133
commandments, assuming burden of,
    140
Connell, R.W., 73
conscientious objection, 68; in Turkey,
    67, 81–3
conscripts: military, view of, 72; war
    trauma of, 83 *see also* Mehmetçik
Curtis, Tony, 220
cycles of stories in Islamic culture, 158–
    9
Cyrus, 246

dancing of men, 45–6, 50
darb 'ashara (masturbation), 184
Davis, Dick, 160–1
desire, invisible, 190–3
Dir Mashmoushah school, 268, 270
disappeared people, 82
Don-Yehiya, Eliezer, 129, 140

Dunne, Bruce, 190

earlocks *see payess*
East Jerusalem, general strike in, 115
education, of boys, 263–72 (French-language, 269, 270, 271)
effeminacy, 173, 182; (*khinath*), 190
Egyptian novel, sexual treatment in, 189
Ellis, John, 218
enemy, military contact with, 132
erotic triangles in literature, 161–2
Ertegün, Ahmet, 84
excision of girls, 26; as *makruma*, 20

face, defence of, 107
Fahim al-Far, Ahmad, 170
fakir, 269, 270
Fanon, Frantz, 112
fatawa hindiyya, 20, 21
fathers, 28, 48, 245; authority of, 266; boys' entry into domain of, 150, 151; duty of circumcision, 38; image of Saddam Hussein, 244; inability to protect children, 107; punishment by, 265; repeated in sons, 265; replication of, 55; ritual role of, 50
Fauzi, Muhammad, 213, 214–15, 221
Feldman, Allen, 114
fellatio, 171
female, proximity to nature, 39
female object, in cinema, 219
female space, in Islamic culture, 148–9
femininity, 127; as social construct, 118, 148, 162, 219; disavowal of, 150; of Iraq, 242; renouncement of, 185
film industry, in Egypt, 199–226; Egyptian, patterned on US models, 202
fiqh, 231; treatment of sexual identity, 172
foreskin, 54; as feminine residue, 41; fruit as, 52; viewed as impure, 41
Freud, Sigmund, 148, 155
fruit, uncircumcised condition of, 52

Gaza Strip, military operations in, 130, 132

al-Gazayirli, Fu'ad, 213
gender: hierarchies of, 118–20; in Islamic story-telling, 147–68; in Israeli armed forces, 136
gender differentiation, 37, 38, 45, 46, 50, 56, 57
gender studies, within Islamic studies, 170
General Chief of Staff (Genelkurmay) (Turkey), 65; European Union Working Group, 67
al-Ghazali, 20, 26
al-Ghitani, Gamal, *Incidents in Zafarani Alley (Waqa'i harat al-Za'farani)*, 178
Gilmore, David, 107, 138–9
Girard, René, 161
Giv'ati unit (Israel), 130–5; composition of, 131; description of, 131; initiation ceremony, 132
golem, creation of, 55
Gönül, Tayfun, 81
Gordon, Pierre, 24
Greece, versions of masculinity, 68–9
guile, as female characteristic, 147–68
Guth, Stephan, 189
Gypsies: life of, 256–7; midwives, 258

hadith, treatment of sexuality, 172
hafalat tarab concerts, 22
Hafiz, 'Abd al-Halim, 213
hair: as symbolic device, 53; long and dishevelled, meaning of, 53–4; tightly controlled, 54
haircut: age of, 56; as act of purification, 53; first, in Judaism, 33–64 *see also halaka*; ritual of, 44–7 (in Islam, 52); sexual meanings of, 53
al-Hajjaj bin Yousif, 244
halaka (haircut ceremony), 45; as secondary circumcision, 50, 52, 56
Halakha religious law, 33
Halal, Ahmad, 274, 279
Hallpike, C.R., 53
hamam, 251–62; architecture of, 254–5; as sexual location, 179, 183; practices of, 27
Hamido, film, 205, 210

Hanbal, Imam Ibn, 172
Hasidim, 33, 34
hassas (passive partner), 187
Hebrew alphabet, letters as bodily
  representation, 42
Herzl, Theodor, 140
heterosexuality, 69, 85, 87, 127, 151, 155,
  160, 161, 185
heyder schooling, 55
hierarchies: of gender, 118–20, 205;
  transformation of, 117–18
High Institute for Acting (Egypt), 200,
  204
Hilmi, Soraya, 207–8
Holden, William, 207
homoeroticism, 151; in Arab daily life,
  174–5; preference for term, 171
homosexual characters in novels, 177–8,
  184
homosexuality, 84, 87, 127, 155, 161, 173;
  and Israeli armed forces, 134; and
  love, 172, 174, 180; as metaphor for
  relation with West, 185–9; as
  'Oriental vice', 191; banned as part
  of modernization of society, 191;
  censorship of, 190; critical non-
  treatment of, 169; in Arab
  metropolises, 175; in Israeli armed
  forces, 129; in modern Arabic
  literature, 169–98; in relation to
  Westerners, 175; 'Mediterranean',
  172; not an identity, 170; not illegal
  in Egypt, 172; passive (*ubna*), 190;
  repetition of sexual acts, 179;
  sociology of, 169
honour, defence of, 107, 113, 114, 202,
  205, 214, 221, 229, 233
Husayn, Taha: attitude to
  homosexuality, 176; *al-Ayyam*, 175–6
al-Husayn b. al-Dahhak, 191
Hussein, a Palestinian, 109, 110;
  achievement of leadership, 111
Hussein, Saddam, 236–48; as image of
  manhood, 247; as modernizer, 241;
  as role model, 247; machismo of,
  242; multiple reproductions of, 241;
  orphan status of, 239; photographed

with children, 243; political
  background of, 240; relationship
  with military, 243; sterility of image
  of, 246

Ibn al-Abd, Tarfah, 264
Ibn al-Jawzi, *Condemnation of Passion*
  (*Dhamm al-hawa*), 173
Ibn Daniyal: *The Man Stricken by
  Passion* (*Al-mutayyam wa-l-yutayyim*),
  174; *The Imaginary Shadow* (*Tayf al-
  khayal*), 173–4
Ibn Hazm, *The Dove's Necklace* (*Tawq
  al-hamama*), 172
Ibn Tufayl, 151
Ibrahim, Hafiz, 191
Ibrahim, Sun'allah: *Honour* (*Sharaf*),
  188, 189; *The Smell of It* (*Tilka al-
  ra'iha*), 189
Idris, Yusuf, *A Leader of Men* (*Abu al-
  rigal*), 181; *A Matter of Honour*
  (*Haditha sharaf*), 171–2
Ihya, 20
interrogation: sexual forms of, 121;
  withstanding of, 111
Intifada: declining status of elders, 117;
  meaning of, 113; rituals of resistance
  in, 103–26; role of youth in, 117
Isaiah, eating of text of, 48
Islam: conversion to, 20; five pillars of,
  26; haircut ritual in, 52
Israel, 33–64; and the Palestinian
  Intifada, 103–26; as civil religion,
  129; central role of military in, 127;
  defeat at the hands of, 278
  (experienced as humiliation, 233);
  militarized nature of, 136; military
  service in, 127–44; viewed as lacking
  in manhood, 114, 116
Israel Defence Force (IDF): as melting
  pot, 127, 129; as socialization agent,
  128; gender distinctions in, 127;
  homosexuality in, 129; sanctity of,
  140; view of Arab enemy other, 141;
  Zionist ideology of, 128
Izmir War Resisters' Association, 81–2

al-Jahiz, *Book of Maids and Lads*
(*Mufakharat al-jawari wa-l-ghilman*),
175
Jahya, grandson of al-Ma'mun of
Toledo, 22
Jamil, a student, dress of, 273
Jews: Ashkenazi, 33, 34, 44, 49, 57;
Mizrahi, 33, 44, 128; Sephardi, 33;
ultraorthodox (*haredi*), 33–64, 133 (as
recent phenomenon, 56;
involvement in national life, 35;
military service of, 128; socio-
cultural codes of, 34)
Joseph, Suad, 214
Joukasizian, Jan Hofanes Grigor, 236;
photographed with Saddam
Hussein, 238
Judaism: primacy of text in, 36; role of
circumcision in, 23–5
al-Jundi, Nadia, 234

Kadare, Ismail, *Broken April*, 276
Kanizak, 156–60; punishment of, 159–
60
Kapferrer, Jean Noel, 233
Al-Kawakib fan magazine, 218–21
Khal, Abdu, 19
al-Khalil, Samir, 241; *The Monument . . .*,
239
Khalil, Sidi, 21
khasi (castration), 21
Khayr Allah, Adnan, 243
Khayr Allah, Sajida, 243
khitan (circumcision), 21
kibbutz: ideology of, 128, 130, 134, 135;
recruitment for elite brigades, 131
killing by soldiers, dehumanization
process of, 133
knowledge, in circumcision, 38–44
Koç Holding company, 74
Kurdistan Workers' Party (Parti
Karkeren Kurdistan - PKK), 66, 78,
79
Kurds, 76, 82, 252; assault on
nationalism of, 78–80, 83; attitude
to military service in Turkey, 77

labia, study of, 258–60
Lacan, Jacques, 36–7
Ladd, Alan, 207
Lag Ba'omer, 44, 45, 47, 50
leadership, 120; among Palestinians,
117; hierarchies, emergence of, 111,
112; urban-based, 118
Levine, Myerowitz, 53
Liebman, Charles S., 129, 140
LOTAR operations (Israel), 132
The Lout, a play, 204
Lover's Revenge, film, 203
Luria Ashkenazi, Rabbi Isaac, 47

Mahfuz, Nagib, 191; *The Epic of Beggars*
(*Malhamat al-harafish*), 177; *Midaq
Alley* (*Zuqaq al-midaqq*), 177; *Sugar
Street* (*al-Sukkariyya*), 177
majority, age of, definition of, 49
Makiya, Kanan, *Cruelty and Silence . . .*,
241
male beauty, acknowledged in Arabo-
Islamic culture, 171
male bonding, 55
male fears, and the Arab media, 227–35
male homosociality, 156, 157
male identity: in Judaism, restructuring
of, 50–5; inculcating of, 35
male redundancy, fear of, 147
male utopias, 151
Malti-Douglas, Fedwa, 147, 153, 155;
Woman's Body, Woman's Word . . .,
151
manhood: achievement of, 43, 109–13,
135; conferred by others, 137;
enhanced by presence of children,
244; equation with reason, 153;
homosocial patterns of, 155
manhood rituals, and military service,
in Turkey, 65–102
Mansour, Fathi, 228
Marcus, Ivan, 49
marriage, requirement of military
service to be completed, 74
masculinity, 66, 87, 221, 230; among
Palestinians, 103–26; as social
construct, 106–7, 148, 162, 172;

definition of, 234; Egyptian, 199; essentialist notions of, 86; hegemonic, 73, 85; ideal version of, generated in the military, 69–71; in Arabic culture, 107; in Iraq, 236–48; in Judaism, 128, 139; in the American cinema, 219; in Turkey, and homosexuality, 84; in Zionism, 127–44; 'makeshift', 139; military as repository of, 69; of Farid Shauqi, 199, 200, 205, 220, 222; questioning of, 87, 129; relationship with honour, 114; role of class background in defining, 76; tested in combat culture, 137; threats to, 229; versions of, in Greece, 69

Matar, Fuad, 238, 240

Mater, Nadire, *Mehmedin Kitabı . . .*, 83–4

Mauss, Marcel, 24

Mazahéri, A., 22

McDonald, Paul, 221

mediators, social role of, 109–10

mehablim, use of term, 141

Mehmetçik ('Little Mehmet') conscripts, 72–3, 78; featured on television, 80

Mehraz, Sidi, 22

Meron, shrine of Rabbi Shimon Bar Yohai, 44–7

milah as circumcision and word, 37

al-Miligi, Mahmud, 204, 205, 206, 210

military: as sanctuary for moustaches, 277; placed in position of sacredness, 130; role in socialization, 138; superiority over civilians, 71

military indoctrination, role in socialization, 136

military performance, importance of, 133

military service: as initiation into manhood, 66, 135–8; as moment of self-discovery, 136; gendered nature of, 136; in family photo album, 77; in Israel, 127–44; in Turkey, 65–102 (as passage to manhood, 74; buying out of, 68; call-up for, 75; delaying

of, 68; departure for, 75; duration of, 68; evasion of, 68, 74, 82, 84, 86, 87; (amnesty for, 69; punishment for, 68); funerals of serving soldiers, 79, 80; in emergency zones, 78–80, 81, 83; legal aspect of, 67; meaning and social impact of, 74–8; precondition for employment, 74)

misogyny, 154, 156

Mission to Tel Aviv (Muhimma fi Tel Aviv), film, 234

Mitchum, Robert, 219

mithliyya jinsiyya (homosexuality), 170

Mitnagdim, 33, 34

modesty codes, violation of, 118

mohel (circumciser), 39

al-Moizz Ibn Badis of Kairwan, 22

moral self, reconstitution of, 115–16

Morocco, 19, 41, 52

Moses, circumcision of, 24–5

mosque, women's section of, 148

mothers: as stock figure of betrayal, 149; as wet-nurse, 153–4; bond with baby, 44; boy's separation from, 39, 54, 55, 56, 57; grieving for dead soldier sons, 80; impurity of, in birth, 41; protection of sons, 119; return to domain of, 151; separation of male child from, 39, 40; stereotypes of, 155

moustaches, 182, 246, 273–80; dating of, 275; 'Douglas', 274, 279; of Che Guevara, 279; protected by the military, 277; reduction of, 274; removed from the undeserving, 275; shaving of, 279–80; swearing on, 275

Muhammmad, Prophet: uncircumcised state of, 21; weighing of, 21

Muhammad 'Ali, 190

Mulvey, Laura, 219

Mura, Layla, 207

Murray, Stephen O., 192

Mus'ad, Ra'uf, *The Egg of the Ostrich (Baydat al-na'ama)*, 180, 189

Musa Sadr, Imam, 270

Al-Nahar newspaper, 228

Nahda era, 190
Nahj al-balaaghah, 271
naming of first son, 263–4
Nasrallah, Yusri, 170
al-Nasser, Gamal Abd, 243, 246, 247
National Security Council (Milli
    Güvenlik Kurulu) (Turkey), 65, 67
National Union Troupe (Egypt), 200
Nationalist Action Party (Milliyetçi
    Hareket Partisi - MHP), 77, 84
Nazhat al-albab, 233
Nazmi, Iris, 210
Nebuchadnezzar, 245–6
Nefzawi, Sheikh, 229; *The Perfumed
    Garden (Al-rawd al-'ater...)*, 230–1
New Era Films (Aflam al-'ahd al-gadid),
    208
Nilüfer, 261, 262
Nir, an Israeli soldier, 129; story of,
    130–5
non-circumcision, 20, 21, 23, 26; of
    fruit, 52
al-Nuwayri, *al-Nihaya*, 172

obscenity (*sukhf*), 173
Öcalan, Abdullah, trial of, 66, 80
Oedipus story, 148, 155
O'Hara, Maureen, 207
O'Sullivan, Maureen, 207
ot, 51; as physical marker and letter, 43
Ottoman empire, 278

pacifism, 81
Palestinian male, reconstitution of, 106
Palestinians: cast beyond the pale, 106;
    emergence of male
    authoritarianism, 120; injured in
    Intifada, 103; moral reconstitution
    of, 115; politicization of, 110–11
paternity, 107
Path of Thorns (Tariq al-Shauk), film, 210
patriarchy: in Arab society, 214;
    structure of, 263
Paul, St, Epistle to the Galatians, 25–6
payess (earlocks), 46–7, 50; phallic
    connotations of, 51, 53
penis *see* phallus

phallus, 230, 231, 259, 261; domination
    of, 173, 174; equated with ear-locks,
    53; length of, 232; valorization of, 28
Philo, 24
Phoenicians, and circumcision, 22
Photoplay fan magazine, 218–21
physical/symbolic relationship, 36
pir'ah (uncovering), 43
poetics of contrast, 116
political action, commitment to, 114
pornography, 230
prison: as consolidating resistance, 121;
    as liminal experience, 112; as rite of
    passage, 120; as university, 111;
    homosexuality in, 189; return home
    and re-entry into community, 113;
    sexual activity in, 179
procreation, as commandment, 34
prison literature, 188; in Egypt, 179
puberty, 152, 262; of boys, 255–6; rituals
    of, 19
purity: access to, 37; in circumcision,
    38–44

Qadhi-Khan, 21
Qadisiya, Battle of, 245
Qaragoz shows, homosexuality in, 170
Qasim, Abdul-Karim, 240
Quran, 21, 26, 184; schooling in, 267,
    268, 270, 272; treatment of male
    beauty, 171

Rabin, Yitzhak, 105, 229
Raghda, daughter of Saddam Hussein,
    238
Ran, an Israeli soldier, 137
Rana, daughter of Saddam Hussein, 238
rape, 185, 188, 189, 229, 241; during
    interrogation, 121; fear of,
    cultivation of, 150–1
al-Razzaz, Munif, 242
RefahYol coalition (Turkey), 66
religion of security, in Israel, 130, 131,
    138–42
repetition: of plot, 148; of acts of
    exclusion of boys, 149
resistance, power of, 111

ribaldry (*mujun*), 173
Rich, Adrienne, 147
rites of passage, 37, 50, 103, 106, 107, 112, 114; military service as, 135–8
ritual, definition of, 138
Rivoli Cinema (Cairo), 188
Rossi, Aldo, 246
Rowson, Everett K., 172
rules of looking, 150
rumours, nature of, 233

'Sabra', 129, 131, 141; image of, 128
Sa'd bin Abi Waqqas, 245
al-Sahib b. 'Abbad, 178
Salah al-Din Pasha, 201
Salaman and Absal, 151, 152–5, 159
Salih, al-Tayyib, 189; *This is What Happened to the Boy . . . (Hadha ma gara lil-shabb . . .)*, 187
Salmawi, Muhammad, *A Game of Backgammon ('Ashara tawila)*, 183
Sami, a Palestinian, 111
al-Samira'i, Abdul-Khaliq, 242
Sandal, Mustafa, 69
Sandbadnamah story cycle, 147, 156–60
al-Sarraj, *Masari' al-'ushshaq*, 173
Saturday Mothers (*Cumartesi Anneleri*) (Turkey), 80
Saudi Arabia, 19
Sayeret Matkal reconnaissance unit (Israel), 130
school initiation ritual, in Judaism, 47–50, 55, 57; origins of, 49
Scott, James, 120
seating position in Arab culture, 110
Sedgwick, Eve, 161
Selim, a boy, 251–62
Selman, Ahmad Bin, 229, 232; *The Rejuvenation of the Old Man (Ruju'u al-sheikh ila sibah)*, 230, 231
separation and removal, laws of, 38
sexual desire, concealed in Arab societies, 174
sexual deviation, in Arab culture, 170
sexual ethics, of Arabo-Islamic culture, 192
sexual intercourse, as exercise of power, 173

sexual violation, of women, 118
sexuality: of women, 233; 'determined by breasts', 257; in Islamic literature, 147–68; relation with the West, 187
Shadia, Egyptian film star, 203
shadow plays, in Egypt, 173
Shafi'i, Imam, 22
shahid, figure of, 151
Shahrzad, 156–7; victory of, 160
Shammas, Anton, 106
Sharaf, Rafiq, 278
Sharif, Omar, discovery of, 200
Shauqi, Farid, 199–226; as 'beast of the screen', 203, 205; as 'king of the cheap seats', 202, 204; earnings of, 207; image in fan magazines, 218, 220, 221; in Shakespeare, 201, 202, 204; marketing of, 220; marriage to Zaynab Abd al-Hadi, 206; relationship with Hoda Sultan, 203, 204, 206, 216–17; self-image of, 217, 218; success at audition, 201; writing and production of own films, 208 *see also* masculinity, of Farid Shauqi
shaving of vaginal hair, 258
Shimon Bar Yohai, Rabbi, 44
shudhudh jinsi (sexual deviation), 170
Shukri, Ghali, 191
silencing of the prince, 158
smoking, 267
sodomy, treatment of, in *hadith*, 172
Son of the Popular Quarter, film, 205
Sophie, an Armenian, 251–62; departure of, 260
spaces of transgression, needed in society, 192
stars, of film, studies of, 221
step-mother, lustful, stereotype of, 154, 155
stones, as weapons of Palestinians, 103, 106, 108, 110, 113, 115, 132
story cycles in Islamic culture, 147
story-telling, 231; by women, 159
structured and non-structured cultures, 138–9
Studio Babylon Photographers, 236
suckling of boys, 40

Sudabah and Siyavush, 157

Sultan, Hoda, 204, 205, 206, 208, 210, 211, 213, 214, 216–17, 221; earnings of, 207; relationship with brother Muhammad Fauzi, 214

al-Suyyuti, Jalal al-Din, 229; *The Book of Explanations . . . (Kitab al-'idah . . .)*, 230

swearing-in ceremonies, 138

synagogue, importance of, 34

Takrit, position of, in Iraqi politics, 239–40

Talfah, Khayr Allah, 240

Talmud, 34, 54, 55

tarboushes: removal of, 280 (from the undeserving, 276)

Tarkan, a pop star, 69, 84; ambiguous sexuality of, 85

Taussig, Michael, 105, 106

Terror on the Set (Ru'b al-Blatoh), film, 217

Teyze Hanım ('Lady Aunt'), 254–5, 261, 262

They Made Me a Criminal, film, 211

Thousand and One Nights, 147, 148, 155, 156–7, 159, 160, 171, 174

al-Tifashi, Ahmad Shehab al-Din, *The Mind's Promenade . . . (Nuzhat al-albab . . .)*, 173, 232, 233

Torah, 33–64; association with baby food and suckling, 55; entering into, 36, 42, 43, 47, 48, 54; study of, 35, 56 (men's privileged position in, 139)

torture, 106, 109; as ritualized art form, 105; of women, 119; sexual, 118)

The Tough Guy, film, 211

Tough Guys of the Husayn District, film, 211

transgression, delegated to Western world, 193

Tunisia, 19, 20

Turk, ideal, creation of, 70–1

Turkey: 1982 Constitution of, 65; armed forces (atrocities committed by, 79; criticism of, 82; discipline in, 72; lack of criticism of, 80, 81; self-perception of, 70); assumed backwardness of, 71; EU candidacy of, 66, 67; key role of armed forces in, 65; military coups in, 66; military service in *see* military service, in Turkey; prosecution of publishers, 83; state of emergency in Kurdish zones, 66

Turkish Military Penal Code (Türk Askeri Ceza Kanunu), 68

Tutinamah story cycle, 147

'Ubayda, Abu, 176

Ülke, Osman Murat, 81; imprisonment of, 82

ultra-orthodox Jews *see* Jews, ultra-Orthodox

Um Fadi, 108

Um Kamel, 117, 119

Umm Kulthum, 206

United States of America (USA), attitude to Palestinians, 108–9

Updike, John, 239

Van Gennep, Arnold, 50, 112, 135, 140

village guard (*korucu*) system, Turkey, 79

violence: as a 'bridge-burning' activity, 112; as consolidating resistance, 121; cultural politics of, in Intifada, 103–2; defused through mockery, 115; domestic, 119, 120; in Northern Ireland, 114; Palestinian attitude to, 109; technology of, in Intifada, 105; transformative process of, 112; women's role in defusing, 116

Wahbi, Yusuf, 200

Wannus, Sa'dallah, 191; *The Rites of Signs and Transformations (Tuqus al-isharat wa-l-tahawwulat)*, 181

War Resisters' Association (Savaş Karşıtları Derneği), 81, 82

Ward al-Nil soap, marketing of, 207–8

Wayne, John, 207

weapons, use of, 131, 135

Westermarck, Edward A., 41

Westernization, 71, 241, 253

wife, as narrator, 156

womb, recreation of, 150, 151

women: and *halaka* ceremony, 45; and military service, in Israel, 127 (barred from combat, 128); and school initiation ceremony, 48; as contamination, 150; banished from circumcision ceremony, 40; beating of, 118; consumption of chewing gum, 229; excluded from military service in Turkey, 67; flight from, 155; in Jewish communities, 34, 39, 57; non-attendance at cinemas, 221; portrayed as insatiable, 154, 227–35; pressure to wear head scarves, 120; regarded as impaired, 39; role in defusing violence, 116; sexual shame of, 205; sexuality of, in Islamic literature, 147–68; torture of, 119 *see also* boys, expelled from space of women *and* mothers

women's baths, 148, 149, 251–62; boys' presence in, 149–50

women's space, 148, 154, 158

Yaqzan, Hayy ibn, 153

al-Yazidi, Abu Muhammad, 176

yeshiva schooling, 55

Yousry, Madiha, 215

Yusuf, 184; beauty of, 171

Yusuf and Zulaykha, 154, 156–7, 159, 160–2, erotic triangles in, 162

Zencir, Vedat, 81

Zionism, 129, 130, 134, 137, 138, 139; institutionalization of military service, 140; masculinity in, 127–44

ZKhR, connection of male and memory in Hebrew, 41, 52

Zohar, 54, 55

Zulaykha, 184